Public Program Evaluation

Public Program Evaluation

A Statistical Guide

Second Edition

Laura Langbein

M.E.Sharpe

Armonk, New York
London, England

Library of Congress Cataloging-in-Publication Data

Langbein, Laura Irwin.
  Public program evaluation : a statistical guide / by Laura Langbein. — 2nd ed.
    p. cm.
  Includes bibliographical references and index.
  ISBN 978-0-7656-2612-7 (pbk. : alk. paper)
  1. Policy sciences—Statistical methods. 2. Evaluation research (Social action programs)—
Statistical methods. I. Title.

  H97.L35 2012
  352.3′5—dc23   2011045685

Printed in the United States of America

The paper used in this publication meets the minimum requirements of
American National Standard for Information Sciences
Permanence of Paper for Printed Library Materials,
ANSI Z 39.48-1984.

SP (p)   10   9   8   7   6   5   4   3   2   1

Contents

Preface

I have been teaching a course on program evaluation to public affairs graduate students for many years. That course introduces students to the conscious choice of defensible and feasible research designs so that they can evaluate whether public programs are doing what they are supposed to do and not doing what they are not supposed to do. Students enter the course after having taken one or more statistics courses. I ask them to select an appropriate, feasible research design and corresponding statistical tools in order to examine whether a particular program of interest is meeting its intended goals (and avoiding unintended consequences). The course focuses on the hardest (and, arguably, the most important) question of program evaluation: Did the outcome result from the program or would it have occurred anyway?

While questions of causal inference are among the most abstract in science, they nevertheless have to be answered in the real world, because program managers, legislators, and funding organizations legitimately want answers to these questions. Thus, the methods of program evaluation must be practical and as valid (or defensible) as possible. The consequence is that program evaluators cannot always use the scientifically ideal design of the randomized experiment to study program effects. Perhaps evaluators should not use randomized experiments very much because in some respects the design may not be ideal—and even ideal designs go awry. What then? There are many other research designs and a great deal of data. Accordingly, there are many research design textbooks—not only in the specialty of program evaluation but also in many other disciplinary fields, especially political science and sociology—and even more statistics (and econometrics) textbooks. But how do you put the two together? Once you have decided that an interrupted time-series design (or some other design) is a practical and reasonably defensible design to analyze the effects of a particular program, no text tells you which statistical techniques are appropriate for that design. The research designs are usually portrayed as pictures, graphs, or tic-tac-toe diagrams with Xs and Os. There is no statistical guide in the research design texts, and there is minimal or no discussion of research design in statistics texts. This book is intended to fill that gap.

I originally filled that gap with my own notes for the program evaluation class. For that class, I asked students to buy a research design text (usually the latest edition of Peter H. Rossi, Howard E. Freeman, and Mark W. Lipsey, *Evaluation: A Systematic Approach*, published by Sage Publications in successively updated editions since 1980). I also asked students to buy a statistics review text, often one or more of the "green books" in the Quantitative Applications in Social Science Series (also published by Sage). My notes (pages of typed weekly handouts) became the foundations of this book. The book is written for my students and for students like them. They are graduate students (and an occasional upperclassman) who have taken at least one statistics course and who are interested in public policy and public programs, not just from a normative standpoint but also from the empirical standpoint of finding out what works. Specifically, this text is written not only for graduate students in professional public affairs master's degree programs (especially the MPP and other policy-oriented master's degrees) but also for students in other empirically oriented public affairs programs. This includes Ph.D. students in political science and sociology, students in applied master's degree programs in economics, and even some advanced undergraduates who have had a course in econometrics or statistical analysis.

This book is dedicated to the students who have taken my American University course, Public Program Evaluation. I asked them not only to learn how to describe, analyze, and critique the various research designs and corresponding statistical analyses that others used but also to complete an original program evaluation in one semester, with no outside funding. They always came through, although it was never clear in the middle of the course whether the project could be completed on time and within the zero-dollar budget. But we (that is, both the students and I) learned how to adapt the design to the data that were available and to apply the most appropriate statistical analysis for that design. After we collected the data, the fun began: crunching the numbers was exciting, we learned a lot during the process, and the end result was new knowledge, producing defensible information about a program that was not known before. Occasionally, the papers were even published in peer-reviewed journals.

I owe special thanks to students who took the time not only to read the draft chapters of this text but also to give me feedback. They were brave enough to tell me when I was unclear, misguided, or just plain wrong. They include Wei Song, Xiaodong Zhang, Reina Rusnak, and Pablo Sanabria. I owe the biggest thanks to my coauthor, Claire Felbinger. Without her supportive but continual nudges over the years, this book would not have been written. Of course, I am to blame for the remaining errors, obscurity, and lack of wisdom.

Since the original edition was written, Claire Felbinger died. This revision is dedicated to her memory, and to my fond memories of our many lunches where we discussed politics, performance measurement, and program evaluation.

I hope that you have as much fun systematically analyzing real data about real programs as my students and I have had.

Public Program Evaluation

1

What This Book Is About

WHAT IS PROGRAM EVALUATION?

Program evaluation is the application of empirical social science research methods to the process of judging the effectiveness of public policies, programs, or projects, as well as their management and implementation, for decision-making purposes. Although this definition appears straightforward, it contains many important points. Let us deconstruct the definition.

What We Evaluate: Policies, Programs, and Management

First, what is the difference between public programs, policies, and projects? For the purposes of this book, policies are the general rules set by governments that frame specific government-authorized programs or projects. Programs and projects implement policy. Programs are ongoing services or activities, while projects are one-time activities that are intended to have ongoing, long-term effects. In most cases, programs and projects, authorized by policies, are directed toward bringing about collectively shared ends. These ends, or goals, include the provision of social and other public services and the implementation of regulations designed to affect the behavior of individuals, businesses, or organizations.

While the examples in this text refer to government entities and public programs or projects, an important and growing use of program evaluation is by private organizations, including for- and not-for-profit institutions. Not-for-profit organizations frequently evaluate programs that they support or directly administer, and these programs may be partly, entirely, or not at all publicly funded. Similarly, for-profit organizations frequently operate and evaluate programs or projects that may (or may not) be funded by the government. Further, many organizations (public, not-for-profit, or for-profit) use program evaluation to assess the effectiveness of their internal management policies or programs. Thus, a more general definition of program evaluation might be the application of empirical social science research methods to the process of judging the effectiveness of organizational policies, programs, or projects, as well as their management and implementation, for decision-making purposes. I chose to focus on program evaluation in a public context because that is the predominant application of the field in the published literature. Private sector applications are less accessible because they are less likely to be published. Nonetheless, the research designs and other methods that this book elaborates are entirely portable from one sector to another.

The distinction between policy, program, and project may still not be clear. What looks like a policy to one person may look like a program or project to another. As an example, Temporary Assistance for Needy Families (TANF) can be regarded at the federal level as either a policy or

3

a program. From the state-level perspective, TANF is a national policy that frames fifty or more different state programs. Further, from the perspective of a local official, TANF is a state policy that frames numerous local programs. Similarly, from the perspective of a banker in Nairobi, structural adjustment is a policy of the International Monetary Fund (IMF). The loan, guaranteed by the IMF and serviced by the banker, funds a specific development program or project in Kenya, designed to carry out the market-building goals of structural adjustment policy. But from the perspective of an IMF official in Washington, DC, structural adjustment is just one of the programs that the IMF administers. So, whether one calls a particular government policy initiative or set of related activities a policy or a program (or project) depends on one's location within a multilevel system of governments. The distinction does not really matter for the purposes of this book. One could call this volume a book about either policy or program or even project evaluation. However, perhaps because the bulk of studies pertain to specific, ongoing, local programs, either in the United States or elsewhere, the common usage of the set of methods discussed in this book is to characterize them as program rather than policy evaluation. We regard projects as short-term programs.[1] (See Figure 1.1 for an example of the policy-program-project hierarchy.)

These examples also underscore another point: The methods in this book apply to government-authorized programs, whether they are administered in the United States or in other countries. While data collection may sometimes encounter greater obstacles in developing countries, this text does not focus on specific problems of (or opportunities for) evaluating specific programs in developing countries.[2] The logic of the general designs, however, is the same no matter where the research is to be done.

Finally, the logic of program evaluation also applies to the evaluation of program management and implementation. Evaluators study the effectiveness of programs. They also study the effectiveness of different management strategies (e.g., whether decentralized management of a specific program is more effective than centralized management) and evaluate the effectiveness of different implementation strategies. For example, they might compare flexible enforcement of a regulatory policy to rigid enforcement, or they might compare contracting out the delivery of services (say, of prisons or fire protection) to in-house provision of services.

The Importance of Being Empirical

As the first phrase of its definition indicates, program evaluation is an empirical enterprise. "Empirical" means that program evaluation is based on defensible observations. (I explain later what "defensible" means.) Program evaluation is not based on intuition. It is not based on norms or values held by the evaluators. It is based not on what the evaluators would prefer (because of norms or emotions) but on what they can defend observationally. For example, the preponderance of systematic empirical research (that is, research based on defensible observations) shows that gun control policies tend to reduce adult homicide.[3] An evaluator can oppose gun control policies, but not on the basis of the empirical claim that gun control policies do not reduce adult homicide. Evidence-based evaluation requires a high tolerance for ambiguity. For example, numerous studies, based on defensible observations show that policies allowing people to legally carry concealed weapons act as if they make it more risky for criminals to use their weapons because, empirically, these policies appear to reduce homicides rather than increase them. Equally defensible studies raise serious questions about the defensibility of that conclusion.[4] This example suggests that evaluation results based on defensible observations can sometimes produce ambiguous results. Most people's intuition is that it is dangerous to carry concealed weapons, but defensible observations appear to produce results that cause us to challenge and question our intuition.

Figure 1.1   **The Policy-Program-Project Hierarchy**

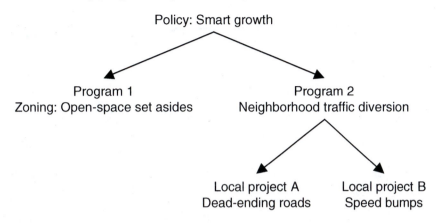

Although "empirical" refers to reliance on observations, not just any observations will do for program evaluation. Journalists rely on observations, but their observations are selected because of their interest, which may mean that they are atypical (or even typical) cases. Journalists may claim that the case is "atypical" or "typical" but have no systematic way to justify the empirical veracity of either claim. By contrast, program evaluation relies on the methods of science, which means that the data (the observations) are collected and analyzed in a carefully controlled manner. The controls may be experimental or statistical. In fact, the statistical and experimental controls that program evaluators use to collect and analyze their observations (i.e., their data) are the topic of this book. The book explains shows that, while some controls produce results that are more valid (i.e., defensible) than others, no single evaluation study is perfect and 100 percent valid. The book also sets forth the different kinds of validity and the trade-offs among the types of validity. For example, randomized experimental controls may rate highly on internal validity but may rate lower on external validity. The trade-offs among the different types of validity reinforce the claim that no study can be 100 percent valid.

The existence of trade-offs among different types of validity also makes it clear that observational claims about the effectiveness or ineffectiveness of public programs are not likely to be defensible until they are replicated by many studies, none of which is perfect. When many defensible studies, each imperfect in a different way, reach similar conclusions, we are likely to decide that the conclusion is defensible overall. We can act as if the conclusion is true. Note that we do not claim that the conclusion about the program is true, only that we can act as if it were true. Because no method of control can be 100 percent valid, no method of control leads to proof or truth. Mathematicians do proofs to analyze whether claims are true. Because program evaluators do not perform mathematical proofs, the words "prove" and "true" should not be part of their vocabulary.

Lenses for Evaluating Effectiveness

Program evaluation uses controlled observational methods to come to defensible conclusions about the effectiveness of public programs. Choosing the criteria for measuring effectiveness makes program evaluation not purely scientific; that choice is the value or normative part of the program evaluation enterprise. Programs can be evaluated according to many criteria of effectiveness. In fact, each social science subdiscipline has different core values that it uses to evaluate programs. Program evaluation, as a multidisciplinary social science, is less wedded to any single normative value than most of the disciplinary social sciences, but it is important for program evaluators to recognize the connection between a criterion of effectiveness, the corresponding normative values, and the related social science subdiscipline.

For example, the core value in economics is allocative efficiency. According to this criterion, the increment in social (i.e., private plus external) benefits of a program should equal the increment in social (i.e., private plus external) costs of the program. This view leads economists to examine not only the intended effects of a program but also the unintended effects, which often include unanticipated and hidden costs. For example, the intended effect of seat belts and air bags is to save lives. An unintended effect is that, because seat belts and air bags (and driving a sport utility vehicle [SUV]) make drivers feel safer, protected drivers sometimes take more risks, thereby exacerbating the severity of damage to other vehicles in accidents and endangering the lives of pedestrians.[5] Thus, program evaluators, particularly those who are concerned with the ability of public programs to improve market efficiency, must estimate the impact of seat belts (or air bags or SUVs) not only on drivers' lives saved and drivers' accident cost reductions but on the loss of property or lives of other drivers or pedestrians.

A primary concern of economics that is also relevant to program evaluation is benefit-cost analysis, which ascribes dollar values both to program inputs and program outputs and outcomes, including intended as well as unintended, unanticipated, and hidden consequences. Program evaluation is critical to this exercise. In fact, program evaluation must actually precede the assignment of monetary values to program consequences, whether positive or negative. Specifically, before assigning a dollar value to program consequences, the evaluator must first ascertain that the result is attributable to the program and would not have occurred without it. For example, if program evaluation finds that using cell phones in automobiles had no effect on increasing accidents,[6] there would be no reason to place a dollar value on the increased accidents to measure an external cost of cell phones. That is, if a defensible conclusion is that cell phones in autos have no direct impact on increasing accidents, then the cost of the additional accidents cannot be ascribed to (or blamed on) cell phones in autos. In this example, the external cost of automobile cell phones in respect to increasing accidents would be zero. Program evaluation is critical to determine the beneficial (or harmful) effects of programs; it does not monetize the value of these effects.

Similarly, if a publicly funded job-training program fails to have an independent impact on improving employment outcomes for those in the training program, then it is clear that the program, which uses public resources, is not efficient. Any activity that uses resources and produces no valuable outcomes is clearly not efficient, although it might have other meritorious, noneconomic attributes. Moreover, ascribing consequences (whether positive or negative) to programs requires that the consequences can be attributed to the program, not to something else (e.g., an improving economy). This is a task for program evaluation, and it precedes benefit-cost analysis of the program.

Economists use program evaluation to assess program efficiency. Other social science subdisciplines have different core values and correspondingly different criteria for measuring effectiveness. Sociologists often focus on the core value of equality or social justice. Thus, a sociologist might evaluate welfare reform (the 1996 change from Aid to Families with Dependent Children [AFDC] to TANF) according to whether it lifts people out of poverty or reduces poverty gaps between blacks and whites. By contrast, an economist might evaluate welfare reform according to whether it makes people (including taxpayers and program beneficiaries) better off than they were before. Psychologists (and others) might examine how welfare reform affected child welfare or parent–child relations. For program evaluation, all of these outcome criteria are relevant.

Political science and public administration, a close relation to political science, examine programs according to responsiveness or accountability. In political science, responsiveness might mean whether the program conforms to the preferences of voters or meets with the satisfaction of its clients. Political scientists might evaluate government services according to citizen or client satisfaction. For example, they might compare citizen or parent satisfaction in school districts that allow parents to choose schools with satisfaction in school districts that do not.[7]

Satisfaction is also important in program administration and management. For example, program managers often seek to satisfy clients, not only because satisfied clients might be one signal of program effectiveness but also because satisfaction helps to legitimize programs.[8]

Accountability examines whether the program is implemented in accordance with the preferences of the legislators who collectively authorize the program, appropriate money for it, write the detailed (or vague) rules for how it is to be implemented, and play a role in selecting the political appointee tasked with administering the program. As an example of accountability or bureaucratic responsiveness to political oversight, political scientists have found that aggressive implementation of environmental controls is more likely when political controls are in the hands of proenvironmental legislatures and political executives.[9]

Public administrators and program heads also have another core value: program effectiveness, gauged by empirical measures of program outputs and outcomes. Program outputs are usually short-term, countable results. Evaluations of program outputs may ask questions such as these: How many people are employed because of their participation in a training program? How much have achievement scores increased because of an education program or policy change? How many additional workplace inspections for compliance with environmental or workplace health and safety regulations were conducted as a result of a policy change? Does participation in school lunch programs increase school attendance?[10]

Compared to evaluations of program outputs, evaluations of program outcomes usually ask longer-range questions. Rather than examining the impact of job training on employment, outcome evaluations might assess long-run earnings. Similarly, rather than examine the impact of a school reform on achievement scores, an outcome evaluation may examine whether the reform resulted in higher graduation rates or better jobs. Or evaluators might examine whether more inspection leads to less pollution or enhanced workplace safety or if privatizing solid waste collection leads to long-run cost savings.[11]

The basic point is that program evaluation uses multiple lenses to assess program performance. These include the norms of economic efficiency, equality and social justice, responsiveness and accountability, and aspects of effectiveness measured by short-term outputs or long-term outcomes. For program evaluation, the general rule is to be attentive to multiple values and multiple perspectives. This means that program evaluators should use multiple outcome indicators that correspond to multiple values in judging program performance. Evaluators must also pay particular attention to the values and perspectives held by important stakeholders in the program. Stakeholders include important political decision makers, interested groups and individuals, program managers, program clients, and perhaps others as well. Their input helps to ensure that program evaluations examine multiple goals that are important to at least one of the affected parties. The result is that evaluators usually conclude that programs are effective and perform well in one dimension but not in another.[12] Another result is that evaluations may engender or contribute to political debate, improving the ability of legislators to do their job of representation.[13]

Providing Deliverables

A final point in deconstructing the definition of program evaluation is that it is used "for decision-making purposes." This point sets program evaluation apart from academic research. Academic social science research may meet all of the foregoing criteria because it is empirical research based on defensible observations and uses multiple evaluation criteria.[14] But, unlike research conducted for program evaluation, academic research does not need to be practical, on time, and clear to non-academics. The primary audience is likely to be other academics in the author's field. Academic research will not be published until it has undergone blind review by peers, who have an incentive to look for reasons not to publish someone else's research (but to publish their own). Peer review is time-consuming. It is not uncommon for five years to elapse between the time the data are collected and analyzed and the publication of study results. Before publication, many studies undergo reanalysis and revision during multiple peer reviews. Under this system, while academics labor under budget constraints, they do not face severe time constraints, especially if they are tenured.

In contrast, program evaluation information, which usually does not undergo blind review by peers, is most useful only when decisions have to be made. If the legislative vote on program reauthorization is next Thursday, then the information that arrives on the following Friday is no longer useful, at least for affecting the vote. If the program manager's budget request is due on September 1, information that arrives on September 8 is not very useful. If the program evaluation report is framed in theoretical terms, then it is less likely to be attended to by program administrators and other decision makers, though it is more likely to be published in an academic journal. For example, if an evaluator were to frame a study of the impact of performance pay on teacher effectiveness in terms of theories on optimal incentive systems, incomplete contracts, adverse selection, moral hazard, and rational choice, decision makers might ignore it. If the same study is framed less abstractly, decision makers will be more likely to pay attention to its findings. (There is a large and growing academic literature on the rationale for and impact of linking teacher pay to student performance. There is less evidence that the literature actually influences the choice of pay systems for teachers.[15])

Further, the information must be clear. Academics can talk about unbiased regression parameter estimates, t-scores, p-values, homoscedasticity, and the like, but program evaluators have to explain what this shorthand jargon means. Further, brevity is an important component of clarity: for program evaluators, a crisp 300-word abstract or executive summary or a few (less than five) PowerPoint® slides (backed by a more detailed report) is critical for communication to busy decision makers.[16]

In addition to timeliness and clarity, program evaluation faces another constraint that academic research may not confront. Because its primary consumers are decision makers and not other researchers, those who demand (and authorize the payment for) program evaluation may not value the intricacies of defensible research as much as evaluators themselves do. The result is that decision makers are often reluctant to support adequate budgets for evaluation research. Evaluators thus face not only time constraints but also budget constraints that shape the research designs that they use. The most valid design from an academic perspective may be infeasible for the program evaluator, who often faces more binding money and time constraints.

TYPES OF PROGRAM EVALUATIONS

While program evaluations share a common definition, there are several kinds of program evaluation studies. Each asks a somewhat different question. There are four basic types of program evaluation questions. Each type can be classified in terms of its methodology and in terms of its substantive focus. In terms of method, program evaluations can be largely descriptive or they can be focused on assessing causal claims. In terms of substance, evaluations can focus on program inputs or outputs and outcomes.

Focus on Method: Descriptive and Causal Evaluations

Descriptive methods are essentially "bean counting." They are used to describe a population often (but not always) based on a random sample.[17] Descriptive evaluations might estimate the characteristics of a target population of potential clients. For example, if the target population is preschool children in families below the poverty level, a descriptive evaluation might assess their nutritional status, their overall health, their verbal and numerical abilities, and so on. "Needs assessments" are a common type of descriptive program evaluation that describes a target population of potential clients. Another type of target population is the population not of clients but of existing programs. For example, this type of descriptive evaluation might assess the characteristics of the population of local recycling programs. Such an evaluation might estimate their average budget, describe who administers the program (e.g., the government itself or a contractor), characterize the type of program (e.g., curbside pickup, payment for bottle return, or per-pound charge for curbside waste), or describe the types and tons of waste recycled. Thus, descriptive programs may assess program inputs, outputs, or both.

Another type of program evaluation is causal. As the term implies, causal evaluations aim to assess cause: Did the program bring about desired outputs and outcomes and avoid undesired outputs and outcomes? This is equivalent to asking the question in terms of cause: Did the program cause the desired outcomes (without causing undesired ones)? Another way to ask the same question is to ask whether the output or outcome would have happened anyway. For example, if clients would have found above-minimum-wage employment even without the job-training program, then it would be difficult to credit the job-training program with causing the outcome. Conversely, if a particular extent of school segregation would occur even without a program to bus children to magnet schools, it would be difficult to blame the program for causing the adverse outcome.

Substantive Focus: Implementation and Output and Outcome Evaluations

In terms of the substantive focus of the program evaluation, some evaluations center on the implementation of programs, while other evaluations focus on the outputs or outcomes of programs.

Examples of evaluations that examine implementation include assessments of program accountability and program management that are common in public administration and political science. They are often referred to as formative evaluations. For instance, studies of whether programs are implemented "as planned" or "on time" and "on budget" fall into the class of implementation or formative evaluations. Similarly, studies of program management also fall into this class of process or implementation evaluations. These studies might examine whether the program services are contracted out or run by the agency; whether the program activities are organized functionally or geographically; whether programs are administered centrally or locally; or whether the program staff is paid based on individual or program performance or face flat pay or a mix of flat and variable pay.

By contrast, evaluations that (exclusively) examine outputs or outcomes are most common in psychology, economics, and sociology. They are often referred to as summative evaluations. For instance, common output measures in assessments of education programs are standardized test scores, while outcome measures might include graduation rates or postgraduation measures, such as employment status or wages and salary. Output measures that are commonly used in the assessment of welfare and job-training programs include number of clients served and number of training hours per client; outcome measures might include clients' earnings, poverty levels, job mobility, and long-term wage increases. Regulatory program outputs include making inspections, assessing penalties, and other indicators of compliance or noncompliance. Regulatory program outcomes include measures of pollution, safety, and health.

Four Types of Evaluations

The two classes of methodological evaluations (descriptive vs. causal) and the two classes of substantive lenses (implementation vs. output/outcome) can be cross-classified as four basic types of program evaluations, as shown in Table 1.1. The types of questions that these evaluations ask are listed in each box.[18]

Using descriptive methods and focusing on program implementation, one type of program evaluation focuses on how the program was implemented. Questions include: What activities does the program support? What is the purpose or goal of these activities? Who performs these activities? How extensive and costly are the activities, and whom do they reach? Are conditions, activities, purposes, and clients fairly similar throughout the program, or is there substantial variation across program components, providers, or subgroups of clients? Were these the intended activities, costs, procedures, and time lines?

Using descriptive methods and focusing on program outputs and outcomes, another type of program evaluation is targeted at the objects at which a program's activities are directed and the coverage that these activities achieve. Questions include: Have program efforts focused on the intended targets or problems? Has the program reached the appropriate or intended people or organizations? Do current resources and targeting practices leave significant needs unmet? Assessing a program's targeting success typically requires not only data on the clients served but also information about the size and distribution of the eligible population, target group, or problem area as a whole.

Using causal methods and focusing on program outputs and outcomes, the third type of program evaluations estimates the impacts of public programs. Questions include: Did the program achieve its intended purposes or outcomes (impact), or would the outcome have happened anyway? Did the program have unintended beneficial or adverse effects? How does the current program compare to alternative strategies for achieving the same end (comparative advantage)? These impact questions center on whether program activities actually resulted in the improvements that the program was designed to produce. That is, the focus is on whether program activities are consistent with the hypothesis that they actually caused these improvements (or adverse effects). For example, a job-training program is expected to show that participation in the program led to significantly higher earnings or more stable employment. Similarly, regulatory programs are expected to show that implementation leads to reduction in the targeted hazard and that the reduction would not have happened otherwise.

Causal evaluations do not always appear in the guise of the explicit language of causality. That is why I frame the first two illustrative causal/output/outcome questions in Table 1.1 in two ways. One version uses the explicit language of causation (Does the use of seat belts cause fewer deaths? Do smaller classes cause higher achievement?). The other version is equivalent, but the word "cause" does not appear in these forms of the question, so the issue of causation is implicit but still central (Do seat belts save lives? Do smaller classes raise achievement?). The absence of the word "cause" does not signify the absence of the causal issue. (See Table 1.1.)

Table 1.1

Four Basic Types of Program Evaluations

Methodological focus	Substantive focus	
	Implementation	Output/Outcome
	Illustrative types of questions	
Descriptive	How many are enrolled? How many classes are offered? How many inspections were carried out? What is the ratio of servers to clients? What are the costs per client? Does the program operate • on budget? • on time? • in compliance with rules? What percentage of eligibles is served? Of those served, what percent is ineligible? Are clients in high-poverty areas (or in different jurisdictions) served more or less than those in other areas?	How many/what percent of clients are/is employed/above poverty/in school? What is the number/rate of workplace: • accidents/toxic substances observed? • pollutants emitted? What are scores on standardized tests? How do the above measures vary: • by jurisdiction? • by program need? What is the overall crime rate? • property crime rate? • violent crime rate? How do the crime rates vary: • by jurisdiction? • by poverty rate?
Causal	Why do (what causes) some jurisdictions (to): • implement regulations more strictly? • delay implementation? • provide more generous/extensive benefits/services? • offer a different mix of services? Does management affect implementation? Does contracting out save money/speed implementation? Does decentralized management: • reduce case worker discretion? • improve program performance?	Do seat belts save lives? (i.e., Do seat belts cause fewer deaths?) Do smaller class sizes raise achievement? (i.e., Do smaller classes cause higher achievement?) Do computers in classrooms raise student achievement? Do stricter regulations: • increase compliance? • reduce illness/pollution/accidents? Does training/education increase probability/quality of employment? Does increasing/targeting police patrol reduce crime rates? Does decentralized management result in better client outcomes?

A third version of a causal question about outcomes appears as seeking an answer to "Why?" For example, if one asks why some people are homeless, one is asking an implicit causal question: What causes some people (and not others) to be homeless? Program evaluators may ask questions in this form because the answer may cast light on program impacts. For example, evaluators may find that among the causes of homelessness are various policies that restrict or reduce the supply of low-income housing, such as zoning laws, restrictive rent control policies, and community development activities. Thus, causal questions about outcomes (or outputs) appear in various guises:

Does program X cause outcome Y?
Does program X have outcome Y (i.e., does X cause Y to occur?)?
What causes outcome Y to vary (among persons or places or over time)?
Why does outcome Y vary (i.e., what causes Y to vary?)?

Using causal methods and focusing on program implementation, the fourth type of program evaluation pays more attention to "why." It asks: Why are programs implemented differently? Why are some states more generous with welfare programs than others? Why do state taxes vary? Why do some cities contract out refuse collection (or other services) and others do not? Why are some school districts more supportive of school choice initiatives than others? But the underlying issue is still a causal question about program implementation, management, or administration: What causes some jurisdictions to be more aggressive or generous or speedy at implementing a program than others?[19]

Hybrid Evaluations

It is important to note that the 2 × 2 classification in Table 1.1 omits an important class of causal program evaluation questions. The omitted class represents the intersection of causation, implementation, and outcome. These evaluations explicitly link implementation to outcome, asking whether a characteristic of the implementation *caused* the outcome. The causal link is critical to these evaluations because, if the outcome would have occurred anyway, the causal claim about the method or mode of implementation cannot be sustained.[20] A typical question in this hybrid class of evaluation questions might be whether smaller classes (a question of implementation) cause higher achievement (an outcome).[21] The Student Teacher Achievement Ratio (STAR) experiment carried out in Tennessee in the 1980s suggests that smaller class size improves student test scores in the lower primary grades.[22] Another hybrid evaluation question asks whether increasing levels of implementation of a regulation cause higher compliance (an intended output) and lower pollution or better health (intended outcomes). Some studies have shown that additional health inspections, or inspections imposing penalties, decrease workplace injuries,[23] while other studies show that penalties imposed by the Occupational Safety and Health Administration (OSHA) are too small to have any significant deterrence incentive for employers to reduce workplace injury.[24] Studies that compare the impact of private, public, and nonprofit service delivery (e.g., trash collection, hospitals, K–12 schools, job training, prisons) on costs, outputs, or outcomes are also examples of hybrid evaluations.

Causal Evaluations

This book centers on the general class of causal questions because they are the hardest to answer. Although all the criteria for assessing the validity (i.e., defensibility) of descriptive claims are also used to assess the validity of causal claims, the reverse is not true. Specifically, as Chapter 2 explains, there are four general criteria for validity: external, measurement, statistical, and internal validity. Causal claims are unique because they have to meet one validity criterion, internal validity, which is not applicable to descriptive claims. All the other validity criteria apply to both causal and descriptive evaluations. Thus, while this book concentrates on methods for improving the defensibility or validity of causal claims about program impact, it will also apply, by logical extension, to methods for assessing the validity of descriptive claims about public programs.

In practice, most observational program evaluations fall into more than one category of the typology drawn above. For example, virtually all evaluations of program impact describe the "typical" program in the sample that is being studied and the variation from, say, one region to another or the variation in the size of the programs that are being studied. Similarly, most researchers who study why programs are implemented differently in various jurisdictions also describe variations in the range of programs under study. And, as noted earlier, some evaluations are hybrids.

Hybrid evaluations not only fall into both classes of causal evaluations but often also include descriptive components. These evaluations examine why programs are implemented differently in different jurisdictions (causal/implementation) and the impact of different implementation strategies on program outputs or outcomes (causal/output or outcome). They also describe the level and variation in both implementation and outputs or outcomes (descriptive implementation and output/outcome). Thus, evaluations like these fall simultaneously into all four categories displayed in Table 1.1. For example, Scholz and Wei describe how state and local governments implement OSHA workplace safety regulations and levels of firm compliance.[25] They also examine why OSHA workplace regulations are implemented more rigidly in some areas than others. That is, they ask: Why are enforcement activities (e.g., inspections) more frequent and penalties more severe in some jurisdictions than others, even when the characteristics of the firms are similar? Thus, they are asking what causes variation in implementation strategies. The same study then goes on to examine whether more rigid enforcement causes increases in levels of compliance.[26]

BASIC CHARACTERISTICS OF PROGRAM EVALUATION

Retrospection

This is a book about empirical, or observationally based, program evaluation. Program evaluations like these, whether descriptive or causal, are retrospective or contemporaneous. That is, evaluators cannot use observational data to describe or assess the actual impact of programs that do not (or did not) exist. Decision makers may use evaluators' assessments about previous or ongoing programs to make conjectures about the program's future characteristics or effects, but the core of program evaluation is a retrospective or contemporaneous assessment of previous or ongoing programs rather than the evaluation of future programs. Evaluators may assess imaginary programs by establishing a trial program and assessing it. However, after the trial program is established, it becomes an ongoing "trial," and it can be assessed as a contemporaneous evaluation.

Comparison

This is also a book about causal program evaluations. The primary purpose of causal program evaluations is to establish defensible causal claims about program implementation and impact. *It is impossible to make causal claims in the absence of comparison.* Two types of comparison lie behind any observationally based causal claim. One type compares entities with the program to those without it, or it compares entities with a lot of the program to those with just a little. Typically, this kind of comparison is called a cross-section (CS) comparison, because two (and often more than two) different entities (with and without) are being compared at the same time. For example, one might compare the academic performance (or the delinquency record) of high school students who participate in competitive sports programs with that of (comparable) students who do not—this is a with-and-without CS comparison. Or one might compare the achievement levels of children whose mothers face fairly lenient TANF work requirements with the achievement levels of similar children whose mothers face stricter or more time-consuming weekly TANF work requirements. This is an "a lot, a little" CS comparison. Or one might compare stakeholder satisfaction with conventionally written administrative regulations to stakeholder satisfaction with (comparable) negotiated administrative rules.[27] This is a "Type A vs. Type B" CS comparison. There are many kinds of CS comparison designs seen in the chapters that follow on experimental, quasi-, and nonexperimental designs.

Another type of comparison is before-and-after, or a time-series (TS), comparison. In this case, one compares the same entity (or set of entities) over time, examining how the entity operated before being subject to the program and then examining the same entity afterward. For example, one can examine whether raising state speed limits from 55 to 65 miles per hour (mph) increases accidents by comparing accident rates in a state before and after the speed limit was raised. Similarly, one might compare smoking rates in states for a period before and after cigarette taxes were raised. TS evaluations like these are particularly useful for "full coverage" programs. In this case, there is no entity that is not affected by the program, making a with-and-without CS comparison impossible. I discuss TS comparisons in the chapters that follow on quasi- and non-experimental designs. A TS-only comparison never applies to true experimental designs.

Sometimes evaluators make both kinds of comparisons at the same time. For example, some states have raised speed limits to 65 mph, while others have not. Some states have implemented TANF work requirements more strictly than others, and they implement (and change) these requirements at different points in time. Some high schools within a single school district adopt work-study programs, while others do not. In these cases, one can simultaneously make before-and-after (TS) and with-and-without (CS) comparisons. For instance, an evaluator can compare accident rates in states before and after each one raised its speed limit from 55 to 65 mph, simultaneously comparing accident rates in states with the lower limit to the rates in similar states with the higher limit. Or one can compare employment rates and salaries within a state before and after state TANF implementation and between states with different TANF implementation. One could compare alcohol sales between states with and without a state monopoly on retail alcohol to sales and simultaneously examine what happens to sales within states that change from monopoly to none.[28] I discuss these mixed TS and CS designs in the forthcoming chapters on quasi- and non-experimental evaluation designs.

In any case, some kind of comparison is necessary for causal evaluation. Causal evaluations with no comparison (that is, with no counterfactual or net effect) are not defensible.[29] Comparison is necessary (but not sufficient) for defensible causal claims. Examining one entity with no comparison at all makes it impossible to answer whether having the program (or not) makes (i.e., causes) a difference. When there is no comparison, the researcher can examine one entity and describe both the program and the level (and the distribution) of the output/outcome variables after the program was implemented. The researcher can even compare the level of the outcome variables to an external standard. This is often done in a performance evaluation, such as those required by the Government Performance and Results Act (GPRA) or the Program Assessment and Rating Tool (PART). But the researcher cannot defensibly conclude that the program caused the outcome because, without some minimal comparison, one cannot rule out the possibility that the level of the outcome would have been the same whether the program was implemented or not.

As an example, an evaluator can describe the elements of a high school work-study program and the achievement levels, delinquency rates, and part-time employment of students in the work-study program after it has been implemented. But without comparison (e.g., to outcomes of the students before participation or to outcomes of similar nonparticipants), no causal claim about the impact of the work-study program on the performance of the students is possible. Note that if the evaluator observed that achievement scores in the target group went up after the program was implemented, she is making a TS comparison. There would also be comparison if she observed that students in the school with the work-study program have higher achievement scores than similar students in the nearby school without the program. This would illustrate a CS comparison. But both of these examples comprise comparison.

Causal claims with no comparison at all are clearly indefensible. Making defensible causal claims about program impact even when there is comparison is not easy. In fact, it is the topic of this book. We will see that some types of comparison are more defensible than others. That is, different types of research designs make different kinds of comparisons, and some of these designs are more defensible for making causal claims. Unfortunately, the designs that are the most defensible in this regard are often less defensible in other ways.

RELATION OF PROGRAM EVALUATION TO THE GENERAL FIELD OF POLICY ANALYSIS

The general field of policy analysis is much broader than program evaluation, which can be regarded as a subfield of public policy analysis. Both fields are explicitly multidisciplinary, drawing on the applied portions of the social and natural sciences. Thus, neither policy analysis nor program evaluation is purely theoretical. Both fields include practitioners with backgrounds from many of the (applied) social and natural sciences. So, program evaluators (or policy analysts) may have degrees in program evaluation (or public policy), but many have degrees in psychology, economics, sociology, political science, chemistry, biology, ecology, and so on. Further, as I indicated earlier, the pure social sciences are not only concerned with abstract theories; they also have core normative values that guide the central theoretical questions of each social science discipline. By contrast, program evaluation, as a general field of study, has no core substantive norm. That is not to say that the field lacks core values. Rather, the core value is using defensible, observationally based (i.e., empirical) evidence on program performance for informing decisions about the termination, modification, continuation, or expansion of public programs. Its core value is allegiance to the scientific method and to its ethical use in applied empirical policy research, not to particular substantive normative values or to disciplinary theory. Rather, it uses multiple outcome criteria in the context of real-world programs and program options.[30] While I argue that program evaluation ought to pay more attention to disciplinary theories (from social and natural science) to frame evaluators' expectations about likely policy or program outcomes, the primary focus of the field is applied, defensible, empirical research about policy or management programs that can be used to inform collective decisions. Its primary task is to provide an answer to the question "What works?" that is as valid as possible.[31]

ASSESSING GOVERNMENT PERFORMANCE: PROGRAM EVALUATION AND PERFORMANCE MEASUREMENT

Program evaluation is not the same as performance measurement. Performance measures are the indicators of outputs or outcomes (or implementation or management strategies) that are used in program evaluation. Program evaluation requires performance measures but entails other demands as well, including multiple types of validity. Selecting the indicators that are used for performance measurement, or in a program evaluation, is a normative and political choice. It is also a choice that can affect how a program operates. As an example, consider the performance measures used for the Workforce Improvement Act (WIA) of 1998, which replaced the Job Training Partnership Act. It requires states to establish measurable performance standards, such as the following:

- the number of adults who obtained jobs by the end of the first quarter after program exit, excluding those employed at registration
- the number of adults with jobs in the first quarter after program exit, and the number with jobs in the third quarter after exit
- the number of adults with jobs in the first quarter after program exit, and the increases in their post-program earnings relative to pre-program earnings.

If program managers want to appear "successful," then they will select for training the least needy of those who are eligible (known as "creaming").[32]

The federal government uses two different systems of performance measurement. (State and local governments use similar systems to assess performance.) The first is the GPRA. Passed by Congress in 1993, it requires all agencies to submit to the Office of Management and Budget (OMB) an annual performance plan covering each program activity set forth in the agency's budget. These plans are to be consistent with the agency's strategic plan and should include the following features:

- the establishment of goals to define the level of performance to be achieved by a given program activity
- the use of goal statements that are objective, quantifiable, and measurable
- the use of performance indicators to measure or assess the relevant outputs, outcomes, or service levels for each program activity
- a description of the operational processes and resources required to meet the performance goals.

It should be apparent from this list that the core of the GPRA is descriptive program evaluation, spanning the description of both outcomes and implementation, and assessing them against externally set goals or standards. Although the GPRA, as applied in some agencies, may require the analysis of whether the program actually causes the outcomes, impact analysis is not the core of the GPRA. For example, under the GPRA, the Internal Revenue Service (IRS) might set, as one measure of compliance, a standard that 95 percent of all individual and corporate tax returns that are supposed to be filed by April 15 will be filed by that date. If that outcome is empirically observed, one cannot conclude that it was accomplished because of any activities or policies or programs of the IRS. In fact, it is even possible that, had the IRS done something else (e.g., changed the penalties for late filing), the compliance rate might have been even higher. Similarly, the WIA performance measures listed previously are outcome measures that might be used in a descriptive program evaluation. Alone, however, these measures cannot establish whether the WIA program, or something else, brought about the outcome. For example, whether adults obtain jobs or increase their earnings may also be attributable to changes in the local or state economy or in the local labor supply.

The executive branch uses a more recent, competing system of performance measurement to manage disparate federal agencies.[33] The PART is administered by the OMB as part of presidential oversight of federal agencies. The first ratings appeared in 2004; by now, nearly all federal programs have PART scores, and many programs have received PART scores in multiple years, to measure change. PART scores are used to assess the following four features of programs:

- clarity of program purpose and whether it is well designed to achieve its purposes
- strategic planning: Does the program have "valid" annual and long-term goals?
- program management, including financial oversight and program improvement efforts
- results that programs can report with "accuracy" and "consistency."

Performance measurement is necessary for program evaluation. Specifically, descriptive program evaluations require valid measures of performance. Forthcoming chapters define validity and describe how to assess it. Causal evaluations, however, start from measuring and observing program performance, but they do not end there. Thus, performance measurement (e.g., the GPRA and PART) undergirds descriptive evaluations. Performance measurement is necessary (but not sufficient) for making causal claims about program impact.[34]

A BRIEF HISTORY OF PROGRAM EVALUATION

Program evaluation began in the 1960s, coincident with the war on poverty.[35] Program evaluation used newly developed applied statistical methods (e.g., computer software programs for multiple regression analysis and for the analysis of large data sets) and new social science research methods (e.g., randomized experiments in the real world, large-scale random-sample surveys). The general assumption was that government programs did work; the purpose of program evaluation was to show how well government programs (especially education and antipoverty programs) worked and how they could be improved.

The first big national evaluations were in the field of education. James Coleman's federally funded study, *Equality of Educational Opportunity* (EEO), looked at the impact of per-pupil spending on educational performance.[36] It was a causal evaluation, using multiple regression analysis of a very large data set. At the time it was published (1966), its findings were nothing short of earthshaking. It showed that, compared with the impact of the socioeconomic status of the students and their peers, additional school spending had little or no impact on improving student performance. Re-analyses of Coleman's data, as well as other analyses, use more advanced statistical methods; they have been less conclusive regarding the impact of spending on educational outcomes.[37] Another major national study, the Westinghouse Head Start study, found that the effects of the Head Start program on academic readiness were short-lived; overall, the evidence appeared to show that the program had no impact.[38] While re-analyses of that data with modern social science methods, and other studies of similar programs, did not uphold that no-impact finding, the Westinghouse study fanned the firestorm started by the EEO study.

This was also a time of large-scale, national, randomized experiments and demonstration programs in the social service area.[39] For example, the negative income tax experiments (similar to the earned income tax credit, but open to those with no earnings as well as those with low earnings) began in several sites, including the state of New Jersey, the cities of Seattle and Denver, and rural North Carolina. The purpose was to see whether a guaranteed income (the negative income tax) would discourage work.[40] The findings, available only long after the study began, generally showed that there was little or no work disincentive, but there were unintended outcomes, including family dissolution. In a different policy area, a housing voucher study in two medium-size Midwestern cities showed that housing vouchers did not appear to raise the price of rental units, as detractors had feared.[41] A national health experiment designed by the RAND Corporation showed that a higher percentage of cost sharing by families on health plans decreases the use of health-care services. However, the reduced service had little or no net adverse effect on health for the average person.[42] A demonstration program in Alum Rock, California, showed that educational vouchers were very popular with parents but appeared to have no impact on achievement.[43]

By the 1970s, support for the big, national impact evaluations of domestic social service programs had waned. Some critics blamed the ideology of the administration of Richard Nixon, arguing that, because conservatives tend to assume that government programs do not work, that empirical evaluation of actual program impact is not necessary to uphold their assumption. Other observers pointed to the role of decentralization of federal authority to states, manifested by the new use of bloc grants to replace categorical grants. Bloc grants gave states more authority in deciding how to spend federally appropriated grant funds, and states usually chose not to spend on program evaluation.

The large-scale federal-level studies have been replaced by small-scale agency management and evaluation studies, as well as by separate state and local program evaluation studies. Many of these fail to provide defensible evidence regarding the impact of programs or management on outcomes, and some of them are methodologically less complex than the large-scale studies they replaced. Nonetheless, units within federal agencies are charged with program evaluation and policy analysis. In Congress, the Government Accountability Office has undertaken the task of evaluating the impact of agency programs (as well as auditing their finances), and similar state legislative oversight agencies undertake similar tasks.

Congress often requires agencies to systematically evaluate the impact of their programs on important outcomes. For example, the 1996 TANF Act requires the secretary of health and human services to evaluate the programs funded under the act.[44] Before the TANF, a federal requirement that states not only evaluate their individually designed welfare programs, but also that they use the most defensible designs, which usually require random assignment, stimulated the growth of evaluation capacity at the state level. The evaluation results generally showed that, compared with traditional AFDC benefits, which did not require work, work requirements were effective in raising recipients' income. Based in part on the program evaluation results, these state-level programs were forerunners of the national welfare reform that culminated in the TANF. But there is still no nationally comparable evaluation data to support large-scale national studies of welfare reform.[45]

Local governments typically have little evaluation capacity, but many local government programs are run in conjunction with nonprofit nongovernmental organizations (NGOs). Nonprofit organizations face considerable pressure to evaluate the programs they run because large organizations (like the Ford Foundation) that provide funds to local NGOs (in the United States and elsewhere) want to know what works. As a consequence, local nonprofit NGOs find that evaluating program impact helps them compete for scarce funds from large donors.

Finally, the increasing political importance of ascertaining that programs work before continuing or increasing their funding has made program evaluation results, particularly at the state level, critical to state funding decisions. This is most apparent in education funding, where testing of schools and students has created large, state-specific databases that evaluators use to evaluate the impact of many educational policies, from reducing (or increasing) class size and the seemingly mundane issue of when the school day should begin and end to the decision of whether a particular school should be closed.

Over the years, program evaluation has become increasingly organized. It has a national professional association (American Evaluation Association), a national conference, many regional and local conferences and professional associations, a code of ethics and standards for practitioners, and at least three journals (*Evaluation Review, American Journal of Evaluation,* and *New Directions in Program Evaluation*). Professional policy analysts also perform program evaluation as a core activity. They, too, have a professional organization (Association for Public Policy Analysis and Management [APPAM]), a professional journal (*Journal of Policy Analysis and Management* [JPAM]), and annual professional and research conferences.[46]

Applied policy researchers in traditional social science disciplines also evaluate programs, even though they may not be members of the American Evaluation Association or APPAM. Their evaluation research appears in journals such as *Social Science Quarterly, Policy Studies Journal, Review of Policy Research* (formerly *Policy Studies Review*), and elsewhere, including disciplinary journals such as *American Economic Review, American Economic Journal: Applied Economics,* and *American Economic Journal: Economic Policy*.

WHAT COMES NEXT

Chapter 2 is a discussion of the different types of validity that make evaluation conclusions more or less defensible. It introduces and briefly explains external validity (generalizability), statistical validity (separating systematic from random effects), and measurement reliability and validity (the relative absence of random and nonrandom measurement error, respectively). These three types of validity apply to both descriptive and causal evaluations. Chapter 3 introduces the concept of internal validity. It applies only to causal evaluations, as it pertains to the ability to separate causal claims about program impact from other causal factors that could also elicit the same outcome.

Causal evaluations are the central topic of this book. The next three chapters outline the three basic research designs that evaluators use to assess causal claims about program impact: the randomized experiment (Chapter 4), the quasi experiment (Chapter 5), and the nonexperiment (Chapter 6). Each chapter describes the characteristics of the class of designs and also introduces variations within each class. Each chapter also discusses each basic design in terms of threats to the various types of validity, especially internal validity, statistical validity, and external validity.

Most important, each of these research design chapters also describes statistical models that can be used to analyze the data that each design generates. For example, knowing how to collect data using a particular type of randomized or quasi-experimental design is not sufficient for understanding how to analyze the data collected in order to maximize statistical and internal validity. While other program evaluation texts introduce the basic evaluation research designs, none of them explain how to analyze the data collected. Data analysis (applied statistics) is a component of each research design chapter in this text.

Data on program management and inputs and data on program outputs or outcomes are often but not always available from existing sources. One of the most common ways to collect original data in program evaluation is to use a survey to ask questions of intended respondents. Program evaluators commonly use surveys to collect data about program benefits (e.g., wages, duration of employment, housing conditions); responsiveness (e.g., client or citizen satisfaction); equity (e.g., wages or satisfaction of white vs. minority trainees); and outputs and outcomes (e.g., health status, engaging in risky behaviors, use of social services; employment status or hours of work). Asking questions to elicit useful information with reliable and valid measures is not entirely an art form, yet it seems easy; we do it all the time. There is actually science behind crafting survey questions. Researchers have learned (often using randomized designs) how to ask questions to produce responses that are as objective, informative, and useful as possible. Chapter 7 summarizes some of that information, discussing how evaluators can write questions to collect data that they can use, especially in quasi- and non-experimental designs. Chapter 7 is not a substitute for an entire text on survey sampling and questionnaire construction, but it does describe much of the current wisdom of the best practice of writing questions used by academics, market researchers, and political pollsters.

Chapter 8, on meta-analysis, is logically the last chapter. It is a "meta-" chapter on how to systematically analyze (or evaluate) evaluations. Meta-analysis is the use of a nonexperimental design to summarize "what we know" based on the cumulative findings from other studies. For example, there are many studies of the impact of class size on student achievement; some find no impact, while others find that smaller classes raise achievement. What is the most defensible overall conclusion regarding the impact of class size? Does the impact of class size even have a most defensible overall conclusion, or does its impact depend on the subject, the grade, or the type of student? Meta-analysis (the analysis of analyses) is critical for making good use of evaluation research, especially when there are many studies with different conclusions.

KEY CONCEPTS

Policies vs. programs vs. projects
Defensible evaluation
Normative lenses
Allocative efficiency
Equality and social justice
Responsiveness and accountability
Outputs and outcomes
Descriptive vs. causal evaluations
Evaluations of implementation vs. outcomes and outputs
Four types of evaluations and hybrid evaluations
Retrospection and evaluation
Comparison and evaluation
Program evaluation and policy analysis
Program evaluation and GPRA or PART
Program evaluation and benefit-cost analysis
Origins of program evaluation
The profession today

DO IT YOURSELF

Locate some examples of program evaluations in your own field of interest. You might find some in your local newspaper; more likely in major national newspapers; in journals like *Journal of Policy Analysis and Management, American Journal of Evaluation, Review of Policy Research/Policy Studies Review, Policy Studies Journal*, and *Social Science Quarterly*; on the Web sites of many evaluation research firms that are paid to do evaluations of federal, state, and local programs (Institute for Policy Research, Northwestern University; various state institutes of government; the Urban Institute; the RAND Corporation, Abt Associates, Inc.; MDRC, Westat; SRI International [formerly Stanford Research Institute], and Mathematica Policy Research; and on the Web sites of various government agencies, including the Government Accountability Office, the Department of Housing and Urban Development's Office of Policy Development and Research, the office on the assistant secretary for policy evaluation at Department of Health and Human Services [HHS], and policy analysis and evaluation offices in the Department of Agriculture, and National Highway Traffic Safety Administration). There are also special evaluation and policy journals in many fields. Evaluation research on the impact of health policy often appears in the *New England Journal of Medicine* and in the *Journal of Health Economics,* while research on the impact of educational policy appears in *Economics of Education* and in *Education Evaluation and Policy Analysis*. Evaluation of public management issues appears in *Journal of Public Administration Research and Theory* and in the *International Public Management Journal.*

Decide whether the evaluation is a descriptive or causal evaluation (or both), and whether it focuses on program implementation, program output and outcome, or both.

Is the evaluation based on observations of real data? That is, is it retrospective? What data does the evaluation use (e.g., surveys, administrative data)? Does the evaluation make comparisons? What is compared? Is the comparison CS or TS or both?

NOTES

1. The text therefore makes no further separation between project and program evaluation. Project evaluation most often implies the use of benefit-cost analysis to evaluate the efficiency of specific projects or programs. While benefit-cost analysis is closely related to program evaluation, program evaluation does not require monetizing program inputs and outputs or outcomes, while benefit-cost analysis does. For more detail on benefit-cost analysis, see Edward M. Gramlich, *A Guide to Benefit-Cost Analysis*, 2d ed. (Long Grove, IL: Waveland Press, 1998); Tevfik F. Nas, *Cost-Benefit Analysis: Theory and Application* (Thousand Oaks, CA: Sage, 1996); Michael C. Munger, *Analyzing Policy: Choices, Conflicts, Practices* (New York: Norton, 2000), ch. 9–11; Anthony Boardman, David Greenberg, Aidan Vining, and David Weimer, *Cost-Benefit Analysis*, 4th ed. (Boston: Prentice Hall, 2011). For other texts on program evaluation (but not benefit-cost analysis), see Joseph S. Wholey, Harry P. Hatry, and Kathryn E. Newcomer, ed., *Handbook of Practical Program Evaluation* (San Francisco: Jossey-Bass, 1994); and William D. Berry and Stanley Feldman, *Multiple Regression in Practice* (Beverly Hills, CA: Sage, 1985).

2. For a discussion of these issues, see Joseph Valdez and Michael Bamburger, *Monitoring and Evaluating Social Programs in Developing Countries: A Handbook for Policymakers, Managers, and Researchers* (Washington, DC: World Bank Publications, 1994); Michael Bamberger, "The Evaluation of International Development Programs: A View from the Front," *American Journal of Evaluation* 21 (2000): 95–102; Miriam Bruhn and David McKenzie, "In Pursuit of Balance: Randomization in Practice in Development Field Experiments," *American Economic Journal: Applied Economics* 1, no. 4 (2009): 200–232.

The discussion in Barbara O. Wynn, Arindam Dutta, and Martha Nelson, *Challenges in Program Evaluation of Health Interventions in Developing Countries* (Santa Monica, CA: RAND, 2005), extends beyond health interventions. For a discussion of the problems of doing survey research in developing countries, see Mitchell Seligson, "Improving the Quality of Survey Research in Democratizing Countries," *PS: Political Science and Politics* 38, no. 1 (2005): 51–56; and Michael Bamburger, Sim Rogh, and Linda Mabry, *Real World Evaluation: Working Under Budget, Time, Data, and Political Constraints* (Thousand Oaks, CA: Sage, 2006), ch. 1. For a discussion of the opportunities for randomized experimental designs in developing countries, see Abhijit V. Banerjee and Esther Duflo, "Giving Credit Where It Is Due." *Journal of Economic Perspectives* 24, no. 3 (2010): 61–79; and Abhijit V. Banerjee and Esther Duflo, *Poor Economics: A Radical Rethinking of the Way to Fight Global Poverty* (New York: Public Affairs, 2011).

3. Gary A. Mauser and Richard A. Holmes, "An Evaluation of the 1977 Canadian Firearms Legislation," *Evaluation Review* 16, no. 6 (1992): 603–617; Mark Duggan, "More Guns, Less Crime," *Journal of Political Economy* 109, no. 5 (2001): 1086–1114; Philip J. Cook and Jens Ludwig, "Firearms," in *Litigation Through Regulation*, ed. W. Kip Viscusi (Washington, DC: Brookings Institution Press, 2002), 67–105; Arthur L. Kellermann et al., "Gun Ownership as a Risk Factor for Homicide in the Home," *New England Journal of Medicine* 329, no. 15 (1993): 1084–1091; Jens Ludwig and Philip J. Cook, eds., *Evaluating Gun Policy: Effects on Crime and Violence* (Washington, DC: Brookings Institution Press, 2003); Philip J. Cook and Jens Ludwig, "Aiming for Evidence-Based Gun Policy," *Journal of Policy Analysis and Management* 25, no. 3 (2006): 691–735.

4. Stephen G. Bronars and John R. Lott Jr., "Criminal Deterrence, Geographic Spillovers, and the Right to Carry Concealed Handguns," *American Economic Review* 88, no. 2 (1998): 475–479; Hashem Dezhbakhsh and Paul H. Rubin, "Lives Saved or Lives Lost? The Effects of Concealed-Handgun Laws on Crime," *American Economic Review* 88, no. 2 (1998): 468–474; John R. Lott Jr. and John E. Whitley, "Safe-Storage Gun Laws: Accidental Deaths, Suicides, and Crime," *Journal of Law and Economics* 44, no. 2 (2001): 659–689; John Donohoe, "The Impact of Concealed Carry Laws," in *Evaluating Gun Policy* (Washington, DC: Brookings Institution Press, 2003), 287–324; W. Manning, "Comment," in ibid., 331–341.

5. For evidence on unintended effects, see Sam Peltzman, "The Effects of Automobile Safety Regulation," *Journal of Political Economy* 83 (1975): 677–725; Michelle White, "The 'Arms Race' on American Roads: The Effect of Sport Utility Vehicles and Pickup Trucks on Traffic Safety," *Journal of Law and Economics* 47, no. 2 (2004): 333–356. For evidence on intended effects, see David J. Houston and Lilliard E. Richardson Jr., "Reducing Traffic Fatalities in the American States by Upgrading Seat Belt Use Laws to Primary Enforcement," *Journal of Policy Analysis and Management* 25, no. 3 (2006): 645–659.

6. Robert W. Hahn, Paul C. Tetlock, and Jason K. Burnett, "Should You Be Allowed to Use Your Cellular Phone While Driving?" *Regulation* 24, no. 3 (2000): 46–55; Robert W. Hahn and James E. Prieger, "The Impact of Driver Cell Phone Use on Accidents," *Advances in Economic Analysis and Policy* 6, no. 1 (2006), www.bepress.com/bejeap/advances/vol6/iss1/art9.

7. Mark Schneider et al., "Institutional Arrangements and the Creation of Social Capital: The Effects of Public School Choice," *American Political Science Review* 91, no. 1 (1997): 82–93.

8. See, for example, E. Allan Lind and Tom R. Tyler, *The Social Psychology of Procedural Justice* (New York: Plenum, 1988); Jodi Freeman and Laura Langbein, "Regulatory Negotiation and the Legitimacy Benefit," *New York Environmental Law Journal* 9, no. 1 (2000): 60–151.

9. B. Dan Wood and Richard W. Waterman, "The Dynamics of Political-Bureaucratic Adaptation," *American Journal of Political Science* 37, no. 2 (1993): 497–528; John T. Scholz, "Cooperative Regulatory Enforcement and the Politics of Administrative Effectiveness," *American Political Science Review* 85, no. 1 (1991): 115–136; John T. Scholz and Wayne B. Gray, "Can Government Facilitate Cooperation? An Informational Model of OSHA Enforcement," *American Journal of Political Science* 41, no. 3 (1997): 693–717.

10. Craig Thornton and Paul Decker, *The Transitional Employment Training Demonstration: Analysis of Program Impacts* (Princeton, NJ: Mathematica Policy Research, 1989); Peter Hinrichs, "The Effects of the National School Lunch Program on Education and Health," *Journal of Policy Analysis and Management* 29, no. 3 (2010): 479–505.

11. Scholz and Gray, "Can Government Facilitate Cooperation?"; William N. Evans, Matthew C. Farrelly, and Edward Montgomery, "Do Workplace Smoking Bans Reduce Smoking?" *American Economic Review* 89, no. 4 (1999): 728–747; Germa Bel, Xavier Fageda, and Mildred Warner, "Is Private Production of Public Service Cheaper Than Public Production? A Meta-Regression Analysis of Solid Waste and Water Services," *Journal of Policy Analysis and Management* 29, no. 3 (2010): 553–577.

12. A large literature in policy analysis discusses the inevitable trade-offs among competing values. Efficiency and equality are sometimes conflicting values (though not always, especially in education). There are notable trade-offs between efficiency and responsiveness, especially when popular choices are not efficient. Similarly, there are trade-offs between responsiveness/accountability and effectiveness, especially when doing what voters and politicians sometimes want (e.g., more aggressive regulatory program enforcement) may reduce effectiveness (e.g., less compliance). On the issue of trade-offs among competing values, see policy analysis textbooks such as David Weimer and Aidan Vining, *Policy Analysis: Concepts and Practice*, 4th ed. (Upper Saddle River, NJ: Prentice Hall, 2005), or Jonathan Gruber, *Public Finance and Public Policy* (New York: Worth, 2007). See also David L. Weimer, "Institutionalizing Neutrally Competent Policy Analysis: Resources for Promoting Objectivity and Balance in Consolidating Democracies," *Policy Studies Journal* 33, no. 2 (2005): 131–146; and William West, "Neutral Competence and Political Responsiveness: An Uneasy Relationship," *Policy Studies Journal* 33, no. 2 (2005): 147–160.

13. Nancy Shulock, "The Paradox of Policy Analysis: If It Is Not Used, Why Do We Produce So Much of It?" *Journal of Policy Analysis and Management* 18, no. 2 (1999): 226–244. For evidence on the effect of information on legislative deliberation in health policy, see Kevin Esterling, "Buying Expertise: Campaign Contributions and Attention to Policy Analysis in Congress," *American Political Science Review* 101, no. 1 (2007): 93–109. For a study of the varying demand for program evaluation and policy analysis more generally, see John Hird, *Power, Knowledge, and Politics: Policy Analysis in the States* (Washington, DC: Georgetown University Press, 2005).

14. John T. Scholz and B. Dan Wood, "Controlling the IRS: Principals, Principles, and Public Administration," *American Journal of Political Science* 42, no. 1 (1998): 141–162.

15. Some of that research is reviewed in a symposium edited by Allison Armour-Garb, "Should Value-Added Models Be Used to Evaluate Teachers?" *Journal of Policy Analysis and Management* 28, no. 4 (2009): 692–712.

16. It is important that program evaluators not ignore academic research. Program evaluators note the importance of program theory in designing their evaluations. Program theory is a representation of how program managers believe their program will operate, but managers' beliefs are not usually based on theoretical expectations from the academic social science disciplines. Evaluators who rely on program theory and ignore disciplinary theory do so only at their own peril, because programs do not necessarily work as managers intend, and programs are not exogenous to those who are affected by them. Academic theories are not just academic. They really explain observed behavior. For example, the law of demand (from economics) and the law of responsiveness (from political science) cannot be ignored just because they are academic. Programs often have hidden costs that are unanticipated by program managers but that nonetheless affect the behavior of target groups. Similarly, programs are chosen by vote-seeking politicians or by politically accountable administrators. These characteristics affect how program impact should be estimated. In the language of research design, these characteristics raise issues regarding the internal validity of quasi and nonexperiments, because they pertain to the identification of relevant confounding variables and simultaneity problems. They

also raise issues regarding the external validity of randomized field experiments, which by definition impose exogeneity on a world in which programs are really self-selected. The forthcoming chapters of this book discuss these issues in more detail. For further discussion of the importance of disciplinary theory for program evaluation, see Laura Langbein, "Estimating the Impact of Regulatory Enforcement: Practical Implications of Positive Political Theory," *Evaluation Review* 18, no. 5 (1994): 543–573.

17. There are many kinds of random sampling. While the text discusses aspects of sampling in subsequent chapters, it does not focus on sampling issues: that topic is widely discussed elsewhere. See, for example, Floyd J. Fowler, *Survey Research Methods* (Thousand Oaks, CA: Sage, 2009); Leslie Kish, *Statistical Design for Research* (New York: Wiley, 1987).

18. The questions listed in Table 1.1 mirror the examples set forth in General Accounting Office, *Program Evaluation: Improving the Flow of Information to the Congress* (Washington, DC: GAO, 1995); see also *Program Evaluation: Strategies for Assessing How Information Dissemination Contributes to Agency Goals* (Washington, DC: GAO, 2002).

19. Joe Soss, "Lessons of Welfare: Policy Design, Political Learning, and Political Action," *American Political Science Review* 93, no. 2 (1999): 363–380; Joe Soss, Sanford F. Schram, Thomas P. Vartanian, and Erin O'Brien, "Setting the Terms of Relief: Explaining State Policy Choices in the Devolution Revolution," *American Journal of Political Science* 45, no. 2 (2001): 378–395. Institutions affect choice: democratic choice is different from autocratic choice (and the outcomes may differ too). See Pedro Dal Bo, Andrew Foster, and Louis Putterman, "Institutions and Behavior: Experimental Evidence on the Effects of Democracy," *American Economic Review* 100, no. 5 (2010): 2205–2229.

20. Another way to tie implementation and output or outcome together is the logic model, which has gained popularity in recent years. Based on program theory (see note 16), a logic model is a conceptual model that describes the pieces of the project to be implemented and the outputs or outcomes, outlining the expected connections among them. A typical model has four parts: project inputs, activities, outputs, and outcomes. For more on logic models, see W.K. Kellogg Foundation, *Logic Model Guide* (2001); Joseph S. Wholey, *Evaluability Assessment: Developing Program Theory* (San Francisco: Jossey-Bass, 1987); Joseph S. Wholey, "Assessing the Feasibility and Likely Usefulness of Evaluation," in *Handbook of Practical Program Evaluation*, ed. Joseph S. Wholey, Harry P. Hatry, and Kathryn E. Newcomer (San Francisco: Jossey-Bass, 1994), 15–39. However, the discussion of internal validity and unbiased estimation in Chapters 3 and 6 shows that the logic model is an insufficient program theory for valid quasi- and nonexperimental evaluations. The logic model omits important confounding variables and assumes that program adoption and implementation are entirely exogenous to the problem to be solved. See Langbein, "Estimating the Impact of Regulatory Enforcement." Some of these issues are discussed indirectly in Government Accountability Office, *Program Evaluation: Strategies for Assessing How Information Dissemination Contributes to Agency Goals* (Washington, DC: GAO, 2002).

21. When implementation is not random, which is most of the time, hybrid evaluations usually require the answer to two related causal questions: Why was an implementation strategy chosen (e.g., why do some districts reduce or raise class size?); and, What is the impact of the change on a relevant outcome (e.g., achievement?). The second question cannot be tested independently of the first. See Caroline Hoxby. "The Effects of Class Size on Student Achievement: New Evidence from Population Variation," *Quarterly Journal of Economics* (November 2000): 1239–1285.

22. Tennessee State Department of Education, *Project STAR Office, Project Star: Final Executive Summary Report—Kindergarten Through Third Grade* (Nashville: Tennessee State Department of Education, 1990); Frederick Mosteller and Robert Boruch, *Evidence Matters: Randomized Trials in Education Research* (Washington, DC: Brookings Institution Press, 2002); Jonah Rockoff, "Field Experiments in Class Size from the Early Twentieth Century," *Journal of Economic Perspectives* 23, no. 4 (2009): 211–230.

23. John Scholz and Wayne Gray, "Can Government Facilitate Cooperation? An Informational Model of OSHA Enforcement," *American Journal of Political Science* 41 (1997): 693–717; Wayne B. Gray and Carol Adaire Jones, "Are OSHA Health Inspections Effective? A Longitudinal Study in the Manufacturing Sector," *Review of Economics and Statistics* 73, no. 3 (1991): 504–508.

24. Kenneth Meier, *Regulation: Politics, Bureaucracy, and Economics* (New York: Plenum, 1985); Robert S. Smith, *The Occupational Safety and Health Act: Its Goals and Its Achievements* (Washington, DC: American Enterprise Institute, 1976). More recent research focuses on cooperative strategies in environmental management (i.e., implementation) and their comparative effectiveness (i.e., outputs and outcomes). See for example W.R.Q. Anton, G. Deltas, and M. Khanna, "Incentives for Environmental Self-Regulation and Implications for Environmental Performance," *Journal of Environmental Economics and Management* 48, no. 1 (2004):

632–654; W. Antweiler and K. Harrison, "Canada's Voluntary ARET Program: Limited Success Despite Industry Cosponsorship," *Journal of Policy Analysis and Management* 26, no. 4 (2007): 755–773.

25. John T. Scholz and Hengfeng Wei, "Regulatory Enforcement in a Federalist System," *American Political Science Review* 80, no. 4 (1986): 1249–1270. See also John T. Scholz, "Cooperative Regulatory Enforcement and the Politics of Administrative Effectiveness," *American Political Science Review* 85, no. 1 (1991): 115–136; John T. Scholz, Jim Twombly, and Barbara Headrick, "Street-Level Political Controls Over Federal Bureaucracy," *American Political Science Review* 85, no. 3 (1991): 829–850; W. Kip Viscusi and James T. Hamilton, "Are Risk Regulators Rational? Evidence from Hazardous Waste Cleanup Decisions," *American Economic Review* 89, no. 4 (1999): 1010–1027; James T. Hamilton, "Politics and Social Costs: Estimating the Impact of Collective Action on Hazardous Waste Facilities," *RAND Journal of Economics* 24, no. 1 (1993): 101–125; Mark Lubell et al., "Watershed Partnerships and the Emergence of Collective Action Institutions," *American Journal of Political Science* 46, no. 1 (2002): 148–163.

26. It is increasingly common for program evaluations to examine the determinants of program use in order to more validly estimate the impact of program use on outcomes. See Chapter 6 on Instrumental Variables. For an example, see Sandra J. Newman and Joseph M. Harkness, "The Long-Term Effects of Public Housing on Self-Sufficiency," *Journal of Policy Analysis and Management* 21, no. 1 (2002): 21–43.

27. Laura Langbein, "Responsive Bureaus, Equity, and Regulatory Negotiation: An Empirical View," *Journal of Policy Analysis and Management* 21, no. 3 (2002): 449–466.

28. See Alexander Wagenaar and Harold Holder, "Changes in Alcohol Consumption Resulting from the Elimination of Retail Wine Monopolies: Results from 5 States," in *Evaluation in Practice,* 2d ed., ed. Richard Bingham and Claire Felbinger (New York: Chatham House, 2002): 283–294.

29. Lawrence B. Mohr, *Impact Analysis for Program Evaluation,* 2d ed. (Thousand Oaks, CA: Sage, 1995); Peter H. Rossi, Howard E. Freeman, and Mark W. Lipsey, *Evaluation: A Systematic Approach,* 6th ed. (Thousand Oaks, CA: Sage, 1999), ch. 7. The discussion of various methods of program evaluation in Government Accountability Office, "Program Evaluation: A Variety of Rigorous Methods Can Help Identify Effective Interventions," Washington, DC, November 2009, makes the need for comparison clear: to have a chance for valid conclusions about program impact, there must be some sort of comparison.

30. A recent statement of these core values appears in American Evaluation Association, "Guiding Principles for Evaluators," *American Journal of Evaluation* 26, no. 1 (2005): 5–7.

31. Many lawyers act as policy analysts. Few act as program evaluators, unless they also have training in social science research methods.

32. For a detailed list of the WIA performance standards, see Carolyn J. Heinrich, "Improving Public-Sector Performance Management: One Step Forward, Two Steps Back?" *Public Finance and Management* 4, no. 3 (2004): 317–351. Heinrich points out that one drawback of descriptive performance standards is that they give an incentive to program managers to limit access to programs to the least disadvantaged of the eligible groups (to "skim the cream"). Causal evaluations, when properly designed, can account for such patterns of deliberate selection, if indeed they exist.

33. For a detailed comparison of these two competing systems of performance measures, see Vassia Gueorguieva et al., "The Program Assessment Rating Tool and the Government Performance Results Act," *American Review of Public Administration* 38, no. 3 (2009): 225–245.

34. By contrast, as I mentioned earlier, benefit-cost analysis does require (causal) assessments of program impact in order to attribute beneficial (or harmful) consequences to a program or to implementation alternatives before monetizing them.

35. Christopher G. Wye and Richard C. Sonnichsen, eds., *Evaluation in the Federal Government: Changes, Trends, and Opportunities* (San Francisco: Jossey-Bass, 1992).

36. James S. Coleman, *Equality of Educational Opportunity* (Washington, DC: Department of Health, Education and Welfare, 1966).

37. Eric A. Hanushek, "The Economics of Schooling: Production and Efficiency in Public Schools," *Journal of Economic Literature* 24, no. 3 (1986): 1141–1177; Sheila E. Murray, "State Aid and Education Outcomes" in *Improving Educational Productivity: Lessons from Economics,* ed. David S. Monk and Herbert Walberg (Philadelphia: Information Age, 2001); Sheila E. Murray, "Two Essays on the Distribution of Education Resources and Outcomes" (Ph.D. diss., University of Maryland, 1995); Gary Burtless, ed., *Does Money Matter? The Effects of School Resources on Student Achievement and Adult Success* (Washington, DC: Brookings Institution Press, 1996); Eric A. Hanushek et al., *Making Schools Work: Improving Performance and Controlling Cost* (Washington, DC: Brookings Institution Press, 1994); David Card and Alan B. Krueger, "School Resources and Student Outcomes: An Overview of the Literature and New Evidence from

North and South Carolina," *Journal of Economic Perspectives* 10, no. 4 (1996): 31–50; Rati Ram, "School Expenditures and Student Achievement: Evidence for the U.S.," *Education Economics* 12, no. 2 (2004): 169–176; Sarah Archibald, "Narrowing in on Educational Resources That Do Affect Student Achievement," *Peabody Journal of Education* 81, no. 4 (2006): 23–42.

38. Westinghouse Learning Corporation and Ohio University, *The Impact of Head Start: An Evaluation of the Effects of Head Start on Children's Cognitive and Affective Development,* vols. 1 and 2, Report to the Office of Economic Opportunity (Athens, OH: Westinghouse Learning Corporation and Ohio University, 1999).

39. David H. Greenberg, Donna Linksz, and Marvin Mandell, *Social Experimentation and Public Policymaking* (Washington, DC: Urban Institute, 2003), presents a history of these experiments and describes their design, their findings, and how they were used in the decision-making process.

40. David N. Kershaw and Felicity Skidmore, *The New Jersey Graduated Work Incentive Experiment* (Princeton, NJ: Mathematica, 1974); Albert Rees, "An Overview of the Labor-Supply Results," *Journal of Human Resources* 9 (1974): 158–180; Joseph Pechman and P. Michael Timpane, ed., *Work Incentives and Income Guarantees: The New Jersey Negative Income Tax Experiment* (Washington, DC: Brookings Institution Press, 1975); Gary Burtless and Jerry A. Hausman, "The Effect of Taxation on Labor Supply: Evaluating the Gary Negative Income Tax Experiment," *Journal of Political Economy* 86, no. 6 (1978): 1103–1130.

41. Garth Buchanan and John Heinberg, "Housing Allowance Household Experiment Design, Part I: Summary and Overview," Working Paper 205–4, Urban Institute, Washington, DC, 1972.

42. Joseph P. Newhouse, *Free for All? Lessons from the Rand Health Insurance Experiment* (Cambridge: Harvard University Press, 1993); Greenberg, Linksz, and Mandell, *Social Experimentation.*

43. James A. Mecklenburger and Richard W. Hostrop, ed., *Education Vouchers: From Theory to Alum Rock* (Homewood, IL: ETC, 1972); Pierce Barker, Tara K. Bikson, Jackie Kimbrough, and Carol Frost, *A Study of Alternatives in American Education* (Santa Monica, CA: Rand Corporation, 1978).

44. Larry Orr, *Social Experiments: Evaluating Public Programs with Experimental Methods* (Thousand Oaks, CA: Sage, 1999).

45. See Greenberg, Linksz, and Mandell, *Social Experimentation.*

46. John Wiley publishes *JPAM.* Sage publishes *Evaluation Review;* the other two are published by the American Evaluation Association.

2

Defensible Program Evaluations

Four Types of Validity

DEFINING DEFENSIBILITY

Program evaluation is not someone's personal opinion about a program or someone's casual observations about a program or even observations based on journalistic or managerial familiarity with the program. Rather, it is based on defensible observations. Defensible observations are those collected in a systematic manner. "Systematic" means that the process by which the observations are collected and analyzed is both replicable and valid.

Replicability means that it does not matter who is doing the research. The basic design is laid out before the research is done. Robert Right or Leslie Left could implement the study design, collect, and analyze the data as prescribed in the study design and come to the same conclusion using the normative criteria also specified in the study design. Most of the research designs that this book discusses are *ex ante* replicable. That is, in advance, the researcher specifies in considerable detail what is to be observed, how it is to be measured, and how the information is to be analyzed. The process is known before the research is begun, but the conclusion is not. While virtually no research is 100 percent *ex ante* replicable, most research designs are quite detailed in specifying how the project is to proceed. Nonetheless, it is common for the researcher to make changes when he is in the field. He may find better ways of measuring some variables and discover that other ways are not possible. He then indicates how the design was modified, so that the audience (decision makers and others) can see, *ex post*, how the design could be replicated. Case study designs, which I briefly mention in Chapter 5 as a type of quasi experiment, have relatively more *ex post* than *ex ante* replicability. By contrast, experimental designs will have relatively more *ex ante* replicability. *Ex post* replicability means that, once the research was done, how it was done (the route that got the researcher from design to actual findings) is clear. *Ex ante* replicability means that, before the research is done, how it will be done (the route that will get the researcher from the design to actual findings) is clear.

Replicability, especially *ex ante* replicability, helps to make empirical claims (whether descriptive or causal) more defensible and objective. Without replicability (and other properties of defensibility), the claim would merely reflect personal opinion and casual observation. Replicability makes conclusions (whether descriptive or causal) traceable. That is, given the process for selecting observations and variables to study, for measuring each variable, and for analyzing the data, one can trace the link between the process and the conclusions. Traceability (or replicability) is at the core of making research objective.

While traceability (or replicability) is necessary for defensible program evaluation, it is not sufficient. If it were, one could defensibly implement a fully outlined research design that uses a process for collecting data that is known to be error prone. Such a design would be objective and replicable. It would not be valid. Validity is the second component of defensible program evaluation.

TYPES OF VALIDITY: DEFINITIONS

The four types of validity are internal validity, external validity, measurement validity (and reliability), and statistical validity.[1] I first define what these terms mean. I then discuss each type of validity in more detail, noting the threats to each type of validity and how to reduce them. The core of this text is on impact, or causal, evaluations. Because this is the province of internal validity, the discussion of internal validity begins in the next chapter. Subsequent chapters further elaborate that topic. By contrast, the discussion of external validity, measurement reliability and validity, and statistical validity will be relatively brief and is generally confined to this chapter. However, I also discuss these types of validity in more detail in forthcoming chapters when they also relate to internal validity.[2]

Internal validity refers to the accuracy of causal claims. Consequently, this type of validity is relevant only when causal evaluations are at issue. Because this is a textbook about causal, or impact, evaluations, it is a textbook about internal validity. For example, suppose that an evaluation study claimed that public school teachers with master's degrees are "more effective" than teachers with only a bachelor's degree. That is, based on the analysis of the observations in the study, the study's causal claim is that, compared with teachers with less education, teachers' additional education (including or beyond a master's degree) "causes" better performance by the students they teach. Suppose further that a subsequent, internally more valid study showed that that claim was entirely inaccurate or partially so, in that it overestimated the impact of public school teachers' advanced degrees on their students' performance. The implication would be that the internal validity of the former study was questionable. Subsequent chapters consider how to assess internal validity. It is important to note here that no study can be 100 percent internally valid. However, some studies are clearly more internally valid, or unbiased, than others. (These two expressions mean the same thing.) Reasonable levels of internal validity are necessary for causal inference if the causal claims of an evaluation are to be credible or unbiased.

External validity refers to the generalizability of research results. Research results are generalizable if they are applicable to other times and places and to the larger population that is of interest. External validity is relevant to both descriptive and causal evaluations. For example, someone interested in generalizing about state-run Temporary Assistance for Needy Families (TANF) programs in the United States would probably question the external validity of a single study of TANF programs in Nebraska, whether descriptive or causal. However, it is important to point out that one applies the criterion of external validity only to the population of interest. If one is only interested in generalizing about TANF programs in Nebraska, then the study above might be externally valid. It would not be externally valid if the population of interest were TANF programs in the United States as a whole. Temporal generalizability is another component of external validity; it is almost always relevant. That is, evaluators hope that findings from a study of ongoing programs (in a given location) will also be applicable to programs (in the same location) in the near future. Hence, findings from studies of alleged gender bias in, say, hiring practices in 1970 would probably not be generalizable to the same topic thirty-five years later, no matter how internally valid the studies were. It is also important to point out that external validity (that is, generalizability) is sometimes not possible. If program results are contingent on the particular subgroup or location in which the program is implemented, external validity is impossible. Worse, ignoring contingency would also make the findings internally invalid if the findings represented a causal claim.

Measurement validity and reliability pertain to the appropriate measurement of all the concepts and variables in the research. Measurement validity concerns the accuracy with which concepts are measured, while reliability pertains to the precision of measurement. Another way of describing the difference between measurement validity and reliability is that valid measures have as little systematic or nonrandom measurement error as possible, while reliable measures have as little random measurement error as possible. I will discuss each of these in more detail. It is important to note that measurement reliability and validity refer not just to outcome or output variables but also to program variables and other variables that the evaluation measures.

Finally, statistical validity refers to the accuracy with which random effects are separated from systematic effects. Measurement reliability pertains to the relative absence of random error in the measure of a single variable. Statistical validity usually pertains to the relative absence of random error from the causal or descriptive claim that there is a systematic relation between variables. Thus, statistical validity usually (but not always) pertains to relations between two (or more) variables; measurement reliability usually pertains to the measurement of variables considered one at a time.

TYPES OF VALIDITY: THREATS AND SIMPLE REMEDIES

With one exception, I discuss each type of validity in greater detail. I reserve all of Chapter 3 to discussion of threats to internal validity, and Chapters 4, 5, and 6 to research designs that, to a greater or lesser extent, minimize those threats to internal validity.

External Validity

External validity refers to the generalizability of research results—that is, their applicability or portability to other times and places. Threats to external validity mainly come from four sources.

1. *Selecting a sample that is not representative of the population of interest.* If the population of interest is large (say, over 500 units of analysis), it may not be feasible or even reasonable from the perspective of costs, time, or ease of administration to study the entire population. So whom should a researcher study if she cannot study every unit in the population? The usual remedy is to select a random sample. Random means that every unit to be selected for study has a *known* probability of being selected. Many samples are simple random samples, where every unit has the *same* probability of being selected for study. More detailed texts on sampling also discuss other kinds of random samples where the probabilities are known but not equal. For example, in stratified samples, small populations may be oversampled to improve the efficiency of estimating population characteristics.[3] For the purposes of this text on program evaluation, there are three important points to make about representative sampling for external validity.

1a. *The unit of analysis is what is sampled and what is counted.* Units of analysis may be people, but often they are not. Sometimes a researcher will select a sample of individual persons from the adult population of a country or from the population of a medium or large city or from the population of students in a medium or large school district. If she selects 2,000 individuals from the population of members of a group whose population numbers about 200,000, she might select them such that each member has .01 probability of being selected. The number of observations in the study would be 2,000. Sometimes the unit of analysis is a collection of people. Suppose a researcher wants to study schools in Maryland. There are about 7,500 schools in Maryland, and he might decide that he cannot study all of them. Instead, he decides on a representative sample, with each school having a .10 probability of being selected for study. He would collect data on 750 schools. The number of observations in his study is 750 schools; the number of observations in the study is *not* the total number of students in the 750 schools.

Similarly, suppose a researcher wants to study the implementation of Title IX programs in universities in the United States. She decides to study a representative random sample, rather than the whole population. Selecting 100 universities from a list of the 1,000 largest universities, she would design a sampling procedure such that every university in that list has a .10 chance of being in the sample. The important point here is that the relevant sample size is 100, not the number of students in the athletic programs in those universities. We revisit the issue of the units of analysis when we talk about experimental designs in Chapter 4. While the application is different, the underlying principle is the same: In selecting units for study, the number of observations in the study is the number of units in the sample, not the number of entities (if any) within the units.[4]

1b. *Small random samples are never representative.* "Small" usually means less than 120, but this is not an absolute rule. However, random samples of, say, thirty are not likely to be representative. What makes random samples representative is their size: Large random samples from a fixed population are more representative than smaller random samples. A 100 percent sample is the population, so it is clearly representative. But a random sample of 10 children is probably not representative, regardless of whether the population from which they are being selected is 300, 3,000, 300,000, or 30 million children.

Sometimes, usually because of budget and time limitations, it is not possible to study a large sample. In that case, it may be best to decide *ex ante* what a typical sample might look like. When samples must be small, rather than rely on the laws of statistical sampling that require a large sample, it is better to deliberately select what appear to be representative units from the population of interest. Such a sample is deliberately rather than randomly representative. For example, in an evaluation of a federally funded Department of the Interior (DOI) initiative to rehabilitate urban parks, the evaluators had funds to collect detailed, on-site information from no more than twenty cities.[5] Rather than select a random sample, the researchers deliberately selected cities from each region of the country; they selected cities of the size that typified those in the program, including some large cities and some small ones, and they studied different types of programs. Although a few programs provided services, most were aimed at improving the physical infrastructure of the parks (e.g., fixing the basketball courts). Consequently, the researchers deliberately selected for study more infrastructure than service programs. Had they selected twenty cities randomly, it is likely that no cities with service-oriented programs would have shown up in the simple random sample, even though they were (a small) part of the DOI initiative under study.

1c. *Random sampling from a small population will not be representative.* This is true for a variety of reasons. First, if the population is small, the random sample will also be small, and, as we have just seen, small random samples will probably not be representative of the population from which they are selected. Second, the usual theory of sampling assumes sampling with replacement. That is, in sampling theory, researchers select one unit at random from a population of, say, 10,000 units, pretend to return that unit to the population, and resample the second unit. They keep doing this until they have their desired sample of, say, 200 units. But, in practice, they do not really return the units to the population. So, the probability of selecting the first unit is 1/10,000 = .0001. The probability of selecting the second unit is 1/9,999, which is only slightly greater than .0001. The probability of selecting the third unit is also only slightly greater than the former probability. In general, when the denominator is large, sampling without replacement (which is what is usually done in practice) is virtually the same as sampling with replacement.

However, selecting a simple random sample of states from the population of fifty states will not be random because the first unit to be selected has a lower probability of selection than the second, which has a lower probability than the third, and so on. If a researcher aims for, say, a sample of thirty, the probability of selecting the first unit is 1/50 = .02; the probability of selecting the second is 1/49 = .0204; the probability of selecting the third is 1/48 = .0208. Every unit in the analysis would have to be adjusted by the probability of showing up in the sample, adding an additional level of complexity to the analysis of the observations in the study. And the final sample may not be representative anyway because it is too small.

2. *Studying "sensitized" units of analysis.* When the units of analysis are individual people who know that they are being studied, their awareness often distorts their behavior, such that the behavior or response in the study is not generalizable to what would be observed in the real world. (Later we see that this is the same as a testing effect, a source of measurement invalidity.) For example, if bank loan officers are told that they are being studied to determine whether they service Federal Housing Administration–guaranteed mortgages differently from their own bank's mortgages, they may well behave differently in the study than they would ordinarily. Teachers who are being observed for a study may also alter their behavior, such that what is observed during a study is not representative of their ordinary behavior. The problem of studying sensitized units of analysis is often called the Hawthorne effect, based on the unexpected 1920s findings from a Hawthorne company plant that manufactured shirts. The plant managers surveyed the workers on the assembly line to see what their needs were; for example, they asked the workers whether they wanted more light to do their work. Surprisingly, the workers' output improved just after the survey, even though the managers had not changed anything. Apparently, the workers worked harder simply because the survey itself changed their behavior, signaling that management "cared."[6]

It would seem that the remedy for the problem of studying sensitized units is straightforward: Do not tell people that they are being studied. Although the respondents to a survey will be aware that they are being studied, the bank officers in our example simply need not be told that they are being studied. Similarly, social service recipients, or other program clients, simply need not be told that they are being studied. The problem with this solution is that, in general, it is illegal and unethical to fail to get informed consent from people whose behavior is being studied in an evaluation of public program implementation or impact. Although there are some exceptions to this rule,[7] the presumption is that informed consent is necessary.

An alternative strategy is to design the study so that it does not rely entirely on reactive data. Although surveys and direct observation are wonderful sources of information, they are obtrusive, and respondents may consequently alter their behavior such that it is not representative of what would be observed outside a study situation. But there are other sources of information. For example, administrative records are a source of information about the activities of teachers and bank officers in two examples that I have used. To reduce the threat to external validity from relying entirely on sensitized units of analysis, one option is to supplement the sensitive data with unobtrusive data on the same units of analysis. If the two sources of information produce similar results, then researchers can be more confident that the reactive data sources are as externally valid as the unobtrusive sources of information.

3. *Studying volunteers or survey respondents.* People who are willing to be studied may not be representative of the intended population. For example, one of the biggest problems in contemporary opinion polling and survey research is the problem of nonresponse. In this case, researchers select a large random sample of people from a specified population and phone them, send them a

survey by mail or e-mail, or visit their homes for a face-to-face interview. Although the researcher selects the intended sample, the respondents select themselves into the actual sample; in effect, they are volunteers. Typical response rates are 70 percent or lower. Even the response rate to the 2010 national census (which is not a sample; it is a tally of observations from the entire population) is only about 75 percent, and it varied considerably across the country. (For example, among states, it varied from about 65 percent in New Mexico to 82 percent in Minnesota.)

Responders are not like the population; they tend to be more educated, wealthier, and generally cooperative people. Depending on the purpose of the study or the nature of the intended sample of respondents in the study, the actual responders might be the ones with the most extreme views or more time on their hands (e.g., retired people). Another class of volunteers participates in many medical studies that compare the effectiveness of a new drug to the current drug or to a control. For example, the National Institutes of Health (NIH) offers summer internships in Washington, DC, to healthy college biology majors to work in the labs with NIH research scientists and take part in controlled drug studies. These volunteers may not be representative of the population to which the researchers would like to generalize. And, of course, many people remember being "volunteered" to be in a study in a sophomore psychology or economics class. Most people would not characterize their behavior then as representative.

Remedies for the problem of studying volunteers will only minimize the problem, not eliminate it. Chapter 7 discusses in considerable detail the steps that researchers can take to increase response rates to surveys, and I will not repeat that discussion here. The problem of generalizing from those who consent to be studied (e.g., school districts that volunteer to be in a study of school integration; college students who volunteer to be in a psychology or medical study) is usually minimized by replicating the studies in other volunteer groups. That is, if similar studies of college students from large universities, small colleges, public universities, expensive not-for-profit colleges, private universities, and the like produce the same results, the implication is that the individual studies are representative. When researchers reasonably expect that nearly all individuals respond similarly to environmental treatments, or stimuli, generalizing from volunteers or single-site studies may be valid. For example, most patients react the same way to common antibiotics, and most consumers react the same way to prices: When prices go up, people buy less. The problem of studying volunteers or sites selected by the researcher because of their convenience or availability is much more of a threat to external validity when the researcher anticipates that reactions may be different for different groups of people. This is the problem of statistical interaction.

4. *Statistical interaction.* Statistical interaction means that the descriptive relation between two variables X and Y (or the causal impact of X, the program, on the outcome Y) depends on the level or value of a third variable, Z. For example, consider a possible causal relation between public school spending and pupil achievement. Suppose that the impact of additional spending (X) on student achievement (Y) depends on the socioeconomic status (SES) of students in the school district (Z), so that more spending (X) appears to bring about ("cause") higher achievement (Y) only in low SES districts ($Z-$) and has no impact in high SES districts ($Z+$). This would be an example of statistical interaction, because spending "works" only in low-income districts. Thus, the impact of spending (X) on achievement (Y) depends on the level of district SES (Z). Similarly, if job training (X) appears effective at raising the earnings (Y) of unskilled adult women (Z_w) but not for unskilled adult men (Z_m), that also would be an example of statistical interaction.

Statistical interaction is a threat to external validity because it means that generalization is not possible. Rather, what characterizes one subgroup in the population of interest does not characterize other subgroups. When a researcher is evaluating the plausibility of causal hypotheses or causal claims, failing to recognize statistical interaction when it is present means that external validity is not possible and reduces internal validity. That is, undetected statistical interaction can lead researchers either to erroneously find a causal relation or to erroneously reject a causal claim. Hence, we discuss the issue further in our consideration of internal validity.

The possibility of statistical interaction may also necessitate larger sample sizes to minimize the threat of small samples to external validity (and to statistical validity, as we will soon see). For instance, African-Americans comprise a small proportion of the U.S. population. If a researcher expects that a program might operate differently for African-Americans than for other groups, she might want to oversample African-Americans to ensure that there are enough African-Americans for externally valid results for that subgroup. If she is studying whether school vouchers improve academic performance among low-income public school students, anticipating that the effects might be different for black students than for white students, she should oversample African-Americans to examine this possibility. Otherwise, if the sample of African-Americans is too small, then the final causal claim about vouchers (whether the claim is "vouchers improve academic performance" or "vouchers do not affect performance") might be externally valid for the larger subgroup (those who are not African-American), but it will be less valid externally (and statistically) for the smaller subgroup of African-Americans. In fact, researchers frequently oversample many subgroups for special study simply because they anticipate statistical interaction. That is, they anticipate that it will not be possible to make one generalization about the population of interest and that the study may find that what "works" or is effective for one subgroup is not so for another.

Statistical Validity

Definition

In making descriptive or causal claims about the relation between variables (or in making descriptive claims about single variables), researchers (and critics) often wonder whether what the observations seem to show is "real" or just a fluke. For example, in the case of a single variable, if a researcher observes that achievement scores in a particular school appear extremely low compared with some external standard, that observation might be a fluke. That is, the researcher might ask, "If I did this study again (say, next week), would I get the same result? Or is the observed score just a random occurrence?" And, in the case of, say, two variables, if the researcher observed that schools with large class sizes have low achievement scores, he might ask, "Is this result real?" or "If I did this study again, would I see the same thing?" (These questions apply to both descriptive and causal claims.) Sometimes what researchers observe is purely random occurrence, especially when the number of observations (i.e., units of analysis) is small. Generalizations based on small samples are prone to random error. For example, it is quite likely that a coin, tossed twice, will show two heads (25 percent), even though it is really a fair coin. More tosses make a more statistically valid test of the hypothesis that it is really a fair coin. Random error decreases as the sample size increases.

More generally, statistical validity refers to the accuracy with which random claims (descriptive or causal) about observations are separated from systematic claims. For example, a random claim might be: "The school performance is just below the standard, but the difference is so small that it is just random." A systematic claim might be: "This school is clearly below (or above) the standard." How can we assess the accuracy of either claim? Alternatively, a random claim may pertain to the accuracy (or, in this case, precision) of a random sample: "53 percent report that they support my candidate, so it looks like my candidate may lose; the difference between winning (50 percent + 1) and 53 percent is just random." Someone else might use the same claim as systematic evidence that the candidate will win. Which claim is more likely to be correct? Assessing statistical validity helps us to evaluate the relative accuracy, or precision, of claims like these.

Sources

Observational studies, whether they are descriptive or causal, have three sources of randomness: sampling, measurement, and human behavior. Consider, first, sampling as a source of random error. Recall that we have already related random sampling to external validity. Specifically, we noted that small random samples are likely to be low in external validity because they may not be representative of the larger population to which the evaluator wishes to generalize. Small random samples also have more random error (called sampling error) than larger samples, and thus they are more subject to problems of statistical invalidity. Statistics texts point this out, and it is not necessary to repeat those lessons here.[8] Although the probability of accuracy increases as the sample size increases, this is true only up to a point. As the sample size becomes exceedingly large (e.g., over 1,000), the probability of accuracy does not go up much, but the costs of the larger sample continue to rise, often at an increasing rate. As a consequence, we rarely observe samples of the U.S. population (or any other sample) that are much larger than 1,000.

The exception to this rule occurs when the evaluator anticipates statistical interaction. In other words, if the evaluator anticipates that, say, the impact of providing a housing voucher on housing consumption may be different for seniors than for others, such that generalization to a single population would be erroneous, then taking two separate, large samples (say, close to 1,000) of each group would increase the statistical validity of conclusions for each subgroup. The important point is that larger samples have less sampling error than smaller ones. Large samples reduce the chance that one will mistake a randomly occurring observation (noise) for a signal that is really there. Of course, larger samples always have higher costs, so researchers must balance the gain in statistical validity against the added monetary costs to determine the optimal sample size.

The ideal sample size also depends on the use that is to be made of the data. For example, we have just seen that if a researcher anticipates statistical interaction, then the ideal sample size should be larger than otherwise. Similarly, if a researcher is interested solely in the estimating population mean of one variable based on sample data, she will probably need a larger sample than if she were interested in evaluating whether a particular program is having its intended impact in a particular city. In the former case, she might need, say, 1,400 randomly selected observations (assuming that there are no issues of likely statistical interaction) in order to be 95 percent confident that an estimated mean is within + or –3 percent of the (unknown) true population mean. In the latter case, she could readily work with, say, only about 120 observations in order to be 95 percent confident that an estimate of program impact (the causal relation between X and Y, given, say, 110 degrees of freedom) is significantly greater in the intended direction than no impact at all. Further, in this case, the 120 observations could be randomly selected from the relevant population, or they could comprise the entire population of the relevant study group. Finally, in this case of impact estimation, while 1,000 observations might be better for statistical validity, it might not necessarily be optimal because of rapidly rising data collection costs. The point is that, for statistical validity, generalizing about a population's value on separate, *single* variables requires larger samples than estimating parameters that characterize causal (or even descriptive) relations *between* variables. Generalizing about the population value of single variables (e.g., mean education and median income) is usually a task for descriptive program evaluation. For statistical (and external) validity, these evaluations may require a larger *n* than causal evaluations.

It is also important to note that reconsidering the unit of analysis can transform what appears at the outset to be an inherently small sample with an *n* of 1 into a larger sample, simultaneously enhancing both external and statistical validity. For example, suppose that the task is to evaluate a specific shelter program that serves homeless women in a particular city. The intention is that the evaluation be generalizable only to that program. This appears to be a case in which the number of observations can only be one which is far too low for statistical or external validity.

But, in fact, this is not the case. The researcher can readily amplify the number of observations by studying a single unit over time. For example, if the shelter program has been operating for 10 years, then the potential *n* is 10 years × 12 months in a year = 120. Alternatively, and even better if it is feasible, he could compare the operation of the focal shelter, using monthly data over the past 10 years (*n* = 120), with that of a different program serving homeless women in the same city, using monthly data for the same period. Now, *n* is 240. Suppose, however, that the shelter has been in operation for only one year or that only the records for the past year are readily available. The researcher cannot then study data over time, but he can observe the entities within the study unit. Suppose the shelter, during the one-year span of time, has served 120 women. Some of the women have found independent living and employment, some are still in the shelter, and some have left and returned. A study can provide descriptive information about the program inputs and outputs for these 120 women (e.g., hours of paid employment) and even begin to examine whether the use of more program inputs "causes" better outputs (or even outcomes). In any case, *n* is 120. If the researcher can collect similar data on, say, 100 homeless women in a different program in the same city, *n* now becomes 220.

The point is that what originally appeared to be a study with one observation can be reframed by extending it over time or, by looking at individuals within a single unit, examined at a microlevel, or both, simultaneously increasing both its statistical and external validity. It may also be possible to increase *n* by adding another set of observations on individuals served by a different, comparable entity, providing a comparison for the focal institution that is being evaluated.

Two remaining sources of randomness also reduce the ability to separate systematic observations or patterns from random occurrences, jeopardizing statistical validity: randomness in measurement and randomness in human behavior. Consider first the case of randomness in measurement. We have already noted that one source of randomness in measuring population values on a single variable is small sample sizes. Just as multiple observations reduce random sampling error, multiple measures reduce random measurement error, especially when what is being measured is an abstract concept.

For instance, suppose that an evaluator is trying to estimate the employment rate of people who have completed a job-training program. Realizing that an estimate based on a random sample of ten might be a fluke, the estimate would be more precise if the random sample were 300 or 1,000. This is an example of statistical (random) error due to small sample size. In the example, employment is relatively easy to measure.

But consider the case of measuring the value of observations on a single, abstract concept like educational achievement or "social adjustment." For example, because of randomness in student performance measures, a student in a study might score low on one day, but if the same test were given the next day, the student might score better (or worse). The observation might be purely random and impermanent, but maybe it is "real" and persistent. If the observation was just a fluke, extremely low scores measured on the first day will go up the next day and extremely high scores will go down; on subsequent days, individual daily scores will fluctuate around the true mean. When there is randomness in an observed variable, any single observation will be a fluke. What is really there will be revealed by repeated measures of (roughly) the same test over time. If the seemingly low score was not a fluke, it will remain low on subsequent days, still fluctuating around the true mean. Thus, in the case of a single variable, especially when it is an indicator of an abstract concept, the best way to reduce randomness in observations or scoring is to have repeated measures or observations.

Multiple indicators, measured at a single point, also help to reduce random measurement error. As an example, consider the design of standard educational achievement tests, such as the Scholastic Aptitude Test (SAT) or Graduate Record Examinations (GRE). Why are these tests so long? Asking multiple questions about the same basic concept increases the reliability of the test (with diminishing returns) by using multiple indicators. A ten-question SAT would contain a much greater random component than the current version. Similarly, a four-question final exam in a math class would be a quicker but much "noisier" measure of a student's true performance than a fifty-item final exam.

In addition, randomness in individual-level measures (the example in these paragraphs) is usually far greater than randomness in collective-level or aggregate data (for example, school-level means or percents compared with individual-level measures), but it does not disappear, especially when the concept to be measured is abstract.

I consider the problem of random measurement error in more detail next and in Chapters 6 and 7. It turns out that random error in measures of outcome or output variables is a particular threat to statistical validity. In addition, the best way to reduce random error in the measurement of abstract concepts is to have multiple indicators or repeated measures. Just as more observations reduce random error in sample sizes, repeated measures or more indicators reduce random error in the measurement of abstract concepts. With diminishing returns, multiple indicators or repeated measures (and larger samples) separate the signal (the systematic component) from the noise (the random component). That is why researchers almost never measure an abstraction like educational achievement with just one indicator. Rather, they measure its separate components (math ability, reading ability, reading comprehension, analytical ability, and so on), using multiple items to measure each one. Multiple indicators of abstract concepts reduce the randomness in the measurement of abstract concepts.

Finally, randomness in human behavior is also a threat to statistical validity. First, randomness in human behavior is one source of random measurement error, which is due not to the measurement process but to the behavior of what is measured. This is a particular problem in survey research, but it is also a problem in other measures, too. For example, sometimes a student does well on a test, and sometimes the same student does not. The student does not know why. Sometimes she just guesses an answer; that is surely random. In surveys (or classroom tests), if students are asked to respond to a question about an issue that they have not thought about before, they respond randomly.[9] We consider the implications of random responses (in tests, surveys, and other measures) in the following paragraphs and in Chapters 6 and 7 in the discussion of measurement reliability and of surveys in evaluation research. In both of these cases, however, randomness in measures attributable to randomness in human responses makes it harder for the evaluator to separate systematic observations from random ones.

The other source of randomness in human behavior is that human behavior is very complex, probably too complex for researchers ever to completely comprehend. Furthermore, in impact evaluation research (i.e., causal evaluation studies), it is not necessary for evaluators to understand all the causes of the human behavior that they are examining. For example, suppose an evaluator wishes to estimate whether and how much a job-training program "causes" recipients to move to higher-paying jobs than they were in before. The evaluator cannot hope to explain everything about the wages of everyone in her sample. She will probably chalk up the unexplainable aspects of human behavior to the "stochastic" or random component of her study.

If the stochastic component is too large, it will be more difficult to separate any systematic impact of job training on wages from random patterns. The forthcoming chapters on research design explain how researchers can (sometimes) make use of pretest scores to reduce the random component of human behavior without having to undertake the impossible burden of explaining it. The basic idea is that the best predictor of a person's wages at a moment in time, t, is to know what that person's wages were at a previous time, $t-1$. Taking account of the predictability or temporal stability of behavior allows researchers to increase the statistical validity of estimates of relations between program inputs and outputs, whether they are intended to be descriptive or causal. And do not forget that a large sample size is also a straightforward if not always convenient way to reduce the random component of evaluation studies. (There is another aspect to the inexplicable, random element in human behavior that is a threat to internal validity. I postpone that discussion to the extensive treatment of that topic in the chapter on internal validity.)

Consequences

Why is low statistical validity a problem? Low statistical validity can lead to important errors of decision. In academic research, these errors may not be costly, except to one's pride, but in program evaluation, where policy makers and program administrators must make "real" decisions based on research outcomes, these errors may well be of external consequence. No matter what its source, statistical validity tends to minimize these decision errors. In statistical language, there are two kinds of decision errors: Type I and Type II. A Type I error occurs when a null hypothesis is rejected when it is actually true; a Type II error occurs when a null hypothesis is accepted when it is actually false. Increasing sample size can reduce each type of error, but the benefit diminishes as the sample size increases. First, I characterize each type of error, and then I provide a simple illustration of how large samples can reduce the chance of each.[10]

In systematic studies, there are two kinds of hypotheses. The null hypothesis (H_0) is the one that is tested. The null hypothesis is also always an exact hypothesis. For example, in descriptive studies of a single variable, the null hypothesis might be that the observed pollution in a stream exactly meets the required (or desired) standard. In causal studies of the impact of a program on an output or outcome, a null hypothesis might be that the training program improved wages by 2 percent. Most often, the null hypothesis is that the program had absolutely no (0) impact. This (exact) null hypothesis is tested against an alternative hypothesis. The alternative hypothesis (H_1) is not exact. In evaluation research, the alternative hypothesis, while inexact, usually has a specific direction. For example, in the case of a descriptive study of a single variable, the evaluator is probably interested in whether the observed pollution in the stream exceeds the required (or desired) standard. If the pollution level is lower than the standard, no action is needed; if the pollution is above the standard, remedial action may be required. Similarly, in the case of causal evaluations, the alternative hypothesis is inexact, but it typically speci-fies a direction. For example, if the program manager has a standard that the training program ought to raise wages by 2 percent, impact estimates that are less than that standard may be a concern for decision makers, while beating the standard may not require action. Similarly, if the null hypothesis is that the program had no impact, the usual alternative of interest to the decision maker is that the program had an impact on the intended direction. (This is not necessarily the case in academic research, but directional alternative hypotheses are the usual case in evaluation research.)

The basic point here is that null hypotheses are exact; alternative hypotheses are inexact and usually specify a direction relative to the null. The evaluator does the study because no one knows *ex ante* which hypothesis is false. One hypothesis is false in the "real" world, but the decision maker does not know which of the two it is. The job of the evaluator is to construct a study, col-lect observations, and analyze the data so as to reduce the chance that the decision maker comes to the wrong conclusion. Figure 2.1 depicts the evaluator's dilemma.

Figure 2.1   **Statistical Errors in Hypothesis Tests**

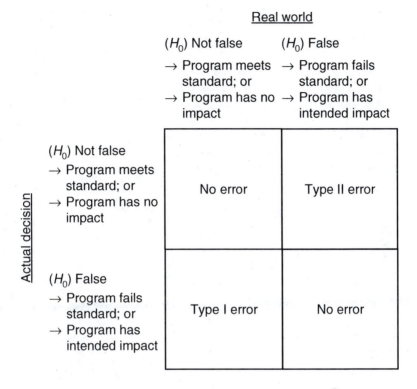

The evaluator does not know which hypothesis statement characterizes the real world. Further, he can test only the null hypothesis and either reject or fail to reject it. It is not possible to "prove" a null (or an alternative) hypothesis about real-world behavior. As I remarked earlier, mathematicians do proofs; empirical social scientists do not. If the data are systematically different from what the evaluator would observe if the null were true, then he would decide that the null is (probably) not true (i.e., H_0 is false) and that the data, if they are in the same direction as the alternative hypothesis, are consistent with that hypothesis. (This does not mean that the alternative hypothesis is "true.")

Having decided that the null is not true, the evaluator may or may not be correct. Having rejected the null, he risks a Type I error, which is the error of rejecting a null that is really true. In that case, the program "really" has no impact, but the evaluator concludes (erroneously) that it does have its (intended) impact. It is also possible that the evaluator decides the null is not true and that it "really" is not true. In that case, there is no error. Alternatively, the evaluator might conclude from the study that the null hypothesis is not false. (This does not mean that the null hypothesis is true.) This might be a correct conclusion; the program may "really" have no impact. But maybe the program "really" does have an impact (in the intended direction). In this case, the evaluator has come to an erroneous conclusion. He concluded that the program had no impact, when it really does. This is a Type II error.

So no matter what the evaluator concludes, the conclusion can be wrong. Statistical validity, which is the ability to separate random from systematic influences, reduces the probability of each type of error. If the program "really" has no systematic effect (or if the sample observations are not "really" different from the standard), then statistically valid studies will reduce the probability of erroneously finding an effect (or difference) when none is there. Similarly, if the program "really" has a systematic effect (or if the sample observations "really" are different from the standard), then statistical validity reduces the probability of erroneously finding no difference when there "really" is a difference.

No study is 100 percent valid, but some studies are more valid than others. Most important, studies with more observations nearly always reduce the probability of each type of error. However, at some point, the increase in observations begins to reduce the probability of error only a little, while the cost of collecting and analyzing more data continues to rise. In other words, at some point, increasing sample size has diminishing returns and increasing costs. So it is not the case that more observations are always better, after costs are taken into account. However, it is the case that some studies can have too few observations. A simple fable illustrates.

The Fable of the Fat Statistician

Imagine a good cookie—rich, moist, with lots of dark chocolate chips, at least two and a half inches in diameter, and one-third of an inch thick. Some cookies meet your standard of a good cookie, and others simply do not. You are a statistician; you are hungry; you are in a strange city. You go to the nearest bakery to see whether the cookies in that bakery meet your standard. You buy one cookie to take back to your hotel and test (by eating it). The null hypothesis is an exact one: The cookie meets the standard (cookie = standard). If the null hypothesis is not false, then you will buy more cookies from the bakery. The alternative (inexact) hypothesis is that the cookie fails the standard (cookie < standard). If the null hypothesis is false (meaning that the cookie appears not to meet your standard), then you will have to go elsewhere for cookies, spending more time on your search. Now you taste the one cookie, and it is OK. But based on just one cookie, you remain uncertain about whether to search further (an unwelcome thought) or to remain with this bakery and forgo a better cookie (also unwelcome). In short, you are really not sure whether to believe (i.e., fail to reject) the null hypothesis and continue to buy from that bakery or to reject the null and incur the expense and time of finding another place to buy acceptable cookies. If you reject the null but make an error in doing so, you incur unnecessary search costs and give up perfectly good cookies (Type I error). If you fail to reject the null hypothesis but make an error (Type II) in doing so, you buy more cookies that are really no good, wasting your money. So how do you reduce the chances of either kind of error? Buy (and eat!) more cookies from the test bakery. That is, you try a larger sample to increase your certainty about your decision (increase your own confidence in your judgment). That is why statisticians tend to gain weight.

The Costs of Type I and Type II Errors

In evaluation research, when policy decisions may be made based on statistical tests of null hypotheses, sometimes one type of error is worse than the other type. For example, suppose that in a political campaign, a campaign manager wants to do some research about the status of her candidate, A, against a competitor candidate, B. Her null hypothesis is that A = B, which means that the two candidates are tied in their rate of support, while her alternative hypothesis is that A > B, which means that her candidate, A, is leading. If the null hypothesis is "really" true, but the campaign manager rejects it in favor of the alternative hypothesis that her candidate is winning (a

Type I error), she may reduce her efforts to win support for her candidate when she should not. If the null is "really" false (i.e., A is actually winning), but the campaign manager accepts the null (a Type II error), then she continues to allocate excessive resources to campaigning.[11] While the Type II error is a waste of time and money, the Type I error is more costly in this case, because it may cause the candidate to lose an election.

By contrast, in impact evaluations, program managers (and program supporters) may regard Type II errors as more costly than Type I errors. For example, suppose that the null hypothesis is that a popular preschool program for poor children (e.g., Head Start) has no impact on school readiness. The alternative hypothesis is that it increases school readiness compared with what one would observe if students were not enrolled in the program. Suppose further that an evaluator, based on the data in the study, failed to reject (i.e., accepted) the null hypothesis, deciding that the program has no impact. The evaluator risks a Type II error; he also risks a storm of protest from program supporters and from the program manager. More important, if the program is canceled, but the evaluator is wrong, the children risk losing the gains in academic readiness that they would otherwise reap from what is "really" an effective program. Compared with the Type II error, the Type I error may be less costly. In that case, the evaluator erroneously rejects the null. The program continues to be funded, even though it is not effective. This too is a waste of resources, but it may not be a waste that draws as much political fire as a Type II error, at least in this case.

As another example, consider the case of the jury in the trial of a suspect who is charged with burglary or robbery. The null hypothesis is that the defendant is innocent. The jury then faces the dilemma of facing two types of errors: putting an innocent person in prison or freeing a dangerous criminal who could continue to harm society. Suppose the jury rules that the defendant is guilty, while in fact he is innocent. The jury then makes a Type I error of putting an innocent person in prison. However, suppose that the jury does not have enough evidence to reject the null hypothesis and decides that the suspect is not guilty. If he really did commit the crime, then the jury makes a Type II error, which will hurt not only the previous victims but also future ones, now that the suspect has been released. Further, the error raises the doubt that the judicial system can really punish criminals. In addition, Type II errors could eventually encourage more (severe) crimes because a few previous innocents may commit crimes hoping the justice system will let them go free. Thus on this occasion, the Type II error is arguably more costly.

In a murder case, the Type I error may be more costly than in other cases. The null hypothesis is that the suspect, charged with murder, is innocent. The jury then faces the dilemma of punishing an innocent person (perhaps with prison for life or even a death sentence), or otherwise letting a dangerous criminal go free, possibly to continue harming society. Suppose the jury does not have enough evidence to reject the null hypothesis and decides that the suspect is not guilty. If the suspect really committed the murder, then the jury would make a Type II error, which will hurt the victim's family and potential future victims. It will also fail to deter other potential killers and raise the doubt that the judicial system can really punish murderers.[12] However, if the jury rules that the defendant is guilty and sentences him to death, while in fact he is innocent, the jury then would make a Type I error. The Type I error is more costly in this case than the Type I error in the previous case of burglary or robbery. In this case of murder, the Type I error might put an innocent person to death and also raises doubts about the integrity of the judicial system.

We have seen that larger samples reduce the probability of both Type I and Type II errors.[13] Later, we will see that using "efficient" statistics and statistical tests can also reduce the probability of both Type I and II errors. Statistics like the mean (e.g., the mean SAT score in a sample of schools, which may be compared to a standard), or the difference between means (e.g., the difference between the mean standardized test scores of third-graders in comparable charter and public schools), are point estimates based on one random sample of n observations. Theoretically, however, other random samples of the same size could produce other statistics. The sample from which we draw our conclusion is just one sample of many that could have been drawn. Another sample would produce a different mean (or a different difference of means). As the number of observations in our sample increases, the variance of possible means (or difference of means, or other statistical summary measures, such as a proportion) diminishes. This is desirable; we want the variation of our observed, statistical summary measure around the unknown but "true" value (that is, its likely distance or variance or standard error around the "true" value) to be smaller rather than larger. As the variation of our sample statistic around the unknown "true" value grows increasingly small, the probability of either a Type I or Type II error will go down because our guess about the "true" value based on the statistic that we actually computed from our sample data is likely to be more precise. In statistics, more precise estimates are called more efficient estimates. Thus, large samples make statistical estimators more efficient; other design aspects (including reducing random measurement error in program variables, which we discuss later) also have the same effect. Finally, we also want to estimate accurately how far our estimate is from the true value (i.e., its variance or standard error). Chapter 6 on nonexperimental designs discusses how to assess whether our estimates of the likely distance between our sample estimate and the "true" value are not only as small (or precise) as possible, but also as accurate as possible.

Alternatives to Type II Error

The issue of Type II errors is particularly vexing for program evaluators. We have already seen that program evaluators often worry more about Type II than Type I errors. For example, suppose that study results show that, of two alternatives being tested, the new alternative is no better than the current one. The evaluator fails to reject ("accepts") the null hypothesis (no difference between the treatment alternatives) relative to the (inexact) "research" hypothesis (the new program is better). But this conclusion could be erroneous because the evaluator, in deciding that the new program is no better than the old one, could be wrong. This is a Type II error. The dilemma is that, unlike null hypotheses, research hypotheses are not exact. The null is an exact hypothesis: The program had no (zero) effect. The alternative or research hypothesis is an inexact hypothesis that includes many exact hypotheses that the program had "some" particular effect in the desired direction. Given multiple sources of randomness, each of these numerous alternative exact hypotheses about program impact, even if they were "true," could produce a "zero impact" result. As a consequence, the probability of the Type II error is hard to calculate, and we do not consider that task here. There are tables of the probability of Type II errors, but the general logic is not as straightforward as that of Type I errors.[14]

However, a practical way to consider the risk of a similar error is to turn one of the alternative hypotheses in the rejection region into an exact one. For example, having decided in step 1 not to reject the null, the evaluator, in step 2, could next test the observed results against a minimum acceptable threshold of desired effectiveness. The minimum threshold becomes an exact hypothesis, and the research proceeds in the usual way. The minimum threshold could be what political decision makers (or program managers) consider minimally acceptable. That level could be outside the .05 rejection region (especially if the sample size is small), but it could still be better than "no impact" from a management point of view. The threshold could be a level determined by legislative statute or court order, or it could be the break-even point in a cost-benefit or cost-effectiveness analysis. So, having accepted the null (no effect) hypothesis test, the evaluator can next test the observed results from the study against the minimum acceptable threshold, which now becomes the exact null hypothesis that is tested in the second stage of the analysis. While the computed p-value from this second stage is technically the probability of a Type I error, it also provides information about the probability of incorrectly deciding that the program does not work (i.e., it fails to meet the standard) when in fact it may work at an acceptable level.[15]

In a similar vein, Jeff Gill suggests paying attention to the confidence interval of a parameter estimate.[16] Confidence intervals decrease as the sample size increases, which is analogous to increasing the power of a null hypothesis test, in which power is the probability that failing to reject the null is the correct decision. This may be less confusing than a hypothesis test, since there is no Type II error in estimating a confidence interval.

In sum, it is particularly important in program evaluation to avoid rigid adherence to a hypothesis-testing model of the 0-null hypothesis using a conventional p-value of .05. In academic research, real careers may depend on statistical decisions, but in program evaluation, real programs, as well as real careers, are at stake. The best advice is to use multiple criteria. If the program is acceptable (or unacceptable) under multiple criteria of statistical validity, then the statistical decision becomes more defensible. However, statistical validity is not the only criterion for the valid assessment of program characteristics or impact. I turn next to the critical issue of measurement.

Measurement Reliability and Validity

Introduction

Valid descriptions of program inputs, outputs or outcomes, and valid assessments of program impact require that the measures of program inputs and outputs or outcomes themselves are defensible. For example, if an evaluator is examining the impact of participatory management on productivity in a school, she needs to have valid measures of management that are more or less participatory and valid measures of output that represent productivity levels.

Abstract concepts like these are particularly difficult to measure. In fact, the overall measurement of "validity" is parsed into separate criteria: reliability and validity. The reliability of a measure is the *absence* of random measurement error (RME) in recorded scores. The validity of a measure is the *absence* of *non*random measurement error (NRME) in recorded scores.

A diagram is the best way to distinguish between reliability (no random error) and validity (no nonrandom error) in measures. Consider a measure of school productivity using test score gains in a first-grade classroom. Call that measure Y. Y has two components. First, there is the "true" score Y_T; we do not know what it is. We only know what we observe or measure, which we call Y_M. Figure 2.2 shows how Y_T is related to Y_M. In this diagram, the measured scores (Y_M) are determined by a random component (μ_Y) and a systematic, or nonrandom, component (Y_T). If most of Y_M consists of μ_Y, then Y_M is a noisy measure of Y_T, with considerable RME. However, if most of Y_M is due to Y_T, then Y_M is likely to be a relatively valid measure of Y_T, with little NRME.

Representing this diagram algebraically is more informative, especially with respect to NRME. Specifically, we write Y_M as a linear function of both Y_T and μ_Y:

$$Y_M = \alpha + \beta Y_T + \mu_Y.$$

In this formulation, if the expected value of μ_Y is small [written $E(\mu_Y)$] (and if it has little variance), then we would conclude that Y_M has little RME. With respect to NRME, $E(\alpha) = 0$ and $E(\beta) = 1$ (and they have little variance), then we would conclude that $Y_M \cong Y_T$, so that the measured and true scores of Y are about the same. One could have a valid measure Y_M with considerable RME:

Figure 2.2 **The Basic Measurement Model**

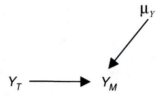

$Y_M = 0 + 1 * Y_T + \mu_Y$. Alternatively, one could have an invalid measure of Y_M with little RME: $Y_M = \alpha + \beta Y_T + 0$, where the intercept is not expected to be 0 and the slope is not expected to be 1.[17]

Below, I discuss examples of both kinds of measurement errors, including problems of likely RME and NRME in test scores of first-graders. To begin the discussion, consider my beloved, but old bathroom scale. In the long run, scales like these have little (but not zero) random measurement error. In fact, I can see the random error on this old analog scale. When I step on it, the indicator bounces around a little before it settles down to a number. Thus, I assume that my scale has relatively little RME: $E(\mu_Y) \gg 0$. However, my scale has considerable NRME. First, it consistently underreports my weight; symbolically, this means: $0 < E(\beta) < 1$. Second, it is anchored at a negative weight, so it registers a slightly negative score when no one is standing on it: $E(\alpha) < 0$.

While a bit lightweight, this example serves to illustrate the two aspects of measurement error (random and nonrandom). It also illustrates the two facets of NRME: constant error or error in the intercept; and systematic error or correlated error in the slope. Examples and implications of these errors for assessing overall measurement reliability and validity follow.

Measurement Reliability

Measurement reliability refers to a measurement procedure that has little RME. I have already suggested some examples of measurement procedures that are likely to contain random components:

- standardized achievement tests
- classroom tests
- athletic ability
- responses to attitude or opinion survey questions, particularly when the issue is unfamiliar to the respondent or when the respondent has ambiguous attitudes or beliefs
- nonhomicide crime rates
- safety (of anything)

Measurement reliability is achieved if different measures of the same phenomenon record the same results. For example, continuing with the example of my bathroom scale, the scale is a reliable measure of weight if I step on it and it reads 112. I step off and then step on it again two minutes later, having done nothing except maybe read a few pages of this book. Once again, the scale reads 112. I conclude (if I did such a test repeatedly, with the same or close to the same results each time) that the scale is reliable.

By contrast, we say that, compared with the bathroom scale, an SAT score is not as reliable an indicator of academic achievement because a student taking the SAT twice in a short period may get different scores, even though her underlying level of achievement remains unchanged.

Similarly, we are accustomed to getting different scores on exams or in athletic competitions, and we often attribute surprising success to "good luck" and surprising failure to "bum luck." The technical term for these casual assessments is "random measurement error."

Test scores may be particularly unreliable, but randomness is greater under some circumstances than others. At the individual level, scores on standardized tests fluctuate randomly. However, larger "samples" reduce randomness. For example, increasing the number of items on a test reduces randomness in the overall test score of an individual. At the classroom, group, or school level, randomness in the group average decreases as the number in the group increases. Thus, test scores for minority groups may contain more "noise" than scores on the same test for nonminorities. Statistically, this is recognized as a problem of heteroscedasticity in measurement. Scholars also point out that failure to recognize random error in test scores (and in measures of test score gains) is likely to result in underestimates of teacher effectiveness.[18]

Responses to opinion surveys provide another, less familiar, example of often-unrecognized unreliability. According to Asher, respondents to opinion surveys commonly feel pressured to say something when they are asked a question in a poll.[19] This reaction is particularly likely when respondents have ambivalent opinions about a complex topic (like the death penalty). It is also likely when respondents know little or nothing about the topic or if the topic is a nonsense question (e.g., "Should the music industry increase the level of hemiola in contemporary music, reduce it, or is the current level satisfactory?"). The actual response will be "random," but it will be indistinguishable from a "real" one, unless the possibility of random response is anticipated.

Even crime rates, which look "real," contain RME, because not all crime is reported, and sometimes the decision of a citizen to report a crime is just a random one. (Sometimes, the decision to report reflects characteristics of the reporter and is not just a random phenomenon; I discuss NRME later.) Homicides, however, are likely to be reported, so they are not likely to be subject to problems of random (or nonrandom) measurement error. This also characterizes accident data. For example, small accidents are not consistently reported to authorities, and some of the non-reporting is undoubtedly random (and some probably reflects characteristics of the reporter, so part of the error is not random). Significant accidents (e.g., those that result in death or hospitalization) are more likely to be reported. Thus, data on automobile fatalities are probably more reliable than data on the number of nonfatal automobile injuries.

RME may also plague what appear to be objective measures of program implementation. Sometimes, what is recorded may reflect random reporting errors or data entry errors. For example, if the evaluator is studying the impact of hours spent in a job-training program on the probability of finding a job, the reported measure of finding a job (yes or no) may be quite reliable. However, the measure of hours spent in training may not be as reliable because random errors frequently plague administrative recordkeeping, particularly when the agency providing the training is not a large bureaucracy that is accustomed to keeping records and can do so at low marginal costs.

Consequences of RME and Strategies for Reducing It

Virtually no measurement is 100 percent reliable, but some measures are more reliable than others. Why should program evaluators, concerned about making their research conclusions defensible, care about reliable measures? It turns out that unreliable measurement has one and sometimes two undesirable effects on validity. First, unreliable measures of outcome variables reduce statistical validity, thus raising the likelihood of both Type I and II errors. Chapter 6 on nonexperimental design discusses this further. Second, unreliability in measures of program variables (but not output variables) also reduces internal validity. The next chapter, on internal validity, makes clear why internal validity is particularly important for defensible program evaluation results, and Chapter 6 explains why NRME in program variables adversely affects internal validity.

Contrary to intuition, it is more important to be concerned that program and treatment variables are measured as reliably as possible than it is to focus attention on reliably measuring outcome or output variables. Yet conventional wisdom is to concentrate on reliable measures of outputs or outcomes, but the cost may be to ignore the development and assessment of reliable measures of program treatment. In program evaluation, it is not clear that the gains in statistical validity from concentrating on reliably measuring outcomes or outputs are worth the losses in internal validity if reliable measures of program treatment are sacrificed. To give some examples, program evaluators tend to concentrate on reliably measuring outcomes or outputs (e.g., achievement scores, wages, recidivism, compliance). If the measures of program treatments (e.g., hours in school, hours in a training program, hours in a drug treatment program, quality and quantity of safety or health inspections) are unreliable, then estimates of the impact of X on outcome Y could be internally invalid even if the outcome Y is reliably measured.

A relatively straightforward way to increase the reliability of measurement is not unrelated to the way to increase statistical validity. Just as increasing the number of observations in a study reduces random error, so does increasing the number of indicators reduce measurement unreliability. I prove this statement in Chapter 7, which discusses measurement of the reliability of responses to survey questions. But the rationale for this statement is easy to demonstrate with a simple example. Suppose that your performance in this (or any other) class was to be assessed with one exam; on that exam, there is only one short-answer question. While students and the instructor would all enjoy the reduced workload, most students would complain that one short question on one exam is not a very reliable measure of their performance in the class. Maybe you will have a cold on that day. Or the question does not touch on what you have spent most of your time working on. Or the question deals with the topic that you found the hardest to understand. Or maybe you got lucky, because the test question represents the *only* thing that you understand from the course. The point is that one item measuring a student's performance in an entire class is an unreliable measure. More items, and more tests, increase reliability.

Using multiple indicators or multiple items to increase the reliability of measurement is particularly important when concepts are hard to measure (e.g., outcome or output measures such as class performance, satisfaction with a program, environmental quality, or wellness). By contrast, when concepts are not so abstract or hard to measure (like weight, hourly wages, or hours of work), multiple indicators are not as important because a single indicator can be reasonably reliable.

Frequently, evaluators combine multiple indicators into a single index. Your grade in this class is such an index, assuming that it is an average (weighted or unweighted) of grades on several tasks. The final score in a baseball game is an index of the performance of each team in an inning. Your overall SAT or GRE score is an index of your performance on each item in the test, and each component of the exam (e.g., the verbal score) is an index of your performance on each item in that portion of the test. Chapter 7, in addition to discussing how to measure reliability, also discusses how to create indexes and assess the reliability of indexes. Indexes that have more components (more indicators) are likely to be more reliable than indexes with fewer components. For example, a ten-item test is usually more reliable than a three-item test. Chapter 7 also discusses how to assess the validity of indexes.

Measurement Validity

Measurement validity is different from measurement reliability. While measurement reliability refers to a measurement procedure that is (relatively) absent of random error, measurement validity refers to a measurement procedure that is (relatively) absent of NRME. NRME means that the measure is biased—that is, it contains a nonrandom component that does not have anything to do with what the researcher really wants to measure, so the measured score Y_M is not equal to Y_T, even with allowance for RME. Recall that there are two types of NRME: bias in the intercept (constant or consistent bias); and bias in the slope (systematic bias in the measured score Y_M that is correlated with the true score Y_T). It turns out that one way to increase measurement validity is the same as the way to increase measurement reliability: Use multiple indicators.

First, let us consider some examples of possible NRME. A common charge is that SAT and GRE scores are biased. Specifically, the charge is that minorities whose true score = Y_T perform more poorly on these tests than nonminorities, so their observed score $Y_T < Y_M$. The deviation is allegedly not random; rather, it is allegedly due to the race or ethnicity of the test taker, which is not what the test is supposed to be measuring. This is an allegation of potential bias due to NRME in SAT, GRE, and other standardized, multi-item, reliable achievement test scores.

If the allegation were true, it would be an example of systematic error. Even if there is no direct connection between underlying true scores and race, racial minorities in the United States typically come from families with low financial and human capital assets. One consequence is low measured test scores, as a result of low assets, not race. Using the basic measurement model to represent this allegation, where $Y_M = \alpha + \beta Y_T + \mu_Y$, there is not only RME but $E(\beta) < 1$, unless race and capital assets (often measured by indicators of socioeconomic status [SES]) are accounted for. In this example, assume $E(\alpha) = 0$; there is no intercept or constant error. Rather, the measurement error affects the relation between Y_M and Y_T, which, unless otherwise accounted for, reflects the direct impact of SES on measured test scores. Figure 2.3 represents this dilemma. Unadjusted GREs, SATs, and other standardized test scores do not account for these alleged sources of systematic, or correlated, bias.[20]

Another example of correlated or systematic NRME is race-of-interviewer effects on responses to face-to-face surveys. Apparently, respondents alter their responses to many (but not all) survey items depending on whether the interviewer is the same race as the respondent.[21]

In addition to distinguishing between constant and correlated NRME, researchers make other distinctions to characterize NRME. These distinctions overlap our distinction between constant and correlated NRME. For example, it is useful to describe three aspects of NRME in the following manner:

1. *Face validity:* Does the actual indicator reflect what it is supposed to measure? For example, students often argue that a final exam did not reflect what was taught in the class or reflected only a small component of what was taught. That is an allegation of face invalidity. I have always wondered whether scores on driving tests (the written plus the behind-the-wheel component) in the United States really indicate a driver's ability to handle a car skillfully and safely. A spelling test alone would, on its face, be an invalid indicator of a student's overall verbal ability.

These are examples not only of face invalidity but also of intercept or constant NRME: The allegation is that a high score on a typical driver's test or spelling-only test overestimates actual driving or verbal ability. Using multiple indicators (e.g., for verbal ability: a spelling test, a test of reading comprehension, and a test of the ability to compose an explanatory paragraph) would go far to improve face validity, just as it improves reliability.

Figure 2.3 **The Model of Systematic Nonrandom Measurement Error**

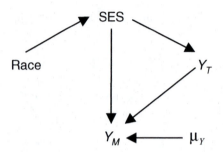

2. *Concept validity:* Are the measured indicators of the same concept correlated with one another and uncorrelated with unrelated concepts? (This is also called convergent and discriminant validity, respectively.) For example, if academic achievement (e.g., grade point average) is correlated with four related indicators (e.g., scores in SAT verbal, SAT math, SAT reading, and SAT reasoning), then we might regard these as valid indicators of the concept "academic achievement." However, if any (or all) of these indicators correlate with an unrelated concept, such as race, we would regard that as a sign of concept invalidity. They are also examples of systematic or correlated NRME.

3. *Predictive or criterion validity:* Do the indicators predict the expected outcome? For example, does the score on a driver's test (written plus behind-the-wheel performance) overestimate or accurately predict a person's ability to drive? Does a high GRE score underestimate or accurately predict a student's performance after she gets into graduate school? In either case, does the prediction depend also on, say, the (unobserved) personality of the test taker? These questions raise issues of predictive validity. They are also instances of both correlated and constant NRME.

Measurement Errors: Threats to Statistical or Internal Validity

Measurement reliability and validity are problems for the validity of evaluation studies for several reasons. First, in causal evaluations, RME in any variable except the output or outcome variable will reduce the internal validity of any causal claim, regardless of whether the claim is "there is an impact" or "there is no impact." NRME in any variable will also reduce the internal validity of a causal claim. Forthcoming chapters, which list and explain threats to internal validity, develop the relation between measurement issues and internal validity. Second, in both causal and descriptive evaluations, RME in variables reduces the statistical validity of the evaluation study. It is never possible to have 100 percent reliable and valid measurement procedures, but some measurement procedures are more reliable and valid than others.

In general, as we have seen, the best way to improve measurement reliability is to use multiple indicators of program treatment and program outcome. Usually, this also improves face validity and may well reduce other sources of NRME. Chapter 1 stressed the normative importance of multiple indicators of outputs and outcomes. Chapter 7 on surveys briefly introduces alpha as a measure of reliability and factor analysis as a tool for assessing the validity of measurement procedures; both are useful whenever there are multiple indicators. Multiple indicators are thus central to measuring complex concepts: Having multiple indicators allows researchers to assess both reliability and validity and also is likely to improve both. Proper model specification for internally valid estimates of program impact, considered in the next chapter, and the use of statistical controls, considered in Chapter 6, are also essential for reducing systematic (or correlated)

NRME. Because of the connection between systematic NRME, RME in program variables, and internal invalidity, separating measurement reliability and validity, the topics of this chapter, from internal validity, the topic of the next chapter, is rather artificial. Thus, it is important to turn to the more general issue of internal validity.

BASIC CONCEPTS

Defensible designs
Replicability
Internal validity: definition
External validity: definition
Statistical validity: definition
Measurement reliability: definition
Measurement validity: definition
Threats to external validity
Unrepresentative sample
Sensitized units of analysis in sample
Volunteer respondents
Statistical interaction
Threats to statistical validity
Random sampling error
    Making n larger
Random measurement error
    Making number of indicators larger: multiple indicators
Random human behavior
Statistical errors
    Type I
    Type II
Costs of statistical error
    Type I costs
    Type II costs
Alternatives to Type II error
Threats to measurement validity: the measurement model
Diagram: RME vs. NRME
Equation: RME vs. NRME
RME: examples
RME: consequences
    RME in program variables (X)
    RME in output/outcome variables (Y)
Reducing RME: multiple indicators
NRME: examples
Constant NRME
    Correlated/systematic NRME
    Face invalidity: constant NRME
    Concept invalidity: correlated NRME
    Predictive invalidity: constant NRME
Reducing NRME: multiple indicators

DO IT YOURSELF

Find an example of an evaluation of a public or nonprofit program, management initiative, or recent reform effort. The evaluation could concern a program in the United States or in another country. The evaluation need not be an impact evaluation. It may simply describe program performance. In the United States, most federal government agencies are required to report their performance according to Government Performance and Results Act standards, and links to that information can be found in agency Web sites. That would be a convenient source of information for this exercise. There are many published or unpublished evaluations of local government agencies, especially school districts, schools, and police departments, either by outsiders or insiders. Newspapers often report the results of these evaluations; the original evaluation is a good source for this exercise. The World Bank continuously evaluates projects that it funds, and so does the Ford Foundation; these provide another source of information for this exercise. Warning: The exercise looks simpler than it is.

The Exercise

Evaluate the "evaluation" according to the following criteria:

- External validity: How generalizable are the conclusions?
- Statistical validity: How well does the report separate the signal from the noise?
- Measurement reliability and validity:
  - How noisy are the measures? (reliability?)
  - Are the measures reasonable estimates of the "true" underlying concept? (constant measurement error)
  - Are the measures likely to be correlated with factors that do not reflect the underlying concept? What factors? (correlated measurement error)

NOTES

1. Richard A. Berk and Peter H. Rossi, *Thinking About Program Evaluation*, 2d ed. (Thousand Oaks, CA: Sage, 1999), also use this classification of the types of validity. Chapter 6 shows that the four types of validity can be reduced to just internal and statistical validity. Measurement reliability and validity (and, arguably, external validity) are important because they are aspects of internal and statistical validity.

2. Readers can refer to Leslie Kish, *Statistical Design for Research* (New York: Wiley, 2004), for external validity and sampling; Madhu Viswanathan, *Measurement Error and Research Design* (Thousand Oaks, CA: Sage, 2005), John McIver and Edward G. Carmines, *Unidimensional Scaling* (Thousand Oaks, CA: Sage, 1981), Edward G. Carmines and Richard A. Zeller, *Reliability and Validity Assessment* (Thousand Oaks, CA: Sage, 1979), Jae-On Kim and Charles W. Mueller, *Factor Analysis: Statistical Methods and Practical Issues* (Thousand Oaks, CA: Sage, 1978), and David Andrich, *Rasch Models for Measurement* (Thousand Oaks, CA: Sage, 1988), for measurement; and Alan Agresti and Barbara Finlay, *Statistical Methods for the Social Sciences*, 4th ed. (Upper Saddle River, NJ: Prentice Hall, 2009), for general statistical topics.

3. Agresti and Finlay, *Statistical Methods for the Social Sciences*.

4. Relevant to the unit of analysis is the issue of ecological inference. If the data in a study are data about schools, one cannot usually claim that the unit of analysis pertains to students. Similarly, if the data in a study are data about cities, one cannot claim that the study results pertain to individuals in the cities. For example, if one finds that high immigration rates in cities have no impact on crime in those cities, one cannot make a straightforward claim about immigrants and crime at the individual level. For further discussion of the problems of ecological inference, see Laura Langbein and Alan Lichtman, *Ecological Inference* (Beverly Hills, CA: Sage, 1978); Christopher Achen and W. Phillips Shively, *Cross-Level Inference* (Chicago: University of Chicago Press, 1995); Gary King, *A Solution to the Ecological Inference Problem* (Princeton: Princeton University Press, 1997). Some studies have multiple

levels of units of analysis. For example, there are studies of students within schools and schools within school districts. One might study immigrants within cities and cities within states. Chapter 6 includes a brief discussion of hierarchical (multilevel) modeling in evaluation research and provides references.

5. William Martineau, Laura Langbein, Richard White, and Peter Hartjens, *National Evaluation of the Urban Park and Recreation Recovery Program* (Washington, DC: Blackstone Associates, 1983).

6. Steven D. Levitt and John A. List report that much of the story of the Hawthorne effect is an urban myth. They actually located the original data, reanalyzed it using the methods described in this book, and found no lighting effect or any clear observational effect. They do not deny that subjects often react to being observed (or surveyed); they point out that the "design" in the original study was deficient. See Levitt and List, "Was There Really a Hawthorne Effect at the Hawthorne Plant? An Analysis of the Original Illumination Experiments," *Applied Economics* 3, no. 1 (January 2011): 224–238.

7. American Evaluation Association, *Guiding Principles for Evaluators*, 2004, www.eval.org/gptraining/GPTraining Final/gp.principles.pdf (accessed July 5, 2011).

8. For example, Agresti and Finlay, *Statistical Methods for the Social Sciences*.

9. Robert Weissberg, Policy, *Polling and Public Opinion: The Case Against Heeding the "Voice of the People"* (New York: Palgrave Macmillan, 2002); Herbert Asher, *Polling and the Public: What Every Citizen Should Know* (Washington, DC: CQ Press, 2001).

10. Mark Lipsey observes that, in a single study, there can be only one type of error. If the H_0 is really true, the only possible type of error is a Type I error. If H_0 is really false, then Type II is the only possible error. It is particularly difficult to assess the probability of a Type II error, because it depends on the (unknown) effect size parameter. Lipsey points to the role of meta-analysis (see Chapter 8) to help assess effect sizes. Based on multiple studies, such effect size estimates can be used to estimate the probability of a Type II error. See Mark W. Lipsey, "Statistical Conclusion Validity for Intervention Research: A Significant ($p < .05$) Problem," in *Validity and Social Experimentation: Donald Campbell's Legacy*, vol. 2, ed. Leonard Bickman (Thousand Oaks, CA: Sage, 2000), ch. 4.

11. In a statistics text, the campaign manager in this situation would not "accept" a null hypothesis; rather, the manager would "fail to reject" the null. In program evaluation, managers often take real actions based on statistical decisions. Thus, if they fail to reject the null, they take action based on the belief that the null is (probably) true. In effect, they act as if the null were true; they effectively "accept" the null.

12. There is controversy over the specific and general deterrence impact of capital punishment. If capital punishment has no deterrent impact, the cost of a Type II error would be considerably less. See Isaac Erlich, "The Deterrent Effect of Capital Punishment: A Question of Life and Death," *American Economic Review* 65, no. 3 (1975): 397–417; Brian Forst, "Capital Punishment and Deterrence: Conflicting Evidence?" *Journal of Criminal Law and Criminology* 14, no. 3 (1983): 927–942; Hashem Dezhbakhsh, Paul H. Rubin, and Joanna M. Shepherd, "Does Capital Punishment Have a Deterrent Effect? New Evidence from Postmoratorium Panel Data," *American Law and Economics Review* 5, no. 2 (2003): 344–376; Robert B. Ekelund, Jr., John D. Jackson, Rand W. Wessler, and Robert Tollison, "Marginal Deterrence and Multiple Murders," *Southern Economic Journal* 72, no. 3 (2006): 521–541. Erlich's article was the first to test and support the deterrence hypothesis; it set off a plethora of empirical research, reviewed by Forst, that raised significant doubt about the deterrence effect of capital punishment. The articles by Dezhbakhsh et al. and Ekelund et al. use newer data and more recent methodological improvements to reaffirm Erlich's original findings. Chapter 6 on non-experiments discusses the panel methods used in those articles.

13. Juries cannot conveniently, legally, or morally increase the sample size. Instead, they can reduce the probability of error by increasing the amount of evidence (not unlike increasing the sample size) for the single case that they are considering.

14. Christopher L. Aberson, *Applied Power Analysis for the Social Sciences* (New York: Routledge, 2010); Jacob Cohen, *Statistical Power Analysis for the Behavioral Sciences* (Hillsdale, NJ: Lawrence Erlbaum, 1988).

15. There are important problems of logic and misinterpretation that surround null-hypothesis significance testing. The most noteworthy logical challenge is posed by Bayes' theorem. The classical model, common in program evaluation (and in this text), asks the question: If the "theory" is true (e.g., the program has no impact; the program meets the standard), what is the probability of observing the results that we got from the data that we collected? Bayes' challenge inverts the question and deals more explicitly with the issue of Type II error. It asks: What is the probability that the theory is true (e.g., the program meets or beats the standard, which is an inexact hypothesis), given the results that we observe from the data we collect?

Misinterpretations are also common. For example, statistical significance in a large sample study should not be confused with real-world importance or substantive significance. Similarly, a given p-value in a large sample study is no more reliable (i.e., less random) than the same p-value from a smaller sample study. It should also be clear from the preceding discussion in this chapter of the "real" costs of Type I (vs. Type II) error in program evaluation, relative to academic research, that Type I p-values of .05 have no particular magic, especially in comparison to a p-value of .049 or .051. Finally, failing to reject the null does not rule out any of the infinite number of competing hypotheses. See David Rindskopf, "Plausible Rival Hypotheses in Measurement, Design, and Scientific Theory," in *Research Design: Donald Campbell's Legacy,* vol. 2, ed. Leonard Bickman (Thousand Oaks, CA: Sage, 2000), ch. 1; and Jeff Gill, "The Insignificance of Null Hypothesis Significance Testing," *Political Research Quarterly* 52, no. 3 (1999): 647–674.

Stephen Ziliak and Deirdre McCloskey, *The Cult of Statistical Significance: How the Standard Error Costs Us Jobs, Justice, and Lives* (Ann Arbor, MI: University of Michigan Press, 2008), and Deirdre Mc-Closkey and Stephen Ziliak, "The Standard Error of Regressions," *Journal of Economic Literature* 34, no. 1 (1996): 97–114, also point to the importance of having the relevant null hypothesis: If the substantive focus is on how much consumption (e.g., of gasoline) responds to higher prices, then the relevant null is probably not that the relation is 0; rather, the relevant null is that demand is price elastic, which implies a null hypothesis of –1.00. In addition, they make the critical point that statistical significance has nothing to do with substantive significance. Results that are statistically significant may be substantively trivial; this is particularly likely with large sample sizes, which can make almost anything look significant. When sample sizes are very small, substantively important results often look insignificant. For example, if a standard of health is "close to" 3,500 units (e.g., white blood cells) per 100 milliliters, and two subsequent random measurements with a known (i.e., valid and reliable) instrument ($n = 2$) report results of 40K and 75K units per 100 milliliters, respectively, further inquiry if not remedial action should proceed, regardless of the outcome of a significance test.

But if a large n (e.g., $n > 50,000$) upholds a null hypothesis of "no impact" (and if other aspects of the research design are defensible), the probability of a Type II error is vanishingly small, making the "no effect" conclusion more credible. For example, see Christopher Carpenter, Sabina Postolek, and Casey Warman, "Public-Place Smoking Laws and Exposure to Environmental Tobacco Smoke (ETS)," *American Economic Journal: Economic Policy* 3, no. 3 (2011): 35–61, who find that laws banning smoking in public places (in Canada) reduce exposure to ETS but have no impact on the number of cigarettes smoked by smokers. In all their analyses $n > 65,000$. In this case, statistical significance is an "easy" standard to reach, and the authors point to the substantive significance of the "significant" results and also to the "significance" of the insignificant results, which with such a large n, is in fact a "hard" standard to reach.

16. Gill, "Insignificance of Null Hypothesis Significance Testing," and Ziliak and McCloskey, *The Cult of Statistical Significance*, also suggest this.

17. See Madhu Viswanathan, *Measurement Error and Research Design* (Thousand Oaks, CA: Sage, 2005), for a complete text on measurement that also distinguishes between random and nonrandom errors of measurement and categorizes nonrandom errors into two basic components: additive (i.e., constant error) and correlational (i.e., correlated) error. Viswanathan further distinguishes between within- and between-measure correlated errors. Most of our examples illustrate between-measure errors. An example of within-measure error occurs when some survey questions on political liberalism are positively worded, while others are negatively worded.

18. See Don Boyd, Pam Grossman, Hamp Lankford, Susanna Loeb, and Jim Wyckoff, "Measuring Effect Sizes: The Effect of Measurement Error" (paper presented at the National Conference on Value-Added Modeling, Madison, WI, April 2008); Eric A. Hanushek and Steven G. Rivkin, "Generalizations About Using Value-Added Measures of Teacher Quality" (paper presented at the annual meeting of the American Economic Association, Atlanta, GA, 2010).

19. Asher, *Polling and the Public.*

20. See Arthur C. Brooks, "Evaluating the Effectiveness of Nonprofit Fundraising," *Policy Studies Journal* 32, no. 1 (2004): 363–374, on the use of adjusted measures of the performance of nonprofits to neutralize the effects of uncontrollable outside forces. See also Arthur C. Brooks, "The Use and Misuse of Adjusted Performance Measures," *Journal of Policy Analysis and Management* 19, no. 2 (2002): 323–328. See also Gary King, Christopher J.L. Murray, Jashua Ajay Salomon, and A. Tandon, "Enhancing the Validity and Cross-Cultural Comparability of Measurement in Survey Research," *American Political Science Review* 98, no. 1 (2004): 191–207, on problems of constant and correlated NRME in survey-based measures of self-assessed visual acuity (and other measures of personal health) in cross-national research and many other applications as well. The authors of the last-named article also suggest a way to adjust observed measures for this bias.

21. Darren W. Davis, "The Direction of Race of Interviewer Effects Among African-Americans: Donning the Black Mask," *American Journal of Political Science* 41, no. 1 (1997): 309–322. See also Gabriele B. Durrant, Robert M. Groves, Laura Staetsky and Fiona Steele, "Effects of Interviewer Attitudes and Behaviors on Refusal in Household Surveys," *Public Opinion Quarterly* 74, no. 1 (2010): 1–36.

3

Internal Validity

THE LOGIC OF INTERNAL VALIDITY

Internal validity is critical to the defensibility of impact evaluations. External validity, statistical validity, and measurement reliability and validity pertain to all program evaluations, whether they are primarily descriptive or causal. In contrast, internal validity pertains only to impact or causal evaluations, and it is key to their credibility because it is defined as the accuracy of the causal claim. If an evaluator claims that program X (e.g., welfare reform) causes outcome Y (e.g., reduced welfare caseloads), and if that claim is accurate, then it is said to be an internally valid claim. Similarly, if an evaluator claims that program X (e.g., political action committee [PAC] contributions to members of Congress) does *not* cause outcome Y (e.g., how members vote on bills relevant to the PAC), and if that claim of no (or little) impact is accurate, then the claim is said to be internally valid.[1]

Logically, the problem of assessing internal validity can be broken into the components of a claim like this one: program X caused output or outcome Y to change by a certain amount (which could be positive, zero, or negative impact). Observed changes (even if it is zero) in Y have three potential sources:

Observed level or change in level of $Y =$
    Effect of intervention or treatment type or level (X)
+   Effects of other systematic variables (Z) related to X. (Z includes correlated/ confounded or extraneous factors, and related design effects from threats to external and measurement reliability or validity)
+   Effects of stochastic or random processes (μ). (The symbol μ includes threats to statistical validity and related design effects from threats to external and measurement reliability)[2]

We can write this relationship as an equation: $Y = \alpha + \beta X + \sum \gamma_k Z_k + \mu$. In the equation, the constant α is the value of Y if the program level is zero and other systematic processes are also at a level of zero. Theoretically, it stands for the base value of Y that would be observed if there was no treatment. However, only under limited circumstances could it be regarded as counterfactual. The variable X is the level or dosage or amount of the program or intervention (e.g., after [vs. before] welfare reform, amount of PAC contribution); β represents the actual magnitude of difference that a one-unit change in X makes on Y, net of Z. It is what we seek to find out. The next term, Z, consists of many subvariables Z_k; it stands for a summary of the level or amount of each extraneous or confounding, but known and measured, variable Z_k; γ_k represents the actual magnitude of effect that each of these k variables has on Y, net of the intervention. Finally, μ is a summary of all the "stuff" that we left out of the equation for Y because we do not know about it or because we cannot measure it. The μ term has no direct measure; we hope that it is a random term that summarizes these omitted, unmeasured factors. Our central interest is in internally valid estimates of β.

We can also summarize the equation as a graphic, shown in Figure 3.1. The graphic clarifies the possibility that X and Z, the treatment (i.e., the intervention) and the confounding (or extraneous) variables, respectively, can be related to one another, in no particular direction and therefore difficult to disentangle. The central problem of internally valid program evaluation is to do just that: to estimate β net of, or independent of, Z, which represents all variables that affect Y and are also related to X.

As an example, consider the case of welfare reform, representing change from no work requirement to a (conditional) work requirement. Let Y be the measure of an important outcome: the number of months that target families are on welfare. Let X be a measure of the intervention: whether the target families had received the traditional welfare program with no work requirements ($X = 0$) or a newer form, which requires recipients to work ($X = 1$). The coefficient β would be the difference that the two kinds of welfare program make on Y; β is unknown but is potentially knowable, and the purpose of our evaluation is to estimate its value as validly as possible. Theoretically, that value could be zero, positive, or negative. A value of zero would mean that being on welfare without ($X = 0$) or with ($X = 1$) a work requirement makes no difference in the number of months on welfare (Y). A positive sign (which is not expected) would mean that the new program increases the amount of time that the family remains on welfare. A negative sign would mean that the new program with work as a condition for receiving the benefit reduces the amount of time that the average family remains on welfare. Z_k is a summary measure that includes all the other factors that are related to being on one kind of welfare compared with the other and that also affect how much time the family is likely to be on welfare. These factors could include the family members' education, race, health, age, place of residence, and many other variables as well; the coefficient γ_k is an estimate of the impact of each of these on Y. Finally, μ represents unmeasured (and unmeasurable) factors that affect Y that are not included in X and Z_k, which are measured in our evaluation study.

As another example, consider estimating the impact of PAC contributions on voting behavior in Congress. We want to evaluate whether the receipt of money causes members of Congress to alter their vote, changing it to reflect the preferences of the PAC donor rather than those of their constituents. Suppose that the bills at issue are ones that the PAC favors. We suspect that β is nonzero and positive. Y is a measure of how members in Congress voted on the target bills; X is a measure of the amount of PAC contributions from the suspect groups. To estimate the net impact of X on Y (that is, to accurately estimate β), we need to account for all the other factors (Z_k) that affect how members vote and that are also related to the receipt of PAC money (X). These factors might include party, ideology, seniority, committee assignments, constituency characteristics, and many other variables. To the extent that we fail to account for these factors, our estimate of β will not be accurate, because it will not separate the impact of PAC money (X) from that of the related, confounding variables (represented by Z_k). That is, it will be internally invalid. We will also need to worry about the last term, μ; it is a summary of everything other than X and Z_k that affects Y. We do not measure the components of μ; we do hope that their overall impact averages out to be zero. We know that we cannot eliminate this random component from our design, but, to

Figure 3.1   **Sources of Variation in Y: The Picture**

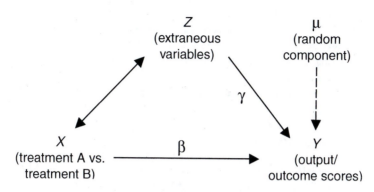

improve the statistical validity of our estimate of β, we want to minimize the random component of our evaluation design.

These two examples of causal claims come from the United States. But program evaluation is critical to the study of international development, and evaluations of program impact are at the center of this growing subfield. Many interventions in developing countries focus on health, education, and financial services. For example, one study examined the impact of health intervention programs in Bangladesh (X) on child mortality (Y), controlling for, among other variables, the mother's education (Z). (In this study, the mother's education not only is a confounding variable but also interacts with X, since the impact of X on Y depends on the level of Z. The health intervention reduced mortality the most when the mother's education was low.[3])

Another study, also in Bangladesh, examined the impact of participation (X) in microcredit programs (such as those sponsored by Grameen Bank) on labor supply, schooling, household expenditure, and assets (respectively, $Y_1 \ldots Y_4$), controlling for many (k) individual and village-level characteristics ($Z_1 \ldots Z_k$). Two of the control variables in this study (gender and income) also interact with the program (X), since the amount of impact of the program depends on income and gender. The program appears to be more effective (the estimate of β is greater) for poor women than for other groups.[4]

There are many evaluations of education interventions in developing countries. For example, one examines the impact of improvements in school quality (X) on school attendance (Y) in Kenya, while another estimates the impact of an expansion in school supply (X) on youth wages (Y) in Indonesia.[5] A third studies the impact of extending tuition-free education (X) on various labor market outcomes for youth (Y) in Taiwan.[6] All these studies control for numerous confounding variables (Z).[7]

In each of these examples, and in causal program evaluations in general, what we really care about is the net effect of X on Y. To estimate that net effect, it is necessary to rule out the other unmeasured systematic factors related to X which also affect Y, as well as the random ones (μ). Failing to account for the components of the random term Z that affect Y and that also are related to the intervention (X) threatens the internal validity of the estimate of β. We also need to rule out the possibility that we may be erroneously attributing a systematic effect (that is, the claim that X, the program or policy, the alleged causal agent, is systematically related to Y, the output or outcome) to a random one (μ). Moreover, it is also necessary to rule out the possibility that a claim of no systematic effect (that is, a claim that X has only a random effect on Y) is really a systematic effect. Chapter 2 (briefly) discussed some of these design effects. That is, Chapter 2 showed that a causal claim of positive, negative, or zero impact may be inaccurate because it is not externally valid, because it is not sta-tistically valid, or because it lacks measurement reliability and validity. Chapter 2 also pointed out that many aspects of threats to external validity and measurement reliability are important problems because they are threats to statistical validity. In the equation $Y = \alpha + \beta X + \gamma Z + \mu$, statistical validity is partly captured by the μ term; by contrast, internal validity concerns the (absence of) a relation between X and μ. Internal validity means that they are uncorrelated: $E(X, \mu) = 0$.

The end of this chapter points out that many threats to internal validity actually relate to ele-ments of external invalidity and measurement unreliability and invalidity. However, all the threats to internal validity can be regarded as Z variables that, if they are ignored and unmeasured, may be confounded with the program variables under study (the X variables) in that they also have a systematic effect on the output or outcome variables (Y). Failure to consider these threats (omitted Z variables) by separating them from X may make the program (X) look effective when it is not or may make the program look ineffective when it is actually effective.

It is important to reiterate that no study is 100 percent valid. No study can simultaneously rule out every threat to each of the four kinds of validity, and no study can ever entirely rule out even one of the four threats to validity. However, some studies are clearly more valid than others in that they do a better job of minimizing threats to validity. The focus here is on numerous threats to internal validity. By providing a checklist, evaluators can anticipate these threats, designing their study to either account for or fend off these threats as well as possible. The poorest studies do not consider these threats at the design stage or analysis phase at all.

MAKING COMPARISONS: CROSS SECTIONS AND TIME SERIES

Before considering these threats to internal validity, recall from Chapter 1 that all causal studies use contemporaneous or retrospective observations. That is, they are based on observations of ongoing or previous activities. All causal analysis also requires comparison. Without comparison, there can be no counterfactual: What would have happened to the outcome (Y) if there were no intervention (X) or if the intervention had been different?

There are two basic ways to make empirical comparisons: a cross-section (CS) study and a before-and-after or time-series (TS) study. Consistent with the idea that no causal claim can be made if there is no comparison, both basic types of design entail comparison.

The *cross-section design* compares two or more similar units, one with the program and one without the program (or one with a different program), at the same time. Thus, one might compare standardized test scores in 2008 in a school district that has school choice with scores in 2008 in a similar district that does not allow school choice. Alternatively, one might examine test scores in two comparable school districts at the same time, one district having year-round schooling while the other has the conventional long summer break. Or one might examine test scores in three comparable districts, one in which teachers face a fixed-pay system, another in which pay is partly fixed and partly variable, depending on improvement in student test scores and principal ratings, and a third in which teacher pay raises are entirely variable. These would all be CS designs.

By contrast, time-series designs compare the same unit at two (or more) points in time; the earlier observations represent preprogram outcomes, while the later observations represent observations during the program. Or the comparison could represent observations before and after a program change. For example, one might compare the number of crimes reported by citizens to police before a community-policing program went into effect to the number reported one year after. This is a simple before-and-after comparison. Another type of TS design might entail more than two data points. For instance, one might compare trends over a period of time in measures of public school outputs or outcomes (e.g., teacher-to-student ratios, standardized achievement scores), before a property tax limit began in the school district to the trend in the same measures in the same district for a period of time after. Each of these is a different kind of TS design. In addition to examining outcomes before and after the inception of a program, it is also possible to examine trends (or levels) before and after a change in the amount of program resources. For example, one could examine crime levels in a city before and after an increase in the number of police on the street.

Some designs combine cross sections and time series. For the purposes of introducing the main threats to internal validity in both kinds of designs, I will not discuss mixed designs here, but I do consider combination designs in Chapters 4, 5, and 6. All designs try to separate the impact of an intervention (X) from the impact of extraneous or confounding systematic factors (Z) and from random influences (μ). The preceding chapter considered many sources of random influences. This chapter considers the problem of systematic factors (Z) related to X that also affect Y. These factors represent *threats* to internal validity. It is not possible to say that one design (e.g., CS) is better than the other (e.g., TS) in reducing threats to internal validity. Rather, both have advantages and disadvantages. Specifically, they are each subject to different threats to their internal validity.

THREATS TO INTERNAL VALIDITY

History or Intervening Events

The threat of "history" or "intervening events" applies to all time-series studies. That is, many events (included in Z) other than changes in the program that is being studied (X) could have happened during the period of the study. It is always possible that the observed change in Y may be due to the intervening event (Z) and not to change in the program being studied (X). For example, if a researcher examines the number of crimes reported to police (Y) by citizens both one year before the implementation of a community-policing program (X) and one year after, the observed change in reporting behavior (or the lack thereof) may not be attributable solely to this program. The reason might be that half a year ago, the government fixed all the streetlights (Z_1), so the level of crime went down and there was just less crime to report. Or maybe a new business opened up in town (Z_2), expanding employment opportunities and reducing the incentive for criminal activity. Similarly, if a researcher is studying the impact on graduation rates of a new work-study program for at-risk high school students by comparing graduation rates before the program to those after, what the researcher observes could be attributable to the new program. But it could also be explained by other events, such as a new principal or a change in the curriculum that affected the school during the same period. The point is that an extraneous event, and not the one under study—the new work-study program—could account for the observed change (even if it is no change) in graduation rates and other output or outcome variables.

These intervening events of history may be difficult if not impossible to disentangle from the treatment that is being studied. The discussion of specific research designs in Chapters 4, 5, and 6 suggests some strategies for doing so. But the greatest threat is the evaluator's failure even to consider history or intervening events (a Z variable) as a possible source of systematic change that is extraneous to the program under study (X) and that may be confounded with the program if it is totally ignored.

Maturation or Secular Change or Trends

In time-series designs, besides the intervention due to the program under study (X), long-term, underlying trends (Z), which can also be characterized as maturation or secular change, may also systematically affect program outputs or outcomes (Y). We may observe a change in Y before and after a program change, but the change may be due to a long-term underlying trend, not to the program. For example, decreasing crime rates may not be due to a certain anticrime program, but occur instead because people are aging. Older people are less likely to commit crimes, so crime rates would go down anyway, even without the anticrime program. Similarly, changes in standardized achievement tests (Y) in schools affected by a new education initiative (X) may also be affected by long-term trends in the demographic composition of the school district (Z). If the school district has a growing population of at-risk minorities or immigrants, school test scores (Y) may be dropping, and it is important to separate this underlying downward trend (Z) from the impact, if any, of the education initiative (X). Another example illustrates why this threat is also referred to as "maturation." Suppose that an evaluator is studying the impact of a new curriculum on third-graders. He examines reading scores in September, before the introduction of the new curriculum, and again in June, after the new curriculum. The scores (Y) improve. Maybe the new curriculum (X) accounts for the improvement, but maybe the cause is maturation (Z). Maturation in this case means that young students age, even between fall and spring during an academic year, and they read faster and with more comprehension because they have additional experience and greater developmental readiness. Consequently, some (or all) of the improvement might have happened anyway, regardless of the curriculum change. Thus, internally valid designs must always try to disentangle the program (X) from confounding factors (Z), such as maturation or underlying trends in these examples.

Some time-series designs make it easier to reduce threats due to long-term trends or maturation than others. For example, it is easier to reduce these threats in designs that have observations at many different points in time. It is impossible to deal with this threat in simple before-and-after designs with only one "before" observation and one "after" observation. In that case, the program (X) is measured as "before" and "after," and the trend (Z) is measured as the very same two data points. Thus, they are identical and cannot be separated. But if there are many pre- and post-program observations, it is easier to reduce this threat by separating the underlying trend from the inception of the program. Subsequent chapters discuss this issue in more detail. Further, the chapter on nonexperiments points out that the threat of maturation or trends corresponds to the problem of auto- or serially correlated data and that it is a threat to both internal validity and to statistical validity. But the greatest threat is for evaluators who use time-series designs to ignore this threat entirely.

Testing

"Testing" refers to instances in which the method of measuring the outcome Y can affect what is observed. This is common in the social sciences. Observing a rock will not change its behavior; observing me will change my behavior if I see that you are looking at me. These kinds of measurement techniques are called obtrusive measures. Not all measures are obtrusive. For example, collecting administrative data about my age, years of employment, place of work, rank, and salary will not affect my behavior, especially if I do not know about it (more about this issue later). Surveys and tests, however, can be obtrusive. Responding to a survey or taking a test can change behavior: surveys may make a respondent aware of new issues, and students learn by taking a test. Testing is a threat to internal validity in both CS and TS designs.

Obtrusive measures are a particular problem in TS evaluations. In TS studies, when repeated measures are obtrusive, taking the test (Z, or the pretest score on the output or outcome measure, Y_{t-1}), and not the intervention or program treatment (X), may cause the outcome (Y, or the posttest measure Y_t) to change.[8] We will be unable to tell whether the observed change in Y is caused by the obtrusive pretest measurement (Z) rather than (or in addition to) the intervention or treatment (X). Chapter 2 explained that taking tests is a threat to external validity. We see now that obtrusive measurement is also a threat to internal validity in time series, and it can be difficult to correct.

An example will clarify. Suppose that a manager, concerned about productivity, surveys the employees in his organization to assess their morale, their networking, and their commitment to the organization's mission. Finding from the survey that morale, networking, and commitment are not at the level that he thinks they should be, he reorganizes the office to make it less hierarchical. Several months later, he resurveys the employees and is glad to see that morale, networking, and commitment have improved. Can the manager attribute the observed change in Y to the reorganization (X)? Not necessarily. Some (or all) of the change could have been due to the very act of pretesting to get the baseline data on Y. Just as in the famed Hawthorne study, pretesting may have sent a signal to the employees that the manager "cared."[9] The signal from the pretest (called either Y_{t-1} or Z), and not the actual reorganization (X), may have accounted for the improved scores on the output measure (Y_t).

Testing effects are difficult to avoid in a TS design when measures of outcome or output are obtrusive. One way to minimize these effects is to use multiple indicators. For example, in addition to the survey, the manager could use other indicators of office morale and commitment, such as objective indicators from administrative data on productivity and absenteeism, or observations of how many people arrive early and work late. These measures are less obtrusive and could supplement the survey. While the survey may be a more direct measure of what the manager wants to know, its disadvantage is that it is obtrusive and therefore subject to testing effects.

Testing is also a threat to internal validity in CS designs. The classic example of this threat is the use of a placebo in cross-section studies of pharmaceuticals. For example, if one were to compare Newpill to Nopill (i.e., "no treatment") (X), the process of administering Newpill (Z) may be inseparable from ingesting the pill itself (X). Administering the treatment requires physician intervention before the pill is ingested. In looking at the impact of X on Y (the duration or severity of a disease), it would be impossible to disentangle X (Newpill vs. Nopill) and Z (physician intervention). Consequently, medical researchers resort to the use of a placebo. One group of patients gets Newpill; the other gets Placebo or Fakepill. Both groups get "treated" with physician intervention. In effect, the use of a placebo turns a testing threat to internal validity into a testing threat to external validity, which is usually considered less severe. (The threat to external validity is that everyone in the study gets a pill, so the study does not really compare Newpill to Nopill.)

Instrumentation

In TS or CS studies, change in the calibration of the measurement procedure or instrument (Z) may partly or entirely cause the outcome (Y) to change, rather than the treatment (X). For example, in a TS study, if one observes a decrease in program costs (Y_t) after the implementation of a new technology (X), the observed decrease ($Y_t - Y_{t-1}$) may be due to the new way that costs are calculated (Z), instead of to program (X) effects. In other words, if Y_{t-1} is measured differently than Y_t, then instrumentation becomes a threat to the validity of a causal claim about the impact of the new technology, because it is impossible to disentangle the new measurement procedure from the new technology.

Similarly, in CS studies, suppose that an evaluator (or a politician) claims that waste collection costs in one community that has privatized the service are less than those in a similar, nearby community, where the government runs the service. If the costs are measured differently in the two communities, some or all of the observed difference in costs (Y) may be attributable to differences in how costs are measured (Z) and not to whether the program is administered publicly or privately (X).

Minimizing this threat clearly requires careful attention to how outcome or output variables are measured over time and between or among the units of analysis at a single point in time.

Regression Artifacts or Regression to the Mean

Subjects are sometimes selected for treatment because of extreme pretest scores on an output or outcome measure (Y_{t-1}). In this case, considering a time-series study, an observed change or difference in outcome (Y_t) may be observed partly or entirely because of the random tendency of extreme scores to return to their normal values. For example, suppose that you took the Scholastic Aptitude Test (SAT) and got an unexpectedly bad score (Y_{t-1} = low). What would you do? Such an extremely poor score (one that is far below your usual or expected score) would increase the probability that you would sign up (and pay) for an SAT-preparation program. After completing the program, your score improves ($Y_t - Y_{t-1} > 0$). Is the improvement attributable to the SAT-prep program (X) or to a regression artifact (Z, or, equivalently, Y_{t-1} = low)? Regression artifacts refer to the tendency of extreme scores to return, by chance, to their mean. The more extreme the score, the more likely it is the next time to bounce back to its mean. In fact, the lower the score at Y_{t-1}, relative to its usual mean, the more likely it is to rise the next time, just by chance. Similarly, the higher the score at Y_{t-1}, relative to its usual mean, the more likely it is to drop the next time, just by chance. So the next time, after the preparation program, it is very likely that your very low initial score would improve. Is the improvement really due to the effect of the program? Maybe, but it might be simply a return of a randomly extreme score to its normal level. Note that those who score unexpectedly high on the SAT are unlikely to sign up for an SAT-preparation program.

Another example concerns sports teams. Sports teams are especially prone to change their manager after a really poor season, but any observed improvement in performance after that may be attributable to the random return to normal that is expected after an especially worse than normal season, not to the efforts of the new manager. As another example, municipal police forces tend to target police in areas that have spikes in crime rates. There is an element of randomness in crime rates (due to measurement error or randomness in human behavior). In a while, after the extra police patrols have been assigned, the crime rate appears to drop. The police chief claims credit, but the effect could be partially or entirely due to a regression artifact, representing the tendency of extreme scores to return to their usual, mean value.

As a final set of examples, bosses (or teachers) often blow up in anger or annoyance at employees (or students) who suddenly perform at poor levels relative to their normal level. Soon afterward, the performance level improves. The boss (or teacher) concludes that anger works, but the improvement may simply represent the tendency of extreme scores to return to normal values. The flip side of this example is that bosses (or teachers) sometimes lavish praise on employees (or students) whose performance is suddenly exemplary. Soon afterward, the employee's (or student's) performance appears to decline, returning to its normal level. The boss (or teacher) concludes that praise does not work, but this, too, may be an invalid inference. The apparent drop in performance may merely represent the tendency of randomly extreme scores to return to their normal level.

These are all examples of the problem of regression artifacts in TS studies.[10] Forthcoming chapters on time-series research designs suggest that one way to reduce the threat is to collect observations over many points in time, so that it is possible to separate normal from extreme scores. Chapter 5 shows that, in CS designs, it is also possible to make use of randomness in pretest scores by constructing a type of natural experiment, called a regression discontinuity design, to reduce many threats to internal validity, including regression artifacts.

Selection (Uncontrolled Selection)

In CS studies, when the groups to be compared differ on factors other than treatment (X), then these differences ($Z_1 \ldots Z_k$) may account partly or entirely for the observed differences in outcome (Y) between those who receive the treatment or program and those who do not. For example, private school students' performance on standard test scores is much better than that of students from public schools. Can we attribute the observed difference simply to attending different types of schools, private or public? Maybe. But students who attend private schools tend to be wealthier and have parents who are more educated than those who attend public schools. Thus, some or all of the observed difference in achievement scores (Y) may be due to the tendency of wealthy, educated parents (Z) to select private rather than public schools (X) for their children. Thus, if one does not account for the selection effect, the impact of socioeconomic status (SES) (the Z variable in this case) on Y, the outcome, would be confounded with the type of school, which is the treatment (X) variable. Figure 3.2 is a graphic of the causal model that depicts this dilemma.[11]

Failure to account for variables (Z) that are related to the program or treatment (X) and that also affect the outcome or treatment (Y) will cause the evaluator to confound or mix up the impact of the program with that of the uncontrolled or unaccounted-for variable. The consequence is a conclusion about causal impact that is likely to be erroneous. In the example, ignoring SES differences between public and private school children is likely to result in overestimating the impact of private, relative to public, school education.

This is also a problem in comparing public schools to one another. For instance, if an evaluator simply compares one public school (say, PS 105) to another (say, PS 4) and finds that the achievement scores at PS 105 are higher than those at PS 4, she cannot simply conclude that PS 105 is a "better" school than PS 4. PS 105 may simply serve a higher SES group of students than PS 4. Some (or all) of the observed difference in outcome (Y) may be due to the difference in SES between the schools (Z), not to any particular programmatic or management differences between them (X).

As a final example, many claim that PAC contributions (X) make legislators vote (Y) the way the contributors want. Symbolically, the claim is that X causes Y, which I diagram in the top panel of Figure 3.3. However, PAC contributions are not randomly distributed. Trade union PACs direct their contributions to representatives from districts with large numbers of union members and liberal Democratic voters. Similarly, business PACs direct their contributions to representatives from districts with many large corporations and Republican voters. Representatives from these districts are likely to vote the way the PAC wants them to, not because of the PAC contributions, but because incumbents want to get reelected and therefore vote the way their constituents prefer. The lower panel of Figure 3.3 represents the causal diagram for this scenario. It shows that some or all of the observed correlation between PAC contributions (X) and representatives' votes (Y) in the direction preferred by the PAC may be attributable to a third variable, constituency preferences (Z), and not to the PAC contributions (X).

Ignoring the selection problem is equivalent to confusing causation and correlation. One cannot attribute correlation to causation except under very special circumstances. To do so is to invite internally invalid causal conclusions.

Selection problems are probably the dominant threat to internal validity in CS studies. There are thousands of examples of them. In fact, except when assignment is random, they are impossible

Figure 3.2   **Causal Model of Selection Threat**

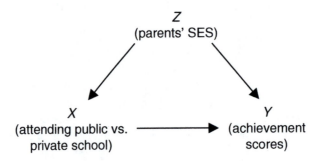

Figure 3.3   **Selection Threat: Does Money Buy Votes?**

(a) The causal claim

X (PAC $) ⟶ Y (vote in pro-PAC direction)

(b) The threat to the internal validity of the causal claim

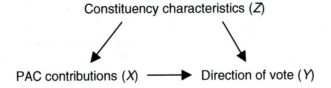

to avoid in CS studies. Even if one controls for one selection threat (factor Z_1), there is always the possibility that another one lurks (factor Z_2). Even if one deals with ten selection threats, there is always the possibility that an eleventh or twelfth threat still looms. In fact, the presence of selection threats in most CS studies makes TS studies particularly desirable from the perspective of minimizing selection threats to internal validity. Many evaluators bemoan the absence of time-series data. Comparing one unit at time 1 to itself at time 2 is a useful way to hold constant many of these confounding (Z) factors that plague CS studies.[12] Often, however, TS data are unavailable or too sparse for statistical validity (that is, too few TS observations are available). So, it is important to be aware of selection threats to internal validity and to design CS studies to minimize these threats.

Uncontrolled (and unknown) pretest scores on outcome measures are also an important selection threat to internal validity in CS studies. This threat is analogous to the regression artifact in TS studies. For example, suppose that an evaluator compares workplace accident rates (Y) in firms that the Occupational Safety and Health Administration (OSHA) inspects (X) to accident rates in firms that OSHA does not inspect. The researcher might find that the accident rate in inspected firms is higher than or even no different from the rate in firms that OSHA did not inspect. The diagram in the top panel of Figure 3.4 illustrates this apparent conclusion. The researcher might

Figure 3.4   **Selection Threats: The Case of Selection Based on Pretest Scores**

(a) Ignoring the pretest score

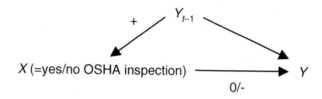

(b) The impact of the pretest score

then infer that OSHA inspections fail to reduce accident rates (0 association) or even increase them (+ association). But suppose that, unknown to the researcher, OSHA targets inspections at firms with unusually high accident rates, as the lower panel of Figure 3.4 illustrates. Accident rates have a large random component, so some extremely high rates are likely to drop, by chance, to their usual expected rate. Thus, in the absence of information about how OSHA selects firms to inspect, and in the absence of information about the problem of regression artifacts, the researcher might well conclude, erroneously, that inspections do not work. But this conclusion could be partly or entirely wrong, because it could be attributable to a regression effect rather than the systematic effect of the inspection program.

More generally, when selection is targeted at needy cases, we can regard previous values of output or outcome variables (Y_{t-1}) as a selection variable (Z) that needs to be accounted for in order to reduce an important threat to internal validity in CS studies. Using CS designs in these cases is, in many circumstances, a poor choice, because, by definition, simple CS studies have no pretest data, so it is impossible to measure and adjust for the selection threat.[13]

Experimental Mortality or Attrition

In TS studies, observed before-and-after differences in outcome scores (Y) may be partly or entirely attributable to a different group of respondents rather than to the treatment (X). For example, suppose that the Department of Housing and Urban Development wanted to study the impact of rental housing vouchers on the recipients' housing location decisions. Suppose that the researchers use a survey to compare where people live before they get the voucher to where they live afterward. The comparison would be valid only if the pre-voucher respondents are the same as the post-voucher respondents. It is hard to follow up with survey respondents, and it is particularly difficult when those respondents are poor and subject to the unpredictable forces of a shaky labor market. Thus, those who respond at time 1 but not at time 2 could be a less-well-off group than the more stable and more employable respondents who actually respond at both time 1 and time 2. The researchers might conclude that the vouchers improved housing outcomes, but maybe it is the difference between the SES (Z) of the respondents at time 2 and time 1, rather than the impact of the vouchers (X), that accounts for the change in Y. When respondents at time 1 drop out at time 2, they are called "attritters"; for the researcher, they represent a "death" (i.e., an experimental mortality) if they cannot be found.

Tracking changes over time in achievement test scores presents another example of an attrition threat. It may illustrate experimental addition, rather than attrition, but it is the same underlying phenomenon. If the test takers are changing, then the changing scores may measure not changes in performance but changes in who is taking the test. There are many examples of this threat in TS studies of student achievement test scores. For example, one reason that SAT scores go down is that more students take the test, and the newest test takers tend to score more poorly than the previous ones. Thus, drops in test scores may not reflect poorly on the schools but may entirely or partly reflect changes in the type of students who take the SATs. Similarly, school achievement test scores (Y) may change from one year to another not because of any response by the school (X) but because the demographics of the students in the school (Z) have changed.

If it is random, attrition itself would not be a threat to internal validity. (It may be a threat to statistical or external validity.) However, as the previous examples illustrate, if the attrition rate is systematically related to the treatment variable (X) or to a confounding variable (Z) that is related to both X and Y, then attrition is a threat to internal validity.[14]

Multiple Treatment Interference

In TS or CS studies, when one treatment (X, the treatment of interest) is confounded with another (Z, where, in this case, Z is another treatment, but not the focal one), then it is impossible to separate the impact of one treatment from the other. For example, suppose that an evaluator, using a CS design, compares the impact of rigid versus flexible curricula (X) in the first grade in otherwise similar schools (or classrooms) on standardized achievement scores (Y). However, it turns out that all the schools (or classrooms) with flexible curricula also have very experienced teachers (Z), while the rigid curricula are taught by teachers with less experience. Then X (the treatment of interest) cannot be separated from another "treatment" (Z) that is not the central interest. Later, Chapter 6 shows that this is also an example of what is called multicollinearity. For now, it is an example of multiple treatment interference, and it is regarded as a threat to internal validity because the two treatments cannot be separated.

Suppose that an international aid agency used a TS design to evaluate the impact of its decision to decentralize the management of agricultural projects in a particular country in Africa. The agency might look at a measure of farm productivity (Y) for some time before projects were decentralized (X) and for a period afterward. However, at the same time projects were decentralized, project budgets were also cut (Z). It is thus impossible to separate the impact of X from that of Z. The two treatments go together, exemplifying the threat of multiple treatment interference in a TS design.

Contamination

In CS studies, sometimes the separation between treatment groups and control groups is less than it should be. For example, if the control (untreated) group receives some of the treatment, then the two groups are no longer distinct, and the treatment is said to be contaminated with the control. Similarly, if some elements in the treatment group do not receive the treatment, then the two groups are once again no longer distinct, and the treatment and control groups are still contaminated.

Unrecognized, this overlap (i.e., contamination) may partly or entirely account for the observed between-treatment difference in outcomes (Y). For example, in a study of drug prevention programs in schools, suppose that one compares the attitudes toward risky behavior (Y) of students in the fourth-grade class that received the program ($X = 1$) to similar fourth-grade students in the same school who did not experience the program in their class ($X = 0$). Nothing prevents students who received the formal program from talking to those who did not. As a result, there is contamination in that some students who did not receive formal training are nonetheless exposed to elements of the program. Similarly, those in the formal treatment group may have chosen not to listen to the antidrug instructor or were absent; the treated group is effectively contaminated with students who were really not treated. Thus, a conclusion about the difference in outcome due to receiving versus not receiving the treatment may not be valid, if those who supposedly received no treatment actually received some treatment or if those who supposedly received treatment actually received none. Using our standard notation, the "pure" treatment-or-no-treatment variable is X, the self-selected treatment is Z, which is often unmeasured, and the outcome is Y. (This is also an example of nonrandom measurement error, as the actual measure of the treatment as a yes-no variable is clearly not valid.)

As another example of contamination as a selection threat, consider a study comparing the impact of classroom education ($X = 0$) to on-the-job training (OJT) ($X = 1$) on employment outcomes (Y). The researcher usually assumes that subjects in the study receive either one treatment or the other. But many who are assigned to OJT ($X = 1$) may also elect to take education training (Z) elsewhere, and those in the education group ($X = 0$) may also elect to take OJT elsewhere (Z). Some in both treatment groups may opt for no training at all. Once again, the two treatments are not as different as the researcher assumes, since one group has clearly been contaminated with the type of treatment offered to the other group. It is invalid to assume that the groups are really as separate as they appear to be.

Because the measure of "type of training" as two mutually exclusive categories (OJT vs. education in the example, or $X = 1$ or 0) is clearly not valid, it represents a threat of contamination (and nonrandom measurement error) to internal validity. In the example, the actual level of training (which I conceptualize as a confounding factor) is self-selected, while the intended level of treatment is what is being studied and measured as X. It follows that, if possible, one remedy for contamination threats is to separate the intent-to-treat variable (X) from the self-selected treatment variable (Z).

In the real world, where treatment (and nontreatment) cannot be forced, the program is an opportunity to receive service, or "intent to treat," not actual receipt of the service. Similarly, "no treatment" is not the same as "no service"; rather, it means that the specific service under study is intended to be withheld, but people cannot be prohibited from selecting it on their own. If X (assigned treatment) and Z (selected treatment) are related, then contamination is an example of a threat to internal validity. Further, this variety of contamination can be a threat to internal validity, even in randomized field experiments, if the assigned treatment affects the treatment that clients actually select. Chapter 4 discusses this dilemma in more detail.

SUMMARY

To summarize, the threats to the internal validity of TS designs are somewhat different from the threats to the internal validity of CS designs. Threats to TS studies alone include history or intervening events; maturation, secular change, or trends; regression artifacts; and experimental mortality or attrition. Threats to cross-section studies alone include selection effects or uncontrolled selection and contamination. Obtrusive testing, instrumentation, and multiple treatment interference are clearly threats to the internal validity of both kinds of designs.

Type of Threat by Design Type

Threat	Design type
History or intervening events	TS
Maturation, secular change, or trends	TS
Obtrusive testing	TS + CS
Regression artifacts or regression to mean	TS
Selection or uncontrolled selection	CS
Contamination	CS
Experimental mortality or attrition	CS + TS
Instrumentation	CS + TS
Multiple treatment interference	CS + TS

Most studies have multiple threats to internal validity, but it is clear that some have more threats than others. For example, simple comparison of outcomes between two groups, one that has received the treatment while the other has not, is almost always subject to selection threats. In fact, unless one has a controlled experiment, which I discuss in Chapter 4, any CS design is subject to selection threats. Although some CS designs are more vulnerable to this threat to internal validity than others are, some researchers argue that the pervasiveness of selection threats in nonrandomized CS designs (which is most of them) makes them less desirable than TS designs. However, as we have seen, TS designs also have special problems.

It is probably the case that no single approach and no single study can ever be causally conclusive, because threats to internal validity are pervasive. But this is not a reason to give up. Rather, when multiple studies, each with different threats to internal validity, all suggest the same causal conclusions, we can act as if the causal claim were upheld. For example, while it is technically true that no study has proved that "smoking causes cancer," multiple studies, each with different threats to internal validity, all suggest that such a conclusion cannot be rejected. In this case of multiple, individually imperfect designs with a consistent finding, it is probably wise to act as if the causal conclusion is in fact empirically warranted. It is also important to observe that this particular causal claim is supported by discipline-based theory; beyond the hopes and casual observations of program managers, there are a lot of theoretical reasons from understandings molecular biology (and related fields) to expect that smoking and cancer are causally linked. (Note that we still do not say that the conclusion has been "proved." Mathematicians do proofs. Empirical social scientists do not.)

THREE BASIC RESEARCH DESIGNS

The issue of internal validity is so critical to impact evaluations that three different ways of reducing threats to internal validity define the three basic types of research designs that evaluators use to estimate program impact. Undoubtedly, the most commonly occurring threat to internal validity is self-selection. Consequently, each of the basic design types reduces the threat of selection in a distinctively different way. (See Table 3.1.)

Table 3.1

Types of Research Designs, by Method of Reducing Threats to Internal Validity

Type of design	Method of reducing threats to internal validity
Randomized field experiment (RFE)	Random assignment by evaluator to program or no program, or to different program levels (e.g., high, medium, low). Evaluator compares outcomes between the groups.
Quasi experiment (QE)	
Cross-section (CS)	Evaluator selects groups with and without the program, or with different program levels or types. Groups are chosen so that they are as similar as possible in all other respects, except the program. Evaluator compares outcomes between the comparable groups.
Time-series (TS)	Evaluator selects a target group, comparing outcomes before and after the implementation of the treatment.
Nonexperiment (NE)	Evaluator collects data on units of analysis that have experienced different levels of the program and compares outcomes in units with different levels of the programs, using statistical methods to control for other differences between the units.

The first type of design is the randomized field experiment (RFE). In the RFE, the evaluator randomly assigns units of analysis to a treatment group ($X = 1$), to a nontreated (or control) group ($X = 0$), or to groups with different levels or types of treatment, to reduce selection and selection-related threats to internal validity.

Second is the quasi experiment (QE). To reduce threats to internal validity in the QE, the evaluator deliberately selects treatment and other groups so that they are comparable or similar in as many respects as possible with respect to confounding or extraneous factors (Z). The idea is to construct groups so that the only difference between the groups is in how much or whether they experience the program being evaluated. In one type of QE, the evaluator selects comparable groups at the same point in time, but one group has experienced the program (or experienced a high level of the program), while the other group has no treatment (or has experienced a low level of the program, or a different form of the program). This is a cross-section quasi experiment (CS QE). In the CS QE, it is rare that the researcher determines whether the group experiences the program or what the program level will be. Usually, that determination has previously been made by political or administrative decision makers, or by self-selection, and the evaluator uses *ex post* or retrospective comparison of (hopefully) comparable sites to evaluate program impact. Another type of QE examines one group over time, so that the before-treatment group is comparable to the after-treatment group because the group is the same, save for the treatment. This is a time-series quasi experiment (TS QE). Some types of QEs use a mixture of TS and CS comparisons.

The third type of design is the nonexperiment (NE). To make groups comparable, this design uses statistical controls to account for as many selection threats (or pre-existing group differences) as possible. The main statistical tools for nonexperimental designs are multiple regression and related methods of multivariate statistical analysis.

Finally, some studies use a mixture of two or even all three types of designs. It is especially common for studies to supplement RFEs or QEs with nonexperimental design elements by adding statistical controls to reduce additional threats to internal validity that cannot be removed by selection or random assignment alone.

The remainder of this book discusses each of the three basic types of designs (RFE, QE, and NE). Even though it may be difficult to separate one type of design from the other, the three basic design types in Table 3.1 represent different approaches to establishing comparison or to establishing a counterfactual. The goal is the same: to find out what would have happened to the outcome or output (Y) if the program (X) had not been implemented or had been implemented differently, net of the effects of the confounding influences of extraneous systematic factors (Z) and random effects (μ). The choice of a design, however, depends on many factors, including the stage of the program (old or new), the type of intervention (targeted or general), and the resources for evaluation. The challenge facing the evaluator is to come up with the most rigorous or valid design (or mix of designs) that is feasible under the circumstances.

RETHINKING VALIDITY: THE CAUSAL MODEL WORKHORSE

Chapter 2 introduced the basic concepts of external validity, statistical validity, and measurement reliability and validity. This chapter used a causal model workhorse to introduce the notion of internal validity. Figure 3.5 reintroduces that causal model to show how each type of threat to validity relates to the fundamental problem of program evaluation. The evaluator's dilemma is to isolate the impact of the program being evaluated (X) from that of the other two influences on the program outcome (Y). The other two influences are, first, other systematic factors (Z_k) that influence Y and that are also related to the program (X), and, second, random influences (μ). Both of these factors (the extraneous, confounding Z_k variables and the random factors μ) can be reinterpreted in terms of how they reflect threats to validity from random measurement error (RME), nonrandomized measurement error (NRME), statistical noise, and uncontrolled Z variables. The top panel of Figure 3.5 illustrates the threats to defensible causal inferences diagrammatically. The lower panel defines the statistical model that will actually be used to do all this work. Considerable demands are placed on this simple statistical model, and forthcoming chapters illustrate the econometric adaptations that need to be made to address these threats.

As shown in the diagram in the top panel of Figure 3.5, internal validity concerns the accurate estimation of β, the impact of the focal program (represented as X), on the focal outcomes or outputs (represented as Y). The core of internal validity concerns our ability to separate the two systematic influences (that is, to separate X from Z_k) on Y. If we cannot disentangle the relation between X and each of the Z_k, then the association of one or more of the Z_k with X will be reflected in our estimator of β (called b), which, for internal validity, should reflect only the impact of X on Y, independent of Z variables.[15]

Statistical validity concerns the accuracy with which we can separate the influence of X on Y from that of μ, the random component. For example, a large sample reduces the μ component, making it easier to separate the "signal" (X) from the "noise" (μ). Measurement (un)reliability refers to RME. There can be RME in treatment (X) or in outcome variables (Y). RME in outcome variables is a source of statistical invalidity; it is also represented by μ. In other words, a small sample size, the main component of statistical invalidity, is one source of random error in Y. RME in Y is another source. Thus, the μ-term captures issues of both statistical (in)validity and measurement (un)reliability, or RME, in Y.

Issues of measurement also affect internal validity. For example, there can also be RME in the program variable, X, which I represent in the diagram by μ_x. By definition, RME in program variables introduces (random) error into the X variable. Oddly enough, but clarified by the dia-

Figure 3.5   The Causal Model Workhorse and Threats to Validity: Diagram and Statistical Model

(a) The diagram

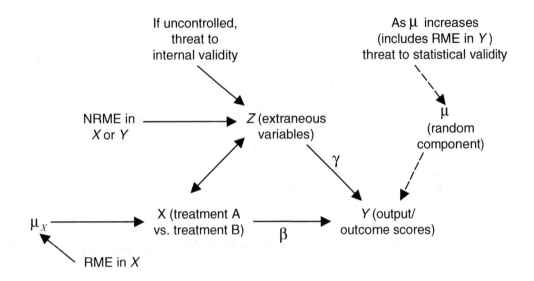

(b) The equation

$$Y = \alpha + \beta X + \gamma Z + \mu.$$

gram, RME in X poses a threat not to statistical validity but, rather, to internal validity because its effects, if uncontrolled, are picked up by b, the estimator of β, which represents the "true" impact of the focal program. Similarly, NRME, or (in)valid measurement of Y (or X), is also a threat to internal validity. Measurement (in)validity refers to the possibility that a nonrandom component (a Z_k term) can slip, undetected, into the measurement of Y (or X), making it difficult to determine whether it is X that affects Y alone or it is X along with an unintentionally invalid instrument for measuring Y (or X), that is affecting Y. Undetected, the invalid measurement of the outcome Y, or the program X, becomes, conceptually, a component of one of the Z variables. The correction is to measure this systematic (measurement) error and to remove it in some way, just as we use different research designs to remove other threats to internal validity by separating the effects of X on Y from those of Z_k.

Even parts of external validity can be clarified using the causal model workhorse. Specifically, statistical interaction means that one causal model might pertain under some circumstances, while another pertains under other circumstances. For example, β might be positive for one group of people but negative for another. The implication is that the model is not generalizable. It is common that a model is conditionally generalizable: It is common for one group or one set of circumstance but not another.

I summarize these as follows:

To attain:	Try to:
Internal validity	Separate the impact of X from Z_k
Measurement validity (same as internal validity)	Separate the impact of X from Z_k
Statistical validity	Separate the impact of X from μ
Measurement reliability of Y (same as statistical validity)	Separate the impact of X from μ
Measurement reliability of X (same as internal validity)	Separate the impact of X from Z_k
External validity (undetected statistical interaction) (same as internal validity)	Establish conditions for causal model

The goal of program evaluation remains unchanged. It is to find out what would have happened to the outcome or output (Y) if the program (X) had not been implemented or had been implemented differently, net of the effects of the confounding influences of extraneous systematic factors (Z_k) and random effects (μ). The causal model workhorse is a useful tool for clarifying the four types of threats to validity or errors of causal conclusions that can happen on the way. The model allows us to see the overlap among these four threats. Some aspects of measurement (un)reliability are really a threat to statistical validity; some threats to measurement (un)reliability, as well as threats to measurement and external validity, are really threats to internal validity. Thus, the pages that follow focus only on the internal and statistical validity of the basic designs because these two general types of validity subsume issues of measurement and external validity.

BASIC CONCEPTS

Internal validity: definition
What makes Y change?
   X Intervention variable(s)
   Z_k Confounding or extraneous variable(s)
   μ Random factors
The basic equation
The graphic of the equation
Examples of Z variables as threats to internal validity
Types of comparison designs
CS designs: examples
TS designs: examples
Threats to internal validity
   History or intervening events
      Definition
      Examples
   Maturation, secular change, or trends
      Definition
      Examples
   Testing
      Definition
      Examples
   Instrumentation
      Definition

Examples
Regression artifacts or regression to the mean
    Definition
    Examples
    (Two-way causation as one example)
Selection or uncontrolled selection
    Definition
    Examples
    (Two-way causation as one example)
Experimental mortality or attrition
    Definition
    Examples
Multiple treatment interference
    Definition
    Examples
Contamination
    Definition
    Examples
The relation between type of threat and type of comparison (CS vs. TS)
Three basic research designs for reducing selection threats
    Randomized field experiment (RFE)
    Quasi experiment (QE)
        Time series (TS)
        Cross section (CS)
    Nonexperiment (NE)
The basic causal diagram and threats to validity
    Threats to internal validity
        Threats due to confounds (Z_k)
        Threats due to RME in X, NRME in X, NRME in Y
        Threats due to undetected statistical interaction or low external validity
    Threats to statistical validity
    Threats due to random components (μ)
    Threats due to RME in Y

DO IT YOURSELF

Suppose that the two causal claims below are the conclusions of actual empirical studies. Without knowing any specifics about the research studies that produced each claim, what are the potential threats to the internal validity of each causal claim? Explain why each one might be a potential threat.

Example for CS Design

1. Decentralized (as opposed to centralized) World Bank projects have a higher rate of return.

Example for TS Design

2. Putting more police on the streets has reduced the crime rate in this neighborhood.

A SUMMARY OF THREATS TO INTERNAL VALIDITY

Definition: internal validity = accuracy of causal claim

1. History or external events: In TS studies, an event (Z_k) other than the change in the treatment (X) might have caused the outcome (Y) to change (or might cause some of the observed net change in Y).
2. Maturation, trend, endogenous change, or secular drift: In TS studies, Y may be changing partly or entirely because of an underlying trend (Z_k), not because of change in the treatment (X).
3. Testing: In TS studies with obtrusive measures, taking the test (Z_k), not change in the treatment (X), may cause the outcome (Y) to change (or might cause some of the observed net change in Y).
4. Instrumentation: In TS or CS studies, change in the calibration of the measurement procedure or instrument (Z_k), rather than the treatment (X), may partly or entirely cause the outcome (Y) to change.
5. Regression artifacts: In TS or CS studies, when subjects are selected for treatment because of extreme scores $(Y_{t-1} = Z_k)$, an observed change or difference in outcome (Y) may be observed partly or entirely because of the random tendency of extreme scores to return to their normal value.
6. Selection: In CS studies, when the groups to be compared differ on factors besides the treatment (X), then these differences (Z_k) may account partly or entirely for the observed differences in outcome (Y).
7. Experimental mortality or attrition: In TS or CS studies, when two or more groups are being compared, observed between-treatment differences in outcome (Y) may be partly or entirely attributable to a differential loss of respondents (Z_k), rather than to the treatment (X).
8. Multiple treatment interference: In TS or CS studies, when the focal treatment treatment (X_1) is confounded with another $(X_2 = Z_k)$, then it is impossible to separate the impact of one treatment from the other.
9. Contamination: In CS studies, when the separation of treatment groups from control groups is less than it should be, or when the control group receives some of the treatment, then the overlap (Z_k) may partly or entirely account for the observed between-treatment difference (or lack of difference) in outcomes (Y).

NOTES

1. For reviews of evaluation evidence regarding the impact of welfare reform on welfare caseloads, see Steven H. Bell, "Why Are Welfare Caseloads Falling?" Urban Institute Discussion Paper 01–02, Washington, DC, 2001; Rebecca Blank, "Evaluating Welfare Reform in the United States," *Journal of Economic Literature* 40 (2002): 1105–1166; Robert Moffitt, "A Primer on U.S. Welfare Reform," *Focus* 26, no. 1 (2008): 15–25; Caroline Danielson and Jacob Alex Klerman, "Did Welfare Reform Cause the Case Decline?" *Social Service Review* 82, no. 4 (2008): 703–730.

For evidence on the impact of PAC contributions on votes in Congress, see Janet M. Grenzke, "PACs and the Congressional Supermarket: The Currency Is Complex," *American Journal of Political Science* 33, no. 1 (1989): 1–24; Laura Langbein and Mark Lotwis, "The Political Efficacy of Lobbying and Money: Gun Control in the U.S. House, 1986," *Legislative Studies Quarterly* 15, no. 3 (1990): 413–440; Thomas Mann, "Linking Knowledge and Action: Political Science and Campaign Finance Reform," *Perspectives on Politics* 1, no. 1 (2003): 69–83; John Gilbert and Reza Oladi, "Net Campaign Contributions, Agricultural Interests, and Votes on Liberalizing Trade with China," *Public Choice*, online first October 19, 2010; James DeVault, "Swing Voting and Fast-Track Authority," *Southern Economic Journal* 77, no. 1 (2010): 63–77.

2. Rindskopf regards simultaneity, or two-way causation, between X and Y as a fourth source of observed change in Y. I regard simultaneity as one instance of a type of confounding or extraneous factor, and I discuss it in that context below. See David Rindskopf, "Plausible Rival Hypotheses in Measurement, Design, and Scientific Theory," in *Research Design: Donald Campbell's Legacy*, vol. 2, ed. Leonard Bickman (Thousand Oaks, CA: Sage, 2000: 1–12).

3. See Pradip K. Muhuri, "Health Programs, Maternal Educations, and Differential Child Mortality in Matlab, Bangladesh," *Population and Development Review* 21, no. 4 (1995): 813–834.

4. See Mark M. Pitt and Shahidur R. Khandker, "The Impact of Group-Based Credit Programs on Poor Households: Does the Gender of Participants Matter?" *Journal of Political Economy* 106, no. 5 (1998): 958–996.

5. See Michael Kremer, "Randomized Evaluations of Educational Programs in Developing Countries: Some Lessons," *American Economic Review* 93, no. 2 (2003): 102–106; Esther Duflo, "The Medium Run Effects of Educational Expansion: Evidence from a Large School Construction Program in Indonesia," *Journal of Development Economics* 74, no. 1 (2004): 163–197.

6. Chris Spohr, "Formal Schooling and Workforce Participation in a Rapidly Developing Country: Evidence from 'Compulsory' Junior High School in Taiwan," *Journal of Development Economics* 70, no. 2 (2003): 291–327.

7. Program evaluations in developing countries are numerous. See, for example, Barbara O. Wynn, Arindam Dutta, and Martha I. Nelson, *Challenges in Program Evaluation of Health Interventions in Developing Countries* (Santa Monica, CA: RAND, 2005); Jessica Cohen and Pascaline Dupas, "Free Distribution or Cost-Sharing? Evidence from a Randomized Malaria Prevention Experiment," *Quarterly Journal of Economics* 25, no. 1 (2010): 1–45; Shaohua Chan, Ren Mu, and Martin Ravallion, "Are There Lasting Impacts of Aid to Poor Areas? Evidence from Rural China," *Journal of Public Economics* 93 (2009): 512–528; Robert Chambers, Dean Karlan, Martin Ravallion and Patricia Rogers, "Designing Impact Evaluations: Different Perspectives," International Initiative for Impact Evaluation Working Paper 4, New Delhi, India, 2009.

8. The notation Y_{t-1} or Y_{t-j} indicates pretreatment or preintervention measures of output or outcome variables. Usually, the $t–1$ subscript implies just one pretest score, while $t–j$ implies more than one pretest score. For example, there could be observations for five years before the intervention. Similarly, Y_t implies a single posttest observation, while Y_{t+j} implies multiple postintervention observations.

9. Fritz J. Roethlisberger and William J. Dickson, *Management and the Worker: An Account of a Research Program Conducted by the Western Electric Company, Hawthorne Works, Chicago* (Cambridge: Harvard University Press, 1939). Recall that Levitt and List could not replicate the results from the original data; see Steven D. Levitt and John A. List, "Was There Really a Hawthorne Effect at the Hawthorne Plant? An Analysis of the Original Illumination Experiments," *Applied Economics* 3, no. 1 (January 2011): 224–238. Nonetheless, the problem of obtrusive measurement that the "Hawthorne Effect" represents remains a threat in general.

10. Regression artifacts exemplify the problem of reverse causation or simultaneity as a threat to internal validity. Often, previous values of the outcome (Y_{t-1}, or Z) determine selection for treatment (yes or no) (X), and treatment is supposed to affect the subsequent outcome (Y_t). In the absence of TS data (that is, in the absence of the value of Y_{t-1}, it will be unclear whether the chicken causes the egg ($X{\rightarrow}Y$) or whether the egg begets the chicken ($Y{\rightarrow}X$). Some researchers regard simultaneity as a separate threat to internal validity. In this example, I regard Y_{t-1} as a potentially uncontrolled Z variable and as a type of regression artifact. See Rindskopf, "Plausible Rival Hypotheses."

11. This is the fundamental problem of social science research in general. Many years ago, Hubert M. Blalock Jr., *Basic Dilemmas in the Social Sciences* (Beverly Hills, CA: Sage, 1984) framed the problem as one of causal inference when Z and X are related to each other, and both affect the dependent variable.

12. Timothy Besley and Anne Case, in "Political Institutions and Policy Choices: Evidence from the United States," *Journal of Economic Literature* 41, no. 1 (2003): 7–73, make this dilemma very clear in the case of examining the causal impact of political institutions (e.g., the size of state legislatures, term limits) on policy outcomes. On the importance of comparing one unit itself over time (e.g., within-state, over time comparison), see also Luke Keele and William Minozzi, "How Much Is Minnesota Like Wisconsin? States as Counterfactuals," www.polmeth.wustl.edu/media/Paper/kmpolmeth2010.pdf (accessed July 10, 2011).

13. As Chapter 4 shows, the (well-designed and implemented) randomized control experiment is the exception to this generalization.

14. E. Michael Foster and Grace Y. Fang, in "Alternative Methods for Handling Attrition: An Illustration Using Data from the Fast Track Evaluation," *Evaluation Review* 28, no. 5 (2004): 434–464, present a nontechnical discussion of the attrition problem and suggestions for dealing with it statistically. Steven Tenn, "The Effect of Education on Voter Turnout," *Political Analysis* 15, no. 4 (2007): 446–464, finds that using nonattriters in the Current Population Survey (CPS) panel minimizes the selection threat from unobserved confounding variables (Z) in his study. (A panel data set requires repeat observations on the same individuals.)

15. It is important to note that, just as the arrow linking X to Z has no causal interpretation, the arrow linking Z to Y also has no causal interpretation. The coefficients linking each Z variable to Y measure the relation between Z and Y, controlling for X, but reflect only statistical association. The central focus of program evaluation is on the impact of X on Y, where we do seek a causal interpretation.

4

Randomized Field Experiments

Many evaluators regard the randomized field experiment (RFE) as the gold standard of program evaluation.[1] In theory, if implementation of this design encounters few or no glitches, it is the best way to guard against selection and selection-related threats to internal validity. That is, with randomized designs, estimates of program impact on the outcomes of interest will be, relative to other designs, less biased.

BASIC CHARACTERISTICS

Random assignment of the units of analysis in the study to different groups is critical for these designs.[2] Units of analysis can be individuals or identifiable, separable groups of individuals, such as schools, villages, churches, cities, or work groups. Each individual or group in an experiment is randomly assigned to a different program or treatment, and there are many ways to do this. To select a treatment randomly for each unit, you can flip a coin. As I point out, there must be multiple units of analysis, which means that there must be multiple coin tosses. You could throw a die (odd versus even, if there are two treatment variations; or outcome 1 to 6, if six treatment variations are being tested; or die outcome 1–2, 3–4, or 5–6, if three treatment variations are being tested). You could also use computerized random number generators. For example, if you get an even number for the first unit of analysis in the study sample, you can assign that unit to group A (or $X = 1$, the group that gets the new program, called the treatment group). If you get an odd number, you assign the unit to group B ($X = 0$, the group that gets no program, or the current program, called the control group). Such random assignment is said to be blind because the die, the coin toss, or the computer picks the treatment variation for each unit of analysis. The program manager does not make the choice; the affected client (the unit of analysis) does not make the choice; even the evaluator does not make the choice. The evaluator chooses the random process to be used (computer or coin or die). But after the random process is chosen, the process determines the treatment choice for each specific unit of analysis in the study. In all these examples, there must be the equivalent of multiple coin tosses or rolls of the die, with one "toss" for each unit of analysis; the standard rule of thumb is that there should be at least about 30 units available for (random) assignment to each treatment. If there are multiple units of analysis available for each treatment (i.e., multiple tosses of the coin or rolls of the die), the units assigned to each treatment group are very likely to be comparable on all confounding variables (Z_k), whether they are measured or not. Thus, any observed difference on the outcome, Y, will, in theory, be attributable to treatment differences ($X = 1$ or $X = 0$), not to pre-existing differences in confounding variables (Z_k). Thus, RFEs, in theory, are likely to be internally valid.

It is rare that the control group gets no treatment at all. Even in medical experiments, the control group gets a placebo (a sugar pill), while the experimental group gets the new drug whose efficacy is being tested. The same is true in program evaluation. In program evaluation, the most common experiments entail random assignment to program or treatment A versus program or treatment B. Program A may be the new program, while B is the current program. Often, experiments examine the relative impact of more than two alternatives—for example, comparing the impact of programs A, B, C, and D on outcome Y.[3] An evaluator could also compare the impact of different levels (or dosages in medical experiments), such as high, medium, and low levels, of exposure to the program (X) on outcome variables (Y). It is also possible to delay treatment, so applicants for a program with limited space can be randomly assigned to treatment now and treatment later. Although this text often uses the language of random assignment to treatment and control groups, it is important to remember that, in practice, there may be many treatment groups and no control group with no treatment at all.

The use of the adjective "field" to describe this experimental design is not casual. "Field" means that the random-assignment experiment happens in the real world. Just as random assignment is critical to improving the internal validity of this design, its implementation in the real world is critical to enhancing its external validity. Many randomized experiments originated in laboratory conditions, but they are not field experiments. For example, medical researchers carry out experiments on rats in laboratories. But, in many clinical and behavioral situations, rats respond differently than humans. Thus, it is hard to generalize from the impact of new versus old drugs randomly assigned to rats to what would happen if the same drugs were randomly assigned to people. Consequently, drug and medical innovations must show their efficacy not only in randomized laboratory experiments but also in randomized field experiments. This means that, in field experiments, the units of analysis for random assignment to treatment and control groups are people, not rats; further, they are people in "real world" settings that resemble the population targeted by the policy or program that is being studied. The same is true in program evaluation, where the units of analysis that are randomly assigned are either individual people or groups of people in a real-world setting, not in experimental labs. Furthermore, in program evaluation, the types of people who are assigned to the different treatment groups are not likely to be college sophomores but, rather, people who are typical of the program's target group.

BRIEF HISTORY

In the United States, randomized field experiments have been used since the early 1960s.[4] RFEs are sometimes used in such policy areas as early education, job training, criminal justice, and, most recently, primary education. But the first RFEs evaluated the impact of cash support for the poor on their incentive to work during the war on poverty. They were federally funded, large-scale, experimental tests of alternative ways to provide financial support and other services to poor people.

The first experiment involved a guaranteed income, known as a negative income tax (NIT). The guaranteed income experiments were carried out during the 1960s and early 1970s in one state (New Jersey), two cities (Seattle and Denver), and one rural area (in North Carolina).[5] Each study at each site compared various guarantee levels and various tax rates (the rate at which federal payments would be reduced as earnings went up) to the welfare status quo at that time, known as Aid to Families with Dependent Children (AFDC). Higher guarantee levels and tax rates ($X1$ and $X2$, respectively) were expected to reduce the incentive to work (Y), among other outcomes, and this was the primary hypothesis that the RFE was designed to test. The target group in this design consisted of people who were eligible for AFDC in their state of residence (specifically, people who were receiving welfare or were eligible for AFDC but not receiving it). The researchers selected a random sample of this subpopulation and (in most of the study sites) asked for their consent to be in the study. After consent was given, the individuals were then randomly assigned to thirteen experimental groups and one control group, which remained eligible for AFDC.

Random assignment of each unit of analysis (individual families, in this case) to the treatment and control groups is what makes this an *experiment* and reduces selection threats. The random process determined which eligible families got which of the multiple treatments (of which one was the then-prevailing policy); the program administrator did not make the choice nor did the persons in the study. The units of analysis were families in the target group, making this a *field* experiment. Random *selection* of individuals from the larger target group population for the final study sample does not make this a random experiment; rather, random *assignment* makes it an experiment. Random selection enhances the external validity of the study but has no direct impact on internal validity. After the sample is selected (randomly, in the NIT experiment, or nonrandomly in many other studies), each unit in the sample is then randomly assigned to the experimental and control subgroups. Random sampling is not necessary for the RFE. Rather, random assignment of each element in the sample, which may or may not have been selected randomly, to a treatment alternative is what defines the RFE. (One of the treatment alternatives may be the status quo alternative or a control group.)

There were other large-scale randomized experiments during this period. One of the most prominent was a national health insurance experiment, in which the treatment groups faced different co-payment rates and the control group was the status quo. Investigators examined the comparative impact of each treatment alternative, including a control group or status quo option (X), on health-care usage (Y).[6]

Financial support for national, large-scale randomized field experiments waned after the 1960s, but the use of smaller experimental designs to evaluate programs increased in the 1970s and increased even more in the 1980s and 1990s and continues today. Most of these designs were studies of various ways to provide job training and job search assistance. There were also studies of counseling, case management, electricity rate structures, police and prison practices, and rental vouchers.[7] During the 1990s, states were allowed to exercise discretion in how they delivered federal welfare funds to recipients; for example, they could set caps or time limits on the amount of funding that recipients could get. The price of this discretion was that the state had to test the impact of its treatment relative to the status quo on various output and outcome measures, and the RFE was the method for evaluation preferred by Congress. The results from these waiver experiments became a foundation for the 1996 transformation of AFDC into Temporary Assistance for Needy Children (TANF).[8]

There has been an increasing number of small, randomized field studies in education, including one on class size, an assessment of the Teach for America program, and several studies of voucher programs.[9] The No Child Left Behind (NCLB) Act of 2001 called for using "scientifically based research." Specifically, it advocates (and funds) the use of the RFE, going as far as saying that the RFE is the only sure way to establish "strong evidence of effectiveness" while discrediting all other designs. In the past, evaluation research in primary and secondary education had been notable for the absence of RFEs, especially in comparison to other social and education-related service areas.[10] Ironically, it probably would not be possible to use an RFE to evaluate NCLB. A recent evaluation relies on a type of quasi experiment discussed in Chapter 5.[11]

It is notable that most RFEs focus on poor people in developing countries; poor people in the United States who are dependent on publicly provided, means-tested social services; people in prison; and enlistees in the military. By contrast, there have been few RFEs to test aspects of regulatory policy and public management. For example, there are none that compare collaborative against coercive means of implementing or enforcing rules. Nor do RFEs compare detailed ("complete") procurement contracts against general ("incomplete") contracts or evaluate the impact of different "dosages" of inspection frequency on workplace safety.

CAVEATS AND CAUTIONS ABOUT RANDOMIZED EXPERIMENTS

Selecting Control Groups

RFEs are not easy to do. They require considerable advance planning. Nor are they applicable for all kinds of programs. In general, they are most applicable when the likely impact of a new program idea, or a modification of an existing one, is at issue. It is often politically impractical or awkward to use random assignment to study the impact of ongoing programs, but it is not impossible, especially when there is considerable uncertainty about the effectiveness of ongoing alternative arrangements. It is rarely feasible (politically or ethically) to assign treatment to one group and to deny it to another, even when units are randomly (and thus fairly) assigned. Rather, it is more defensible to compare one treatment ($X = A$) to another ($X = B$), or to vary the magnitude of treatment, or just to delay treatment (now versus later).

For example, there is controversy about the impact of larger or smaller classes for at-risk primary school students, which can be tested using random assignment of students to small classes of about fifteen students compared with large classes of about twenty-two students.[12] Years ago, random assignment was used to test the impact of the ongoing Big Brothers Big Sisters mentoring program on a variety of school-related outcome variables. In order to avoid reducing or denying services to those in need, the researchers selected only agencies with large caseloads and waiting lists. Then they randomly assigned youths who had applied for the program to a treatment group and a control group; those in the control group were put on the waiting list.[13] Services were not denied, only delayed. The Mexican antipoverty program called Progresa is another example of the use of delayed treatment in an RFE.[14]

Sample Size Issues and the RFE

Another property that makes RFEs hard to implement is that they require a large number of subjects. Thirty is the bare minimum number of units required in each group. First, a large n in each treatment group increases the likelihood that units are comparable on all confounding (Z_k) variables, adding to internal validity. Second, if the researcher wants to minimize the probabilities of both Type I and II errors (that is, to increase statistical validity), a far larger number of units in each treatment group will be required. Determining the optimal number of units in each group depends on other factors as well. If the researcher expects only small "effect sizes," then the number in each group should be larger. Suppose, for example, that a researcher anticipates that the difference between treatments A and B will be noticeable, but not large (say, 0.05 of a standard deviation unit change in a standardized test score each year). Then a large n will be required to obtain a statistically significant but substantively small effect.[15]

It is also important to stress that the unit of analysis is defined by what is randomly assigned. Suppose that program managers at the U.S. Agency for International Development wanted to design a study comparing the impact of written versus pictorial information (X) on maternal health-care practices (Y) in a developing country. Suppose further that the evaluators proposed to "randomly" assign treatment $X = 1$ (pictorial information) to all 1,000 women in Eastville and treatment $X = 0$ (written information) to all 1,500 women in nearby Westville. The n in this study is 2, not 2,500. Such a small n (1 in each treatment group) is not really random assignment, just as a "random sample" of two is not random. (A design comparing the different treatments in two presumably similar villages is a quasi experiment. This type of design is the topic of Chapter 5.)

To turn the study of two villages into a considerably more valid RFE, the evaluators could draw up a list of the 2,500 women in the two villages and individually assign each woman (perhaps by tossing a coin once for each of the women) to receive either pictorial or written instructions.[16] This design would be a true RFE, but it would undoubtedly suffer from contamination problems, because the women with different treatments could easily talk with one another. Carving each village into, say, thirty separate neighborhoods, for a total of sixty neighborhoods, would minimize (but not eliminate) the threat of contamination. Each of the sixty neighborhoods could then be randomly assigned to one of the two treatments. This modification would minimize the contamination threat while preserving an acceptable level of statistical validity. In addition, using neighborhoods from two villages rather than one in this hypothetical design may aid external validity. It also creates a larger pool of neighborhoods available for random assignment, enhancing statistical validity and the internal validity of random assignment.[17] Below, I discuss blocking as a method to better handle this common dilemma.

The need for a large n is exacerbated if the researcher expects different impacts in different subgroups. In that case, the number of separate subgroups randomly assigned to each treatment group must meet these "large number" standards. For example, suppose, first, that the researcher is not interested in studying different subgroups, seeking instead to generalize to "all students in the (imaginary) state of Uforia, USA." To detect effect sizes and to reasonably protect statistical validity, it might be sufficient to randomly assign, from a pool of 1,000 eligible students in the target group, 500 students to treatment A (opportunity for state-sponsored school vouchers) and 500 to treatment B (no such opportunity).

But consider what happens if researchers expect that vouchers may have different effects in different racial/ethnic subgroups. Then, it is necessary to randomly assign the treatment alternatives (vouchers or the status quo) within each of four different subgroups—white students, African-American students, Hispanic students, and Asian students. To maintain the same statistical validity as the original design, which anticipated no subgroup differences, it would still be necessary to have 500 in each treatment subgroup. There would now be eight groups: a treatment and a control group for each of the four racial/ethnic subgroups. In this case, budget constraints and issues of administrative feasibility make it unlikely that there could be 500 in each treatment group. Such a design would require a pool of 4,000 eligible students in the target group, randomly assigning 500 whites to each of the two treatments ($n_1 = 1,000$), 500 African-Americans to each treatment ($n_2 = 1,000$), and so on for the other two subgroups. The more subgroups that are of interest, the more likely it is that budget constraints will make it necessary to sacrifice statistical validity for the separate subgroup analyses. In this example, suppose that the budget constraint of 1,000 in the study target group is binding. Then, to study four subgroups, the evaluator could randomly assign 125 students to each treatment ($X = 1$ and $X = 0$) within each of the four subgroups without sacrificing acceptable levels of statistical validity. However, if the subgroup n's (i.e., $n_1, \ldots, n_4$) become very small (say, less than thirty), then internal validity for each of the subgroups may have to be sacrificed as well. I will show that some types of RFEs can minimize statistical validity problems by making use of pretest data on outcome variables. (Chapter 6 shows how statistical controls can also be used to mitigate some of the adverse effects of small sample sizes on internal validity when random assignment is not or cannot be carefully implemented.)

It is important to note that, in RFEs, there is no need for equal n's in each experimental group. The rationale for randomly assigning equal or roughly equal numbers to each group has nothing to do with internal validity as long as the number in each group is reasonably large. For internal validity, it would be reasonable to assign 100 individuals to the more expensive treatment group and a larger number (e.g., 150) to the less expensive treatment group. Budget constraints might make such an allocation necessary, and such an allocation would not sacrifice internal validity.

The reason for equal or roughly equal numbers in each group is to aid statistical validity. Most statistical procedures assume that, whether group means are equal or unequal, their variances are equal. (Statistics texts call this the assumption of homoscedasticity.) In general, when numbers of observations are smaller, variances are larger. So the group with 100 randomly assigned units in it may have a larger variance in the Y variable than the group with 150 units. However, statistical techniques (specifically, heteroscedastic-corrected tests of statistical significance) are readily available to test and adjust for different between-group variances. Chapter 6 discusses this process in more detail. The main point is that, as long as the n in each group is reasonably large, equal numbers in each treatment group are usually not necessary for internal or statistical validity, unless the imbalance is severe. Even in that case, the error is remediable.

This discussion has repeatedly emphasized the importance of a large number of observations in each randomly assigned treatment group in the RFE.[18] But two factors set a limit to large n studies. As we have seen, the first is the budget. More observations add to project costs. The second is to recognize that n's over 1,000 or so in each group to which the researcher wishes to generalize add progressively little to statistical or internal validity. For example, suppose that the sample size cannot exceed 1,000 and that the evaluator needs to compare as many as fifteen different treatments using random assignment. If the evaluator were not interested in subgroup analyses, an average of 66 or 67 units could be assigned randomly to each of the fifteen treatment groups within the constraint of a sample size not to exceed 1,000. The relatively large number in each group would be sufficient for statistical validity and probably for internal validity as well. (As we shall see, the use of pretest scores in the RFE makes it even easier to assure both internal and statistical validity when budgets and other considerations of practicality constrain the sample size.) Of course, if one needs to do analyses of separate subgroups, the n's in each subgroup should be large enough for both internal and statistical validity, but budget constraints frequently necessitate sacrificing observations, consequently threatening these validity criteria.

"Blocking" the observations before random assignment is a useful addition to the RFE toolkit that has two important advantages: It improves statistical validity with fewer observations than the typical RFE, and it also improves internal validity.[19] "Blocking" before random assignment in an RFE is analogous to "matching" before comparison in the quasi experiement (QE). The idea of "blocking" means that, having selected the units of analysis to be randomly assigned to different treatments, the evaluator deliberately sorts the units into homogeneous groups, or blocks, and then randomly assigns the treatment within each (homogeneous) group. The sorting should be done on confounding variables (Z_k) that are expected to affect the relevant outcome. The blocks need to include enough observations to make random assignment possible, which means the blocks should be based on discrete variables or categories of continuous variables (e.g., observations within with the same letter grade in a required freshman math class; or observations within + or − 0.1 standard deviation units on a pretest). In some cases, it may be even be possible to closely sort observations simultaneously on a large set of "k" measurable and relevant characteristics (Z) likely to affect Y and to randomly assign a small number of blocks to one treatment and a small number of (comparable) blocks to the control or other treatment. However, as the number of confounding variables increases, the ability to form blocks that are comparable on all k variables drops. Additionally, when the number of blocks that are randomly assigned is small, it becomes particularly important to verify that they are indeed comparable on all of the (measureable) confounding variables.

Even without blocking simultaneously on all k (measurable) confounding variables, there are numerous advantages to blocking before random assignment. With respect to internal validity, it is always possible (but not likely), even with a large n, that the (unblocked) randomly assigned treatment group will wind up being all female, or all smart, while the (unblocked) control group will wind up as the opposite. Blocking makes this (unlikely) outcome impossible because it integrates the process of assessing that groups are similar, or balanced on relevant confounding variables, with the process of random assignment itself. And blocking increases the statistical power of a design, making it less likely to produce Type II errors. King et al. (2007) also point out that blocking reduces the damage from nonrandom drop out: If one block leaves or decides not to participate, you still have the others. This may reduce external validity, but it does no damage to internal validity.

In addition, some statistical procedures use data more efficiently than others. That is, for a fixed n, some statistical procedures have greater statistical validity than others at no cost to internal validity. Specifically, the use of multiple regression with dummy variables is often more efficient than separate subgroup analyses using 2×2 tables. Compared with tabular analysis, multiple regression allows evaluators to meet budget constraints with only a small sacrifice in statistical validity and no sacrifice of internal validity. I introduce the use of regression with dummy variables later in this chapter. Chapter 6 shows how dummy variables can be used in multiple regression with statistical controls.

Random Selection ≠ *Random Assignment*

A final property of random assignment is to point out what it is not. Specifically, random selection of n units from a specified population to which the evaluator wishes to generalize is not random assignment of n units to different treatments. The word "randomization" alone is not clear because it could pertain either to random selection of observations, random assignment of units of analysis to different treatments, or both. Random selection of n units from a given population promotes external validity. It does not define an RFE. Pollsters, market researchers, and others who use random-sample surveys as a source of data about a specific population of interest are concerned with external validity. Evaluators may also be concerned with external validity, and as Chapter 2 pointed out, they take random samples of a focal population for this purpose. But the RFE does not require a random sample. Evaluators can (and often do) ask for volunteers to participate in a randomized experiment. After they have assembled a list of volunteers who are otherwise eligible for the RFE (e.g., they have incomes below a certain threshold), the evaluator then assigns (hopefully, after blocking) each of the n volunteers to one of k treatments. The volunteers are not a random sample, but the study is still an RFE as long as there is random assignment. Sometimes (not often), RFEs will entail both random selection and random assignment, but random selection is neither necessary nor sufficient for the RFE. Rather, it is random assignment to treatments that defines the RFE. (While this point may seem an obvious, beginners often confuse pollsters' random samples with evaluators' use of the RFE.)

TYPES OF RFEs

RFEs come in three basic types, as outlined in Table 4.1. The key to reading the table is that X denotes the treatment, and its absence denotes the control group. The control group may get no treatment or

Table 4.1

Basic Types of RFEs

			Basic Characteristics
I. No pretest; random assignment (R) only			
	X	Y_E	Basic design. No pretest
R			Needs large N
		Y_c	
II. Pretest + R			
Y_E''	X	Y_E'	Pretest for both groups
R			Greater internal and statistical validity with statistical
			control for pretest
Y_c''		Y_c'	Testing is threat to external validity
III. Four-group = (pretest + R) + R			
	X	Y_E	Combines I and II
R			Can measure separate effects of testing and treatment,
R		Y_c	and test for possible interaction of testing and
			treatment
Y_E''	X	Y_E'	
R			
Y_c''		Y_c'	

program, a different treatment or program, or a different level of the treatment or program. There can be more than two groups, but, for now, I discuss the experiment in the context of just two groups. I will point out how the analysis needs to be modified if there are more than two groups. R denotes that, in all cases, assignment of each unit of analysis in the study to treatment or control is random. Thus, the first line of part I of the table denotes the treatment or experimental group and the second line denotes the control group. The R between the lines denotes random assignment. Y is the set of output or outcome indicators, measured at some point after the program is expected to show impact. Y_E stands for a "column" of posttest measures for the n_E units of analysis in the experimental (or treatment) group, while Y_c represents the "column" of post-treatment measures for the n_C units of analysis in the control group, where $n_E + n_C = n$ units of analysis in the RFE.

There is no pretest (or pretreatment) measure of the output or outcome variables in this basic experimental design. When pretest scores are not available, but the RFE is a feasible design, it is advisable to have a large enough n in the study to make sure that the randomization actually worked. It is advisable to check whether the randomization worked by testing whether the two randomly assigned groups are statistically equivalent on whatever Z variables have been measured. However, without pretest data, it is impossible to check whether the randomization completely worked. That is, if the n is "large enough," randomizing the assignment of units to treatment and control groups will make it likely that the groups will be statistically equal on pretest scores and other preexisting differences. But in the absence of pretest data, it is impossible to verify whether the two groups began the different treatments with statistically equivalent scores on the pretest value of the outcome variable. Even with a large n, things can go wrong with the randomization process. Without pretest data, however, one cannot see whether anything actually did go wrong, and, if it did, it is almost impossible to adjust for the mishap.

The second basic type of RFE (II in Table 4.1) reduces the chance of such mishaps by using a pretest. The pretest can enhance the statistical as well as the internal validity of an RFE. In this type of RFE, observations are pretested on the outcome variables. Then they are randomly assigned to treatment alternatives (either before or after being pretested). They undergo the randomly assigned treatments for an appropriate duration of time; then each observation is measured again on Y, creating a posttest score. Because the pretest score on Y is known, it is possible to ascertain whether the groups actually scored equally on the pretest. Theoretically, random assignment is supposed to create this statistical equality, but the creation of statistical equality will come about most predictably if n is large and nothing else goes wrong in the random assignment process.[20] Blocking prior to random assignment would make this outcome more likely.

The internal validity of an RFE that passes the test of pretest statistical equality between groups to which observations have been randomly assigned is demonstrably more defensible than an RFE (with equal n) in which no pretest information is available. Further, we will see that statistical controls for pretest scores reduce the noise in observed posttest scores, adding to the statistical validity of the pretest RFE, compared to the posttest-only RFE.

However, the pretest RFE has an important drawback. Because both groups are pretested, the design can be used only for observations on groups that are or can be pretested. Pretesting may limit the external validity of this design. When pretest information is readily available in administrative records, this may not be a matter of concern. For example, pretest information on many outputs or outcomes, such as test scores or measures of employment or health status, is readily available for students and social service recipients, respectively. However, when pretest information on intended outcomes is not routinely available, collecting that information may become obtrusive. Persons in such pretest RFEs have agreed to be pretested and know that they are being tested and observed. In this case, the external validity of the pretest RFE is limited to persons who are aware of being observed. If this awareness affects behavior, it becomes a threat to the external validity of such a design.

The third type of RFE is a response to this threat. Often referred to as a "Solomon four-group design" (III in Table 4.1), this RFE allows researchers to examine whether the results of the treatment alternatives (X) on the outcome (Y) occur not only for observations that undergo the pretest but also for randomly assigned observations that are not pretested. In this design, the evaluator randomly assigns the units to one of four groups. The first two groups take no pretest, but one of these groups is randomly treated, while the other is not. The second two groups both receive a pretest; one (randomly) gets treatment, but the other does not. This design can measure the separate effects of testing and treatment, both of which are randomly assigned. Nonetheless, evaluators are usually more concerned with the impact of the treatment than with the impact of the pretest.

Compare this four-group design to design II. In design II, all the treatment groups are tested. Since the treatment groups are treated equivalently, testing is not a threat to internal validity in design II. It may be a threat to external validity, but if pretesting is a normal component of the program that is being evaluated (which is the case in many education and social service programs), it is not even a threat to external validity. Consequently, I do not present the statistical model for the analysis of design III. Its practical application in program evaluation is, at best, rare, but it is commonly mentioned in research design textbooks.

The practical application of design III in program evaluation most likely has nothing to do with the problem of pretesting. It is more likely to be used when the evaluation anticipates interaction. Specifically, a four-group, or nested, design might be used if the researcher anticipates that the impact of one treatment ($X_1 = 1, 0$) is contingent on the presence or absence of another randomly assigned condition ($X_2 = 1, 0$). To test that hypothesis using the RFE, she might randomly assign levels of X_1 in two stages: one when X_2 is present, and one when it is not. As an example, suppose that the impact of class size (X_1 = 15 or 25) depends on the heterogeneity of the class with respect to ability (X_2 = hetero- or homogeneous). Then, in the first stage, the researcher might randomly assign students to heterogeneous versus homogeneous classes. In the second stage, students in the mixed classes get randomly assigned to large or small classes; students in the homogeneous classes are similarly assigned to large or small classes.

The Posttest RFE: The Diagram

The basic posttest RFE is a common, essential design. As long as the n is large and the random assignment process works as intended, it produces internally valid estimates of the impact of X on Y. Effective random assignment makes it likely that there is no selection threat to internal validity. Such random assignment (with a large n) means that treatment and control groups do not differ significantly on Z variables (including the unobserved pretest value of Y) that relate, in any direction, not only to the presence or absence of the treatment (X) but that also affect Y. The certainty that treatment and control groups do not differ on these Z-type variables increases (with diminishing effects) as n increases. For nonrandom cross-section (CS) comparison designs, the selection threat means that Z variables compete with X as an explanation for any observed association between X and Y (Figure 4.1a). As long as n is large, random assignment removes the association between Z variables and the treatment (X), so that the Z variables can no longer compete with X as an explanation for any observed association between X and Y (Figure 4.1b). In effect, random assignment turns confounding Z-type variables into purely stochastic (i.e., random) terms that have only a direct effect on Y, just like the μ component.

The Posttest RFE: The Statistical Model

The theoretical model that corresponds to the RFE is the simple linear equation:

$$Y_i = a + BX_i + \mu_i.$$

The corresponding statistical model to estimate B, the parameter that stands for the impact of X on Y in an RFE, is a simple (bivariate) regression of an outcome or output variable (Y) on the program variable (X):

$$Y_i = a + bX_i + e_i.$$

In this model, Y_i is assumed to be a continuous variable that records the values of the outcome or output variable for each of the $i = 1 \ldots n$ units of analysis that were randomly assigned in the RFE. If Y is a continuous variable, the method of analysis is a regression. If Y is a two-category categorical variable with 1 or 0 values for each of the n units of analysis, the method of estimation is logit (or probit). If Y is a multicategory categorical variable, the method of estimation is multinomial logit; if Y is an ordinal variable, then the method of estimation is ordinal logit. But the basic logic in all the cases is the same as that in regression, which is what I discuss here. (For information on the other methods of estimation, and for more information on regression, see one of the many econometrics texts that do not require calculus and matrix algebra[21] or one of those that do.[22] A discussion of the data format for the basic regression appears in Chapter 6.)

In the simplest case, when just two program alternatives are being tested (e.g., the program is present versus absent, or the program operates at a high versus low level), then X is a dummy or

Figure 4.1 **The Effect of Randomization: Posttest Only RFE**

(a) Selection threat in the nonrandom
Cross-Section (CS) design: present

(b) Selection threat in the large
N RFE: absent

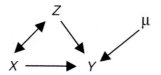

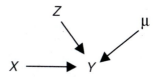

indicator variable. "Dummy" means that X is coded 1 for the n_E experimental units that got the high (or regular) treatment level, and coded 0 for the n_c control units that received the low (or zero) treatment level, where $n_E + n_c = n$ units of analysis in the RFE. The estimate of program impact is the slope, b. That is, b is the estimate of how much the mean outcome or output measure Y changed as a result of being in the group coded 1, compared with being in the group coded 0. So, if $b = 4.2$, then the $X = 1$ group mean is 4.2 points higher than the $X = 0$ group. If $b = -4.2$, then the $X = 1$ group mean is 4.2 points lower than the $X = 0$ group. The intercept is the estimate of the "starting" level: It is the mean on Y for those in the $X = 0$ group, and b is the estimate of the change from that mean as a result of the (randomly assigned) treatment alteration.

In an RFE, b is the estimate of causal impact. We want that estimate to be as internally valid as possible. Random assignment in the RFE reduces selection threats to the internal validity of that estimate. (I will discuss other threats to the internal validity of the estimate next.) The estimate of b is composed of the systematic effect and a random component. We want the estimate of the systematic effect not only to be as internally valid as possible but also to be as statistically valid as possible. The t-statistic associated with the estimate of b helps us make the assessment of statistical validity. As long as the n is large (> 120), the random component is expected to be normally distributed; the t-statistic separates the systematic from the random component at acceptable levels of statistical validity.

The regression coefficient b that we report is an estimate of the unknown, true effect, which I represent by B in this chapter. (I used β in Chapter 3. Both are common ways to represent the central unknown parameter of interest.) Specifically, the t-statistic tests the null hypothesis of no true impact, written as H_0: $B = 0$ (i.e., there is no systematic effect of X on Y) against the alternative that there is a systematic effect (H_a: $B > 0$ or H_a: $B < 0$, depending on what the desired or expected direction of impact is). (Uppercase letters are used to denote hypothesized effects, and lowercase ones to denote the actual, estimated test results; the subscript "a" means alternative hypothesis, which is always inexact.) When the n is large enough (> 120), the t-statistic is normally distributed around the value expected by the null hypothesis (usually 0). Suppose the evaluator uses the conventional .05 probability of a Type I error. Then, a t-statistic larger than 1.65 (if the alternative hypothesis is $B > 0$) will lead the evaluator to conclude that the program has a statistically significant impact in the expected (and presumably intended) positive direction. Similarly, t-statistics less than -1.65 (if the alternative hypothesis is $B < 0$) lead the evaluator to conclude that the program has a statistically significant impact in the expected (and presumably intended) negative direction.[23]

Researchers conventionally use analysis-of-variance (ANOVA) F-tests to statistically analyze the results from an RFE when there are more than two treatment groups. (See Table 4.2.) When there are two treatment groups, researchers conventionally use the t-test for the difference of

Table 4.2

Main Methods of Statistical Analysis for Basic Types of RFEs

I. No pretest; R only	Difference of means with t-test if two groups
	ANOVA and F-test if more than two groups
	Simple regression of Y (outcome) on X (treatment dummy or dummies) with estimate of treatment regression coefficient(s) and t-statistic(s)
II. Pretest and R	Multiple regression of Y_t on X and Y_{t-1}
	Control for Y_{t-1} improves internal validity if N is small or if there are problems with random assignment and Y_{t-1} is causal
	Always improves statistical validity (reduces standard error of b)

means to analyze the results from an RFE. However, instead of using F- and t-tests for the difference of means, it is better to use the regression approach. It is more general, provides more information, and is the basis for the analysis of all research designs, whether experimental, quasi experimental, or nonexperimental, no matter how many treatment groups there are. In the case of the two-alternative (i.e., two-group) RFE, the bivariate regression t-test gives the same results as the conventional difference-of-means t-test. In the case of multiple groups, the F-test for the regression sum-of-squares is also the same as the F-test in an ANOVA. With multiple groups, the regression coefficients (b) are the differences of means that the ANOVA also reports, but the regression also reports the significance of the differences between each treatment and the reference treatment (usually the status quo), which the ANOVA does not report. Moreover, it is no longer necessary to distinguish between ANOVA for more than two groups and t-tests for two groups. In fact, they are equivalent because squaring the two-group t-score is the same as the F-test for a two-group ANOVA.

If k levels or types of program alternatives are being compared, then X in fact becomes $k - 1$ dummy variables in a multiple regression, as follows:

$$Y_i = a + b_i X_{1i} + b_2 X_{2i} + b_3 X_{3i} + \ldots + b_{k-1} X_{k-1,i} + e_i.$$

Each of the regression coefficients is an estimate of the difference between the specified program level and the omitted one, also called the reference group. Thus, b_1 is the estimate of the difference in average values of Y for the group labeled 1 and the omitted kth one, which is often the lowest treatment level group, or the control group (called the reference group, which is X_k). Similarly, b_2 is the estimate of the difference in average values of Y for the group labeled 2 and the omitted (or reference) group. And b_{k-1} is the estimate of the difference in average values of Y for the group labeled $k - 1$ and the reference group. The amount of difference between, say, b_3 and b_1 is the estimate of the difference in the mean of Y between treatment 1 and treatment 3.

Just as the t-statistic in the bivariate regression separates random from systematic coefficients, so do the $k - 1$ t-statistics associated with each of the regression coefficients. Their interpretation is the same as in the bivariate case. That is, to claim that the treatment (say, X_3) is significantly different (in a particular direction) from the baseline, reference treatment, we want the t-statistic to exceed 1.65 (if the expected impact is positive) or be less than -1.65 (if the expected impact is negative). The greater the difference between the estimated t-statistic and this cutoff (critical) value of t, the more statistical confidence we have in our results, at least from the perspective of avoiding Type I errors. Note that statistical significance is not the same as substantive significance.

Example: How to Analyze Results from an (Imaginary) Posttest RFE

Consider the following hypothetical but plausible case. Suppose that a national statistics report showed that teen pregnancy rates in the state of Alpha were among the highest in the country and that they had been growing in recent years. The alarmed state officials determined to take action, but they disagreed about the best way to proceed. Some lawmakers were convinced that abstinence-only, "just-say-no" sex education should be launched in all the middle and high schools in the state. Others thought, with equal passion, that conventional sex education programs that examined abstinence as well as the alternatives, and the risks and benefits of each, should be implemented. And a third group thought that both of these options were probably going to be another waste of government money and that sex education belonged in the churches and families, certainly not in the schools.

To resolve their dispute (and to delay making a decision), the policy makers agreed to study the matter further. They contracted with the Program Evaluation Group (PEG) at Alpha State University to undertake a study of some pilot programs in some schools and see which program, if any, worked the best. For the pilot programs, the PEG investigators selected ninety schools from the population of middle and high schools in the state. These schools were selected because the principals of these schools were willing to cooperate with the study. They were enticed by the extra funding that they would get not only for running the programs but also for complying with the additional paperwork burden imposed by the reporting requirements of the study. The evaluators (without blocking the schools first) then randomly assigned each of the ninety schools to one of three groups. One treatment group would receive funding for the abstinence-only sex education program ($X1$). The other treatment group would receive funding for the conventional sex education program ($X2$). The control group was to leave sex education to the community ($X3$); there was to be no formal sex-education program in the schools in this group.

The main outcome variable, Y, was a multi-item scale. The scale was based on a postprogram data collection instrument. Part of the data came from a random sample of students in each of the ninety schools; the remainder of the information came from administrative data collected in each school. The survey-based component of the multi-item scale measured students' attitudes and behavior with respect to sexual activity, with a high score indicating "better," less-risky behavior. While student attitudes to risk avoidance, the survey-based component of the index, might be available at the student level of analysis, the unit of random assignment is schools, not students; consequently, the survey-based school average score was part of the index. The other components were school-based reports from school nurses and counselors from confidential student records of problems related to risky sexual behavior. The units of analysis in this study are schools, not students. It follows that the units of analysis (i.e., the units of random assignment) are the same as the number of observations ($n = 90$) in the study. The outcome measure, Y_i, was the index score, which could range from 1–10, which is a school-wide average of the items in the multi-item scale after one academic year of the program. The treatment programs began in September; the data were collected in June.

Statistical models for randomized experiments use dummy variables to distinguish treatment groups from control groups and to distinguish treatment groups from one another. In the example, one central question that divided the lawmakers was whether abstinence-only sex education was better than conventional programs. Neither of these two groups of lawmakers was really interested in the "do-nothing" alternative. So the first statistical model that we will evaluate simply contrasts the two programs, ignoring the control group. The second statistical model uses all three groups, comparing the abstinence-only and conventional program with the control group and to one another.

For the first analysis, consider only the sixty schools ($i = 1 \ldots 60$) that were randomly assigned to the two different programs. Let $X1_i = 1$ for the thirty schools in the abstinence-only treatment group, and $X1_i = 0$ for the other thirty schools in the conventional program treatment group. The second analysis uses the entire sample of ninety schools ($i = 1 \ldots 90$) that were randomly assigned to one of the three alternatives. Continue to let $X1_i = 1$ for the thirty schools in the abstinence-only treatment group; $X1_i = 0$ for the sixty schools in the two other groups. Let $X2_i = 1$ for thirty schools that were randomly assigned to the conventional programs; $X2_i = 0$ for the sixty schools in the other two groups. The reference group, with no abstinence education program, has no dummy variable; the estimate of that group's score on Y_i is captured by the intercept. We use regression to analyze the results for both studies. In both models, Y_i is the average score for each school. The regression model for the first study is:

$$Y_i = a + b_1 X1_i + e_i. \qquad \text{\textit{Regression (1)}}$$

The regression model for the second study is:

$$Y_i = a + b_1 X1_i + b_2 X2_i + e_i. \qquad \text{\textit{Regression (2)}}$$

Table 4.3 shows the regression results from the two (imaginary) studies. What do those numbers tell us?

Consider first the results from the first study. Before examining the results, it is important to recall what the specific issue is. In the first study, the question is which type of sex education program works best at improving risk-avoidance behavior. The dispute between the two sides (conventional vs. abstinence-only) is so divisive that the only sensible null hypothesis is that there is no difference between the two groups, ignoring the do-nothing alternative. Thus, Regression 1 tests this null hypothesis:

$$H_0: B1 = 0.$$

Given the controversy, the only sensible alternative hypothesis is that there is a difference, but the direction cannot be specified *ex ante* based on either theory or politics, at least in this case. It follows that the alternative hypothesis is:

$$H_a: B1 \neq 0.$$

The results from the first study appear in the column of Table 4.3, under the heading Regression 1. The first number to consider is the t-statistic for the treatment variable at issue, $X1$: $t = -3.117$. The probability of observing a t-statistic this large, if the null hypothesis was true, given the $n = 60$ and the degrees of freedom ($60 - 2$) in this study, is extremely small. Usually the regression program prints out the p-value. Tables report either the t-statistic or the p-value. The t-statistic associated with the estimated regression coefficient ($b_1 = -1.003$, in the example), together with the degrees of freedom (df), determines the p-value. In this case, based on the t-statistic of -3.117 and the df, the p-value is $p = .01$. The p-value means that the regression coefficient would occur only once in 100 samples of size $n = 60$ from a population in which the null were true. Consequently, we conclude that the null is probably not true. We reject the null hypothesis that there is no difference between the two programs, concluding tentatively, based on the sign of the regression coefficient, that risk-avoidance scores in the average abstinence-only school is lower than the risk-avoidance

Table 4.3

Regression of Risk-Avoidance Scale on Type of Sex Education Programs
(*t*-statistic in parentheses)

Description	Regression (1) Comparison of abstinence with conventional program (= reference)	Regression (2) Comparison of abstinence and conventional with no program (= reference)
Intercept	4.876	4.235
	(2.822)	(2.494)
X1 (abstinence-only education)	−1.003	−2.367
	(−3.117)	(−2.865)
X2 (conventional education)		0.076
		(1.158)
N of observations	60	90
R^2	0.15	0.17

scores in the average conventional program school. The regression coefficient of −1.003 tells us that the abstinence-only schools' ($X = 1$) score, on average is about 1 point lower on the 10-point risk-avoidance scale than the conventional schools' score. The difference is statistically significant at conventional levels ($p < .01$).

The intercept in the same column is the mean value of the outcome measure Y_i when $X1 = 0$. That is, in this study, the intercept is the mean risk-avoidance scale score for the conventional program schools on the 10-point scale. Given the description of the problem, the mean is not high, even in the conventional program schools. It is only about 4.9 on a 10-point scale of risk-avoidance. The associated t-statistic exceeds the critical value of |2.000| in this two-tailed test. Thus, the score is significantly higher than the lowest scale score of 0.[24] Overall, we would conclude from the first study that conventional program schools in the study do not score particularly high on the risk-avoidance scale, but the abstinence-only schools score lower. The difference is statistically significant, and it may be substantively significant, too.

The column in Table 4.3 under the heading Regression 2 shows the results from the second study. The second study compares both treatment alternatives with the do-nothing option. Consequently, the number of observations in the second study is 90 because it uses all three of the treatment groups in the statistical analysis. Given the controversy, the null hypotheses that are tested in this study continue to reflect the presumption that all the sides can be wrong or right. Hence, the nulls are "no impact," and the alternative hypotheses are two-sided:

$$H_0{:}B_1 = 0 \text{ and } H_0{:} B_2 = 0;$$
$$H_a{:}B_1 \neq 0 \text{ and } H_a{:}B_2 \neq 0.$$

The results for the abstinence-only alternative roughly mirror those from the first study. The t-statistic of −2.865 for $X1$, the abstinence-only education program dummy, continues to exceed the critical value of |2.000| in a two-tailed test. The value of the regression coefficient is still negative, but changing the reference group by adding the do-nothing control group to the data makes it even more negative. The p-value implied by the t-statistic for the regression coefficient of $X1$ is $p < .01$. It tells us that the probability of observing a regression coefficient of the (positive or negative) magnitude of $b_1 = -2.4$ (the observed value) is less than 1 in 100 samples of $n = 90$ if the null hypothesis of no difference (H_0: $B_1 = 0$) were true. Thus, we reject that null in favor of the alternative hypothesis that the abstinence-only option is significantly different from the do-nothing option, the reference group.

Recall that the values of the coefficients in Regression 2 are based on a slightly different set of observations than those in Regression 1. Regression 2 includes dummies for both treatments, comparing them with the do-nothing control group. The significant regression coefficient for $X1$ (the abstinence-only group dummy) tells us that the risk-avoidance scale score for schools with the abstinence-only program is about 2.4 points lower on the 10-point scale than that for schools in the do-nothing control group.

Regression 2 added the second treatment ($X2$) to the results. The t-statistic associated with the conventional program dummy ($X2$) is less than |2.00|. The small t-statistic implies a p-value considerably larger than .05. By conventional standards, the probability of observing a regression coefficient of $b_2 = .076$ is fairly likely ($p > .05$) in samples of $n = 90$ if the null hypothesis of no-difference between conventional and do-nothing programs was true. We therefore cannot reject that null hypothesis.

The intercept in Regression 2 continues to be significant, just as it was in Regression 1, since the t-statistic remains larger than the critical value of |2.00|. Its value is slightly lower than in Regression 1. It tells us that schools in the do-nothing control group score about 4.2 out of 10 on the risk-avoidance scale. While the t-statistic (and implied p-value) tells us that the score is significantly different from 0, the score is still pretty low compared with the top score of 10.

Overall, these (hypothetical) results suggest that the abstinence-only program arguably may make things worse. The results would do little to resolve the controversy between the conventional option and the do-nothing option.

Discussion of (Imaginary) Results

I leave the political conclusion to the reader's imagination. Note that, all things considered, these would be defensible results, at least in terms of internal validity. The use of random assignment, together with a reasonably large number of observations, justifies this assessment. However, we could be more confident of the internal validity of the causal assessment if the n were larger or if there were pretest data. We would also like to know whether the three groups are comparable on other characteristics of the schools that also may affect the score on Y, such as the size and location of the school and the demographic and academic characteristics of the students in each school. Any of these remedies would make us more confident that the three groups are similar on all unmeasured confounding variables and that they differ only on the program variable. Random assignment makes this comparability likely, but empirical checks would give us more assurance.

Note that the R^2, the percentage of variance in Y_i explained by variance in the treatment condition $X1$ (and $X2$), is low in both (hypothetical) studies. It is clear that the type of sex education programs does little to explain why these schools vary in the students' mean risk-avoidance behavior. Other, omitted, variables surely also affect risk avoidance behavior. However, because of random assignment, we can be reasonably confident that, relative to doing nothing, our (imaginary) conclusions that abstinence-only programs appear to be counterproductive, reducing risk-avoidance behaviors, and that conventional programs do little one way or the other, are defensible. More important, the magnitude of R^2 gives us no information about the internal validity of a study. Subsequent chapters make this point more explicit. In this study, random assignment tells a lot about internal validity,[25] but the low R^2 is not informative about the absence of internal validity. Similarly, a high R^2 would not be informative about the presence of internal validity, even in the presence of random assignment.

There are remaining possible threats to the internal validity of the imaginary study by PEG. For example, multiple treatment interference could be a problem. The PEG evaluators should ascertain that other remedies or programs were not accompanying each program under study. For example, if the schools with conventional sex education programs were also introducing other programs to reduce risky behaviors that other schools in the evaluation were not getting, then that difference could challenge the validity of PEG's conclusions. The evaluators also assumed that the index-measure of risk avoidance is constructed and implemented similarly in each group of schools; this would be an uncontrolled source of nonrandom measurement error. They also assume no contamination between treatments, so that each school in each treatment group actually experiences different and distinct programs. Threats like these can affect any RFE. The RFE only reduces selection threats due to uncontrolled (i.e., nonrandom) selection of treatments.

The statistical validity of the evaluator's conclusions is minimally satisfactory. The results imply fairly low probabilities of a Type I error, but the n is only minimal. The evaluators failed to reject the null hypothesis about the conventional program, concluding that it is really no better (or worse) than doing nothing. This introduces the chance of a Type II error, which could be reduced by having more observations. More observations could have made this result look significant. Nonetheless, it was simply not feasible to elicit more schools to participate in the study.

This raises the issue of the external validity of the conclusions. PEG would like to generalize to all the middle and secondary schools in Alpha, but the study schools were not a random sample of that population. The study was based on the schools that agreed to participate because they thought that the monetary compensation was worth the cost and bother of participation. The study had a limited budget. PEG might have elicited more schools to participate if it had more money, but the evaluators felt lucky to get ninety participants, none of whom dropped out. PEG evaluators thought that the schools in the study were broadly representative of the target schools in Alpha; it would be appropriate in a real study to use available data to back up this conclusion.

The weakest part of this study concerns measurement reliability and validity. PEG evaluators have stipulated only that the risk-avoidance scale is a multi-item index based both on survey responses from students and on administrative data from each school. The evaluators have not said anything about what the individual items are or whether the index is reliable or valid. The low R^2 implies that the risk-avoidance scale, even though it has multiple indicators, could still be noisy, containing considerable random measurement error. It would be important in a real study to report the results from such an assessment of both reliability and validity. In the example, the use of multiple indicators reinforces the earlier point that multiple indicators are critical for reliable and valid measurement. In this particular case, the evaluators should make use of the methods discussed in Chapter 7 to assess the reliability and validity of the multiple-indicator index that they construct.

The Pretest RFE: The Diagram and the Statistical Model

Confidence in the defensibility of the results from a posttest RFE against selection threats to internal validity rests on two properties of the design. One is observable: Is the n large? The other is not: Are the mean pretest scores in the treatment alternative groups statistically equal? In the pretest RFE, the pretest means are observable: Before the treatments are administered, both (or all) of the groups are (or will have been) pretested. Pretesting means that the evaluator collects information on the baseline value of the output or outcome variables (Y_{t-1}) for all the units of analysis in the study at a time before the implementation of the (randomly) assigned treatments. (Y_t denotes the posttest value of these variables.)

This design has numerous advantages over the previous design in both internal and statistical validity. But it does have one possible disadvantage that I mention first. Under certain circumstances, because all the units that are randomly assigned are pretested, the results may apply only to observations that undergo a pretest, and this may not be the sort of population on which one wants to generalize. When measures are not routinely collected and when their collection is obtrusive, people (or even groups of people) may alter their behavior as a result of being observed. In that case, pretesting may detract from the external validity of this type of RFE. (We considered examples of this kind of reactive behavior in the section in Chapter 2 on external validity.) However, if the units that are randomly assigned cannot react to the pretest (e.g., they are not aware of the pretest because the information is routinely collected or readily available from administrative records), then pretesting is unlikely to have much effect. In that case, pretesting is unlikely to be a threat to external validity. However, if pretesting is part of the program alternatives being evaluated, then it may be desirable to generalize to pretested populations. In that case, pretesting may actually enhance external validity. Despite its possible challenges to external validity, the pretest RFE has considerable advantages.

Most important, with random assignment, if n is large, the treatment groups will all have the same mean score on the pretest (and confounding) variables, so the pretest scores are uncorrelated with the treatment variable X (see Figure 4.2a). In effect, the large n, together with random assignment, turns the pretest scores into noise or a random factor. What if the n is not large? What if the random assignment process does not work as flawlessly as the researcher had hoped, and the pretest scores are correlated with the treatment? With pretest data, one can preserve much of the internal and statistical validity of the failed RFE by controlling for the pretest score Y_{t-1} in a multiple regression (see Figure 4.2b). Thus, collecting pretest data provides a sort of experimental insurance against the possibility that the random assignment does not work as it was intended or the experiment has fewer subjects than planned.

Regardless of whether the random assignment process is flawless or faulty, the statistical analysis model for this design is the following[26]:

$$Y_{it} = a + bX_i + cY_{i,t-1} + e_i.$$

In panel (a) of Figure 4.2, assuming that n is large and that random assignment has been implemented with few or no flaws, multiple regression of Y_t on X and Y_{t-1} is not necessary for internal validity. However, controlling statistically for Y_{t-1} by regressing Y_t on both X and Y_{t-1} improves statistical validity by reducing unexplained variance in Y_t. Under these assumptions, in a large-n, well-implemented, randomized design, Y_{t-1} effectively becomes a measured component of the stochastic μ term. Controlling for it is not necessary for internal validity, but it does enhance statistical validity by reducing the unexplained variance in Y_t, which also reduces the variance (i.e., increases the precision) of the estimated regression coefficient b.

Panel (b) of Figure 4.2 represents the case in which n is small or the implementation of randomization is flawed, so that random assignment, as implemented, is not independent of the treatment. (Note that the model assumes that Y_{t-1} is a cause of Y_t.) Consider an example of caseworkers' behavior in an RFE evaluation of shelters. In this experiment, caseworkers, having indicated their willingness to participate in a randomized design to examine the impact of emergency shelters, compared with none, on the future life circumstances of the homeless, turned out to be reluctant cooperators. Because the number of applicants exceeded the number of available shelter beds, random allocation by lottery is fair. However, on cold and rainy nights, the caseworkers did not comply with random assignment. Instead, they admitted all homeless women with children to

Figure 4.2   **The Effect of Randomization: Pretest RFE**

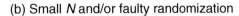

(a) Large *N:* Randomization worked

(b) Small *N* and/or faulty randomization

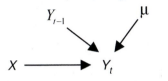
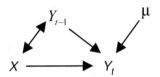

the shelter; the rest were randomly assigned. Thus, instead of randomly assigning all who had applied, as the researcher had instructed, the most needy (sometimes) received the "treatment."[27] In this case of flawed implementation, controlling for the pretest not only improves the statistical validity of *b*, the estimate of treatment impact; it also enhances internal validity of that estimator by controlling for a type of *Z* variable. This is represented by the pretest scores Y_{t-1}, a measure of current life circumstances, which was ordinarily recorded for all applicants.[28]

Using a pretest in randomized designs is also important for another reason. It allows evaluators to consider the possibility of statistical interaction between the treatment (*X*) and the pretest Y_{t-1}. Statistical interaction means that the evaluator expects that the impact of the treatment is contingent on the level of the pretest. For example, prison terms (compared with supervised community treatment) may be effective in deterring crime for offenders with previous nonviolent criminal records, but have a deleterious effect on offenders without previous criminal records, enhancing the probability that they will commit more crime after they are released. Without information about the pretest scores (previous offenses), but with random assignment and a large *n*, an evaluator might conclude that the treatment (*X*) (prison vs. supervised community treatment) had little or no impact on the posttest score (Y_t). However, even though the assignment was random and the *n* was large, this conclusion could still be erroneous (that is, internally invalid). Rather, as in the example, suppose that the impact of the treatment was positive for low values of the pretest score; that is, spending time in prison raises the number of crimes committed by those with no previous criminal record. Suppose further that the impact is negative for high values of the pretest score; that is, going to prison lowers the rate of crime by those with a previous record. In that case, any estimate of impact that ignored the interaction would be biased; a single estimate that pools the positive and negative effects would look like no impact. But, in fact, the single estimate is incorrect because it ignores the interactive effect.

Without data on pretest scores, it would be impossible to test for these possibilities. Interactive effects are not implausible. For example, there is considerable evidence that the impact of small classes on raising primary school student achievement scores is greater for those who begin with low scores than for those who begin with high scores.[29] Similarly, grouping students by ability (*X*) interactively affects their performance (Y_t). It appears to help those who start with low performance (low Y_{t-1}) while it may hurt those who start with higher performance levels (high Y_{t-1}).

The statistical model for the case of statistical interaction can be readily explained. Begin with the basic model for the pretest, randomized experiment:

$$Y_{it} = a + bX_i + cY_{i,t-1} + e_i. \tag{1}$$

The conjecture is that the value of *b* depends on the pretest scores:

$$b = b_1 + b_2 Y_{i,t-1}. \tag{2}$$

Then, by substitution, the estimating equation is:

$$Y_{it} = a + (b_1 + b_2 Y_{i,t-1})X_i + cY_{i,t-1} + e_i \tag{3}$$

and

$$= a + b_1 X_i + b_2 Y_{i,t-1} X_i + cY_{i,t-1} + e_i. \tag{4}$$

The expression for b in Equation (2) shows that its value (the estimate of the impact of the treatment X on Y) depends on the level of the pretest. Given the estimate of b_1 and b_2 in Equation (4), the evaluator can then estimate values of b in Equation (2) for particular values of the pretest score. Once again, in the absence of information about pretest scores, an inquiry of this type would be impossible.[30]

ISSUES IN IMPLEMENTING RFEs

Ethics: Delaying Rather Than Denying Treatment

There are ethical issues involved in implementing randomized experiments. Withholding treatment is often not justifiable, especially when the treatment is known to be beneficial, is a right, or is a currently available social service for which designated groups of people are eligible. In that case, rather than withholding a treatment, evaluators should simply use random assignment to compare one type or level of treatment to another. For example, in education experiments, no one withholds schooling from any group, nor are social services withheld from those who are eligible. Rather, evaluators compare one randomly assigned method of delivering education or social services to another. For example, they compare large to small classes.[31] Similarly, evaluators might compare different ways of delivering job training or different ways of implementing welfare (with or without work requirements, for example).

When withholding treatment is not ethically or politically justifiable, evaluators might be able to delay treatment. For example, when slots are limited, evaluators might randomly assign poor persons who sign up for a one-month training program to different starting dates. One group begins in September; others start the same program six months later. If the n is large enough, the evaluators can compare the employment status after six months of those who were assigned to the early program with the employment status of those who had not yet begun the program. In sum, even when treatment cannot be denied, the program can still be studied experimentally. Using random assignment, different versions of the treatment can be compared, and treatment can be delayed randomly rather than denied.[32]

Another way of dealing with ethical issues of random assignment is not to delay the treatment but, rather, to delay random assignment. This is particularly helpful when ongoing programs are being studied.[33] For example, consider an ongoing job-training program. Staffers have considerable experience (and anecdotal, observational evidence) about what type of training program works best for certain types of people. Rather than force unwilling staffers to assign their clients (i.e., the researcher's subjects) randomly to treatment A, B, or C, it may be better to let the staffer decide who gets which type of training. It is likely that the number of people assigned to A training will exceed the number of slots available. The same is likely to be true for those assigned by staff to B and C training. It is only then that random assignment occurs. In other words, after the staff has said that treatment A is best for a particular client, but when the slots for treatment A are limited, a random process is used to decide whether the client gets the treatment now or goes on the waiting list (or is denied treatment). Such a process is more likely to ensure compliance by staff members who must be willing to help implement the RFE, and it is more likely to be viewed as defensible. Figure 4.3 outlines the steps.

Figure 4.3   **Delaying Random Assignment**

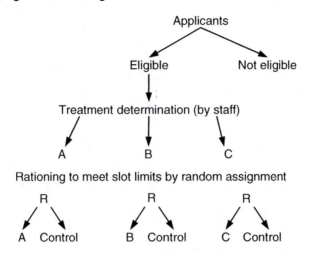

From a research perspective, this process has advantages and disadvantages. It preserves randomization, which, if implemented earlier at the point of treatment determination, might simply not be politically feasible or ethically defensible. The disadvantage is that the RFE with delayed randomization cannot be used to compare the treatments directly.[34] Rather, the researcher uses the RFE design to compare treatment A to no treatment, treatment B to no treatment, and treatment C to no treatment. The information that such an experimental adaptation might produce is often useful, and the internal validity of the design adds to its value in assessing the efficacy of specific treatment modalities, against a no-treatment alternative. However, the experimental design cannot be used to compare the treatment modalities with one another.

Ethics: Is Random Assignment Fair?

It is important not to be squeamish about random experiments in the real world. In many cases, random assignment has ethical virtues. Random assignment is arguably the fairest way to allocate scarce resources. Even if the policy imposes some costs, citizens are more likely to support a policy if they know that the process of implementing the policy is fair.[35] When the difference between treatments A and B is unknown or when a scarce, valued resource is to be allocated and eligible applicants outnumber resources, then blind or random allocation may be not only a good research strategy but also a morally defensible way of allocating scarce resources that are not allocated by price. Lotteries are occasionally used to allocate scarce services; they also provide a useful research vehicle for program evaluation.[36] For example, a joint study by the Department of Housing and Urban Development (HUD) and the Centers for Disease Control and Prevention evaluated the impact of providing housing for homeless or unstably housed persons on the transmission of HIV and the health of persons living with HIV. The treatment group received housing vouchers, which is a preferable benefit compared with the normal HUD housing resources that were received by the comparison group. Because the number of vouchers was limited, the researchers allocated the housing vouchers by lottery.[37]

At the same time, it is important to recognize that random assignment is to be handled with care for ethical, legal, and practical reasons. Institutional review boards (IRBs) should scrutinize RFEs before they are carried out.[38] The IRB at most research organizations, or the evaluation client, will require that subjects are informed about the experiment and that subjects give their consent. That is, the subjects must be told that they may get treatment A, B, or C or no treatment at all; subjects must agree to this process of assignment. Agreement is likely to be forthcoming as long as none of the treatments can make the subjects worse off than the status quo. Most of the examples that we have discussed meet that criterion. The point here is that it is the informed subject, not the researcher, who must make that judgment. Informed consent, which enables the subject to make that judgment, is a legal and moral requirement for carrying out RFEs.

When Random Assignment Is Not Feasible

Over and above ethical issues, not all evaluation questions can be answered with RFEs. For example, many policy-relevant variables (although they are not program variables) cannot be randomly assigned. Race and ethnicity, for example, are policy-relevant variables that cannot be randomly assigned. Behavioral choices, such as cigarette smoking, overeating, and attending religious services, are other examples.

Consider the problem in the case of smoking. Strictly speaking, the American Tobacco Institute is quite correct when it says that there is no experimental "proof" of a causal link between smoking and disease in humans. Smoking is a behavioral choice that cannot be randomly assigned to humans. (An RFE in which the evaluator said, "Heads, you smoke for the next ten years; tails, you don't" would be infeasible, unethical, and unenforceable, at best.) Consequently, no RFE testing the impact of smoking on humans has ever been carried out. Yet, both biological theory and considerable quasi- and nonexperimental evidence support the causal claim that smoking causes cancer and other diseases. In this case, it is prudent to act as if the causal statement is true, even without evidence from an RFE.

The most extensive studies on health risks of smoking are two studies by the American Cancer Society, each of which involved a sample of more than 1 million people.[39] The studies gathered data on individuals' demographic information, medical history, and behavior and estimated the risk of death for smokers compared with nonsmokers. The detailed information together with the large sample size helped to isolate the effect of smoking from other "nontreatment," confounding factors on risks of death.[40]

These studies, and other studies of smoking, are not RFEs. All of them have flaws. But they all produce evidence consistent with the causal claim regarding the link between smoking and disease.[41] Nonetheless, the experimental dilemma still plagues these non-RFE findings: Cigarette smoking cannot be randomly assigned to human beings. The same is true of overeating and many other behavioral choices that are relevant to public policy, especially policies regarding risky or many personal choices. In studying the social consequences of policy-relevant behavioral choices, the RFE is probably not a scientifically or ethically defensible design. However, while RFEs cannot be used to study the impact of many behavioral choices on social outcome, RFEs can be used to study the impact of policy on behavioral choices. For example, random assignment of interventions to affect the decision to drive unsafely, to drink and drive, to smoke, or to diet and exercise are ethically defensible and common choices by evaluators.[42]

Random Assignment and "Intent to Treat"

Contamination raises two issues in implementing RFEs. First, it is a threat to internal validity, as will soon be discussed, but it also entails an ethical issue. Contamination problems in an RFE mean that, despite random assignment to different treatments or to a treatment versus a control, subjects cannot be prohibited from selecting their own treatment. The consequence is that the so-called RFE treatment is not entirely selected by a random process. As a consequence, the RFE becomes subject to selection threats, even if the n is large.

For example, suppose that researchers randomly assign subjects who have consented to participate in the study to particular types of job-training services (e.g., on-the-job training versus classroom training versus counseling on how to apply for a job). The researchers cannot practically or ethically prevent those assigned to counseling from voluntarily taking a training class, nor can they force those assigned to classroom training to attend class. That means that those assigned to treatment group A may also be choosing treatment B or C or that those assigned to treatment A may not actually receive it. Thus, in practice, treatments may be contaminated by each other, and they may be partially self-selected.

Another example concerns education voucher studies that are based on the RFE. In these studies, researchers solicit volunteers; usually, there are more volunteers than vouchers. In the RFE evaluations, the vouchers are allotted randomly among the eligible volunteers. The vouchers entitle the recipient to a particular amount of funding so that the eligible student can attend a private school. However, the researchers cannot force those in the voucher group to actually use the voucher to go to a private school. Nor can the researchers prevent those who did not win the lottery from attending private school on their own, without voucher support.

In these cases, the researchers must be careful about interpreting their findings. Suppose, for example, that the evidence shows that the on-the-job training treatment results in higher-wage jobs than the classroom-training treatment. The researchers cannot claim that on-the-job training is better than classroom training in terms of its impact on wages. Rather, they can claim only that, among those who volunteered to participate in the study, having the opportunity for on-the-job training raises wages more than does having the opportunity for classroom training. The same is true for vouchers. If students who won the lottery perform better in school than the losers, then all the researchers can claim is that, among the eligible volunteers, having an opportunity for vouchers appears to improve education outcomes. The direct impact of vouchers themselves is not obvious from the RFE because the direct impact is partly self-selected. In these examples, what is randomly assigned is the opportunity for service ("intent to treat"), not the service itself. The interpretation of the findings should mirror that distinction.[43]

RFEs and the "Black Box": Why Did This Happen?

One of the criticisms of RFEs is that they are "black box" designs. You put in X (treatment A versus B) and see what happens to Y. According to this charge, RFEs do little to help researchers or program managers understand why the treatment did or did not work or for whom the treatment works best or worst. This is a valid charge, but it is remediable (with qualifications) if researchers decide at the outset to collect information on more than the input (X) and output or outcome (Y) variables in the RFE. In an RFE, particularly one with a large n, collecting information about nontreatment variables (including pretest scores) that affect outcomes is not necessary for internal validity. Theoretically, if the n is large and the randomization process works as intended, it is not necessary in such an RFE to control for likely sources of confounding (Z) variables (including pretest scores), because the design turns these systematic variables into noise. However, in an RFE, it is important to collect such information to increase the chance of understanding why the researchers got the results they got.

For example, suppose that an evaluator randomly assigns participants to one of three different job-training options (classroom training, counseling, on-the-job training) and finds that on-the-job training has significantly better outcomes than the other options. She might want to know whether this effect is typical for all subgroups in the study and whether it works because of poor reading-comprehension skills or low trust of authority figures (teachers, counselors) among the low-income participants in the study. If the evaluator does not collect information on reading comprehension and trust or on race, gender, ethnicity, and so on, she will not be able to examine why she got the results she got. Thus, even though these characteristics will not differ significantly among the treatment groups as long as the random assignment process was effective, it may still be prudent and possibly necessary to collect information about these characteristics of the subjects in an RFE, particularly if the researcher wants to open the "black box" to find out why she got the results that she observed.

However, it is important to point out that, in an RFE, when the evaluator regresses Y on X (the randomly assigned treatment) and Z_k (the pretreatment covariates), as in

$$Y = \alpha + \beta X + \sum \gamma_k Z_k + \mu,$$

only the estimate of β, the impact of X on Y, can be considered causal. The parameter estimates of γ_k describe the relation between each Z_k and Y and may help to elucidate why X affects Y, but they do not meet the same standard of internal validity as the estimate of β, representing the impact of the randomly assigned X on Y. Note that, because this is an RFE, the Z_k variables are not confounding variables: If n is large and the random assignment was effective, each of the treatment groups, represented by X, will not differ on the control variables Z_k. Hence, in the RFE, the Z_k are just covariates that affect Y, not confounds related to both X and Y. In addition to the descriptive properties of adding statistical controls for the covariate variables, using controls may improve statistical validity by reducing noise in the Y variable and by reducing error in the parameter estimate of β.[44]

THREATS TO THE VALIDITY OF RFEs: INTERNAL VALIDITY

RFEs are (arguably) the gold standard of evaluation research, but they are not immune to threats to validity. In fact, they remain subject to threats to their internal, statistical, external, and measurement validity. Their claim to fame is, in fact, more limited: Compared with other designs, if they are carried out with few flaws, they are subject to fewer threats to internal validity than other designs. This section outlines these remaining threats.

Contamination

We have already seen that contamination is a potential threat to the internal validity of many (if not all) RFEs. Whenever subjects can refuse the treatment to which they were randomly assigned (for example, simply by not showing up or not showing up for the full course of the treatment), the RFE becomes subject to self-selection. When subjects can refuse, they effectively are selecting their own treatments, and this choice is unlikely to be randomly distributed.

Contamination is much less likely to be a problem in medical research than in practical program evaluation because subjects are often in hospitals and may have little control over their own treatment. But compliance with treatments remains an issue, even in medical research: Just because a patient is assigned to the green pill does not mean that he will take it or that he will take the full dose.

The client's discretion in choosing treatment is a threat to internal validity in social program evaluation, but it may enhance external validity. Researchers cannot require clients (the research subjects) to participate in social service programs to which they have been admitted, whether the admission is by random assignment, self-selection by the client, or assignment by a program official. As we have already seen, when admission is random, what is randomly assigned is the opportunity for treatment, not the treatment itself.[45] However, such an intent-to-treat interpretation adds to the external validity of RFEs. If the experimental treatment is to be implemented in a postexperimental, "real" world, it is unlikely that subjects will be forced to take the treatment or to take the full dose. Thus, contamination can be ruled out by proper interpretation of what is really randomly assigned; in fact, its presence may add to the realism of RFEs. Other threats to the internal validity of RFEs remain, however. They must be anticipated and dealt with at the design stage in order to preserve the internal validity of the RFE.

Multiple Treatment Interference

One of the remaining threats to the internal validity of the RFE is multiple treatment interference. Multiple treatment interference occurs when one (or some, but not all) of the groups in an RFE differs in factors that are totally confounded with, and thus inseparable from, the treatment itself. Multiple treatment interference is a likely threat to internal validity in an RFE whenever evaluators forget that it is the units of analysis, not the treatments, that are randomly assigned. That is, in the RFE, evaluators randomly assign units of analysis to different treatments; evaluators do not usually randomly assign different treatments to units of analysis.

As an example, suppose that an evaluator uses the RFE to study the impact of class size on student achievement. Suppose that he has a sufficiently large number of students whose parents consent to the experiment. Students are randomly assigned to small classes (say, twelve in a class), medium-size classes (say, seventeen), and large classes (say, twenty-five). No one is made worse off than the status quo (classes of about twenty-five or larger) by this study. The n is large enough to ensure that student characteristics (IQ, sex, race, ethnic background, parental education and income, etc.) are, on average, equal among the experimental groups. Pretest data back this up. So there are no apparent threats to the internal validity of this design.

But multiple treatment interference remains a threat. Suppose that an experienced teacher instructs students in the small classes, while a considerably less experienced teacher teaches the large class. Then class size (the supposed treatment, or X variable) is not separate from another, unmeasured treatment (teacher experience). In fact, the intended treatment (class size) is collinear with (that is, inseparable from) teacher experience, so statistical control to separate their effects is not even possible.

Again, the basic point is to recognize that the units of analysis (the students) are randomly assigned to different treatments. Those who deliver the treatments are (often) not randomly assigned. In the class-size example, it may be impracticable to randomly assign teachers to classes. Given a fixed budget, there would be too few teachers to make use of the large n that random assignment would require. Within a school, the population of teachers and classes is too small to make random assignment of teachers or classes for the study a reasonable option. Randomly assigning one teacher to each of three class sizes is not really random. Even if the RFE were a larger-scale version (with, say, ten schools and thirty classes of varying size), the numbers are still too small to satisfy the law of large numbers that random procedures require.

One way to reduce the threat of multiple treatment interference is for the evaluator to ensure, at the design stage, that the teachers in the class-size study are roughly comparable in experience. Another option is to randomly assign students to one of six class-size (small/medium/large), teacher experience (less/more than four years) treatment pairs. A third way to reduce the threat of multiple treatment interference by using random assignment of both the treatment and its delivery is to randomly assign teachers to classes within larger units. In the example, students are randomly assigned to classes within each school. The teachers could be randomly assigned to classes within each school district. Blocking within schools before random assignment of teachers is another option that would mitigate the problem somewhat.

In sum, random assignment of students (together with the large n) makes it likely that students in each of the different treatment groups are comparable. But it does not ensure that the treatments differ only on the intended treatment variable. If the randomly assigned units of analysis differ in other treatments that are not randomly assigned, then the other treatments may be confounded with the intended treatment, marring the internal validity of the RFE.

Medical researchers use placebos to reduce the problem of multiple treatment interference. Without placebos, the experimental group would get the pill whose efficacy is being studied; the control group would get nothing. The patients are randomly assigned to each group, so the characteristics of the patients are, on average, the same in the two groups as long as the n is large. But these groups differ in two respects: As intended, they differ in a treatment (test pill vs. nothing), but they also differ in who gets medical attention (those who get the pill also get medical attention because a doctor gives them permission and instructions to take the pill; the control group gets none of this attention).

This is another example of multiple treatment interference. Using a placebo removes this threat. The placebo is a device that makes both groups comparable in the receipt of medical attention; the groups differ only in the intended treatment (the "real" pill). With the placebo, one group gets "real pill + attention"; the other group gets "sugar pill + attention."

Unfortunately, in most policy research, placebos are not readily available. The threat of multiple treatments must be reduced by other deliberate actions by the researcher to make sure that the intended treatment is the only treatment that distinguishes the experimental and control groups from each other.

Instrumentation

If the procedure or instrument for measuring outcomes for the experimental group is different from that of the control group, then the measurement instrument, rather than the treatment, may account for the observed differences between (or among) the experimental groups, even if the RFE is otherwise properly designed. Not unlike the problem of multiple treatment interference, the measurement procedure must, on average, be identical for every unit of analysis in the study. Random errors are tolerable, but not systematic ones. Medical researchers guard against instrumentation threats by not telling the attending physicians or nurses which treatment the patient is receiving. In that way, when it is time to measure the outcome, the attending doctor or nurse (who may have preferences favoring or opposing the new drug or medical procedure) cannot systematically bias reports or measures of patient outcomes, because they do not know whether they are dispensing treatment A or B.

In fact, I have just described and justified the double-blind method that medical researchers routinely use in controlled trials. That is, the use of a placebo reduces the threat of multiple treatment interference: A physician attends to everyone in the study. The placebo is the first blind: Even the control group gets a (fake) treatment from a physician. Keeping the medical staff in the dark as to which patient is receiving the treatment or control reduces the threat of instrumentation bias by the attending staff: It is the second blind. While these "remedies" (pun intended) are clearly suitable for evaluating medical procedures that can be administered in the controlled environment of a hospital or doctor's office, it is not clear that they are useful in other environments. Nonetheless, it is important to document the general logic behind these common remedies.

Experimental Mortality (Attrition)

Suppose that subjects, randomly assigned to treatment and control groups, drop out (i.e., they disappear or exhibit experimental "death") during the study period at rates that differ between treatment and control groups before the outcome is measured. Then the subjects that were randomly assigned (and would have been measured at the pretest, if there was a pretest measurement) are not the same as the subjects that are measured at the posttest. In effect, subjects chose who leaves and who stays for the full course of the treatment and control. The self-selection choice is unlikely to be random, and it is a threat to internal validity if it is confounded (or correlated) with the treatment.

Two cases should be considered. In one case, the attrition is not random, but it is not a threat because it is constant across treatments; in the other, the attrition is not random, but it is a threat because it is not constant across treatments. Consider job training RFEs as an example of the first case. Assuming the n is large, the subjects' motivation to work will not differ among the different experimental groups, each of which gets different types of training. However, if the less-motivated subjects drop out, but if levels of motivation do not differ among the treatment groups, then the dropout rates are not different among the groups, so attrition is not a problem.[46] In this case, the attrition may be a threat to external validity, but it is not a threat to internal validity.

Consider next an example in which dropout occurs at different rates. In experimental studies of social service programs, families randomly assigned to the higher-benefit-level treatment groups are less likely to drop out than those in lower-benefit-level treatment groups. When it is time to measure the posttest outcomes (Y), the subjects to be measured are not just a random subsample of those who were originally randomly assigned. Rather, the posttest subsample in the high-benefit treatment group is different from the posttest subsample in the lower-benefit treatment group. In this case, the composition of the posttest subsample is partly self-selected by the nonrandom properties of those who choose to stay in the experiment. If those properties are associated with the treatment (higher-benefit-level treatment has lower attrition rates) without adjustment, it is impossible to separate the treatment (X) from the properties of those who chose not to drop out of the study (Z). Thus, in this case, attrition is a clear threat to internal validity.[47]

In short, experimental mortality is not a clear threat to internal validity if dropout patterns (i.e., within-group compositions) are the same among subjects randomly assigned to different treatment groups in an RFE. Attrition is a threat if the dropout patterns differ, because then the between-treatment differences (X) cannot be separated from the (unobserved) between-treatment differences among those who decide to leave or stay (Z). If we ignore the correlated attrition rates, we would fail to separate the observed differences in outcome scores (Y) from the impact of the (randomly assigned) treatment (X) or from the effects of self-selected and unobserved differences in the propensity to drop out (Z).[48]

Internal Validity of the RFE: Conclusion

Despite these threats to the internal validity of even a well-administered RFE, it is important to remember that these are also threats to the internal validity of any study that uses comparison groups, irrespective of the design. The important advantage of RFEs relative to other comparison-group designs is that they rule out most selection threats that are related to the characteristics of the subjects (units of analysis) that are randomly assigned, even the characteristics that are not measurable. This relative advantage is important enough to make the RFE the gold standard of impact evaluations.

THREATS TO THE VALIDITY OF RFEs: EXTERNAL VALIDITY

Most experiments in social sciences occur in relatively controlled, laboratory-like conditions. For example, many experiments randomly assign students (or other players) to computer games that simulate the "rules" in real-life situations, such as the impact of group size on the decision of individuals to cooperate with a group even if cooperation is not in their narrow, immediate self-interest.[49] But the charge is that the results of these experiments are not general. Program evaluators rarely use these kinds of experiments. Hence, this book refers not to random-assignment experiments in general but only to RFEs that occur in real-life situations. Nonetheless, concerns about external validity (i.e., generalizability) remain. There is growing evidence that results from both laboratory experiments under highly controlled conditions and field experiments are highly contingent on the external environment in which they occur. Results may depend on prevailing norms and institutions that are not part of the experimental design. Thus, the external validity of RFEs cannot be assumed.[50] In addition to the dependence of results on the context (or subjects) in which the experiment is carried out, three issues of external validity remain.

Studying Volunteers

It is not ethical or legal to randomly assign real people to one treatment or another unless they give informed consent to participate in a study in which the treatment to which they will be assigned and the expected outcome are both uncertain. If the people who agree to participate in such studies are not representative of the people for whom the program is intended, then the results may not be externally valid. However, if the RFE is designed to evaluate feasible alternative treatments whose outcome is promising but unknown and not likely to make anyone worse off, then eliciting participation from typical subjects is unlikely to be a major problem. Enrolling representative participants is sometimes time consuming, but it is not a major impediment as long as none of the treatments being studied is clearly worse than the status quo.

Testing

Informed consent means that study participants know that they are being tested. The behavior of those who are conscious that they are under study may be different from ordinary behavior. People frequently behave differently when they know that they are being observed; they alter their behavior to meet the observers' expectations. More important for RFEs is that the study treatments are not permanent. When study participants know that an alternative to which they have been randomly assigned is temporary, their response may differ from what it would have been if the treatment were relatively permanent. For example, if an RFE offers random assignment to a child-care benefit (versus cash) to TANF recipients, the impact of the in-kind benefit on job search activity (the outcome being measured) may be different from what it would have been if the benefit were more permanent. The awareness of being tested combined with the impact of the time horizon on behavior is a common external validity problem in RFEs.

The Problem of Scale

It can sometimes be problematic to generalize from small-scale RFEs to large-scale "real" policy changes. Sometimes, results from small-scale experiments can show effectiveness, but extrapolation to a national program could be hazardous. For instance, suppose that an RFE assigned 300 unemployed single mothers, randomly selected from ten metropolitan statistical areas, to six months of job training versus six months of remedial education, for a total n of 3,000. Suppose further that the results clearly showed that the job training was more effective in raising wages than education. Would these results be generalizable to a national program? Compared with a study of 3,000, if all single, unemployed women in the United States received job training, they might flood the national labor market so much that wages would drop, diluting the effects of job training. The same problem of generalizing from small-scale studies to national policy could apply to randomized experiments in housing, education, and other services for the poor.

THREATS TO THE VALIDITY OF RFEs: MEASUREMENT AND STATISTICAL VALIDITY

Measurement threats are not unique to RFEs; they plague any design. Chapter 2 discussed them; I simply want to point out here that RFEs are not exempt from these problems. Outcome (Y) and treatment (X) variables in any study, including RFEs, must be measured as reliably and validly as possible. Random error in outcome measures in any design has no impact on internal validity. It introduces random noise into the design and therefore reduces its statistical validity, meaning that it is harder to reject the null hypothesis of no impact and to find a small effect size if it is really there. But if the n is as large as it should be for the random assignment process to work, random error in output and outcome measures is unlikely to be of great consequence, unless it is excessive. Using multiple indicators for the outcome measure, and combining them to make an index (discussed in Chapter 7), is a practicable way to reduce random error in any variable.

Counterintuitively, random error in X (treatment) variables is a greater problem than random error in Y (outcome) variables because it reduces the internal validity of any design, even that of RFEs. In large-scale RFEs, this could be a problem if treatment differences or levels are not accurately measured. (Such accuracy is more likely in small-scale studies, because it is easier to check the quality of data in smaller studies.) For example, in studies that randomly assign TANF participants to different benefit packages and tax treatments (the rate at which benefits are reduced as earnings increase), the complexity of the treatment options could be a source of random measurement error and thus a source of internal invalidity of the reported findings. The point is that it may be more important to pay attention to the accuracy (i.e., reliability) with which treatments are measured than to the accuracy with which outcomes are measured, even in RFEs.

Nonrandom measurement error (NRME) in any variable is a threat to the internal validity of any design. In the case of RFEs, systematic measurement error is a problem only if it is confounded with the treatment variable. Suppose, for example, that evaluators use an RFE to study the impact of class size on standardized achievement scores. If the standardized test is administered differently in large classes than in small ones, then the administration of the test is confounded with the treatment, and the impact of class size cannot be validly discerned. In effect, then, NRME in a RFE is equivalent to the instrumentation threat that we discussed earlier.

CONCLUSION

Properly designed and implemented, RFEs are better than the quasi- and nonexperimental design alternatives that the following chapters discuss, but they are not immune to threats to their validity. Specifically, in the best of all possible worlds, the only threat that they escape by virtue of their random assignment design is the selection threat to internal validity. Nonetheless, without careful attention to the administration and measurement of the treatments, the measurement of outcomes, the recruitment and retention of subjects, and other details, even the results from an RFE cannot "prove" that X causes Y. Rather, the results from an RFE can be viewed only as more conclusive than those based on quasi- and non-experimental designs. Further, they are more conclusive only because they are less subject to selection threats to internal validity. Immunity from this threat is critical to the validity of any causal claim. It is important for evaluators to explore whether an RFE is possible in any particular case that they confront. However, it is also important to recognize that immunity to selection threats is only a necessary but not a sufficient condition for the overall validity of a causal claim that one treatment or program or management option (X) is "better" than another with respect to its impact on Y. The next two chapters turn to nonrandomized designs, which also play a critical role in evaluating what works, why, and how much.

SOME COOL EXAMPLES OF RFEs

The RFE by Bertrand and Mullainathan (2004) examines the difference that a name makes in the labor market by randomly assigning names to résumés. The design is used in many RFEs to study labor market discrimination, and Bertrand and Mullainathan cite these studies. What is particularly attractive about this design is not only how clever it is but also how clearly it discusses issues of actually implementing an RFE in the real world.

The article by Gerber et al. (2003) illustrates the growing use of RFEs to study political action: It looks at the impact of contacting voters (face to face, by phone, no contact at all) on voter turnout, as well as how repeating the same RFEs can be used to produce new knowledge.

The research by Dee and Keys (2004) is also clever; it reanalyzes data from an RFE study of class sizes in Tennessee. The original study was aimed at studying the impact of class size on student performance. Both teachers and students were randomly assigned in order to minimize multiple treatment interference. The new study, listed next, takes advantage of the random assignment of teachers to examine an entirely different topic than what was originally intended.

The article by Glazerman et al. (2006) is another study of schools, focusing on the random assignment of low-income students to Teach for America (TFA) teachers (who have no formal certification for teaching but had strong academic records in college) compared with "regular" teachers (and regular novice teachers). The study compares the math and reading scores of students assigned to TFA vs. regular teachers. The study deserves special mention not only because of its findings (TFA teachers improve math achievement scores compared with regular teachers) but also because of its careful use of blocking within schools before random assignment.

The research published by Barrera-Osorio et al. (2011) is another study in education but is illustrative of the use of randomized field experiments in developing countries. Students in many developing countries often face substantial fees (e.g., for books and uniforms) to attend school, which is particularly costly for low-income students. Students in two areas of Bogotá, Colombia, applied for a cash transfer program that offered subsidies to attend school or subsidies were paid only after school completion. Because more students applied than could be enrolled, subsidies were awarded by lottery (that is, randomly). In general, both types of subsidies (immediate and delayed payout) increased attendance, and delaying payment was particularly effective in increasing re-enrollment in subsequent years among the poorest children.

These studies all stand out because of the clarity with which they explain the experimental set-up, show the corresponding estimating equation, and report the results.

1. Marianne Bertrand and Sendhil Mullainathan, "Are Emily and Greg More Employable Than Lakisha and Jamal? A Field Experiment on Labor Market Discrimination." *American Economic Review* 94, no. 4 (2004): 991–1013.

2. Alan S. Gerber, Donald P. Green, and Ron Shachar, "Voting May Be Habit Forming: Evidence from a Randomized Field Experiment." *American Journal of Political Science* 47, no. 3 (2003): 540–550.

3. Thomas S. Dee and Benjamin J. Keys, "Does Merit Pay Reward Good Teachers? Evidence from a Randomized Experiment." *Journal of Policy Analysis and Management* 23, no. 3 (2004): 471–488.

4. Steven Glazerman, Daniel Mayer, and Paul Decker, "Alternative Routes to Teaching: The Impacts of Teach for American and Student Achievement and Other Outcomes," *Journal of Policy Analysis and Management* 25, no. 1 (2006): 75–96.

5. Felipe Barrera-Osorio, Marianne Bertrand, Leigh L. Linden, and Francisco Perez-Calle, "Improving the Design of Conditional Transfer Programs: Evidence from a Randomized Education Experiment in Colombia." *American Economic Journal: Applied Economics* 3, no. 2 (2011): 167–195.

BASIC CONCEPTS

Random assignment of units of analysis to treatment alternatives in the real world
Alternatives to no-treatment control groups include:
    A vs. B
    More vs. less
    Now vs. later
Small n is not random
n = number of units of analysis that are randomly assigned
Assigning individuals vs. communities (classes, schools, villages, municipalities)
    Advantages and disadvantages
Random selection $\neq$ random assignment
Types of RFEs
    Posttest only: table, diagram, and equation
    Posttest with pretest: table, diagram, and equation
    Four-group: table
The advantages and disadvantages of the pretest score
    Internal validity (advantage)
    Statistical validity (advantage)
    External validity (disadvantage)
Ethical issues
    Alternatives to no treatment
    Random is sometimes fair
    Random assignment is sometimes not possible
Random assignment and intent to treat
Random assignment and explaining why things happen
Threats to the validity of the RFE
    Threats to internal validity
        Contamination
    Multiple treatment interference

Instrumentation
Experimental mortality or attrition
Threats to external validity
Volunteers
Testing
Threats to measurement reliability and validity
RME in Y: threat to statistical validity
RME in X: threat to internal validity
NRME in X: possible threat to internal validity
NRME in Y: threat to internal validity

DO IT YOURSELF: DESIGN A RANDOMIZED FIELD EXPERIMENT

Design an RFE to compare the relative effectiveness of two or more policy, program, or management alternatives that are a matter of current public dispute. Describe the alternatives you are examining, the outcome measures you will use, and the procedures you will use to select the subjects for study and then to assign the subjects to different treatments. Your description of the experiment should be detailed enough to clarify your strategy for attaining internal, external, statistical, and measurement validity (and measurement reliability). Explain how you would analyze the data that your experimental results will produce: What statistical model will you use, and how would you interpret the main experimental results?

Be prepared to defend the overall validity of your experimental design. (You may defensibly choose to sacrifice external for internal validity, feasibility, and ethical considerations.)

NOTES

1. There is a nontrivial amount of controversy about this claim for RFEs (also called randomized control trials, or RCTs). See, for example, the cautions about the use of RFEs in Michael Quinn Patton, "The Paradigms Debate," in *Utilization-Focused Evaluation,* ed. M.Q. Patton, 3d ed. (Thousand Oaks, CA: Sage, 1997), ch. 12. See also Richard P. Nathan, "The Role of Random Assignment in Social Policy Research," *Journal of Policy Analysis and Management* 27, no. 3 (2008): 606–615, and the related discussion in Maureen Pirog, ed., "The Role of Random Assignment in Social Policy Research," *Journal of Policy Analysis and Management,* 28, no. 1 (2009): 164–181; Burt S. Barnow, "Setting Up Social Experiments: The Good, the Bad, and the Ugly," *Journal of Labor Market Research* 43, no. 2 (2010): 91–105. Randomized experimental designs are commonly used in many evaluations of (local) programs in international development. See Abhijit V. Banerjee and Esther Duflo, "Giving Credit Where It Is Due." *Journal of Economic Perspectives* 24, no. 3 (2010): 61–79; and idem, *Poor Economics: A Radical Rethinking of the Way to Fight Global Poverty* (New York: Public Affairs, 2011). RFEs are clearly regarded as the gold standard in education evaluation by the U.S. Department of Education. See the guide on evidence-based evaluation at Institute of Education Sciences, "New Guide on Evidence Based Education," http://www2.ed.gov/about/offices/list/ies/news.html; and U.S. Department of Education, Institute of Education Sciences, and National Center for Education Evaluation and Regional Assistance, *Identifying and Implementing Educational Practices Supported by Rigorous Evidence: A User Friendly Guide* (Washington, DC: Council for Excellence in Government, December 2003), www.ed.gov/rschstat/research/pubs/rigorousevid/rigorousevid.pdf. The pages that follow discuss some of these issues.

2. Numerous books about research design in program evaluation outline the basic characteristics of experimental design. The mechanics of the basic design are not in dispute. What this chapter adds is the statistical model to estimate the impacts. Each chapter makes continuing use of the multiple regression workhorse to see the unity in all the designs that this text (and others) discuss. For some useful references on experimental designs, see Peter Rossi, Richard Freeman, and Mark Lipsey, *Evaluation: A Systematic Approach*, 7th ed. (Thousand Oaks, CA: Sage, 2004); William R. Shadish, Thomas D. Cook, and Donald T. Campbell, *Ex-*

perimental and Quasi-Experimental Designs for Generalized Causal Inference (Boston: Houghton-Mifflin, 2002); Robert L. Schalock, *Outcome-Based Evaluation,* 2d ed. (New York: Kluwer Academic, 2001); Larry L. Orr, *Social Experiments: Evaluating Public Programs with Experimental Methods* (Thousand Oaks, CA: Sage, 1999); Lawrence W. Sherman, ed., "Misleading Evidence and Evidence-Led Policy: Making Social Science More Experimental," *Annals of the American Academy of Political and Social Science* 589 (2003): 6–19; Donald P. Green and Alan S. Gerber, eds., "Experimental Methods in the Political Sciences," *American Behavioral Scientist* 47, no. 5 (2004): 485–487. Some of these sources provide considerably more detail than this text provides in this survey of a large field, and others provide less detail. None of them provides a general statistical model for estimating results.

3. While the text refers to outcome *Y*, it is important also to recognize that outcome *Y* may be more validly measured with multiple outcome indicators Y_1, Y_2, Y_3, and so on. Sometimes these indicators may be combined into a single index, while at other times they may be separate. Chapter 7 on survey design and analysis discusses index construction more completely. This note is intended to point out that even though the text refers to outcome or output *Y*, the symbol may stand for multiple indicators.

4. For an overview of the history of social experimentation in the United States, see David Greenberg, Donna Linksz, and Marvin Mandell, *Social Experimentation and Public Policymaking* (Washington, DC: Urban Institute, 2003). The book considers both large- and small-scale experiments, including the income maintenance experiments (guaranteed income maintenance), the health insurance experiments, the welfare-to-work experiments, the unemployment insurance experiments, and a nursing home incentive reimbursement experiment, the smallest of those in the study. See also David Greenberg, Mark Shroder, and Matthew Onstott, "The Social Experiment Market," *Journal of Economic Perspectives* 13, no. 3 (1999): 157–172; David Greenberg and Mark Shroder, *The Digest of Social Experiments*, 3d ed. (Washington, DC: Urban Institute, 2004).

5. David N. Kershaw and Felicity Skidmore, *The New Jersey Graduated Work Incentive Experiment* (Princeton, NJ: Mathematica, 1974); Albert Rees, "An Overview of the Labor-Supply Results," *Journal of Human Resources* 9 (1974): 158–180; Joseph Pechman and P. Michael Timpane, eds., *Work Incentives and Income Guarantees: The New Jersey Negative Income Tax Experiment* (Washington, DC: Brookings Institution Press, 1975); Gary Burtless and Jerry A. Hausman, "The Effect of Taxation on Labor Supply: Evaluating the Gary Negative Income Tax Experiment," *Journal of Political Economy* 86, no. 6 (1978): 1103–1130.

6. Joseph P. Newhouse, *Free for All? Lessons from the Rand Health Insurance Experiment* (Cambridge: Harvard University Press, 1993).

7. Many of these are cited in Greenberg, Shroder, and Onstott, "Social Experiment Market." See also John Goering and Judith D. Feins, ed., *Choosing a Better Life? Evaluating the Moving to Opportunity Social Experiment* (Washington, DC: Urban Institute, 2003). For other examples, see Campbell Collaboration, *What Helps? What Harms? Based on What Evidence?* www.campbellcollaboration.org/index.html, which includes program evaluations (and RFEs) in social welfare, education, and criminal justice; the What Works Clearinghouse of the Institute for Education Sciences of the U.S. Department of Education; and, in the area of criminal justice, Lawrence W. Sherman, Denise Gottfredson, Doris MacKenzie, John Eck, Peter Reuter, and Shawn Bushway, *Preventing Crime: What Works, What Doesn't, What's Promising*, www.ncjrs.gov/works.

8. Orr, *Social Experiments*, 28; Jacquelyn Anderson and Karin Martinson, *Service Delivery and Institutional Linkages: Early Implementation Experiences of Employment Retention and Advancement Programs* (New York: MDRC, 2003); Carol Harvey, Michael J. Camasso, and Radha Jagannathan, "Evaluating Welfare Reform Waivers Under Section 1115," *Journal of Economic Perspectives* 14, no. 4 (2000): 165–188; Rebecca M. Blank, "Policy Watch: The 1996 Welfare Reform," *Journal of Economic Perspectives* 11, no. 1 (1997): 169–177.

9. Orr, *Social Experiments*; David Greenberg and Mark Shroder, *Digest of Social Experiments* (Washington, DC: Urban Institute Press, 1997); Robert F. Boruch, *Randomized Experiments for Planning and Evaluation: A Practical Guide* (Thousand Oaks, CA: Sage, 2004); Paul T. Decker, Daniel P. Mayer, and Steven Glazeman, "Alternative Routes to Teaching: The Impacts of Teach for America on Student Achievement and Other Outcomes," *Journal of Policy Analysis and Management* 25, no. 1 (2006): 75–96. Two research firms specialize in (mostly nonnational) RFEs, focusing on social programs: Mathematica Policy Research (www.mathematica-mpr.com) and MDRC (www.mdrc.org).

10. Thomas Cook, "Randomized Experiments in Education: Why Are They So Rare?" *Educational Evaluation and Policy Analysis* 24, no. 3 (2002): 175–199. See also Frederick Mosteller and Robert Boruch, *Evidence Matters: Randomized Trials in Education Research* (Washington, DC: Brookings Institution Press, 2002). For recent examples of the increasing use of RFEs in education, see the Web site of the What Works

Clearinghouse of the U.S. Department of Education, www.w-w-c.org; and U.S. Department of Education, Institute of Education Sciences, and National Center for Education Evaluation and Regional Assistance, *Identifying and Implementing Educational Practices Supported by Rigorous Evidence: A User Friendly Guide* (Washington, DC: Council for Excellence in Government, December 2003), www2.ed.gov/rschstat/research/ pubs/rigorousevid/index.html. See also the U.S. Department of Education policy stating its preferences at http://www2.ed.gov/news/fedregister/index.html (enter <RIN 1890-ZA00> in the search field).

11. Thomas S. Dee and Brian Jacob, "The Impact of No Child Left Behind on Student Achievement," *Journal of Policy Analysis and Management* 30, no. 3 (2011): 418–446.

12. Jeremy D. Finn and Charles M. Achilles, "Answers and Questions About Class Size: A Statewide Experiment," *American Educational Research Journal* 27, no. 3 (1990): 557–577; Eric A. Hanushek, "Some Findings from an Independent Investigation of the Tennessee STAR Experiment and from Other Investigations of Class Size Effects," *Educational Evaluation and Policy Analysis* 21, no. 2 (1999): 143–163. For a review of field experiments on class size from before World War II, see Jonah Rockoff, "Field Experiments in Class Size from the Early Twentieth Century," *Journal of Economic Perspectives* 23, no. 4 (2009): 211–230.

13. Jean Baldwin Grossman and Joseph P. Tierney, "Does Mentoring Work? An Impact Study of the Big Brothers Big Sisters Program," *Evaluation Review* 22, no. 3 (1998): 403–426.

14. T. Paul Schultz, "School Subsidies for the Poor: Evaluating the Mexican Progresa Poverty Program," *Journal of Development Economics* 74 (2004): 199–250.

15. Howard S. Bloom, Carolyn J. Hill, and James A. Riccio, "Linking Program Implementation and Effectiveness: Lessons from a Pooled Sample of Welfare-to-Work Experiments," *Journal of Policy Analysis and Management* 22, no. 4 (2003): 551–575; Howard S. Bloom, "Using 'Short' Interrupted Time-Series Analysis to Measure the Impacts of Whole-School Reforms: With Applications to a Study of Accelerated Schools," *Evaluation Review* 27, no. 1 (2003): 3–49; Howard S. Bloom, Johannes M. Bos, and Suk-Won Lee, "Using Cluster Random Assignment to Measure Program Impacts," *Evaluation Review* 23, no. 4 (1999): 445–469.

16. In this discussion of RFEs, I equate the unit of assignment with the unit of statistical analysis. In the example, if one randomly assigned the pictorial and the written information to the two sites (rather than to each of the 2,500 individual women), the number of assignment units is two, which is far too small for analysis as a RFE. Such a study should be regarded as a nonexperiment; in that case, the *n* would be 2,500 statistical units of analysis (see Chapter 6). If the two sites were selected to be as comparable as possible on confounding variables, yet they had received different treatments, the study would then be regarded as a quasi experiment. The *n* would still be 2,500 statistical units of analysis (see Chapter 5).

17. In general, RFEs should randomly assign individuals to treatment alternatives when individuals are the treatment target (e.g., in education or job training). However, this is not always feasible. Communities can and should be randomly assigned when they are the treatment target (e.g., in evaluations of public safety or public health programs). Randomly assigning units rather than individuals raises some special issues. See Howard S. Bloom, ed., *Learning More from Social Experiments* (New York: Russell Sage, 2005). Also, Boruch and Foley argue that, despite the special problems of randomly assigning aggregate communities (e.g., classrooms, schools, villages) as units in an RFE, doing so has special advantages. It may enhance both external and internal validity because it is more realistic and less subject to contamination threats, respectively. They present many examples. See Robert F. Boruch and Ellen Foley, "The Honestly Experimental Society," in *Validity and Social Experimentation*, ed. Leonard Bickman (Thousand Oaks, CA: Sage, 2000), ch. 8. A similar claim is made in articles in Robert F. Boruch, ed., "Place Randomized Trials: Experimental Tests of Public Policy," *Annals of the American Academy of Political and Social Science* 599 (May 2005). For example, the contributions by Cook, by Smith, and by Weisburd note that there are fewer ethical objections to random assignment of communities rather than individuals. The articles by Cook, by Sikkema, and by Weisburd observe not only that communities are often a policy target but that communities also affect how much individuals respond to different polices. Randomly assigning communities (or places) to different treatments has disadvantages, too. Articles by Bloom and Riccio and by Smith point out that not only is there a loss of statistical power but that the statistical analysis of the RFE becomes considerably less straightforward than the one presented in this chapter. See Howard S. Bloom and James A. Riccio, "Using Place-Based Random Assignment and Comparative Interrupted Time-Series Analysis to Evaluate the Jobs-Plus Employment Program for Public Housing Residents"; Kathleen J. Sikkema, "HIV Prevention Among Women in Low-Income Housing Developments: Issues and Intervention Outcomes in a Place-Based Randomized Controlled Trial"; Thomas D. Cook, "Emergent Principles for the Design, Implementation, and Analysis of Cluster-Based Experiments in Social Science"; David Weisburd, "Hot Spots Policing Experiments and

Criminal Justice Research: Lessons from the Field," and Herbert Smith, "Introducing New Contraceptives in Rural China: A Field Experiment."

18. It is important not to underestimate the feasibility and informational value of large-scale RFEs. St. Pierre and Puma discuss the Comprehensive Child Development Program (CCDP), a five-year RFE with $n = 4,000$ children in twenty-one projects that showed consistent positive effects on most outcome variables. The authors point out that this RFE is far superior to one-group, pretest quasi experiments, which cannot show causation because there is no counterfactual. The large-scale (and large n) RFE can best show what would have happened had parents not participated in the CCDP. See Robert G. St. Pierre and Michael J. Puma, "Toward the Dream of the Experimenting Society," in *Validity and Social Experimentation: Donald Campbell's Legacy,* ed. Leonard Bickman (Thousand Oaks, CA: Sage, 2000), ch. 7. Recent large-scale field experiments have moved from social programs in the United States to large-scale tests of social programs in developing countries and to large field experiments in politics and nonprofits in the United States. See Gary King, Emmanuela Gakidou, Nirmala Ravishankar, Ryan T. Moore, Jason Lakin, Manett Vargas, Martha Maria Téllez-Rojo, Juan Eugenio Hernández Ávila, Mauricio Hernández Ávila, Héctor Hernández Llamas, "A 'Politically Robust' Experimental Design for Public Policy Evaluation, with Application to the Mexican Universal Health Insurance Program," *Journal of Policy Analysis and Management* 26, no. 3 (2007): 480–506; Steven D. Levitt and John A. List, "Field Experiments in Economics: The Past, the Present, and the Future," *European Economic Review* 53, no. 1 (2008): 1–18; Alan S. Gerber, Donald P. Green, and Christopher W. Larimer, "Social Pressure and Voter Turnout," *American Political Science Review* 102, no. 1 (2008): 33–48; and Dean Karlan and John A. List, "Does Price Matter in Charitable Giving? Evidence from a Large-Scale Natural Field Experiment," *American Economic Review* 97, no. 5 (2007): 1774–1793.

19. Howard S. Bloom, "Using Cluster Random Assignment to Measure Program Impacts: Statistical Implications for the Evaluation of Education Programs," *Evaluation Review* 28, no. 4 (1999): 445–469; King et al., "A 'Politically Robust' Experimental Design for Public Policy Evaluation"; Ryan Moore, "Blocking Political Science Experiments: Why, How, and Then What?" *Newsletter of the APSA Experimental Section 1,* no. 1 (2010): 3–5; Miriam Bruhn and David McKenzie, "In Pursuit of Balance: Randomization in Practice in Development Field Experiments," *American Economic Journal: Applied Economics* 1, no. (2009): 200–232.

20. Recall Murphy's Law: If anything can go wrong, it will. There is a corollary to Murphy's Law: Murphy was an optimist.

21. For example, Damodar N. Gujarati and Dawn C. Porter, *Basic Econometrics,* 5th ed. (Boston: McGraw Hill, 2009); Joshua D. Angrist and Jorn-Steffen Pischke, *Mostly Harmless Econometrics* (Princeton: Princeton University Press, 2009); Stephen L. Morgan and Christopher Winship, *Counterfactuals and Causal Inference: Methods and Principles for Social Research* (New York: Cambridge University Press, 2007).

22. For example, William H. Greene, *Econometric Analysis,* 5th ed. (Upper Saddle River, NJ: Prentice Hall, 2003).

23. In statistics texts, most hypotheses are two-tailed hypotheses. That is, the null hypothesis is $H_0: B = 0$, while the alternative is H_1 (or H_a): $B \neq 0$. However, in the case of program evaluation, including RFEs, two-tailed tests are not likely to be used. In almost all RFEs, there is an expectation that one treatment is better than the other. The RFE is a test of whether the expected direction of impact actually occurs (against an alternative hypothesis of no or random effect). Thus, in this text, almost all the hypotheses about program impacts use one-tailed tests. Subsequent chapters mention exceptions to this generalization.

24. Even if the null hypothesis for the intercept were a target score of 10 on the risk-avoidance scale, the conventional schools would still be significantly different from that null.

25. For a discussion of what random assignment alone does NOT reveal, see Bruhn and McKenzie, "In Pursuit of Balance."

26. The text indexes each variable with the time subscript t when it is necessary to distinguish between pre- and posttests. It also indexes each variable with the unit-of-analysis subscript i to indicate that each unit of analysis may have different values on the treatment (X_i) and output or outcome variables (Y_i). Even if the i subscript is not shown, it is still assumed to be present.

27. Robert G. Orwin et al., "Pitfalls in Evaluating the Effectiveness of Case Management Programs for Homeless Persons: Lessons From the NIAAA Demonstration Program," *Evaluation Review* 18, no. 2 (1994): 153–207; Millicent H. Abel et al., *Evaluation of Project Connect: Final Report* (Louisville, KY: University of Louisville, Urban Research Institute, College of Urban and Public Affairs, 1991).

28. See Jennifer Hill, Donald Rubin, and Neal Thomas, "The Design of the New York School Choice Scholarships Program Evaluations," in *Research Design: Donald Campbell's Legacy,* vol. 2, ed. Leonard

Bickman (Thousand Oaks, CA: Sage, 2000), ch. 7. They argue that, in addition to using pretest scores, using propensity score matching can also improve the internal and statistical validity of pretest RFEs, especially when the random assignment process is not flawless. Chapter 6 discusses propensity score matching.

29. Jeremy D. Finn, "Small Classes in American Schools: Research, Practice, and Politics," *Phi Delta Kappan* 83, no. 7 (2002): 551–560; Rockoff, "Field Experiments in Class Size from the Early Twentieth Century."

30. For specific information about how to interpret regression coefficients and test for significance when analyzing cases of statistical interaction, see James Jaccard, Robert Turrisi, and Choi K. Wan, *Interaction Effects in Multiple Regression* (Newbury Park, CA: Sage, 1990) and Thomas Brambor, William Roberts Clark, and Matt Golder, "Understanding Interaction Models: Improving Empirical Analyses," *Political Analysis* 14 (2006): 63–82. When there is statistical interaction, individual coefficients have no single value; their estimated value is contingent on a third variable. For instance, in the example, when there is no ability grouping ($X = 0$) the performance level of students is described by:

$$Y_{it} = a + cY_{i,t-1} + e_i.$$

However, where there is ability grouping ($X = 1$) the performance level of students is described by:

$$Y_{it} = a + b_1 + (b_2 + c)Y_{i,t-1} + e_i.$$

31. Tennessee State Department of Education, Project STAR Office, *Project Star: Final Executive Summary Report—Kindergarten Through Third Grade* (Nashville, 1990). Even in this evaluation, students (and teachers) were randomly assigned to a relatively narrow range of "small" and "large" class sizes, ranging from 15 to 23 students, respectively. See Rockoff, "Field Experiments in Class Size from the Early Twentieth Century."

32. Mexico's Education, Health, and Nutrition Program (Progresa) is a good example of this strategy. Among 505 eligible very low-income municipalities, 320 were randomly assigned to treatment starting in 1998, while the rest (185) began treatment in 2000. For discussion, see T. Paul Schultz, *Final Report: The Impact of Progresa on School Enrollments* (Washington, DC: IFPRI, 2000); Schultz, "School Subsidies for the Poor"; Paul Gertler, *Final Report: The Impact of Progresa on Health* (Washington, DC: IFPRI, 2000).

33. Orr, *Social Experiments*, 19–21.

34. To do so requires reconceptualizing the design as a quasi- or non-experimental design, the topics of subsequent chapters. In other words, the same data can be analyzed, but the relevant statistical design is that of a quasi- or non-experiment and not one appropriate for the RFE.

35. Colin F. Camerer, George Loewenstein, and Matthew Rabin, ed., *Advances in Behavioral Economics* (New York: Russell Sage Foundation, 2004). RFEs are even used to show how conceptions of fairness affect people's propensity to be cooperative. See, for example, Bruno S. Frey and Stephan Meier, "Social Comparisons and Pro-Social Behavior: Testing 'Conditional Cooperation' in a Field Experiment," *American Economic Review* 94, no. 5 (2004): 1717–1722.

36. William G. Howell et al., "School Vouchers and Academic Performance: Results from Three Randomized Field Trials," *Journal of Policy Analysis and Management* 21, no. 2 (2002): 191–217.

37. A description of this project and the results can be found in Richard J. Wolitski, Daniel P. Kidder, Sherri L. Pals, Scott Royal, Angela Aidala, Ron Stall, David R. Holtgrave, David Harre, and Cari Courtenay-Quirk, "Randomized Trial of the Effects of Housing Assistance on the Health and Risk Behaviors of Homeless and Unstably Housed People Living with HIV," *AIDS Behavior* 14, no. 3 (2010): 493–503.

38. J. Michael Oakes, "Risks and Wrongs in Social Science Research: An Evaluator's Guide to the IRB," *Evaluation Review* 26, no. 5 (2002): 443–479.

39. Paul Slovic, ed., *Smoking: Risk, Perception and Policy* (Thousand Oaks, CA: Sage, 2001), p. 12.

40. General Accounting Office, *CDC's April 2002 Report on Smoking: Estimates of Selected Health Consequences of Cigarette Smoking Were Reasonable* (Washington, DC: U.S. General Accounting Office, 2003).

41. Jerome Cornfield, William Haenszel, E. Cuyler Hammond, Abraham M. Lilienfeld, Michael B. Shimkin, and Ernst L. Wynder, "Smoking and Lung Cancer: Recent Evidence and a Discussion of Some Questions," *International Journal of Epidemiology* 38, no. 5 (2009): 1175–1191.

42. See, for example, Fabio Ferlazzo, Sabrina Fagioli, Francesco Di Nocera, and Stefano Sdola, "Shifting Attention Across Near and Far Spaces: Implications for the Use of Hands-Free Cell Phones While Driving," *Accident Analysis and Prevention* 40, no. 6 (2008): 1859–1864, which recorded driver performance

responses to various randomly assigned stimuli placed in their car (e.g., hand-held, earphone-operated, or loudspeaker-operated cell phones); and Samuel G. Charlton, "Driving While Conversing: Cell Phones That Distract and Passengers Who React," *Accident Analysis and Prevention* 41, no. 1 (2009): 160–173, which recorded driver performance of drivers with randomly assigned combinations of in-car passengers, hands-free cell phones, and remote passengers who could see the driver's current situation. Diets can be randomly assigned to estimate their impact on weight loss. See, for example, Helen Truby, Sue Balc, Anne deLooy, Kenneth R. Fox, M. Barbara E. Livingstone, Catherine M. Logan, Ian A. Macdonald, Moira A. Taylor, and D. Joe Millward, "Randomised Controlled Trial for Four Commercial Weight Loss Programmes in the UK: Initial Findings from the BBC 'Diet Trials,'" *British Medical Journal* 322 (2006): 1309–1311. They found no between-diet differences and a slight loss in weight between any diet and none at all.

43. Truby et al., "Randomised Controlled Trial for Four Commercial Weight Loss Programmes in the UK," make this point very clear. The researchers restrict their conclusions to those who volunteered to be in the trials (probably a group motivated to lose weight) and label the study as an "intent-to-treat" study, since they could not make subjects comply with the diet to which the subject was randomly assigned or prevent subjects from choosing another diet on their own.

44. Donald P. Green and Peter M. Aronow, "Analyzing Experimental Data Using Regression: When Is Bias a Practical Concern?" March 7, 2011, http://ssrn.com/abstract=1466886/ (accessed July 15, 2011).

45. See Stephen G. West and Brad Sagarin, "Participant Selection and Loss in Randomized Experiments," in *Research Design: Donald Campbell's Legacy*, vol. 2, ed. Leonard Bickman (Thousand Oaks, CA: Sage, 2000), ch. 6. West and Sagarin discuss methods of dealing with participant self-selection into actual use of treatment compared with an intent-to-treat estimate of impact. See also Howard S. Bloom, "Accounting for No-Shows in Experimental Evaluation Designs," *Evaluation Review* 8, no. 2 (1984): 225–246.

46. This assumes no statistical interaction between motivation and treatment.

47. It may be possible to find a variable (called an instrumental variable) that predicts the likelihood of dropout (Z) but is not directly associated with Y. In that case, investigators can use the predicted value of Z ($= Z'$) for those who remain in the study to estimate the impact of X on Y by regressing Y on both X and Z'. Chapter 6 discusses the use of instrumental variables. Good instruments are hard to find.

48. See West and Sagarin, "Participant Selection and Loss." They discuss methods of dealing with participant self-selection into attrition (i.e., dropping out) before a posttest in RFEs. (They also elaborate on the analogy between self-selection into dropping out, or attrition, and self-selection into actual use, or into contamination.) See also Robert Brame, Michael G. Turner, and Ray Paternoster, "Missing Data Problems in Criminological Research," *Handbook of Quantitative Criminology* 3 (2010): 273–288; Robert Brame and Raymond Paternoster, "Missing Data Problems in Criminological Research: Two Case Studies," *Journal of Quantitative Criminology* 19, no. 1 (2003): 57–78.

49. Donald R. Kinder and Thomas R. Palfrey, *Experimental Foundations of Political Science* (Ann Arbor, MI: University of Michigan Press, 1993), ch. 3; Elinor Ostrom and James Walker, ed., *Trust and Reciprocity: Interdisciplinary Lessons from Experimental Research* (New York: Russell Sage Foundation, 2003). There are numerous examples of randomized experiments in political communication and organization management that have considerable policy relevance. While they are not field experiments, the authors present considerable evidence to defend the external validity of their findings. See, for example, Diana Mutz and Byon Reeves, "The New Videomalaise: Effects of Televised Incivility on Political Trust," *American Political Science Review* 99, no. 1 (2005); Jordi Brandts, Tatsuydshi Saijo, and Arthur Schram, "How Universal Is Behavior? A Four-Country Comparison of Spite and Cooperation in Voluntary Contribution Mechanism," *Public Choice* 119 (2004): 381–424; John R. Hibbing and John R. Alford, "Accepting Authoritative Decisions: Humans as Wary Cooperators," *American Journal of Political Science* 48, no. 1 (2004): 62–76. Field experiments are sometimes feasible, however. See Frey and Meier, "Social Comparisons and Pro-Social Behavior."

50. Benedickt Herrmann, Christian Thoni, and Simon Gachter, "Anti-Social Punishment Across Societies," *Science* 319, no. 5868 (March 2008): 1362–1367, which describes how results from lab experiments differ across countries; and Angus Deaton, "Instruments, Randomization, and Learning About Development," *Journal of Economic Literature* 48 (June 2010): 424–455, which describes problems of generalizing from RFEs, especially in developing countries.

5

The Quasi Experiment

DEFINING QUASI-EXPERIMENTAL DESIGNS

The quasi experiment (QE) includes many different kinds of designs, usually used to evaluate the impact of an ongoing program (X) on one or more indicators of output or outcome (Y). QEs have two characteristics in common.

First, they make before-and-after (pretest–posttest or over time) time-series (TS) comparisons. That is, they compare outcomes at one time or multiple times $t = t - j \ldots t - 1$ in a location i before the current program began (or was changed) to outcomes at one time or multiple times $t = t, t + 1 \ldots T$ in the same location after it began (or was changed). Alternatively, quasi experiments make cross-section (CS) with-and-without comparisons. That is, they compare outcomes at time t in a location or locations $i = 1 \ldots n_1$ without the program to the same outcomes at time t in a location or locations $i = 1 \ldots n_2$ with the program (or with a different program). (Like RFEs, in a QE, n_1 need not equal n_2, just as the number of pretest and posttest observations need not be exactly equal.) Thus, CS quasi experiments compare different units at the same time, while TS quasi experiments compare the same unit at different points in time. Many QEs use both kinds of comparison in the same design. (The following chapter shows that these characteristics also apply to many nonexperimental [NE] designs.)

Second, and unique to the QE, the researcher selects the groups to be compared so that they are as similar as possible in all respects, except that one group has the program and the other group does not or has a different program. This means that the QE compares ongoing programs that have *not* been assigned by the researcher. Instead, the programs have been politically or administratively assigned or chosen by a process in which she is usually a passive observer. She carefully selects for study among the ongoing programs so that the units of analysis are as comparable as possible, except that one unit has the program (or it has program A) and the other comparable units do not (or they have program B). In the quasi experiment, because the units must be as comparable as possible on potentially confounding (Z) variables, often only a subset of potentially relevant units of analysis are selected for study.

By contrast, in the NE, the researcher is less picky about the units of analysis for study, selecting for study all (or nearly all) relevant units of analysis (e.g., all school districts in the United States, all schools in the district, or all villages in the province) or a random or representative sample of them. However, in both the QE and the NE, the researcher is a passive observer of how programs are selected or assigned to each unit of analysis. Only in the randomized field experiment (RFE) does the researcher control the allotment of programs to units of analysis, using a random procedure.

Table 5.1 outlines the most common QE designs. The columns of Table 5.1 classify QE designs in terms of types of over-time or TS designs. The last column in the table denotes designs that are not really TS designs at all, because they have only a posttest measure of the outcome Y. The designs in this column measure outcomes after the treatment, but not before; they have no baseline. They are not true TS designs because they have no pretest measure of the output or outcome measure Y, measuring Y_t but not Y_{t-1}. By contrast, the first column denotes the simplest types of TS design. These are QE designs with only one pretest (Y_{t-1}) and one posttest (Y_{t+1}) measure; these are simple before-and-after comparisons. The next column denotes designs with multiple pre- and posttest measures. These are true TS designs.

The rows in Table 5.1 denote that some QE designs have no CS comparison group; others have one or more CS comparison groups. Comparison groups are separate groups that are selected to be as comparable with one another as possible on Z-type variables, differing only on the type of treatment they receive (i.e., the value of the X variable).

We see that designs in row 1 have no group-type comparison; they are single-group designs. Designs in the last column have no temporal comparison. Designs in columns 1 and 2 of row 2 combine both group and temporal comparisons. A discussion of each design follows. The first design that I discuss is the worst. Picking among the best of the rest may depend more on data availability than on what may (arguably) be theoretically "best." In fact, if more than one QE design is feasible, then the optimal, most defensible strategy is to use them all. If multiple designs yield the same result about program impact, then the conclusion becomes more defensible.[1]

For illustrative purposes, the discussion of each type of QE proceeds using the case of evaluating a new program in an imaginary elementary school: Little Orley.[2] The example, however, applies not only to the evaluation of policies or programs but also to the evaluation of different ways of managing or implementing programs, in any context. I discuss the statistical model that corresponds to each QE design that uses comparisons, whether they are between-group comparisons, over-time comparisons, or both. In effect, each QE design indicates which information to collect. The corresponding statistical model tells how to analyze the data, once it has been collected, using methods that enhance both internal and statistical validity. With respect to statistical validity, the examples also illustrate how to design evaluations so that they have a large number of observations (say, 300 students) even when the number of comparisons appears to be small (say, two schools).

THE ONE-SHOT CASE STUDY

The one-shot case study is neither an evaluation nor an assessment because there is no comparison, either between groups or over time. It is merely a description. If you want to do a program impact evaluation or assessment, it is an example of what *not* to do.

> Example: Under the (imaginary) Companion Computers in the Classroom (CCC) program, (equally imaginary) Little Orley Elementary School received six new computers in September 2003. In June 2004, 80 percent of its students scored at or above their grade level on the statewide reading test.

The research design that corresponds to observations like these is the one-shot case study. In row 1, column 3 of Table 5.1, Y_t, is the observed outcome (the reading score) measured sometime after the inception of the program. The information is descriptive and possibly informative, but there is no comparison. There is only a treated group, with no TS or CS comparison. Consequently, the

Table 5.1

Types of Quasi-Experimental Designs

	Before-After or Time Series		Single time
	1 pretest/1 posttest	Multiple pre- and posttests	Posttest Only
	Pretest-posttest	Single interrupted time series	No comparison group (One shot case study)
Single group	Y_{t-1} X Y_{t+1}	$Y_{t-j}\ldots Y_{t-1}$ X Y_t $Y_{t+1}\ldots Y_T$	Y_t
Multiple group	Pretest-posttest comparison group (or nonequivalent control group)	Single interrupted time series with (multiple) comparison group(s)	Posttest only comparison group
	Y'_{t-1} X Y'_{t+1} Y_{t-1} Y_{t+1}	$Y_{t-j}\ldots Y_{t-1}$ X_1 Y_t $Y_{t+1}\ldots Y_T$ $Y_{t-j}\ldots Y_{t-1}$ X_2 Y_t $Y_{t+1}\ldots Y_T$ $*$ $*$ $Y_{t-j}\ldots Y_{t-1}$ X_{k-1} Y_t $Y_{t+1}\ldots Y_T$ $Y_{t-j}\ldots Y_{t-1}$ X_k Y_t $Y_{t+1}\ldots Y_T$	X Y'_t Y_t

impact of the new computers ($X = 1$) on the outcome measure (Y) cannot be assessed because there is no comparison to a time or case in which $X = 0$. Comparison is a necessary (but not sufficient) condition for any impact assessment. An example of this kind of "design" would be a survey of program participants that was administered after the program. There is no pretest survey and no survey of a similar group that had not participated in the program (e.g., qualified applicants who were not admitted because there was no capacity).

THE POSTTEST-ONLY COMPARISON-GROUP (PTCG) DESIGN

The Posttest-Only Comparison-Group (PTCG) is the first real QE. It compares postprogram outcome scores (Y'_t) in a school with the CCC program (or in all the schools with the CCC program) to the outcome scores (Y_t) for a *similar* school (or schools) without the program (or with a different program). For example, one might compare, using a t-test for the difference of means, the average achievement (or attendance) scores ($\overline{Y}'_t$) for students in a school with the program ($X = 1$) to the average achievement (or attendance) scores ($\overline{Y}_t$) for students in a similar school that does *not* have the program or that has a different program ($X = 0$).

> Example: Little Orley Elementary School received six new computers in September 2003. Located in the same district, Big Worm Elementary School, similar to Little Orley in size, ethnicity of students, percentage of students receiving free or reduced-price lunches, percentage of students taking English as a Second Language (ESL) courses, number of classrooms and resource teachers, and so on, had only the normal allotment of computers. In June 2004, Little Orley students scored an average of 65 on the standardized statewide reading test, whose scores range from 20 to 100, compared with an average of 60 on the same test in Big Worm. In column 3, row 2, of Table 5.1, the program is X and the posttest score in the treatment school (Little Orley) is Y'_t; Y_t is the posttest score in the comparison school (Big Worm). The scores are both measured at the same point in time (June 2004). In this example, the difference in the means is five points.

Statistically, this comparison of the means between the two groups is identical to regressing the outcome reading scores Y_i for all the students in both the schools on a dummy variable X_i (= 1 for students in Little Orley, the treatment school, and = 0 for students in Big Worm, the comparison school) ($i = 1 \ldots n$ students in the two schools). The regression equation is

$$Y_i = a + bX_i + e_i.$$

This equation corresponds to the PTCG design. The number of observations in this PTCG design is the number of students in the two schools who took the reading test. It could thus be quite sizable for the purpose of statistical validity. The t-test for the regression coefficient b is the same as that for the difference of means. The treatment variable X_i is a dummy variable, scored 1 for all the students in the treatment school and 0 for all the students in the comparison school. The regression coefficient is interpreted as the difference in the mean Y_i scores between the comparison school that received the treatment ($X_i = 1$) and the one that did not ($X_i = 0$). The constant in the regression is the mean Y_i for students in the school for which $X_i = 0$, which is the comparison school, Big Worm. Big Worm students scored a mean of 60 on the posttest, while Little Orley students, in the treatment school, scored an average that was five points higher on the same posttest instrument. As a result, in the regression, we would estimate the constant as $a = 60$ and the regression coefficient as $b = 5$.

The advantage of the regression approach to this design emerges when there are more than two groups. For example, there may be two versions of the CCC program (CCC1 vs. CCC2), and the evaluator wishes to compare them against each other and against the no-program (status quo) option. Suppose now that three roughly comparable schools are in the evaluation. A simple difference of means test on the outcome measure among the three schools would not be applicable because there is now more than one difference. In this case, since there are three schools, there are three differences. Which difference is the evaluator to test with the difference of means?

The advantage of the regression approach in this example is that it can be used no matter how many different treatments there are. Y_i remains the scores for the n observations among all of the treatment groups. In this example of three treatments (CCC1, CCC2, and the no-treatment school), there is a dummy variable for each of the *two* different treatment groups. Specifically, X_1 is a dummy variable scored 1 for all the students in the school with CCC1 and 0 for the students in the other two schools with CCC2 and the status quo. And X_2 is another dummy variable scored 1 for all the students in the school with CCC2 and 0 for students in the CCC1 and status quo schools. There should be no dummy for the no-treatment, baseline school. Assuming the schools are selected to be comparable in other respects, differing only on the treatment options being evaluated, the regression equation is:

$$Y_i = a + b_1 X_{1i} + b_2 X_{2i} + e_i.$$

Each observation is denoted with the subscript i, where $i = 1 \ldots n$ students in the three schools. The first regression coefficient is the difference between the mean reading scores of students in the CCC1 and the status quo schools; the second is the difference between the mean reading scores of students in the CCC2 and the status quo schools. The constant is the mean reading score of the students in the comparison, status quo schools. The t-tests for each of the regression coefficients are the significance tests for the differences between the corresponding means. (It is also possible to estimate the difference of the means and test for the significance of the difference between the performance of the CCC1 and CCC2 schools by comparing b_1 and b_2 using the appropriate formula for the significance of the difference between regression coefficients.[3])

This design has many threats to valid causal inference. With respect to statistical validity, note that the n is not 3. Rather, it is the total n of students in all three schools. Compared with a comparison of schools, the ability to use students as the units of analysis enhances statistical validity. In this example, students are the target and should be the units for statistical analysis. Usually, the n of students in three schools is probably sufficient to pass minimum tests of statistical validity for a regression ($n - k > 120$, where $k = 3$ in this example).

With respect to design threats to internal validity, the most important are the selection threats. Consider, first, the two-group comparison. Little Orley, the treatment school, and Big Worm, the baseline comparison group, were selected because they appear to be similar. More specifically, they can be regarded as comparable if they are similar on the multiple confounding (Z) variables (such as their demographic composition) that could affect their chance of selection into the CCC program and that affect the outcome measure as well. It is also important to stress that the two schools are in the same district. Thus, they are subject to similar rules, administrations, and political oversight.[4]

Nonetheless, Little Orley and Big Worm (and the other school in the three-group comparison) may not really be comparable. They could be different in many ways. Even though they seem alike, the parents of students at Little Orley could be more educated than Big Worm parents, but there may be no data to tell whether this is the case. That difference, if it exists, and not the computers, could account for the difference between the schools. That is, Little Orley might have scored higher even without the CCC program.

Another threat to internal validity is multiple treatment interference. Suppose that, at the same time that Little Orley adopted the CCC program, it also got a new principal. It would be impossible to separate one change from the other. As long as the testing instruments to measure outcomes Y_i are standard measures that are commonly and similarly used by both schools (and as long as Little Orley, the treatment school, does not "cheat" in the administration of the outcome measure), instrumentation and testing should not be a threat to internal validity in this design.

The evidence is still consistent with the hypothesis that the CCC program works. So, at least for now, if the t-test is significant and the difference of means (or the regression coefficient) has the expected sign, there is (arguable) evidence of program impact. Nonetheless, there are still some important threats to the validity of this causal conclusion.

For example, what if Little Orley had started out in September 2003 with higher reading test scores than Big Worm and had aggressively applied to the CCC program in order to continue to excel? In that case, it is no surprise that it scored higher than Big Worm in June 2004. This is a form of selection threat. Alternatively, suppose that the CCC program deliberately selected treatment schools because of *poor* reading scores. There would still be a selection threat. In the case of either type of threat due to self-selection or administrative selection on pretest scores, if there are data on the pretest reading scores for the two schools for both September 2003 (i.e., baseline data) and June 2004, we should use a different QE. Specifically, we should use the pretest posttest comparison-group design shown in row 2, column 1, of Table 5.1. I discuss that design next.

But, first, it is important to consider versions of the PTCG design that make the PTCG close to (but not the same as) randomized field experiments, even though the researcher has not deliberately randomized assignment and even though there is no baseline or pretest data.[5]

The PTCG "Natural" Experiment

It is important to consider instances in which this simple PTCG design might actually approximate the RFE. Sometimes, there may be some naturally occurring, better ways to select similar treatment and comparison groups compared with groups that the researcher selects because they appear to be alike on measureable Z variables. Some evaluators call these "natural" experiments because they occur "naturally" and may approximate what might be observed had random assignment been deliberate. While opportunities for the natural experiment do not occur often, there are several ways that these approximately random comparison groups emerge naturally.

The Waiting List

One of the most common ways to select a natural comparison group is to use those on the waiting list for a service as a comparison group. Persons (or institutions) on the waiting list show the same initiative or motivation as those who have already been selected for the program. That they applied later may indicate less motivation, but it may not. In general, those on a waiting list to receive a public service have already been certified as eligible, and they have shown motivation to apply for a program with limited slots. A waiting list may be created when program managers decide to allocate limited resources based on "first come, first served." This is frequently the case in applications for publicly supported housing in the United States (and elsewhere). The same may also characterize applications for publicly supported job-training programs. As an example, if Little

Orley already had the CCC program and Big Worm had applied, met the eligibility criteria, and was on the waiting list for the CCC program for next year, it would be a good comparison school.

The Lottery

Sometimes, when there are limited slots or space available, program managers solicit applications from the public, certify eligibility, and create a list of eligible applicants. If that list is longer than the number of spaces available, then, rather than allocating limited resources based on "first come, first served," program managers may decide that allocation by lottery is fairer. For example, some cities that desire to clean up abandoned residential properties decide to give the properties to qualified, eligible people. If more people than properties are certified as qualified and otherwise eligible, the program managers may use some random mechanism (a lottery, rolling dice or drawing straws, computer-generated random odd or even numbers) to decide who gets the homes. Later, researchers can regress the outcome scores (Y_i) (e.g., housing conditions, employment status) on the treatment variable X_i, where $X_i = 1$ for those who "won" the lottery and $X_i = 0$ for those who "lost" the lottery. Even when there is not oversubscription, managers may allocate clients to programs randomly, because it is perceived as fair and without bias. Colleges often allocate students to sections of required entry-level courses randomly, and random allocation then makes it possible to examine the impact of other course differences on outcomes.

As an example of a lottery, the Homestead Housing Preservation program in Washington, DC, enabled residents to purchase abandoned houses for as little as $250. In exchange, homeowners must rehabilitate the property, reside in the property for a minimum of five years, and return it to the real property tax rolls. Because there were always more applicants than available houses, the program held an annual lottery to allocate the housing units. The impact of this form of homeownership on focal output and outcome variables (such as housing quality or employment status) could be estimated using a PTCG QE that approximates the RFE. In the example, the comparison groups (winning homeowners vs. lottery losers) should be statistically comparable, especially if the list of eligible applicants was reasonably large and the number of housing units that were given away was also reasonably large (say, more than thirty).[6] For internal validity, there is no requirement that the number of losers in the lottery equal the number of winners, as long as the *n* is reasonably large. If the number in each group is substantially unbalanced, that is a threat to statistical validity. (Chapter 6, on NE designs, discusses the adjustment that must be made when group sizes are unbalanced.)

As an example of random allocation in the absence of oversubscription, a recent study examined the impact of early start time on academic achievement by comparing early-start freshman classes at the U.S. Air Force Academy to later-start freshman classes; as it happens, most of the freshman students are assigned by lottery to class/instructor "slots" of classes.[7]

The Birthday

Sometimes, eligibility for a program is determined by birthday. For example, the Social Security Amendments of 1983 raised the age of retirement to be eligible for full Social Security benefits from sixty-five to sixty-seven. Consequently, those who were born between January 1, 1937, and December 31, 1937, could retire with full benefits at age sixty-five. Those born between January 1, 1938, and December 31, 1938, only a year later, could not retire with full benefits when they turned sixty-five.[8] These groups should otherwise be quite comparable. Thus, an evaluator could estimate the impact of early retirement or other age-related benefits on health, employment, and other outcomes of interest, by comparing the difference, if any, in these outcomes between naturally occurring comparable groups like these.[9]

Another example investigates the impact of a universal prekindergarten program in Tulsa, Oklahoma, with strict eligibility criteria, including birth date. Since birth date partly determined eligibility, it was possible to compare June 2002 test scores of children with an August 1996 birthday (eligible for enrollment during 2001–2002) after one year of pre-K to 2002 pretest scores of children born in September 1996 (ineligible for enrollment in 2001–2002, but eligible for enrollment in September 2002). Birth in August or September 1996 is likely to approximate a naturally random event.[10]

A variation on selecting comparable groups based on arbitrarily determined birth dates is to study twins. They have the same "nature" (i.e., birth date and biological characteristics), but they sometimes do not share the same "nurture." Twins are commonly used as comparison groups to study the impact of family and education on outcomes based on the assumption that the twins are otherwise comparable in their endowments.[11]

The Cut-Point

Another source of comparability occurs when programs are designed so that eligibility is determined by a cut-point on a scale that contains random sources of error, including measurement error. This kind of design is also called a regression discontinuity design (RDD), but it is basically a natural experiment that uses a PTCG design. For example, if selection for a special reading program in an elementary school is determined by scoring below some criterion, X_c, on a standardized reading test, then those who score just below the cut-point are probably quite comparable with those who score just above it. This is especially true since reading and other similar tests are known to contain a certain amount of random error.

The same is true when program eligibility is determined by an income cut-point. Those who earn just a bit over a $13,000 cut-point (say, an intact family of four with an income between $13,000 and $13,499) are probably quite comparable with families who fall just below the cut-point (say, an intact family of four with an income between $12,500 to $12,999). Thus, we can use the PTCG regression to compare the output or outcome scores (Y_i) of those just a bit over the selection cut-point who receive the reading program ($X = 1$) with the scores of those who score just below the cut-point and do not receive the program ($X = 0$).[12]

As another possible use for a RDD, assignment to special education programs is often based on test scores. Those tests undoubtedly contain considerable random measurement error (RME), especially at the individual level. Children just over the cut-point are not likely to be significantly different from those just below the cut-point. These groups, if the n is large enough, arguably form a natural experiment with which to evaluate the impact of special education programs on academic and other outcome variables.

The Seemingly Random Selection

Sometimes the allocation of treatment is seemingly random simply because the environment is chaotic. This might be the case in allocating treatment to families after a natural disaster. Another example concerns the distribution of information about the importance of using condoms to reduce the incidence of HIV/AIDS on a street in Calcutta where brothels are concentrated. Peer educators were dispatched to distribute this information (along with free condoms) in no particular order. The probability of contact, according to the researchers, was seemingly random, as was the order of the follow-up survey (i.e., who was interviewed first, second, third). The researchers made use of the seeming randomness of both interventions (receipt of the information and the order on the follow-up survey) to examine the impact of education on condom use and then to examine the impact of condom use on other outcomes.[13]

The Natural Experiment: Other Considerations

In the absence of any other adjustments, the natural experiment would be analyzed using the same regression setup as the RFE. But this requires assuming that the results from a natural experiment can be interpreted as if random assignment (with a large *n* from a large population) had occurred. Dunning notes that such an assumption can often result in invalid inference from a natural experiment.[14] Seemingly random occurrences, such as living across the street from each other but in different political jurisdictions with different policies, are not necessarily random. Exogenous random shocks (like winning a lottery, or a sudden, large stock market gain or loss, or an infrequent, unpredictable weather event or natural disaster, or an unanticipated policy change that is exogenous to the target observations) are random, but they are poor proxies for more permanent conditions (like many policies and public programs) whose impact is the focus of study. Winnings from a lottery or sudden, unanticipated stock market losses are an imperfect proxy for relatively long-term participation in public programs. Such random occurrences pose a challenge to both the internal and external validity of all but the best examples of a natural experiment. It is always advisable to look for opportunities for natural experiments that approach random assignment to evaluate policy impacts. However, it is also always advisable to supplement the natural experiment with qualitative evidence that the hypothesized process really did occur or with other QE and NE designs to reanalyze the same or similar data. I discuss these designs next.

The PTCG: Extensions

In the absence of a good natural experiment, the PTCG remains a weak design.[15] It is difficult to find exact matches. The more units in the study, the greater the statistical validity, but the harder it is to find an exact match. Frequently, the matching is inexact. Matching requires that confounding variables, on which treated and untreated units are to be matched, are known and measurable. The more confounding variables there are, the harder it is to find even a close match, but increasing internal validity requires matching on multiple confounding variables.

There are, however, alternatives to simple matching designs. Rather than select closely comparable units (one with the program, one without), it enhances both statistical and internal validity to study multiple but roughly comparable units, some with the program and some without, and then use direct statistical controls for multiple, confounding variables. We discuss the use of statistical controls in Chapter 6 on nonexperiments.

Another alternative is to use information about the confounding Z variables to predict the probability that each unit is selected for treatment. Using a PTCG design, researchers can then compare outcomes in units with close to the same predicted probability of selection (say, predicted probability = .45 − .55) but different actualities of treatment (some were selected and some were not). This is called propensity score matching. I discuss this as a type of NE design in Chapter 6.

A third alternative is to make use of pretest information. When pretest scores on outcome measures (Y_{t-1}) are available and stable,[16] it is possible to match units of analysis that have the same baseline scores, yet some are selected for treatment and some are not. For example, some unemployed (Y_{t-1}) men (of similar age, race or ethnicity, and education) receive job training in a particular month (e.g., January 2005) and some do not. The employment (versus unemployment) of these two groups can then be compared in March 2005 (Y_{t+1}). In this example, the groups are selected to be comparable on confounding (Z) variables (age, race or ethnicity, and education). They are also comparable on pretest scores (Y_{t-1}). It is then possible to regress[17] the posttest scores (Y_i) of the outcome variable (employment status) on receipt of training (X_i), knowing that the groups are comparable in many other respects, including their baseline employment status.

But this kind of pretest matching is not always possible, especially when pretest information is not available. Even when pretest information is available (and especially if it represents a continuous measure, like weeks worked, earnings, or test score results), exact or even close matches may not be possible. When pretest information is available, regardless of its level of measurement, it should be used to adjust posttest results for treated and untreated groups. In that case, rather than match on pretest scores, consider using the pretest posttest comparison-group design.

THE PRETEST–POSTTEST COMPARISON-GROUP (PTPTCG) (THE NONEQUIVALENT CONTROL-GROUP) DESIGN

In the absence of opportunity for a natural experiment (which is most of the time), the pretest-posttest comparison-group (PTPTCG) design is more defensible than the usual, nonrandom PTCG. This design adds a baseline, or pretest, from which to measure change in both the treated and untreated group (or groups). In this design (shown in row 2, column 1, of Table 5.1), there is comparison between groups and comparison over time. There is, however, just one pretest and one posttest measure of the output or outcome variable(s). Consider how this design improves the original Little Orley/Big Worm PTCG design by reducing the selection threat from baseline differences in pretest scores.[18]

> To examine the impact of the CCC program in Little Orley school, we want Little Orley and Big Worm to be comparable not only in terms of students' race and ethnicity, percentage of students receiving reduced-price or free lunches, and so on, but also in terms of pretest (September 2003) reading scores. We hope that the only difference between the schools is the presence of the CCC program in one of them. If the school characteristics (including baseline scores, students' race, etc.) are identical, or nearly so, we expect, if the CCC program is effective, the June 2004 reading scores in Little Orley to exceed substantially those in Big Worm.
>
> Alternatively, suppose the pretest reading scores in the two schools are not the same, but the schools are similar on the other dimensions. Then, if the CCC program is effective, we expect the *improvement* in scores from September 2003 to June 2004 in Little Orley to exceed the *improvement*, if any, observed in Big Worm's September and June scores. In other words, if the CCC program in Little Orley is effective, even if Little Orley customarily lags Big Worm in reading scores, we expect "value added" from the CCC program, so that the improvement in Little Orley's scores should exceed that in Big Worm's, even if Little Orley still lags Big Worm in June 2004.
>
> In the PTPTCG design in Table 5.1, Y'_{t-1} is the September 2003 (before treatment, pretest) average reading score in Little Orley. Y_{t-1} is the September 2003 average pretest reading score in Big Worm, the comparison school, which does not have the CCC program, but is similar to Little Orley in other relevant dimensions. X is the implementation of the CCC program in Little Orley. The posttest score Y'_{t+1} is the June 2004 (after one year of treatment) average reading score in Little Orley (i.e., the posttest score in the treatment group). The compa-

rable June 2004 posttest score in Big Worm, which does not have the program, is Y_{t+1}. The pretest scores for each of the schools are the reading scores measured before the inception of the CCC program in Little Orley; because the schools are similar, they are expected to be equal. If they are in fact equal, then $\overline{Y}'_{t-1} = \overline{Y}_{t-1}$. In that case, a simple measure of program impact is $\overline{Y}'_{t+1} - \overline{Y}_{t+1}$. Just as in a PTCG, the t-test for the difference of means would indicate the statistical significance of the measured difference. Otherwise, the simple measure of program impact is $\left(\overline{Y}'_{t+1} - \overline{Y}_{t+1}\right) - \left(\overline{Y}'_{t-1} - \overline{Y}_{t-1}\right)$ (a difference-of-difference in means score). In this case, the t-test for the difference of these mean differences would indicate the statistical significance of the difference.[19]

However, simple measures of program impact such as these rely on t-tests for the differences of means, or the difference-of-difference of means. The cost of such simplicity is that measures like these differences in means do not allow the inclusion of confounding variables to adjust for the common fact that the comparison groups really are not quite comparable, and differences in means are awkward to use when there are multiple treatment groups. Just as in the case of the PTCG design, the regression approach is more general and informative than a simple t-test for the difference of means. In the case of the PTPTCG design, two regression-based approaches are appropriate.[20] When the investigator is convinced that pretest values of Y causally determine posttest scores, and when assignment to the comparison and treatment groups is based on the pretest score, the corresponding regression equation is:

$$Y_{i,t+1} = a + bX_i + cY_{i,t-1} + e_i. \qquad (1)$$

Pretest scores are likely to influence posttest scores when the Y variable is stable: for example, body weight is stable, and so is wealth (but not income), and academic ability in, say, math; in all cases, being overweight (or wealthy, or good at math) at time 1 directly affects the likely response at time 2 (and often determines assignment to programs). In this case, the regression equation (1) models the underlying theoretical model (i.e., the underlying data generating process). The pretest score $Y_{i, t-1}$ is related to the treatment X_i and affects the outcome measure $Y_{i, t+1}$; consequently, the pretest score should be controlled on the right-hand side. Just as in Table 5.1, $Y_{i, t+1}$ corresponds to the posttest scores. In this case, it represents the posttest scores for all the students in both the treatment school ($Y'_{i,t+1}$, where $i = 1 \ldots j$ students in the treatment school) and the comparison school ($Y_{i, t-1}$, where $i = j + 1, j + 2, \ldots n$). If there is a total of n students in these two schools, there are n observations of $Y_{i, t+1}$ in equation (1) above, where $i = 1 \ldots n$. In this regression, we examine the impact of the treatment ($X_i = 1$ for the students in the treatment school and 0 for the students in the comparison school) on the posttest score, controlling for the baseline score of all the students ($Y_{i, t-1}$).

The PTPTCG equation (1) estimates two regression coefficients. The regression coefficient c is the estimate of the impact of the pretest score on the posttest score. Given the stability of most scores, even outside education, this coefficient is likely to be close to unity. But it may not be unity.[21] The focal regression coefficient in the PTPTCG Equation (1) is b. It is the one that estimates program impact, adjusting for the baseline. It is an estimate of the change (hopefully positive in this example) in average posttest reading scores between the school with the CCC program ($X = 1$) and the school without the program ($X = 0$). This coefficient is interpreted as the difference in mean reading scores between the two schools relative to (i.e., controlling or adjusting for) the difference in their baseline scores. It is a direct estimate of the value added by the CCC program.

However, Equation (1) relies heavily on the assumption that the pretest score really causes the posttest score. When scores are not stable, that assumption may be questionable: For example, indicators of income, and indicators of many attitudes and opinions, measured as responses to questionnaires, are not especially stable. While there may be some cases of stable attitudes (e.g., party identification), most cases (e.g., satisfaction with the local public transit system, weekly wages, or hours of employment among the poor) are unlikely to exhibit stability. In this case, a regression of gain scores on the treatment variable is more likely to provide an unbiased estimate of program impact:

$$(Y_{i,t+1} - Y_{i,t-1}) = a + bX_i + e_i. \tag{2}$$

Equation (2) is a difference-in-difference model: It compares difference in treatment ($X = 0$ or $X = 1$) to change in the outcome scores. It does not rely on levels. Treatments are usually assigned based on levels, not differences; poor people, needy schools and noncompliant businesses get "treatments" intended to mitigate the problem. To assure that treatment and comparison groups are really comparable, it is necessary to select them so that they are comparable on the levels of multiple confounding variables. In the absence of random assignment, this is improbable if not impossible. The advantage of examining changes is that, while levels on confounding variables Z affect both the likelihood of treatment (X) and levels of Y, it is unlikely that changes (or differences) in the *levels* of the confounding variables affect the likelihood of treatment (X). Thus, the omitted confounding variables can be more safely ignored in this version of the PTPTCG design. The design relies on differences not levels. (Of course, it is also possible to include confounding variables in any regression, including this one.)

It is not *a priori* clear whether Equation (1) or (2) is "best" for the analysis of data collected using the PTPTCG design; when the issue of causality between pretest and posttest scores is uncertain and when the assignment of treatment based on pretest scores is also uncertain, the best advice is to use both equations. Comparable results from the two estimates would enhance the defensibility of the results.

Both versions of the PTPTCG design rely on regression, rather than a comparison of means. Among the advantages of the regression approach relative to the simple comparison of means is that it is easy to adapt to the case of more than two treatments. Just as in the PTCG design, suppose that there is one comparison school that represents the status quo and two nearby, generally comparable schools with two versions of the CCC program. In this case, we represent the treatments with two dummy variables. $X1_i$ is a dummy variable scored 1 for all the students in the school with CCC1 and scored 0 for the students in the other two schools with CCC2 and the status quo. And $X2_i$ is the other dummy variable scored 1 for all the students in the school with CCC2 and 0 for students in the CCC1 and status quo schools. Assuming the schools are selected to be roughly comparable, they may still differ in pretest scores. Of course, they also differ on the treatment options being evaluated. In this case, the dual treatment version of regression Equation (1) is:

$$Y_{i,t+1} = a + b_1 X1_i + b_2 X2_i + cY_{i,t-1} + e_i. \tag{1a}$$

The regression coefficient associated with the pretest score has the same interpretation as it does in Equation (1). The coefficient associated with the first dummy variable (b_1) is the estimate of the difference in the mean reading scores between the school with the CCC1 program ($X1_i = 1$) and the status quo school ($X1_i = 0$), controlling for the differences, if any, in the baseline reading scores between the schools. Similarly, the coefficient associated with the second dummy variable (b_2) is the estimate of the difference in mean reading scores between the school with the CCC2 program ($X2_i = 1$) and the status quo school ($X2_i = 0$), controlling for the differences, if any, in the baseline reading scores between these schools. Just as in the multiple-group PTCG design, the t-tests for each of the regression coefficients are the significance tests for the differences between the corresponding means. (Just as in the PTCG design, the difference between b_1 and b_2 is an estimate of the difference of the means between the performance of the CCC1 and CCC2 schools. Using the appropriate formula for the significance of this difference between these two regression coefficients produces the test statistic t.)[22]

Similarly, the dual treatment (in this case, CCC1, CCC2, and the comparison) version of regression Equation (2) is:

$$\left(Y_{i,t+1} - Y_{i,t-1}\right) = a + b_1 X1_i + b_2 X2_i + \ldots + e_i. \tag{2a}$$

The regression coefficient associated with $X1$ is the estimate of the impact of the difference between treatment 1 and no treatment on the change in the outcome measure, and the regression coefficient associated with $X2$ is the estimate of the effect of the difference between treatment 2 and no treatment on the change in the outcome measures. It is also possible to compare the differences between the two treatments.

Compared with the PTCG design (unless it is a natural experiment), the PTPTCG design goes far to improve the internal validity of the estimate of program impact. The use of the pretest score as a baseline (whether it is on the right-hand or left-hand side of the equation) makes the estimate of program impact, over and above the pretest, a better measure of the value added by the program. Controlling for the pretest score in a regression equation or using a change score as dependent variable (because the focal independent variable is also a change or difference) helps to reduce selection threats that are pervasive in comparison-group designs. To see why, consider the causal models in Figure 5.1.

In the first panel, unless the PTCG design is a good natural experiment, so that the groups being compared are really comparable on the confounding Z variables, differing only in the treatment X variable, selection threats are likely to challenge the internal validity of any estimate of program impact. Rarely are comparison groups sufficiently comparable to rule out other confounding variables symbolized by Z.

The second panel represents the pretest-control version of the PTPTCG design (Equation 1). While that design does not explicitly control for confounding Z variables, it does explicitly control for baseline scores by "lagging" the dependent variable; the pretest scores of the dependent variable are explicitly assumed to affect the posttest scores. In many cases, the long-run confounding Z variables that affect posttest output or outcome (Y) scores at time $t + 1$ are the same long-run forces that affect the same (Y) scores at $t-1$. To the extent that this is the case, controlling for the pretest scores is an effective way to control for these Z variables without actually identifying and measuring all of them. The second panel represents this possibility.

The third panel represents the pretest–posttest difference version of the PTPTCG design (Equation 2). In that case, the confounding Z' variables are variables that are both related to selection for treatment and control *and* also affect the difference (not the level) of the outcome measure. The set of variables in Z' is likely to be a small subset of the variables in Z; this is the strength of the difference-in-difference PTPTCG design compared with the pretest-control version.

However, it is important to recognize that both versions of this design may suffer from omitted confounding variables. That is, even though Little Orley and Big Worm were selected to be

Figure 5.1   Comparing the PTCG and PTPTCG Designs

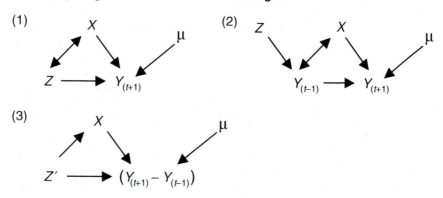

comparable in terms of parental socioeconomic status, and even though the researcher accounts statistically for the students' pretest scores, the schools may still differ on some unmeasured, unknown Z variable whose impact on $Y_{i,\,t+1}$ is not picked up by the pretest control variable, $Y_{i,\,t-1}$ or whose impact on $(Y_{i,\,t+1} - Y_{i,\,t-1})$ is confounded with X. For example, parents' involvement in their children's education may be greater in Little Orley, and that characteristic, not the CCC program, could account for the estimated achievement score or improvement in achievement score (erroneously) credited to the CCC program. However, parental involvement is often hard to observe and measure. If it is not measured, it cannot be controlled statistically. (And if it is measured with an unreliable or invalid instrument, it may be better left out.)

In short, no amount of matching or statistical manipulation can approach the advantages of random assignment for reducing selection threats. But random assignment is not always practicable. Simple comparison groups may not be trustworthy, because they may not really be as comparable as the evaluators think. Incorporating pretest or baseline scores into the basic PTCG design goes far to improve comparability, turning the simple PTCG design into a PTPTCG design. Baseline scores are often measurable, and using them as statistical controls or as gain scores goes far to reduce selection threats.

But sometimes, even when pretest data are available, groups cannot really be regarded as comparable. For example, in extremely heterogeneous school districts, simple controls for pretest scores or the use of gain scores may not be sufficient to claim comparability between schools that differ in respect to size, ethnicity, and demographic composition, or to corresponding changes in the levels of these variables. In this case, evaluators should drop the comparison group approach to quasi experiments and consider, instead, the advantages of the TS designs, which, by comparing posttest scores in one group to that same group's own pretest scores, avoids selection threats entirely. The following sections discuss TS designs. As we see, some TS designs are considerably more defensible than others.

THE PRETEST–POSTTEST (SINGLE-GROUP) DESIGN

This is really half of the previous PTPTCG design. It just does not have a cross-section comparison group. If the comparison group in the previous design is really not very comparable, it may be better not to have a comparison group at all. If there is no comparison group, there can be no selection threat. However, as I note below, there are other, major threats to the internal validity of this particular design, rendering it minimally useful. This pretest–prepost (PTPT) single-group design requires baseline, pretest data. It compares outcomes in the treated group after the program has been running for, say, a year $(Y_{i,\,t+1})$ to outcome measures in same group before the program began $(Y_{i,\,t-1})$.

For example, suppose that Little Orley is still the target school for the CCC program, which is designed to improve reading scores. In row 1, column 1, of Table 5.1, Y_{t-1} is the average September 2003 preprogram reading score at Litte Orley, and Y_{t+1} is Little Orley's average reading score in June 2004, after the program has been in operation for a year. If the program is effective, then Y_{t+1} should be substantially higher than Y_{t-1}. Using this approach, the relevant statistical test would not be a difference-of-means test because the observations are not independent. That is, the students who take the posttest are (mostly) the same as those who took the pretest. Hence, a more appropriate statistical test would be a single sample t-test against the null hypothesis that the average of each individual difference score is zero. Specifically, the null is H_0: $\sum_i (Y_{i,t+1} - Y_{i,t-1})/n = 0$; the alternative is H_A: $\sum_i (Y_{i,t+1} - Y_{i,t-1})/n > 0$. The number of observations (n) in this design is the number of students at Little Orley who take both the pre- and posttest.[23]

Such an approach hides a major threat to the internal validity of this simple statistical test that the regression approach makes transparent. Using regression to analyze the data in a PTPT design, the dependent variable is each posttest score in the treated group, while the independent variable is the corresponding pretest score. In the example, the evaluator regresses the posttest score for each student on that student's pretest score. The number of observations remains n = number of students who have pre- and posttest scores.

$$Y_{i,t+1} = a + bY_{i,t-1} + e_i.$$

Viewing the PTPT design in this framework (a regression equation) reveals a fundamental flaw in this type of design. The regression coefficient, b, is an estimate of the impact of the pretest score on the posttest score. It represents the change in the posttest score for each unit increase in the pretest score. It is likely to be very close to 1. If $b = 1$, then the regression approach is equivalent to the t-test on the differences of means above. But, beyond that, the meaning of the estimate for b is not clear at all. It could be a measure of the underlying trend (maturation) that affects the internal validity of TS designs like this one. In other words, it could reflect the tendency of children to score higher on reading tests as they grow older and as they become more experienced readers. While this is not clearly a causal effect of pretest on posttest, it would be a clear case of maturation. Although CS designs are subject to selection threats and TS designs are not, TS designs are plagued with maturation threats and CS designs are not. This PTPT design, represented as a regression, greatly reduces the trend problem by measuring and statistically controlling for it, a clear advantage, but it comes with great costs.

For one, there is another possible interpretation of the regression coefficient, b. It may measure the (causal) impact of taking the pretest on the posttest score, a clear case of a testing effect. But now there are two interpretations of the regression coefficient, and neither of them involves an estimate of the impact of the CCC program on reading achievement. The problem is: Where is the estimate of program impact?

If the slope coefficient estimates the testing effect or the underlying trend, the only other estimator is the intercept coefficient (a). It is an estimate of the value of the posttest score if the pretest score were zero. It is hard to argue that this represents an estimate of the impact of the CCC program, unless the pretest score before the CCC program is expected to be zero. If there are many pretest observations of zero, then the intercept is the estimate of program impact. For example, if the outcome that was to be measured was a test of knowledge of how to use the new computers, the pretest scores might well be zero. Or suppose that the program under study was the impact of an introductory statistics class (X) on the ability to do statistics (Y). If the outcome was the score on a statistics final in December ($Y_{i,\,t+1}$), then the pretest scores on a similar statistics test given in September ($Y_{i,\,t-1}$), or most of them, might well be expected to be zero. In that case, it might be justifiable to use this design, analyze it using multiple regression, and use the intercept as the estimate of program impact. But, in the Little Orley example, the question concerns the impact of the CCC program on a general academic skill (i.e., reading comprehension). These scores are not expected to be zero at the pretest. The question is whether computer learning improves reading comprehension over and above what would be normally expected (beyond the normal trend). In this case, neither the regression coefficient nor the intercept has a clear interpretation. The PTPT model is said to be underidentified. That is, there is no separate coefficient representing the impact of the program.

A published example of the use of the PTPT design comes from a study of museum attendance conducted by Bickman and Hamner.[24] This study evaluated whether a visit to Yad Vashem, the Holocaust history museum in Israel, had any influence on the attitudes and knowledge of Israeli high school students toward the Holocaust. Evaluators administered survey questionnaires to the students before and after the visit to assess the changes in their attitudes and knowledge by comparing the pretest and posttest scores. Results indicated little change in attitudes or knowledge. But this is not a very strong design, because it is impossible to separate the impact of the treatment (the visit) from testing effects or from any underlying trend. As a result, the internal validity of the no-impact conclusion is not very convincing.

What if the researcher had a longer time series—that is, what if she had more preprogram scores and more postprogram scores? Then, she might be able to measure the preprogram trend and to observe whether the CCC program coincides with a change in that basic trend. With that kind of data, the researcher could use a single interrupted TS design.

THE SINGLE INTERRUPTED TIME-SERIES DESIGN

Row 1, column 2, of Table 5.1 (page 112) displays the single interrupted time-series (SITS) design. In that design, measures of the output or outcome variable, repeated for several time periods before a policy or program or management change, portray the counterfactual pretreatment status quo. Output or outcome measures of the same variable, repeated for several time periods after the change, are taken to reveal the impact of the change. In the figure, there are T time periods, composed of j pretest observations and $T-j$ posttest observations. The number of pre- and posttest observations does not have to be identical. For purposes of statistical validity, there should be a bare minimum of fifty or so total observations, with a reasonable distribution among pre- and posttreatment scores. While there is no magic number, three pre- or posttest observations out of a total of fifty would not be acceptable, while twenty would be.

As an example, recall that the CCC program began in September 1997 at Little Orley. Assume that the sponsor wants an evaluation after the first year, so there is not enough time for a long postprogram time series. Suppose further that there are test scores for ten years before the program, but only one postprogram observation, which is not enough for statistically valid hypothesis tests. A minimum of fifty observations is necessary to discern a trend, and, while they do not need to be exactly balanced between before and after program inception, about one-third of the observations should be postprogram observations. So what do we do?

One simple solution is to use a different outcome indicator, searching for one that is more frequently measured.[25] Test scores are reported, at best, only twice a year. But attendance records are kept daily. Assuming that the school year is 180 days, attendance records would provide 180 yearly postprogram school-level observations. For example, daily school-level attendance records for the past four years would produce 720 daily pretest scores, along with 180 daily posttest scores. We might also use monthly attendance rates. The following example uses monthly data. (Although daily data might improve the statistical validity of the design, collecting the data may require additional effort at a cost that exceeds the benefit.) Reflecting the evaluator's decision to use a frequently measured, but still important, outcome (attendance) rather than one that is arguably more important, but infrequently measured (test scores), the expectation is that the CCC program should improve attendance at Little Orley.

SITS Designs: Pictures and Means

With monthly data, the researcher could collect attendance records for each month of four years preceding the September 2003 start of the CCC program at Little Orley and also for each month of the first year after the inception of the CCC program, up through June 2004. Assuming that each school year comprises ten months, there would be ten times four years (1999–2004) or 40 preprogram observations and 10 postprogram observations, for a total n of 50. One can graph the data. If there is a change in the pattern that coincides with the implementation of the CCC program, showing increased attendance rates, there would be evidence that is consistent with the hypothesis of program impact.

Some typical patterns might look like those shown in Figure 5.2. Panels (a), (b), (c), and (f) are consistent with the hypothesis of program impact. Outcome patterns such as those in panels (d) and (e) in Figure 5.2 would not support that hypothesis.

A common, and erroneous, statistical technique for the analysis of TS data such as these is to compare preimplementation means with postimplementation means. The problem with this method is that it fails to separate maturation (trends) from program impact.[26] Compare panel (e) to panels (a), (c), and (f). In panel (e), there is a clear, steady, upward trend in attendance rates that has been going on for the entire five-year period. That is all that is going on; the CCC program appears not to have altered that trend at all. Yet, we would expect the program to affect the underlying trend if it were having any impact, whether in the intended direction or not. If the impact is in the intended direction, we should observe an upward alteration in the underlying trend and a downward alteration if the impact were adverse. Nonetheless, if we simply examined pre- and posttest means from panel (e), the mean scores in the months before the CCC program would be lower than the mean of the postprogram scores. We would erroneously conclude that the program was effective. Yet, the observed difference in pre- and postintervention means reflects only an overall upward trend that existed before the inception of the CCC program and continues afterward. Consideration of the trend would reveal that the program has had no impact.

Another example elaborates the point. Compare panel (e) to panel (c). In panel (c), there is no trend in attendance scores. However, as we did for the data in panel (e), if we compared mean pre- to mean posttest scores, the posttest mean would exceed the pretest mean. But in this case, the program is effective. That is, simple comparison of pre- and postintervention means in the case of panels (e) and (c) would be the same, but the underlying process is different. In panel (e), the program clearly has no impact, while in panel (c) it clearly does. Yet, in both cases, the postprogram mean is higher than the preprogram mean.

Similarly, the pattern of outcome scores in panels (a) and (f) would also generate a posttest mean that exceeds the pretest mean. Both panels show underlying upward trends as well as program impact, but in (a) the impact is gradual while in (f) it is immediate. A simple comparison of means would fail to reveal that distinction. Panel (b) portrays another example of program impact that reverses a downward trend. A simple comparison of post- to preprogram means would show no difference or even a lower postprogram mean. This approach ignores other evidence in the data. Using all the information in the SITS, a program that reverses a negative trend might be regarded as a sign of positive impact.

Clearly, from the perspective of internal validity, simply comparing pre- and posttest means is not a valid approach. It does not make use of all the information in the SITS design. Rather, we need a statistical approach that allows us to separate underlying trends (maturation) from program impact.[27]

SITS Designs: Regression Models

Once again, regression provides a solution.[28] There are several possible regression models.[29] Consider the simplest first, which simply separates the trend from a hypothetically immediate impact of the program. We represent the trend by a counter for each successive time period. In this example, the trend would be measured by a score of 1–50 for each of the sixty months in our data, from five years before the inception of the program through the first year of the program's operation. (Remember, the school year is assumed to comprise only ten months.) Call this countervariable T for trend. The program variable, as usual, is X_t, has a score of 1 for the ten months that the CCC program has been in operation and 0 for the preceding fifty months. The outcome variable is the monthly attendance data, Y_t, where $t = 1 \ldots 50$ time periods. Thus, each of the variables has fifty observations for the $t = 1 \ldots 50$ time periods. We regress the outcome on both the trend variable and on the program indicator variable:

$$Y_t = a + bX_t + cT_t + e_t. \tag{5.1}$$

Using this model, the coefficient c is the estimator for the underlying trend, if there is any. If there were no underlying trend, as in panel (c) or (d) of Figure 5.2, coefficient c would be statistically equal to zero. Otherwise, if there is an underlying positive trend, as there is in panels (e) and (f), the estimator will be significantly different from zero and positive. The coefficient b is the estimator for the impact of the program, over and above the underlying trend. It is the measure of program impact that we seek. If b is significant and positive, it is an estimate of the change from no program ($X_t = 0$) to the implementation of the program ($X_t = 1$) on the outcome measure (Y_t), independent of the underlying trend. If both b and c are significant and positive, then panel (f) is the graph of the underlying process: there is both an underlying upward trend and a positive program impact. If only coefficient b is significant, and c is not, then panel (c) is the graph of the underlying process: There is no trend, but there is program impact.

Finally, the process in panel (a) requires a different regression equation. In panel (a), there is an upward trend, just as in panel (e) and panel (f). But unlike panel (f), where there is an immediate impact, in panel (a) the impact is gradual. There, the program has no immediate impact, but only a gradual one. The impact of the program appears only to effect a change in the slope. The slope b changes in magnitude, but its level or intercept a does not change. If we expect such a model as shown in panel (a), we should estimate the following regression equation:

$$Y_t = a + b'X_tT_t + cT_t + e_t. \tag{5.2}$$

This equation differs from the previous Equation (5.1) only in the representation of the program variable. The program variable is now multiplied by the trend variable. The product (X_tT_t) will be a vector

Figure 5.2 **Pictures of Possible Outcomes Using the SITS Design**

(a) Impact on Slope: Upward Trend; Gradual Impact

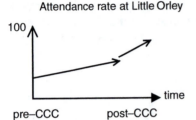

(d) No Impact: No Trend, No Impact

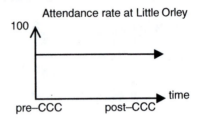

(b) Impact on Slope and Intercept: Downward Trend, Immediate Impact, Reversal of Trend

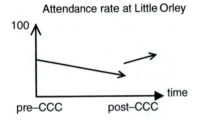

(e) No Impact: Upward Trend, No Impact

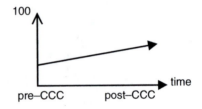

(c) Impact on Intercept: No Trend, Immediate Impact

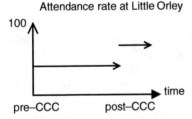

(f) Impact on Intercept: Upward Trend, Immediate Impact

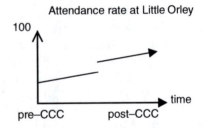

of zeros for all the preprogram months because $X_t = 0$ for those months. That same product (X_tT_t) will be a vector of the month numbers for all the postprogram months because $X_t = 1$ for those months.

How did we get this representation? Begin with the basic model equation (5.1). That simple model will not represent the process pictured in panel (a), where the program has only a gradual impact, changing the underlying slope. In the basic model of Equation (5.1), the program impact is sudden. In the modified model of Equation (5.2), the program impact is not sudden. Rather, its impact is on the underlying trend. Before the program, there is an underlying trend; after it is implemented, the program shifts the trend. So we can say that program impact, represented by coefficient b from the original equation (5.1), depends on the month of the observation: $b = b'T_t$. Substituting this into the basic equation (5.1) gives us the result (5.2). Specifically,

$$Y_t = a + bX_t + cT_t + e_t = a + (b'T_t)X_t + cT_t + e_t = a + b'X_tT_t + cT_t + e_t. \qquad (5.3)$$

For the preprogram months, when $X_t = 0$, the entire second term in the equalities of (5.3) is zero, and the underlying trend is estimated by c, which we hypothesize is positive and significant. For the postprogram months, when $X_t = 1$, assuming that b' is statistically significant, the new trend is $(b' = c)$.[30] The measure of program impact is b', which represents the difference between the pre- and postintervention trend. In this example, the direct impact of the program on Y_t depends on how long the program has been in operation, over the ten months of implementation. In panel (a) of Figure 5.2, and in the corresponding equation, the impact of the program grows as time goes on, at least for the ten months of postprogram data in our study. Thus, the program affects the underlying trend in the outcome, having no direct effect on the level of Y_t.

Neither of these regression models characterizes what is going on in panel (b). In panel (b), we expect that the program has both an immediate impact on the level of Y_t as well as an impact on the direction (or slope) of the trend in Y_t. In that case, we represent our expectation by the following regression:

$$Y_t = a + b_0 X_t + b' X_t T + c T_t + e_t. \tag{5.4}$$

Why this form of the regression model? Start again with the basic regression model (5.1). But now program impact b is expected to affect both the level and the trend of Y_t: $b = b_0 + b'T$, where b_0 is the immediate impact on the level of Y and b' is the gradual impact on the trend. Substituting this into Equation (5.1) yields Equation (5.4). In Equation (5.4), for the preprogram months, when $X_t = 0$, the second and third terms in (5.4) both equal zero, and c, the trend coefficient in the fourth term, represents the underlying preprogram trend, just as it did in (5.1). For the months when the program is in operation and $X_t = 1$, the second and third terms are not expected to be zero. Assuming the coefficients in both terms are significant, then b_0 is the immediate impact of the program X_t on the level of Y_t, while b' represents the impact of the program on the trend of Y_t, or the gradual impact. In effect, this model combines (5.1) and (5.2).

Overall, these SITS designs build internal validity because they do not have a comparison group and therefore are not subject to selection threats. In addition, properly executed, they automatically reduce the threat of maturation by controlling for it statistically.[31] Assuming that a long enough time series of observations is available, so that n is large, they will be relatively robust with respect to statistical validity.

But the SITS design has remaining threats. History and multiple treatments remain potentially important threats to internal validity. For example, events other than the CCC intervention (e.g., a new principal) can account for the observed results. If that event occurred at a different time than the intervention itself, it would be an example of a history threat. In that case, it may be possible to reduce that threat by creating an additional dummy variable for the event, so that the dummy variable (e.g., separating the old from the new principal) is 0 before the event and 1 afterward. Adding this dummy variable (call it variable P_t) to any of the regression models above allows the evaluator to separate the impact of the extraneous event (P_t) from the impact of the policy intervention (the inception of the CCC program, represented by variable X_t) that is the focus of study.

However, suppose that the extraneous event is temporally very close to the inception of the focal program, happening at nearly the same time. Then, it may not be possible to separate the extraneous event from the one under study. They will be collinear, so, together, neither will be statistically significant. Moreover, adding more variables to any of the regression models, without adding more observations, may reduce the degrees of freedom for hypothesis testing, consequently challenging the model's statistical validity. If the extraneous event happens at exactly the same time as the intervention (e.g., the CCC program and the new principal arrive during the same month), it will not be possible to separate these two events. This is an example of a multiple treatment threat. It is not clear that there is a straightforward remedy to this threat, at least using the SITS design.

Nor is there a straightforward remedy to the threat that the estimated impact coefficient is merely a regression artifact, which is the tendency of extreme scores to return to their normal value. For instance, suppose that the CCC program was adopted because of an extremely poor attendance rate in the months just before its inception; the score is likely to return to normal anyway. The dummy variable marking the adoption of the program is also marking the extreme score, and they will not be separable. As another example, suppose that an anticrime program is adopted because of an extremely high crime rate in the neighborhood or that an antipollution program is adopted at a time of extremely high air pollution. In my neighborhood, a mini–crime wave (one rape and one attempted break-in) elicited a neighborhood watch team and more frequent police patrols. When the crime rate immediately dropped to its usual level of zero, the police and the neighbors congratulated themselves on the effectiveness of their efforts.

In all these cases, the program is inseparable from and collinear with the extreme score, which, by chance, is likely to return to its usual level. The best way to reduce this threat is to have a reliable instrument for measuring the outcome that, by definition, is relatively free of random error. Multi-item instruments (such as a crime index or a multi-item pollution index) may be particularly advantageous in this situation. Using monthly rather than daily data, or yearly rather than monthly data, is another way to "smooth" the measure, reducing random error in indicators. This advantage, however, may come at the cost of a smaller number of observations, reducing statistical validity: An extreme score in the context of a large number of observations will not have much of an effect. Using difference scores may also mitigate the problem.

Instrumentation remains a threat to the SITS design as well; the evaluator needs to ensure that the measurement instrument has not changed during the study. If the instrument did change, it will be necessary to document that change by including the date of change on the right side of the regression as a dummy equaling 0 for the time periods before the change and 1 after it. If the instrument change accompanies the inception of the program, then the two cannot be disentangled; they are hopelessly collinear. If the instrument change is temporally separate from the inception of the program, adding a variable to mark the time of the change in the measurement instrument to the equation may reduce the statistical validity of impact estimates by reducing degrees of freedom and possibly increasing collinearity, even as it improves internal validity. Nonetheless, statistically controlling for an instrument change by including it as a pre-/post-dummy variable in the regression may be a practical way to reduce the threat of instrumentation changes, which are common in TS data.[32]

Related to the issue of measurement, all designs, including SITS, should ascertain that the measurement procedure, whether or not it changes during the course of the study, is as valid and reliable as possible. For example, using an index consisting of the sum of multiple items to represent a complex outcome Y_t (e.g., the overall performance of charter schools relative to public schools in the same district, measured over time) may enhance reliability and thus reduce statistical error. But it may actually harm internal validity if the overall construct validity of the measure is poor. If the index measure of Y_t does not measure what it purports to measure, then the estimate of the impact of an intervention X_t (e.g., a change in the procedure for approving charter schools) on Y_t will be invalid.

Finally, the external validity of the SITS is probably its weakest characteristic. For example, in the case of the imaginary CCC program, we can generalize the results from the SITS design only to Little Orley, the school that is under study. If the sponsor of the CCC program at Little Orley is the audience for the study, then that limited degree of external validity may be sufficient for the evaluation. Nonetheless, it is often practicable to replicate the design in numerous sites to extend its external validity. As an example, investigators have used the SITS design in many different cities to study the impact of community policing initiatives in each city that adopts it. When results from separate sites converge to a single picture, it may be possible to general-ize about the overall impact of community policing programs.[33] If the results do not converge, researchers may use a meta-analysis to try to explain why they estimate different outcomes in different sites.[34]

Adding a comparison group to this design may reduce the threat of history or multiple treatments that often plagues the SITS design. For example, what if other things, besides the implementation of the CCC program, are occurring in the school district? Suppose there is a new superintendent? Or expanded use of teachers' aides? Or a new reading curriculum? What if these, or other, changes coincide with the new CCC program? Then we might want to use, along with the time series of attendance data for Little Orley, a coinciding time series of the same information for a school that is just like Little Orley and is experiencing many of the same sorts of changes, but it does not have the CCC program. In that case, we would select a different quasi-experimental design, the interrupted time-series comparison-group (ITSCG) design, the next topic.

THE INTERRUPTED TIME-SERIES COMPARISON GROUP (ITSCG) DESIGN

This design, shown in row 2, column 2, of Table 5.1, has multiple preprogram $(Y_{t-j}, Y_{t-(j+1)} \ldots Y_{t-1})$ and postprogram $(Y_t, Y_{t+1} \ldots Y_T)$ measurements of the outcome in the treatment school (or class-room) and also multiple measures at the same point in time for one comparison school (or class-room). There may be multiple comparison groups, as there are in Table 5.1.[35] Like the PTPTCG design, the ITSCG design uses both comparison across groups (as in a CS design) and comparison over time (as in a TS design). But unlike the PTPTCG design, the ITSCG design has multiple pre- and posttest observations, so there is a full time series in the treatment group, which experiences the intervention, and in the comparison group, which experiences a different intervention or none at all. There may also be multiple groups (i.e., multiple cross-sections).

If there is program impact, one expects an alteration (in the intended direction) of the TS data after the program is in operation in the treatment group. There should be no such alteration of the data in the comparison group (or groups), where the focal program is not in operation. In the con-text of our example, Big Worm might be a comparison school for Little Orley, the focal treatment group. The graphs for this ITSCG design might look like one of the three panels in Figure 5.3. (These examples are not exhaustive.) All are consistent with the hypothesis of program impact, but the process of impact is different in each graph.

ITSCG Designs: Pictures

In panel (a) of Figure 5.3, there is an underlying trend in both groups and an immediate impact in the treatment group. Having the comparison group is useful because it helps to rule out extraneous events. For example, if both Little Orley and Big Worm are in the same school district, then both schools are subject to the same districtwide events. Assume that only Little Orley implemented the CCC program. Then districtwide events, such as a new superintendent or an infusion of class-room aides, which affect both schools, can be ruled out as threats to the conclusion that Little Orley's CCC program was effective in boosting attendance. In panel (b), the program impact is gradual, affecting the underlying trend of the outcome measure. In panel (c), the program has both an immediate and a gradual impact over time, affecting both the level and the trend in the outcome measure.

ITSCG Designs: Regression Models

Basic regression continues to serve as the statistical model for this design. Let Y_{it} be the outcome measure for every time period ($t = 1 \ldots T$) in both groups ($i = 1 \ldots K$). In the example, Y_{it} = attendance rates in both Little Orley ($i = 1$) and Big Worm ($i = 2$), measured for the same sixty-month period ($t = 1 \ldots 60$) in both schools. The total number of observations in this study is $n = K * T = 120$. Let X_{it} be a dummy variable for the CCC program. It is 0 for all sixty monthly observations for Big Worm, which is the comparison group. It is 0 for the first fifty months of observations for Little Orley, the treatment school. After Little Orley implements the CCC program, the value of X_{it} becomes 1. There is a clear trend, which, if uncontrolled, would threaten the internal validity of any conclusions. We continue to measure the trend with a monthly variable, T_{it}, which counts the months, and is scored from 1 to 60 for Little Orley and the same way for Big Worm. Both schools are subject to the same districtwide changes, and we control for them by including Big Worm in the analysis. Represent Big Worm with a dummy variable, BW_{it}, coded 1 for all the observations associated with that school and 0 for all the observations associated with Little Orley. This dummy variable allows us to separate the CCC event, unique to Little Orley, from the impact of other districtwide events that are common to both schools. In addition, including a comparison school in the analysis doubles the number of observations from 60 to 120, improving statistical as well as (possibly) internal validity.

For panel (a) of Figure 5.3, where the impact of the CCC program on the level of Y_{it} is expected to be sudden, the regression is:

$$Y_{it} = a + bX_{it} + cT_{it} + dBW_{it} + e_{it}. \tag{5.5}$$

The estimated coefficient b represents the immediate impact of the CCC program in Little Orley, controlling for the underlying upward trend (T) in attendance rates that are common to the district and for the events that are unique to Big Worm, represented by the dummy variable BW. Coefficient c is the underlying trend, and d is the impact of factors unique to Big Worm, represented by the dummy variable for Big Worm, which is in the same district as Little Orley.

In panel (b), the impact of the program is expected to be gradual, affecting only the underlying growth rate in Y_{it}. The regression model now resembles that for the corresponding SITS design, with the addition of the control for the comparison group:

$$Y_{it} = a + b'X_{it}T_{it} + cT_{it} + dBW_{it} + e_{it}. \tag{5.6}$$

In this model, when $X_{it} = 0$, c represents the upward trend in both Little Orley before the CCC program and in Big Worm. While the level of attendance may be different between the two schools (represented by coefficient d), c is the slope of the trend, representing the average increase in attendance rates for each additional month for the two schools before program implementation in Little Orley. But after the program is implemented in Little Orley, when $X_{it} = 1$, the trend shifts from c to $(c + b')$ in Little Orley; the trend remains c in Big Worm. Thus, b' represents the impact of the program, but it is important to interpret this properly as the gradual impact of the program on the underlying trend of Y_{it}.

Figure 5.3   **Diagrams of Possible Outcomes From the ITSCG**

(a) Attendance rate

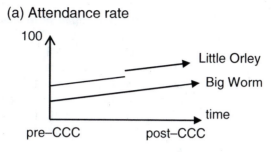

pre–CCC   post–CCC

(b) Attendance rate

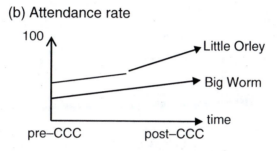

pre–CCC   post–CCC

(c) Attendance rate

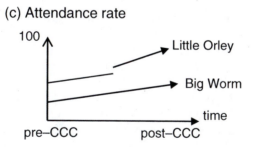

pre–CCC   post–CCC

Similarly, the regression for panel (c), where the impact of the program is expected to be both immediate and gradual, also resembles that for the corresponding SITS design, with the addition of the control for Big Worm. As before, Big Worm represents characteristics unique to the comparison school. The new equation is:

$$Y_{it} = a + b_0 X_{it} + b' X_{it} T_{it} + c T_{it} + dBW_{it} + e_{it}. \qquad (5.7)$$

If $X_{it} = 0$, then c is the underlying trend. When $X_{it} = 1$ (i.e., the CCC program has commenced in Little Orley), there are two possible effects, estimated by $(b_0 + b'T)$. One is the immediate impact of X_{it} on the level of Y_{it}, estimated by b_0. The remaining component is the gradual impact on the underlying trend, represented by the additional increment in Y_{it} for each passing month during which the program is in operation, b'.

It is important to note what the dummy for Big Worm does to strengthen the internal validity of this model. It controls not only for the unmeasured factors in the school district that are common to both Big Worm and Little Orley, but it also controls for unobserved differences between Big Worm and Little Orley that might explain why the attendance rates are different between the schools, yet have nothing to do with the primary program difference between the schools. In other words, adding comparison groups to a SITS design and then controlling for the unobserved characteristics of these groups by including a dummy variable in the model is a simple way to reduce the threat of confounding variables, even when they cannot be measured. This kind of dummy variable is called a fixed effect. Added to the bargain are the extra observations that the comparison group brings, increasing statistical validity, relative to the single interrupted time series. When the comparison group is very similar to the treatment group, the use of the comparison group is particularly effective. For example, some studies use age as a natural experiment that induces treatment differences: Often nineteen- and twenty-year-olds are not subject to the law (e.g., a minimum legal drinking age), while eighteen-year-olds are subject to the law, creating a good comparison group.[36]

More test and comparison groups may help, especially when comparison by natural experiment is not feasible. When there are multiple comparison groups with TS data on each one, the design becomes a multiple comparison-group design or a panel design. I discuss this variation of the ITSCG design next.[37]

THE MULTIPLE COMPARISON-GROUP TIME-SERIES DESIGN

The multiple comparison-group TS design usually has more than two comparison groups, each with outcomes measured over a period of time. One subset of groups within the set of comparable groups may have received the treatment, while another subset has not. Often, all groups receive the treatment, but some receive it earlier than others. Sometimes, all receive treatment, but each subset of comparison groups receives a different level or type of treatment at some point during the time series. However, no matter how many comparison groups there are, the overall set of test and comparison groups should still be roughly comparable to one another with respect to values on confounding Z variables.

In the example, the schools should all be in the same district. But the schools need not be perfectly homogeneous in other respects. In the two-group ITSCG design, we selected Big Worm and Little Orley because they are apparently homogeneous. Including the BW dummy in the model recognizes that the schools are not likely to be identical in all respects, except for the presence of the CCC program. In the multiple comparison-group (interrupted) TS design, we would select all the schools in the same district. They operate with the same political and administrative bosses and with the same overall budget, in the same state, and with the same weather conditions, which might affect attendance rates. And school districts are often relatively homogeneous with respect to demographic characteristics.[38] In that way, we hold many possibly confounding Z variables constant, but not all.

Even though the schools are in the same district, they are not completely homogeneous. We control for the unobserved differences in the schools by representing each one as a dummy variable and including it in the regression. In other words, the multiple group TS (or panel) design includes a time series of output or outcome scores for each (treatment or experimental) school in the district with the CCC program and for each (comparison) school without. Such a design is one type of time-series, cross-section (TSCS) design.

In the context of the CCC program at Little Orley, suppose that we want to use all the primary schools in the district as comparison schools, not just Big Worm. Suppose further that there are ten primary schools in addition to Little Orley. Little Orley is the only school with the CCC program in the district. We now have eleven schools and sixty months of data for each school, resulting in 660 observations. We then form ten dummy variables, one for each comparison school. Each comparison group is now represented by a separate, fixed-effect, dummy variable. Each dummy variable for school i is a column of 660 school-by-month observations scored 1 when the months stand for school i and 0 when the months stand for the other schools. However, there should be no dummy variable for Little Orley, the treatment school. There is also a treatment dummy variable X_{it} that equals 1 for the ten months of treatment at Little Orley and 0 for the remaining fifty months of nontreatment at Little Orley and 0 for the sixty school-months in each of the nontreatment schools. We also include a trend variable T_{it}, whose values range from 1 to 60 for each time period, but is constant for all $i = 1 \ldots 11$ schools. (The next chapter clarifies what the data and variables in this TSCS design look like.) The full equation (assuming here only an immediate impact and no interaction with the trend, meaning no gradual impact) is:

$$Y_{it} = a + bX_{it} + cT_{it} + d_1D1_{it} + d_2D2_{it} + \ldots + d_{10}D10_{it} + e_{it}. \tag{5.8}$$

The set of fixed-effect dummy variables $D1$ to $D10$ represents all the factors (known and unknown) that distinguish the school with the program (Little Orley) from those without the program.[39] Consequently, using a set of fixed-effect dummy variables adds to the internal validity of any comparison-group design. By adding more observations, the multiple comparison-group design augments statistical validity as well. In this example, which assumes eleven primary schools and sixty months of data, all from one school district, the total number of observations is eleven schools (or comparison groups) times 60 months, or 660 units of analysis, which is clearly ample for statistical validity.

But TSCS designs have their own limitations. One drawback of any TSCS design such as this is that it may reduce statistical validity by introducing nonindependent and nonidentically distributed observations. These mar standard hypothesis tests, but they are also remediable if appropriate statistical methods are used. Further, in real life, compared with an example, when evaluating the effect of public program implementation in different localities, it is often very difficult to find many similar or highly comparable observations. Consequently, additional statistical controls, beyond the use of dummy variables, is necessary.[40] Chapter 6 discusses these issues.

SUMMARY OF QUASI-EXPERIMENTAL DESIGN

There are many kinds of QE designs. Some compare by using groups with and without the treatment or treatments, while others compare by examining the same group before and after the inception of treatment. While no one QE is inherently more internally valid than another, there are two that are clearly inferior. One is the QE with one posttest and only one group. This is a design with no comparison; without comparison, impact assessment is not possible. The second is the TS QE with only two points of comparison. In this design, there is one group, composed of members, each with one pretest observation before the treatment and one posttest observation after the treatment. This design, the PTPT, is only conditionally inferior. It is particularly weak when testing effects are likely or when maturation or trends are likely. While the first condition is not ubiquitous, the second probably is. The remaining designs remain widely useful, and the challenge for the evaluator is to realize the options available in any particular application. Frequently, it is possible to use more than one design at a time. If two different designs, each of which is subject to different threats to internal validity, reveal consistent estimates of program impact, then the validity of the estimate is more defensible than it would be if only one QE is used.

Evaluators need to push themselves to think about design possibilities. If a posttest-only (PTCG) design seems easiest at first, the evaluator should first consider if a natural experiment would be possible. If there is no obvious natural experiment, the evaluator should consider if pretest scores are available. If they are, then he should pick the PTPTCG along with (or instead of) the PTCG. Maybe a time series of pre- and posttest scores is available for the treatment group only; if so, he can add the SITS design to his toolbox for that application. Often, changing the unit of analysis (e.g., from schools to students or the reverse; from office sites to individuals working within each site or the reverse; from units of people to units of time or the reverse) can open up new design options. Another way to think of evaluations is to consider not what happens when programs begin, but to evaluate what happens when they stop.

The logic of QE design is to use multiple designs. The responsibility of the evaluator is to make full use of the QE tool kit, even to invent new designs. But it is important to realize that QE designs, especially the cross-section QE designs, still suffer from selection threats. With the possible exception of the natural experiments, the QE is not equivalent to the RFE in respect to internal validity. Even the best QE designs, including the multiple comparison-group design with fixed effects (ITSCG, with multiple groups) and the natural experiment PTCG design, use statistical controls. With statistical controls, they become indistinguishable from the NE design, to which we turn in Chapter 6.

BASIC CONCEPTS

Basic characteristics of the QE
    Types of comparison: CS or TS
    Selection of comparable groups
Types of QE designs
    Inferior designs
        PT only (one group)
        PTPT
    CS design: PTCG
    TS design: SITS
    Mixed TSCS designs:
        PTPTCG
        ITSCG
        TSCS
PTCG design
    Diagram or picture
    Equation and coefficient to estimate impact
        Two groups (treatment and comparison, or two comparison groups)
        More than two groups
    Threats to validity
    The PTCG natural experiment
        Waiting lists
        Lotteries
        Birthdays
        Cut-points (regression discontinuity design)
        Seemingly random selection

PTPTCG design (nonequivalent control group)
    Diagram or picture
    Equation and coefficient to estimate impact
       Two groups (treatment and comparison or two-comparison groups)
       More than two groups
    The causal model and selection threats
    Threats to validity
SITS design
    Diagrams or pictures
    Equations and coefficient to estimate impact
    Threats to validity
ITSCG design
    Diagrams or pictures
    Equations and coefficient to estimate impact
    Threats to validity
Multiple comparison-group time-series design (TSCS)
    Equation and coefficient to estimate impact
    Threats to validity

DO IT YOURSELF

Design a *feasible* QE to evaluate the effectiveness of an ongoing policy or program or management alternative (or to compare the relative effectiveness of two or more ongoing alternatives). Describe

1. the alternative(s) you are examining
2. the outcome measure(s) you will use
3. the particular type of QE design
4. the statistical controls that may be necessary to improve internal validity
5. the data you will collect
6. the statistical model you will use that corresponds to your design; and
7. then identify the coefficient (or coefficients) in that model that estimates program impact

Indicate why you are choosing that particular type of QE. The description of the QE should be detailed enough so that your strategy for obtaining internal, external, and statistical validity and measurement reliability and validity will be evident. Your design should be feasible. The data should be data that are routinely collected by others and are publicly available, or data that you (and others) can reasonably be expected to collect.

Next, consider whether another type of QE is embedded in your original QE. (For example, a SITS design is embedded in an ITSCG.) Write the statistical model for that design and identify the coefficient that estimates program impact. If no other QE is embedded in your original design, develop a feasible companion QE that accomplishes the same evaluation. Write the statistical model for that design, and identify the coefficient that estimates program impact.

Evaluate each design in terms of likely threats to its overall validity. In your example, why is using two designs better than one alone, or is there no particular advantage to using two designs in your example?

NOTES

1. Shadish also stresses the use of multiple designs as an important principle of the QE. He advises multiple analyses (and multiple outcome measures). If the results are stable and are not sensitive to different assumptions about designs, comparisons, and measures, then the results' overall defensibility is enhanced. See William R. Shadish, "The Empirical Program of Quasi-Experimentation," in *Research Design: Donald Campbell's Legacy,* vol. 2, ed. Leonard Bickman (Thousand Oaks, CA: Sage, 2002), ch. 2.

2. Lumpy Brannum, *Little Orley: His Adventures as a Worm* (New York: Decca, 1950).

3. Damodar N. Gujarati and Dawn C. Porter, *Basic Econometrics*, 5th ed. (Boston: McGraw Hill, 2009), 246–248.

4. Shadish, "Empirical Program," lists the selection of internal rather than external controls as the first in his list of general principles of QE. That is, it is best to select comparison groups from within the same district, village, county, state, or country to minimize the impact of external, contextual differences as threats to internal validity. Thomas Pluemper, Vera E. Troeger, and Eric Newmayer, in "Case Selection and Causal Inference in Qualitative Research" (April 27, 2010), http://ssrn.com/abstract=1439868/ (accessed July 28, 2011), argue that matching works best when cases are similar on multiple confounding variables (but not necessarily the pretest value of Y); it is also important to have maximum variation in X and to ensure that the confounding variables Z_k on which cases are matched are not hopelessly correlated with the focal variable, X. Such a strategy also suggests a critical role for comparison case studies in evaluation research or comparison of similar units within a larger "case." I do not view the case study as a special type of research design outside of those considered in this text; rather, case studies are almost always types of comparison group quasi experiments. See John Gerring, "What Is a Case Study and What Is It Good For?" *American Political Science Review* 98, no. 2 (2004): 341–354. See also the discussion on the use of in-depth studies of a single case site as a method for controlled comparison to understand causal inferences in Jasjeet S. Sekhon, "Quality Meets Quantity: Case Studies, Conditional Probability, and Counterfactuals," *Perspectives on Politics* 2, no. 2 (2004): 281–289. Luke Keele and William Minozzi, in "How Much Is Minnesota Like Wisconsin? States as Counterfactuals" (presented at American Political Science Association Annual Meeting, September 2010; available at ssrn.com/abstract=1643236) point out that states are actually poor counterfactuals and argue for within-state comparison. The following discussion of the single interrupted time series can also be regarded as an example of the case study, with comparison of the same unit over a time period before and after the intervention. In this view, most QEs that rely on internal controls (i.e., selection of comparable units within a single case) can be regarded as types of comparison case studies.

5. For an example of a PTCG design that selects groups thought to be comparable on numerous Z-type variables but also uses statistical methods to control for other Z-type variables, see Laura Langbein, "Responsive Bureaus, Equity, and Regulatory Negotiation: An Empirical View," *Journal of Policy Analysis and Management* 21, no. 3 (2002): 449–466.

6. As another example of a lottery at a cut-point, consider how training is allotted to unemployment insurance (UI) claimants who have a high probability of exhausting their benefits. UI claimants who have a high probability of exhausting their benefits are forced to take job training as a requirement for receiving continued benefits. But there is a capacity constraint in the number of training slots that are allocated to these clients. The UI program uses a 1–20 profile score of UI claimants that predicts each claimant's likely duration of unemployment. If 16 is the cut-point that separates the long-term claimants from the others, and if, in a given quarter, there are fifty with that score but only ten slots remain, then the slots can be allotted randomly to claimants in any one round. Over multiple rounds, the reemployment difference (Y_i) between those at the cut-point who "win" the training lottery ($X_i = 1$) can be compared with those at the cut-point who lose it ($X_i = 0$), using a "natural" experiment that approximates the RFE. See Dan A. Black, Jeffrey A. Smith, Mark C. Berger, and Brett J. Noel, "Is the Threat of Reemployment Services More Effective than the Services Themselves? Evidence from Random Assignment in the UI System," *American Economic Review* 93, no. 4 (2003): 1313–1327. The Vietnam War draft lottery in the United States assigned draft numbers randomly and provides another example of a lottery as a natural experiment; various studies compare "winners" (with high numbers, who were not drafted) to "losers" (with low numbers) with respect to the impact of the draft on political attitudes, smoking, and future schooling and earnings. See Robert S. Erikson and Laura Stoker, "Caught in the Draft: The Effects of Vietnam Draft Lottery Status on Political Attitudes," *American Political Science Review* 105, no. 2 (2011): 221–237; Daniel Eisenberg and Brian Rowe, "The Effect of Smoking in Young Adulthood on Smoking Later in Life: Evidence Based on the Vietnam Era Draft Lottery," *Forum for Health Economics and Policy* 12, no. 2 (2009), Article 4 (www.bepress.com/fhep/12/2/4/); Joshua D. Angrist

and Stacey H. Chen, "Schooling and the Vietnam-Era GI Bill: Evidence from the Draft Lottery," *American Economic Journal: Applied Economics* 3, no. 2(April 2011): 96–118; Sebastian Galiani, Martin A. Rossi, and Ernesto Schargrodsky, "Conscription and Crime: Evidence from the Argentine Draft Lottery," *American Economic Journal: Applied Economics* 3, no. 2 (2011): 119–136.

7. Scott E. Carrell, Teny Maghakian, and James E. West, "A's from Zzzz's: The Causal Effect of School Start Time on the Academic Achievement of Adolescents," *American Economic Journal: Economic Policy* 3, no. 3 (2011): 62–81. Random assignment (by the Academy, not the researchers) makes the causal claim that a late start improves achievement credible.

8. This information is available at the official Web site of the Social Security Administration, "Social Security Fact Sheet: Increase in Retirement Age," www.ssa.gov/pressoffice/IncRetAge.html. See also Richard Morin, "Undepressing Findings About Retirement," *Washington Post*, July 9, 2002.

9. For example, Susan M. Dynarski, "Does Aid Matter? Measuring the Effect of Student Aid on College Attendance and Completion," *American Economic Review* 93, no. 1 (2003): 279–288.

10. William J. Gormley Jr. and Deborah Phillips, "The Effects of Universal Pre-K in Oklahoma: Research Highlights and Policy Implications," *Policy Studies Journal* 33, no. 1 (2005): 65–82.

11. Bruce D. Meyer, W. Kip Viscusi, and David L. Durbin, "Workers' Compensation and Injury Duration: Evidence from a Natural Experiment," *American Economic Review* 85, no. 3 (1995): 322–340; Jere R. Behrman, Mark R. Rosenzweig, and Paul Taubman, "Endowments and the Allocation of Schooling in the Family and in the Marriage Market: The Twins Experiment," *Journal of Political Economy* 102, no. 6 (1994): 1131–1174; Paul Miller, Charles Mulvey, and Nick Martin, "Family Characteristics and the Returns to Schooling: Evidence on Gender Differences from a Sample of Australian Twins," *Economica* 64, no. 253 (1997): 119–136; Heather Royer, "Separated at Girth: U.S. Twin Estimates of the Effects of Birth Weight," *American Economic Journal: Applied Economics* 1, no. 1 (2009): 49–85 (which looks at impact of birthweight differences between twins on academic achievement and other outcomes).

12. Christopher Carpenter and Carlos Dobkin, in "The Effect of Alcohol Consumption on Mortality: Regression Discontinuity Evidence from the Minimum Drinking Age," *American Economic Journal: Applied Economics* 1, no. 1 (2009): 164–182, compare drinking and driving behavior of nineteen- to twenty-three-year-olds, using a cut-point at twenty-one, which is the minimum legal age. Victor Lavy, in "Performance Pay and Teachers' Effort, Productivity and Grading Ethics," *American Economic Review* 99, no. 5 (2009): 1979–2011, uses random measurement error in the variable that was used to assign teachers to performance pay (or fixed pay) on teacher effectiveness. For an extended, practical discussion of the regression discontinuity (cut-point) design, see David S. Lee and Thomas Lemieux, "Regression Discontinuity Designs in Economics," *Journal of Economic Literature* 48, no. 2 (2010): 281–355. They find that the RDD approximates the RFE when the comparison is very close to the cut-point and when neither subjects nor administrators can manipulate the assignment. For example, it is likely that random measurement error (RME) in the assignment variable is not manipulable.

13. Vijayendra Rao et al., "Sex Workers and the Cost of Safe Sex: The Compensating Differential for Condom Use Among Calcutta Prostitutes," *Journal of Development Economics* 71, no. 2 (2003): 585–603.

14. See Thad Dunning, "Improving Causal Inference: Strengths and Limitations of Natural Experiments" (paper presented at the annual meeting of the American Political Science Association, Washington, DC, August 31–September 5, 2005). Some examples of posttest comparison-group designs that also embed natural experiments are in Mark R. Rosenzweig and Kenneth I. Wolpin, "Natural 'Natural Experiments' in Economics," *Journal of Economic Literature* 38, no. 4 (2000): 827–874; and Harry J. Holzer, John M. Quigley, and Steven Raphael, "Public Transit and the Spatial Distribution of Minority Employment: Evidence from a Natural Experiment," *Journal of Policy Analysis and Management* 22, no. 3 (2003): 415–441. Another natural experiment is to compare the obesity rate of children whose schools are less than .1 mile from a fast food restaurant to that of children whose school are between .1 and .25 miles from a fast food restaurant; while restaurants may try to locate near schools, the location within a quarter-mile radius is assumed to be random. The hypothesis is that closeness raises obesity; the results supported the hypothesis (for children, not parents). See Janet Currie, Stefano Della Vigna, Enrico Moretti, and Vikram Pathania, "The Effect of Fast Food Restaurants on Obesity and Weight Gain," *American Economic Journal: Economic Policy* 2, no. 3 (2010): 32–63.

15. Even the natural experiment is weaker than a well-designed and successfully implemented RFE. While it is stronger in resisting selection threats than most PTCG designs, it still may need to be supplemented with the same kinds of remedies that apply to the normal PTCG, including statistical controls. However, there is also evidence that a well-designed simple PTCG design (especially with careful matching on pretest scores) or a well-designed "cut-point" natural experiment (also regarded as a regression discontinuity design)

produces the same results as a well-designed RFE. See Thomas D. Cook, William R. Shadish, and Vivian C. Wong, "Three Conditions Under Which Experiments and Observational Studies Produce Comparable Causal Estimates: New Findings from Within Study Comparisons," *Journal of Policy Analysis and Management* 27, no. 4 (2008): 724–750.

16. "Stable" means that the scores contain little RME. It follows that scores with little RME are likely to be measures of outcome states (e.g., pass or fail, employed or unemployed, pregnant or not) rather than outcome quantities (e.g., test scores, days employed, amount of risky behavior).

17. In this example, since the outcome is a dichotomy, it would be appropriate to use logistic regression. The logic is identical to ordinary regression, though the interpretation of the regression coefficient as an odds ratio is slightly different than in an ordinary regression. Logit regressions also produce predicted probabilities, making it possible to compare the probability of different outcomes depending on different treatments, when other confounding variables are held constant at some specified value. Most texts on regression explain regression of qualitative dependent variables.

18. For a general defense of the importance of pretest scores to increase the internal validity of comparison-group designs, see Tricia A. Seifert, Ernest T. Pascarella, Sherri I. Erkel, and Kathleen M. Goodman, "The Importance of Longitudinal Pretest-Posttest Designs in Estimating College Impact," *New Directions for Institutional Research* (Winter 2010): 5–16.

19. The *t*-test for the difference of means in this case would be for nonindependent samples, since the pretest difference is not independent of the posttest difference.

20. Paul Allison, "Change Scores as Dependent Variables in Regression Analysis," *Sociological Methodology* 20 (1990): 93–114.

21. For a variety of reasons, and under many (but not all) circumstances, the estimate of the coefficient c, which is the estimated coefficient of a lagged endogenous (or dependent) variable, is internally valid only if n is large. This would be troubling if our central concern were dynamics and rates of partial adjustment in Y_i from pretest to posttest. However, in the context of this text, the central focus is on the coefficient of X, the program variable. There appears to be general agreement that, in the case of the PTPTCG design represented by Equation (1), where the pretest has a causal effect on the posttest, the gains from including a lagged endogenous variable (when it is causal) outweigh the costs. See Peter Kennedy, *A Guide to Econometrics*, 5th ed. (Cambridge, MA: MIT Press, 2003), 313.

22. Gujarati and Porter, *Basic Econometrics*, 246–248.

23. Because the analysis would be based only on students who remain in the school for both the pre- and posttest, external validity may be reduced. The reduction would not be very great if the school enrollment is relatively stable.

24. Leonard Bickman and Karl M. Hamner, "An Evaluation of the Yad Vashem Holocaust Museum," *Evaluation Review* 22, no. 4 (1998): 435–446. Another example of a one-group pretest–posttest study is H. Liu, Z. Hu, X. Li, B. Stanton, S. Naar-King, and H. Yang, "Understanding Interrelationships Among HIV-Related Stigma, Concern About HIV Infection, and Intent to Disclose HIV Sero-Status: A Pretest–Posttest Study in a Rural Area of Eastern China," *AIDS Patient Care STDS* 20, no. 2 (2006): 133–142.

25. Another solution is to use individual students, rather than school-level data, in a PTPTCG design. At present, the focus is restricted to SITS designs.

26. See Richard D. McCleary, "Evolution of the Time Series Experiment," in *Research Design: Donald Campbell's Legacy,* vol. 2, ed. Leonard Bickman (Thousand Oaks, CA: Sage, 2000), ch. 10. McCleary discusses the origin of the SITS design as "pictures on the wall" or the "time series wall of fame," together with the calculation of pre- and postintervention means. Gradually, researchers recognized that trends and nonindependent observations posed threats to the internal and statistical validity of conclusions based on simple comparison of means. This recognition then led to the development of methods to reduce these threats, some of which I discuss in this chapter and in Chapter 6, on nonexperiments.

27. This text, for simplicity, equates "trend" and "maturation." Note 28 points out that there are different forms of time dependence. In addition, specific fields have developed special techniques to reduce the threat of maturation or trends on outcome scores. In economics, longitudinal or TS studies rely on prices corrected for inflationary trends; they report real prices or constant dollars rather than current dollars. Similarly, in education research that relies on individual or aggregate student scores reported over time, evaluators use scale scores that adjust for children's developmental growth rather than raw scores. But these adjustments are rarely sufficient to remove other sources of the effects of underlying trends that have nothing to do with the measurement procedure. Thus, it is (almost) never wrong to include a trend variable in a TS study, even when outcome measures are adjusted for maturation or inflation.

28. Regression is one approach to the analysis of the impact of interventions in single TS designs. Another approach centers on carefully modeling the underlying process that generates the serially related, time-dependent observations on Y_t before and after an intervention. This is the approach characterized by autoregressive, integrated, moving average (ARIMA) models. More closely related to the simple regression model discussed here is generalized least squares (GLS) regression, which uses a form of ARIMA methods to adjust the basic regression. These adjusted regressions enhance the statistical validity with which simple TS regression estimates the impact of an intervention. Chapter 6 discusses these statistical issues in more depth. For a fuller treatment, see David McDowell, Richard McCleary, Errol E. Meidinger, and Richard A. Hay Jr., *Interrupted Time Series Analysis* (Thousand Oaks, CA: Sage, 1980).

29. Examples of SITS designs that use the simple regression approach include Stephen M. Campbell, David Reeves, Evangelos Kontopantelis, Bonnie Sibbald, and Martin Roland, "Effects of Pay for Performance on the Quality of Primary Care in England," *New England Journal of Medicine* 361 (2009): 368–378, which regresses observations of quality-of-care indicators on a dummy variable that marks the period before and after the introduction of pay for performance in some practices in 2004 in England; and Chris Grundy, Rebecca Steinback, Phil Edwards, Judith Green, Ben Armstrong, and Paul Wilkinson, "Effect of 20 MPH Traffic Speed Zones on Road Injuries in London, 1986–2006: Controlled Interrupted Time Series Analysis," *British Medical Journal* 339 (2009): b4469 (published online December 10, 2009, doi: 10.1136/bmj.b4469), which regresses road injuries on the inception of speed zones, controlling for the underlying downward trend in injuries. John Graham and Steven Garber, in "Evaluating the Effects of Automobile Safety Regulation," *Journal of Policy Analysis and Management* 3, no. 2 (1984): 206–224, use a SITS with many statistical controls (including a trend), finding that auto safety regulations overall saved lives.

30. Regression equation (5.3) represents an instance of statistical interaction, in which the impact of the program depends on the amount of time that it has been in operation. Tests of the statistical significance of separate interactive terms like the (XT) product do not really make sense in a truly interactive model. A more appropriate test of significance in the presence of statistical interaction is described in James Jaccard and Robert Turrisi's *Interaction Effects in Multiple Regression*, 2d ed. (Thousand Oaks, CA: Sage, 2003).

31. Chapter 6 on NEs briefly discusses other ways to control for maturation threats. For example, maturation implies an underlying trend, which means that observations at time t are not independent of observations at $t − 1$. This is a threat to statistical validity. A common method of removing maturation (i.e., an underlying trend) is to use first differences, so instead of using Y_t as the dependent variable, use $(Y_t − Y_{t-1})$. Looking at the one-period difference also helps to reduce the threat of omitted confounding variables that affect the level of Y_t and that are also associated with program assignment. Thus, dealing with the problem of maturation can improve both internal and statistical validity.

32. While this is an easy, cost-effective approach to a difficult problem, it probably is not the most valid approach. Sometimes, when instruments change, it is possible to calibrate the differences between them and to use scores on output and outcome measures that reliably and validly adjust for those differences. But more often, program managers or others change instruments without regard to the problem of developing consistent measures over time. In this case, the dummy variable approach is practical and better than doing nothing.

33. David A. Kessler and Sheila Duncan, "The Impact of Community Policing in Four Houston Neighborhoods," *Evaluation Review* 20, no. 6 (1996): 627–669. The authors' results did not converge to a single picture. For a more recent review of evidence on the same question in the context of the United States, see Michael D. Reisig, "Community and Problem-Oriented Policing," *Crime and Justice* 39, no. 1 (2010): 1–53; for a formal meta-analysis, see David Weisburd, Cody W. Telep, Joshua C. Hinkle, and John E. Eck, "Is Problem-Oriented Policing Effective in Reducing Crime and Disorder," *Criminology and Public Policy* 9, no. 1 (2010): 139–172. However, few of the studies in their analysis are SITS designs; many are RFEs, or ITSCG designs, the topic of the following section.

34. See Chapter 8 on meta-analysis.

35. The intervention need not be at the same time in all groups.

36. David N. Figlio, "The Effect of Drinking Age Laws and Alcohol-Related Crashes: Time Series Evidence from Wisconsin," *Journal of Policy Analysis and Management* 14, no. 4 (1995): 555–566.

37. In general, a panel design has a short time series for each observation (e.g., $T = 5$) and many comparison groups. A multiple comparison-group design (or a time-series, cross-section [TSCS] design) has a longer time series for each observation in the comparison groups. It may have few or many comparison groups.

38. For examples of multiple comparison-group (interrupted) TS (panel) evaluations that study the impact of policy changes within a homogeneous environment and use a minimum of statistical controls, see Laura Langbein and Roseanna Bess, "Sports in School: Source of Amity or Antipathy?" *Social Science Quarterly*

83, no. 2 (2002): 436–454; Laura Langbein and Kim Spotswood-Bright, "Private Governments: The Efficiency and Accountability of Residential Community Associations," *Social Science Quarterly* 85, no. 3 (2004): 640–659. For an example of the same design that compares the impact of immigration on crime in nonhomogeneous cities and reports estimates of impact with only fixed-effects controls, see Kristen Butcher and Anne Morrison Piehl, "Cross-City Evidence on the Relationship Between Immigration and Crime," *Journal of Policy Analysis and Management* 17, no. 3 (1998): 457–493. The article also reports estimates of impact with both fixed-effects and statistical controls. In this example, the statistical controls do nothing to challenge the fixed-effects estimates of impact. As a consequence, the design shows the power of the fixed-effects panel model in overcoming selection threats to internal validity.

39. In this example, there is only one school with the program. If there are, as in this example, eleven schools in the district without CCC, there will be ten dummy variables, one for each school, less one (called the arbitrarily designated reference school). In this example, Little Orley is the reference school. In general, there will be more than one unit of analysis with the focal program. In that case, X_{it} will be 1 for the months of treatment in each of the treatment schools and 0 for the pretreatment months in each of the treatment schools. It will also be 0 for each of the pre- and posttreatment months in each of the nontreatment schools. The program could also be implemented for more years in one school than another.

40. For example, John T. Scholz and Wayne B. Gray, "Can Government Facilitate Cooperation? An Informational Model of OSHA Enforcement," *American Journal of Political Science* 41, no. 3 (1997): 693–717; Wayne B. Gray and Carol Adaire Jones, "Are OSHA Health Inspections Effective? A Longitudinal Study in the Manufacturing Sector," *Review of Economics and Statistics* 73, no. 3 (1991): 504–508; John T. Scholz and Hengfeng Wei, "Regulatory Enforcement in a Federalist System," *American Political Science Review* 80, no. 4 (1986): 1249–1270; H. Abbie Erler, "Legislative Term Limits and State Spending," *Public Choice* 133 (2007): 479–494; Thomas S. Dee and Brian Jacob, "The Impact of No Child Left Behind on Student Achievement," *Journal of Policy Analysis and Management* 30, no. 3 (2011): 418–446, looks at the pattern of student test scores from 1990–2007, comparing test scores in states that previously had similar accountability laws (where No Child Left Behind [NCLB] would be expected to have minimal additional effect) to the same test scores states that had no accountability laws, with controls for state fixed effects. Rather than a time trend, the study uses a dummy for each time period. The focal regression coefficient compares the change in test scores in states that became subject to school accountability law (NCLB) to the change in states that had been subject to school accountability laws during the entire time period.

6

The Nonexperimental Design

Variations on the Multiple Regression Theme

WHAT IS A NONEXPERIMENTAL DESIGN?

Nonexperiments (NEs) include any design that uses statistical controls. Any randomized field experiment (RFE) that uses statistical controls for pretest scores (to improve internal or statistical validity) is partly a nonexperiment, though at its core it remains a randomized experiment. Most of the quasi experiments (QEs) discussed in Chapter 5 also use statistical controls, although, at their core, they use elements of matching comparable groups at one point in time or matching the same group or groups before and after a program change. In these two cases, the line between the NE and the RFE and the line between the NE and the QE is not clear. One would describe these as mixed designs: part RFE and part NE or part QE and part NE.

But many designs are purely nonexperimental. For example, if the program applies to everyone, it will not be possible to compare persons or units who are affected by the program to (comparable) persons who are not; everyone is affected. In the United States, for example, we are all subject to speed limits. We are all subject to some sort of method of registering to vote before we actually cast a vote in state or national elections. We all have access to "free" (taxpayer-supported) public primary and secondary education. Further, these policy "treatments" are laws (i.e., public programs) that have been around for a long time. It would be difficult to examine the impact of these laws (i.e., programs) using some sort of pre/post-design. In such instances, constructing either cross-section or temporal comparison groups is difficult, if not impossible. Instead, evaluators study the impact of variations in the level of programs on an outcome Y (or on a set of outcomes, $Y1$, $Y2$, $Y3$). The variable X defines the program variations or level. X might be the average legal speed limit on four-lane highways in counties in the state of interest (say, New York), and $Y1$ might be the accident rate and $Y2$ the fatality rate. Or X might be the number of physical locations where one can register to vote in each county in a state of interest, and $Y1$ the voting registration rate and $Y2$ the turnout rate. X might include more than one variable, because multiple indicators increase both the reliability and validity of a measure, including policy indicators. For example, to measure the accessibility of voting registration, researchers might use multiple indicators, so $X1$ = number of places and $X2$ = average number of hours that these places are open in each county in New York. In the speed-limit example, $X1$ might be the legal speed limit while $X2$ is the observed speed limit or a measure of resources devoted to enforcing the speed limit. In an education evaluation, the X variable might actually be a set of variables measuring the quantity and quality of resource inputs in each public school in the state's school districts (per-pupil expenditure, teacher-to-student ratio, class size, etc.), and Y might comprise a set of variables measuring student achievement in reading, writing, and math.

In cases like these, which involve "full coverage" programs, constructing comparison groups is difficult or impossible. Instead, evaluators resort to relying entirely on statistical controls to keep groups statistically comparable. When everyone is eligible or potentially affected by a program, it is likely to be difficult or even impossible to find comparable groups with different levels of the program. For example, voting registration facilities are likely to be most prevalent in dense urban areas and in areas where turnout is usually expected to be high (e.g., where the population is highly educated). Thus, searching for two comparable counties, one with many registration locations, and the other, comparable to the first, but with fewer locations, is likely to be fruitless. And even if there were a match, the n might be too small for statistical validity and the match too atypical for external validity. The same is true for speed limits and school resources; the level of the program variable differs because the characteristics of the units differ. Similar (comparable) units do not usually have measurably different levels of public school resources, highway speed limits, or voter registration rules. Thus, the only way to examine the impact of schooling, speed limits, or voter registration rules (the X variable or variables) on relevant outcomes (the Y variable or variables) is to make the groups statistically comparable by simultaneously controlling for a multiplicity of confounding or Z variables. Multiple regression, already the workhorse of the RFE and the QE, remains key to the NE, which relies exclusively on statistical controls.

BACK TO THE BASICS: THE WORKHORSE DIAGRAM

In the typical NE, the theoretical causal model of what we expect to find continues to be the general model used in most QE designs (and in imperfectly implemented RFEs).[1] Figure 6.1 reproduces that model. Y_i in Figure 6.1 is the outcome measure (or set of outcome measures), measured for each of the $i = 1 \ldots n$ observations in the study. X_i is the program indicator; often, it is a measure of the level of the program that is available to each unit of analysis in the study. Treatment variable X may be a 0/1 dichotomous variable if the policy or treatment variable is "present" or "absent," a set of 0/1 dichotomies if the treatment is a set of treatment types, an ordinal scale if the treatment has different levels, or a continuous variable if the treatment has finely defined levels, like spending amounts or number of personnel involved in service delivery. In the case of most NE designs, X is unlikely to be a dichotomy, but it may be. As in other designs, the units of analysis can be individuals or groups of individuals within policy-relevant units of analysis, such as schools, villages, work groups, counties, provinces, or countries.

For instance, one might study the impact of average actual speeds on county highways (X_i, a continuous variable) on fatalities per 10,000 vehicle miles traveled in those counties (Y_i, also continuous) where $i = 1 \ldots n$ counties. Or someone might examine the impact of per pupil spending (the X_i variable) on student outcomes (Y_i), where $i = 1 \ldots n$ schools (or school districts). X_i might also represent an aggregation of indicator variables representing school resources (e.g., an index of per-pupil spending, class size, and other aspects of school resources). Similarly, the student outcome variable Y_i could also represent an aggregate index of indicator variables, not just one indicator alone. For example, it might be an index of achievement scores, daily attendance rates, and graduation rates. As another example, one might wish to evaluate the impact of the ease of voting registration (X_i) in each precinct ($i = 1 \ldots n$ precincts) on voter registration rates (Y_i) in one particular state. But in none of these examples can we simply examine the relation between X_i and Y_i. Self-selection by individuals or selection by politicians

Figure 6.1 **The Causal Model Workhorse Diagram**

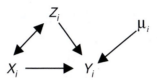

and administrators means that the assignment of the level of X_i is unlikely to be random. As a consequence, the units are unlikely to be comparable on variables that are related to *both* X_i and Y_i. These are the Z_i variables.

For example, speeds (X_i) are likely to be high in counties where there is little traffic (low density) $(Z1_i)$ and where there are many interstates $(Z2_i)$. If a two-variable analysis found that high speeds (X_i) in counties are not associated (or correlated) with higher fatality rates (Y_i), one should not conclude that speed does not kill. Rather, the absence of a relation may be due to the facts that the low-density $(Z1_i)$ counties have high speeds (X_i) and that the high-density counties have low speeds, so $Z1_i$ and X_i are negatively related. Low-density counties may also have lower fatality rates, so $Z1_i$ and Y_i are also related. But the interstates $(Z2_i)$ may predominate in the high-density counties, increasing speeds (X_i) and reducing fatalities (Y_i). How can we disentangle this mess of factors? That is what multiple regression does. Using multiple regression, we control statistically for density $(Z1_i)$ and interstate presence $(Z2_i)$ (and other variables), and then we examine the impact of X_i on Y_i, net of the confounding factors for which we statistically control.

The same is true in the other examples. To examine the impact of specific school resources $(X1_{ij}, X2_{ij}, X3_{ij})$ on an index of student outcomes (summarized by Y_{ij}), it is necessary to control for other factors that relate to both of them. Note the subscripts in this example. The unit of analysis in the example is $i = 1 \ldots n_j$ students; each student attends one of $j = 1 \ldots J$ schools. For example, each student's socioeconomic status needs to be held constant in order to determine if school resources (X_{ij}) affect outcomes (Y_{ij}), independent of the individual resources (the Z_{ij} variables) that each student brings to school. Within each school, we would measure student's individual resources, or socioeconomic status, by the income, education, and occupation of each student's parent(s), the student's race or ethnicity, whether English is spoken at home, whether the student is from a single-parent family, and so on. In the case of voting registration rates, voting registration facilities per person (X_i) might be highest in precincts where voters are educated and older $(Z1_i$ and $Z2_i)$. Older and educated groups of persons are likely voters (Y_i). Evaluators who did not control for the age and education of the voting-age population (the Z_i variables) might conclude that more registration facilities (X_i) result in higher registration rates (Y_i). But such a conclusion could be erroneous, since these groups are the most likely to register (and vote) anyway, regardless of the proximity of registration facilities.

The NE uses statistical controls for these Z_i variables to see if X_i appears to have an impact on Y_i once these confounding variables are held constant. Note that, for internal validity, we do *not* have to control for *all* the things besides X_i that might affect Y_i. It is only necessary to control for Z_i variables that *both* relate to X_i (either because they cause X_i or are caused by X_i) *and* are expected also to affect Y_i. If the variable is expected to affect *only* Y_i, it is necessary to measure it and control for it statistically to increase statistical validity. Controlling for Z_i variables unrelated to X_i and expected to affect only Y_i is not necessary for internal validity.

THE NONEXPERIMENTAL WORKHORSE REGRESSION EQUATION

A simple linear equation (6.1) represents what we expect to find. This equation corresponds to the diagram in Figure 6.1:

$$Y_i = A + BX_i + CZ_i + \mu_i. \tag{6.1}$$

In this equation, Y_i is the outcome value for each observation; X_i is the (set of) values of the program indicators for each observation; and Z_i is the (set of) values of control variables for each observation. As the diagram indicates, the relevant control variables are variables that are likely to affect Y_i *and* that are also likely to be related in some way (direction not known) to the (set of) program variables X_i. The parameters (i.e., what we expect to find, if our theory is true; we do not observe parameters) are represented by the uppercase letters A, B, and C.[2] The intercept is A; it is the value of Y_i that we would *expect* to observe if both X_i and Z_i had values of 0. In many cases, we have no expectation about this value; it is just a benchmark that allows us to scale the other parameters and is usually not of any particular interest. But sometimes, especially when zero values of X_i (and Z_i) are of particular interest, the A term may be important. The discussion that follows does not focus on the intercept.[3]

The key theoretical parameter is B, the value that stands for what we expect the program to do.[4] For example, we expect education programs to improve academic and other outcomes, and we expect that more education resources (X_i) will result in better outcomes (Y_i), even when other factors (Z_i) are held constant. We expect that job training will improve wages and employment opportunities. In short, we often expect B to be positive. This is called the research hypothesis. (Many times, we expect B to be negative; for example, we expect environmental programs to reduce pollution.) The null hypothesis is usually what we do not expect. For example, we usually do not expect programs to have no impact. This is the null hypothesis: B is zero. Null hypotheses are what statistical procedures test; they *must* be exact.

Conventional statistical procedures that we consider here cannot test inexact nulls. The (exact) null is usually set to zero (no impact). The research hypothesis is inexact and often has a sign. For example, the usual expectation is that education improves outcomes, so we expect (hope) the B parameter to be positive. Similarly, the usual expectation is that increasing the number of voter registration facilities will raise voter registration rates and that higher traffic speeds will lead to more fatalities. Alternatively, we expect (hope?) drug treatment programs (X_i) to reduce criminal behavior in the future (Y_i) or tougher enforcement of occupational safety regulations (X_i) to reduce workplace accidents (Y_i). In these cases, the null hypothesis is still that B is zero, but the research hypothesis is that B is negative.

Sometimes there is controversy about expected program impacts. Consider sex education and drug awareness programs in middle and high schools in the United States. Proponents of these programs argue (expect) that these programs will reduce unwanted pregnancies and illegal drug use, respectively. They expect that B will be negative. Opponents of these programs argue (expect) that these programs will do nothing (the null hypothesis of zero) or, worse, that these programs will actually increase the behaviors they are intending to reduce (i.e., opponents expect B to be positive). In cases like these, the null remains unchanged and still exact: $B = 0$. But the research hypothesis (still inexact) is that B may be either positive or negative; that is: $B \neq 0$.[5]

The parameter (or set of parameters) C represents the expected impact of the (set of) control variables (Z_i) on the program outcome (Y_i). The estimated value is not of central theoretical interest, nor can it be interpreted as a causal estimator. However, its value may help evaluators understand why programs work as they do, and estimates of C that behave as they are expected often add credibility to the underlying research design whose focus is to estimate B, not C. Evaluators usually have a standard null hypothesis: $C = 0$. Usually, they have no particular research hypothesis, unless the expectation is obvious from previous research. For example, in the case of education, an indicator of parental income (e.g., the percentage of students receiving free or reduced-price meals) is a typical control variable. If the outcome is a measure of education achievement, the research hypothesis for the income control variable is that $C > 0$. Income might also be a control variable in a study of the impact of speed limits on motor vehicle fatalities; in that case, there may be no clear expectation about the direction of impact of income on motor vehicle fatalities, so that the research hypothesis is $C \neq 0$.

The last value in the theoretical equation is μ_i, which represents the random components that are associated with each individual observation i that affect Y_i but unrelated to X_i (or Z_i). (See Figure 6.1.) These components include random measurement error (RME) in the dependent variable(s) (i.e., the output or outcome measures). The elements of μ_i also include sampling error if the observations are a random sample from a large population. Or, only in the case of a randomized experiment, they include randomness inherent in random assignment of cases to treatments. Finally, μ_i is a good way to represent all the factors that affect behavior that we do not know about or cannot or do not measure (and may not need to measure). We lump these into the random (stochastic) term because we do not know about all the factors that affect Y or because we know about them but are unable to measure them.

Suppose that (some of) the factors in the μ_i term are not entirely random. Instead, μ_i may include variables that are related to the (set of) X_i variables. Suppose further that we are unable to measure these variables or that we do not even know what they are. Then the regression estimate of the impact of X_i on Y_i [represented by b in Equation (6.2)] will be a biased (i.e., internally invalid) estimate of the unknown theoretical parameter B. For internally more valid estimates, it is necessary to figure how to measure these factors, even imperfectly, and include them as Z_i variables in the estimating equation. If, however, the components of μ_i are unrelated to X_i, as they would be in the ideal RFE, it would not be necessary (for internal validity) to figure how to measure and include them in the estimating equation.

In the NE, the researcher collects data on values of X_i, Y_i, and Z_i for each observation $i = 1 \ldots n$ and uses that data to estimate the theoretical parameters A, B, and C. The estimating equation (6.2) parallels the theoretical equation. It is common to represent the estimates of each theoretical parameter with a corresponding lowercase letter:

$$Y_i = a + bX_i + cZ_i + e_i. \tag{6.2}$$

The first term, a, is the estimate for the parameter A; b is the (set of) estimates for the theoretically critical parameter(s) B. The value(s) of b estimate the impact of the program (X_i) (or treatments $X1_i$, $X2_i$ and so on) on Y_i. Finally, c is the (set of) estimates for the parameter(s) C and represents the estimated impact of the set of control variables (Z_i) on Y_i. The observed error, e_i, is the difference between the observed Y_i and the value predicted by the estimating equation (called the residual, or the error term).

Our central interest is in the validity of b as an estimate of B, which represents the underlying "true" program impact. Core to the validity of b is the correspondence between the estimating equation and the theoretical model. That is, the theoretical model must correspond to the diagram in Figure 6.1, in which μ_i is unrelated to X_i. But the actual estimating equation may or may not resemble its theoretical ideal. If it does, the actual estimate b will be an internally valid estimate of program impact. However, to the extent that components of μ_i are actually related to X_i, the internal validity of the estimator b becomes less defensible.

DATA FOR THE WORKHORSE REGRESSION EQUATION

Next I discuss in considerably more detail how to interpret these estimates. But, first, it is important to understand how to structure the data for input into a data set for subsequent multiple regression analysis. All relevant software (Excel®, SPSS®, SAS®, Stata®, etc.) use the same matrix format of rows and columns. Each row is an observation (unit of analysis); each column is a variable. In the simplest case, where there are $i = 1 \ldots n$ observations, one outcome measure (Y_i), one program indicator (X_i), and, say, three control variables $(Z1_i, Z2_i, Z3_i)$, the database looks like the format in Table 6.1. The columns can be in any order, but the order portrayed seems most logical. Often, the order of the columns is the order in which the data are collected, and that is often convenient and perfectly acceptable. Note that one column should include an identification number (ID) so that the researcher knows the identity of each observation. The data should be entirely numeric. For example, if the variables are percentages, the percent symbol (%) should be omitted from the data set for regression analysis. Decimals may be included, but not dollar signs ($), or other nonnumeric characters.

In the case of a simple single interrupted time series (SITS), there is a control only for the underlying trend. This makes SITS close to an NE. The data set for such a design would look like that shown in Table 6.2, in which the year, not individuals or other elements, is the unit of analysis. Note that the year $(Time_t)$ is also a variable in the SITS regression, representing an underlying trend. In the time series, each time-based unit of observation is represented by the subscript t, and the number of observations in the data set is T.

More complicated are time-series, cross-section panel (TSCS) data sets, commonly used in NE and QE designs, that use data on $i = 1 \ldots n$ cross-section observations, each measured at $t = 1 \ldots T$ points of time. Critical to this design is that there are multiple observations over time for each cross-section unit of analysis. These data sets have the format represented by Table 6.3.

As you can see, the TSCS data set is arranged so that all the time periods for the first observation are grouped (in temporal order) together. Then the time periods for the data on the second observation appear, and so on for all n units of observation in the data set. In many TSCS data sets, the actual number of observations is the number of units of observation (n counties, or n nations, or n school districts, or even n individuals), each measured for the same T time periods (e.g., annual data, 1990–2000; monthly data for 2000; decennial data, 1960–2000). In this case there are a total of $n * T$ observations in the analysis, increasing statistical validity of TSCS designs relative to simple time-series (TS) or cross-section (CS) designs alone, which have only T or N observations, respectively.

It is common but not necessary for each cross section to have the same number of TS observations. Often, more years of data on all variables are available for some units than for others. In that case, the total number of observations is the number of cross sections times the sum of the number of time periods observed for each unit, or $\sum_{i=1\ldots N} T_{-1}$.

In the case of simple RFEs with no pretest score, the data layout is very simple. Each observation in the RFE is a row, so there are n rows. The first column should be an identifier for each observation; the second column (or set of columns) should be the values of the outcome measure Y_i (or set of q separate outcome measures, $Y1_i \ldots Yq_i$); and the last column is a dummy variable X_i, which equals 1 for the observations in the treatment group and 0 for the observations in the control group. If there are three groups to which observations are randomly assigned, there will be two columns of dummy variables, where $X1_i = 1$ if the observation is in group 1 and 0 otherwise; $X2_i = 1$ if the observation is in group 2 and 0 otherwise. The coefficient for observations in the third group is captured by the intercept. More generally, if there are J groups in an RFE, there will be $J - 1$ dummy variables. If

Table 6.1

The Typical NE Database Format

ID	Y_i	X_i	$Z1_i$	$Z2_i$	$Z3_i$
1	y_1	x_1	$z1_1$	$z2_1$	$z3_1$
2	y_2	x_2	$z1_2$	$z2_2$	$z3_2$
3	y_3	x_3	$z1_3$	$z2_3$	$z3_3$
.	.	.	.	.	.
.	.	.	.	.	.
.	.	.	.	.	.
N	y_N	x_N	$z1_N$	$z2_N$	$z3_N$

Table 6.2

The Time Series Database Format: The Case of the SITS as an NE

$Time_t$	Y_t	X_t
1	y_1	x_1
2	y_2	x_2
3	y_3	x_3
.	.	.
.	.	.
.	.	.
T	y_T	x_T

the RFE measures the pretest values of the outcome measure, those values ($Y_{i,t-1}$) comprise the last column or set of columns. Sometimes RFE data sets also include observations on confounding variables (Z_i). Randomization implies that means of $Y_{i,t-1}$ and Z_i between control and treatment groups should be the same; collecting the data allows investigators to test this hypothesis of equality and also to use the information to help in understanding the results.

The data format for QEs combines the dummy variable format of the RFE with the use of control variables characteristic of the NE. Dummy variables (X_i = 1 or 0) are used to measure whether the observation is in the treatment or comparison group or which of the comparison groups the observation is in. If there are M comparison groups, there should be $M - 1$ dummies.[6] Pretest values of the outcome measure or other independent variables are used as statistical controls (Z_i).

The next question is: How do we interpret the output from our data? We input the data into a multiple regression "meat grinder." Now, what should we say about what emerges? And should we believe it? I discuss each of these issues here.

INTERPRETING MULTIPLE REGRESSION OUTPUT

R-square

The first thing that most people look at when they examine the output from a multiple regression is the R^2. Most people want a "high" R^2. I show that the R^2 (and the adjusted R^2, or $\bar{R}^2$) is the least

Table 6.3

The Time-Series Cross-Section (TSCS) NE Panel Data Format

ID_i	$Time_t$	Y_{it}	X_{it}	$Z1_{it}$	$Z2_{it}$	$Z3_{it}$
1	1	y_{11}	x_{11}	$z1_{11}$	$z2_{11}$	$z3_{11}$
1	2	y_{12}	x_{12}	$z1_{12}$	$z2_{12}$	$z3_{12}$
1	.	.	.	.	.	.
1	.	.	.	.	.	.
1	T_1	y_{1T}	x_{1T}	$z1_{1T}$	$z2_{1T}$	$z3_{1T}$
2	1	y_{21}	x_{21}	$z1_{21}$	$z2_{21}$	$z3_{21}$
2	2	y_{22}	x_{22}	$z1_{22}$	$z2_{22}$	$z3_{22}$
2	.	.	.	.	.	.
2	.	.	.	.	.	.
2	T_2	y_{2T}	x_{2T}	$z1_{2T}$	$z2_{2T}$	$z3_{2T}$
3	1	y_{31}	x_{31}	$z1_{31}$	$z2_{31}$	$z3_{31}$
3	.2	y_{32}	x_{32}	$z1_{32}$	$z2_{32}$	$z3_{32}$
.	.	.	.	.	.	.
3	T_3	y_{3T}	x_{3T}	$z1_{3T}$	$z2_{3T}$	$z3_{3T}$
.						
.						
N	1	y_{N1}	x_{N1}	$z1_{N1}$	$z2_{N1}$	$z3_{N1}$
N	2	y_{N2}	x_{N2}	$z1_{N2}$	$z2_{N2}$	$z3_{N2}$
N	.	.	.	.	.	.
N	.	.	.	.	.	.
N	T_N	y_{NT}	x_{NT}	$z1_{NT}$	$z2_{NT}$	$z3_{NT}$

important part of a regression table, says nothing about the validity of a regression and should be the last thing that evaluators examine, not the first. The R^2 is not totally uninformative; it describes the proportion of the variance in the dependent variable that is explained by all the independent variables taken together. It is a purely descriptive statistic, ranging from 0 to 1. If R^2 is .43, we say that the independent variables in the regression, taken together, explain 43 percent of the observed variance in the outcome measure. As I point out, this statistic is particularly useful in (a) helping to determine the best functional form of a regression, when theory does not determine the choice; and (b) helping to detect multicollinearity. So the statistic is not useless. (The statistic is particularly useful for those in the business of predicting outcomes, but this task is not central to program evaluation, which is mostly retrospective and causal.)

In practice, when individual persons are the unit of analysis and when the sample of individuals is heterogeneous, R^2 is likely to be low (less than .20). This reflects the fact that human beings have many inexplicable differences. It is very difficult to explain human behavior at the individual level, especially when the people being studied are all very different. For example, regressions of the impact of, say, a training program or an education reform on the wages of people in a heterogeneous target population may typically have a low R^2 (e.g., .10). This may be true even if the estimate of program impact is statistically and substantively significant and also regarded as internally valid, having been generated by a well-designed and carefully implemented RFE. Further, if the outcome measure that is being examined is a variable that contains a lot of RMEs (e.g., individual test scores or responses to a survey instrument), low values of R^2 should be anticipated.

Thus, a low R^2 is not a sign that the evaluation model is a total catastrophe. A low R^2 says little or nothing about the validity of the evaluation design, especially its internal validity. It just reflects the inexplicable variety and randomness in ordinary human behavior.

R^2 has a cousin, $\overline{R}^2$. The adjusted R^2, or $\overline{R}^2$, is usually preferred to the unadjusted R^2, especially when the number of observations is small relative to the number of independent variables. The relation between the two shows how the difference between the two descriptors depends on n and the number of independent variables,[7] K: $\overline{R}^2 = 1 - (1 - R^2) [(n - 1)/(n - K - 1)]$. In general, if $(n - K - 1)$ is less than 120, one should use the adjusted R^2. The reason for the adjustment is that, especially when n is small, adding another independent variable, even if the new independent variable is a set of random values, will increase the R^2. In other words, adding noise can make a regression R^2 look better! The adjusted R^2 is less subject to this ruse. Its use and interpretation are the same as the unadjusted version.

The next portion of a typical regression output table is the F-test (part of an analysis of variance [ANOVA] table). The F-test is often said to be a test of the significance of R^2, where the null hypothesis is thought to be $R^2 = 0$. The test or research hypothesis is said to be that $R^2 > 0$. (Obviously, R^2 is never < 0, and $\overline{R}^2$ is rarely < 0.) But this interpretation is not correct, because R^2 is a descriptive statistic and not a theoretical parameter. Researchers test hypotheses about theoretically expected parameters and not about descriptive statistics. The F-test is more properly described as a test of the null hypothesis that all the theoretical parameters B and C in the regression $Y_i = A + BX_i + CZ_i + \mu_i$ are jointly equal to zero against the alternative hypothesis that the theoretical parameters, taken together, are not zero. If the F statistic is large and its associated probability value (p-value) is "small" (by convention, less than .05), the usual conclusion is that, taken together, the independent variables have a "significant" impact on the dependent variable. Researchers usually report this, but, like the R^2 itself, the particular F-statistic and associated p-value are not critical pieces of information in the context of program evaluation.

Regression Estimates: Statistical Significance and p-Values

The regression portion itself is the most important part of the output. The first part of the table to examine is whether the parameter estimate(s) associated with the treatment variable(s) is (are) statistically significant. The column of p-values associated with each estimated regression coefficient is what gives this information. To understand these p-values, recall that there is an exact null hypothesis that corresponds to each parameter that we estimate and an inexact research hypothesis. The most important null hypothesis is the one about B, the program impact parameter. (There may be a set of null hypotheses if there are multiple treatments or comparison groups or if there are multiple measures or dimensions of the program variable.) In any case, the null hypothesis is $B = 0$.[8] Usually, the research hypothesis specifies an expected (or desired) direction of impact ($B > 0$ or $B < 0$). Sometimes, the direction of likely impact may not be so clear, or it may be extremely controversial; in these cases, the research hypothesis is that $B \neq 0$.

The null hypothesis ($B = 0$) generates the sampling distribution of what the outcomes would look like if the null hypothesis were true (given the sample size, n). In other words, suppose that we replicated our study repeatedly, resampling and re-collecting the data, re-entering the data, and re-estimating the coefficients. Doing this over and over again, we would see random variations from replication to replication. The estimates (b) of a given regression parameter (B) would vary from replication to replication. In the long run, if the null hypothesis of $B = 0$ were true, the repeated estimators b would average out to the population mean given by the null hypothesis of zero. The *p*-value is the probability (i.e., the chance) of getting the regression coefficient that we actually estimated if the null hypothesis ($B = 0$) were true. Here is the common rule of thumb:

- if the *p*-value is low ($\leq .05$), then reject the null (with corresponding probability of Type I error, given by *p*)
- if the *p*-value is high ($> .05$), then fail to reject the null (with some probability of Type II error)

Even if the conventionally used *p*-value of .05 may not make sense, the general idea behind these rules of choice makes logical sense. If the (unknown) parameter B is 0 in the "real" world, then most of the *b* regression coefficients that we would calculate in the theoretically infinite number of possible replications of our study would center around 0. In other words, if the null hypothesis were true, most of the observed (i.e., estimated) regression coefficients in the infinite number of replications would be close to zero, including ours. It would be quite likely, if the null hypothesis were really true and the program had no impact, that we would estimate a regression coefficient close to zero, and the *p*-value would be "high." Suppose the *p*-value is .20. We would say something like this: "In infinitely repeated replications of this study, which has *K* independent variables (e.g., $K = 5$) and is based on a sample size of *n* (e.g., $n = 150$), we would estimate the *b* we got (e.g., $b = .15$) twenty times out of each one hundred replications if we were drawing our sample from a world in which *B* really was 0." (Note that researchers do not actually do all these replications. Sampling distributions are based on the known properties of probability distributions. The most important laws for generating sampling distributions are the central limit theorem and the law of large numbers.)

In this example, the researcher would conclude that the *b* we estimated is fairly likely to be the case ($p = .20$) if she were studying a world in which $B = 0$. So she decides that *B* probably is zero. Of course, she could be wrong. Specifically, many, many other null hypotheses besides $B = 0$ could make the *b* she estimated even more likely to occur than the null of zero that she used. This is the probability of a Type II error; researchers do not usually compute it. Nonetheless, as we saw in the discussion of statistical validity, the Type II error is an area of concern in program evaluation, because it is the probability of deciding that the program has no impact when, in fact, it does. Type II errors are particularly likely when sample sizes are small. Recall from the discussion of statistical validity that a large sample size is the best protection against statistical errors of either type.

Suppose on the other hand that the reported *p*-value is .002. In that case, the researcher would reject the null. The probability of observing the *b* that we estimated ($b = .15$) given that the null is true is very low: only two chances in each of a set of 1,000 replications with a sample size of $n = 150$. So the researcher would decide that the null is probably not true. But the researcher could be wrong; the chance that she is wrong is the *p*-value of .002, which is the chance of a Type I error.

Interpreting *p*-values that are printed in most regression tables depends in part on the alternative hypothesis. If the alternative hypothesis specifies no direction, then we use what is referred to as a two-tailed hypothesis test. The *p*-values that most regression tables list are two-tailed *p*-values. Thus, the *p*-value that is usually reported assumes that the alternative hypothesis is that the underlying impact parameter *B* is *not* zero. But, in program evaluation, this is not the usual alternative hypothesis. Rather, the alternative hypothesis associated with the parameter for each policy alternative being compared is likely to be directional (either positive or negative). It may even be the case that, compared with the current program, one alternative is expected to improve outcomes while another is expected to make outcomes worse.[9] When the alternative hypothesis specifies a direction, we must halve the reported p-value, because we want the one-tailed p-value. In other words, we reject the null if the outcome we observed is unlikely to occur if the null were true *and* if it lies in the direction of the alternative hypothesis.

For instance, suppose that the null is $B = 0$; the research hypothesis is that the program improves outcomes ($B > 0$). Using multiple regression, with statistical controls for various Z variables, we estimate $b = 39$; the associated (two-tailed) p-value is .02. In that case, we would reject the null and decide that the data are more consistent with the alternative hypothesis. The probability that this conclusion represents a statistical error is *not* .02; rather, it is .01, because only outcomes in the direction of the alternative hypothesis would cause you to reject the null. If, under the same null and alternative hypotheses, we estimate $b = -39$ and the two-tailed p-value is still 0.02, we would not reject the null. From this perspective, the negative outcome is no different than an outcome of zero. The negative outcome is not in the desired or hypothesized direction. Hence, when we are testing a null against a one-tailed (or one-sided) alternative, we would reject it only if outcomes lie in just one tail of the sampling distribution—the tail specified by the research hypothesis. Because we are using only half the sampling distribution as the region where rejection of the null is possible, we also halve the reported two-tailed p-value.

Regression Estimates: Statistical Significance, *t*-Statistics, and Standard Errors

Most regression tables also report a t-statistic and a standard error. The standard error is the standard deviation of a sampling distribution. In regression, the usual sampling distribution is the t-distribution. It gives the values of the t-statistic and determines the associated p-value. (In univariate and bivariate statistics involving discrete variables or proportions, the relevant sampling distributions are the z or χ^2 distributions. Earlier, I also referred to the F-distribution, which actually turns out to be a close relation of the t-distribution, because $F = t^2$ in certain cases.) The sampling distribution is the distribution of estimated statistics (means, proportions, regression coefficients, and any other statistic that you calculate) that would theoretically be observed in repeated replications of a study if the null hypothesis (usually, $B = 0$) were true, given the n and the number of variables in the study.

In many cases, if the n is large, the sampling distribution will be normal. This is usually the case for the t-distribution, the one that concerns us here. Every study has its own sampling distribution based on the scale of measurement for its variables, the variance in those variables, the n, and the number of variables. But, rather than calculate a sampling distribution for every study, when n is large relative to the number of variables in the study, it is preferable to standardize each sampling distribution to a normal (z) or near-normal (t) distribution that applies to all studies. For regressions, the formula for that transformation is familiar: It is the statistic minus the parameter given by the null (usually, $B = 0$), divided by the standard error of the statistic, which is s_b in the case of the regression coefficient:

$$t = \frac{(b - B)}{s_b} = \frac{(b - 0)}{s_b} = \frac{b}{s_b}. \qquad (6.3)$$

Note that, when the null is $B = 0$, the t-statistic has the same sign as the estimated regression coefficient. Also note that, when the t-statistic is large, the observed coefficient b is likely to be distant from what would be expected if the null ($B = 0$) were true. Further, when the t-statistic is large, the standard error, which is the square root of the variance of the sampling distribution, will be small. Usually, t-statistics greater or lesser than 2 (i.e., $t > |2|$) will cause us to reject a null at the .05 level, if $(n - K - 1) > 120$. With a one-tailed test, t-statistics greater than 1.65 will cause us to reject a null if the alternative is $B > 0$, and t-statistics of less than -1.65 will cause us to reject a null if the alternative is $B < 0$.

The t-statistic is a standardized measure of an effect size, relative to the null, assuming that n is large enough to make the shape of the distribution normal. The regression table prints the standard t-score of the regression estimate. The t-score transforms the unstandardized regression estimate (b), which is based on the scale of the variables in the study, to a standard, almost normal, score. (The t-distribution is normal when n is large relative to K, the number of independent variables). Since the shape of the probability distribution of t is known for every $(n - K - 1)$, it is easy to calculate the probability of observing the b that is actually estimated (i.e., the p-value). The regression estimate, divided by its standard error, gives the t-statistic, and the t-statistic gives the p-value. It is common to report all this information, which appears in the printed output of a regression table, but it is also acceptable practice to report only the estimated regression coefficient and *either* the p-value or the t-statistic associated with it.

Regression Estimates: Substantive Significance and Regression Coefficients

Statistical significance is not the same as substantive significance. When coefficients are statistically significant (or even if they are close to it), the next task is to interpret the corresponding estimated regression coefficient(s). (Often, the intercept is the first coefficient reported in a regression table, but it is not always the most important. I discuss it later.) In program evaluation, the most important estimate is the regression coefficient of Y on X (b_{yx}, or $b_{yx.z}$ if there are Z_k control variables). If there is more than one program or treatment variable, there will be more than one regression coefficient of particular interest. This coefficient is an estimate of program impact. One would know from the $p < .05$ that it is statistically significant.

The magnitude of the actual estimate of b helps the researcher to judge if the treatment is *substantively* significant. In substantive terms, the regression coefficient is an estimate of the change in Y (measured in the units of Y) for each unit change in X (measured in the units of X), holding constant the other variables (Z_k) in the regression equation. It is an estimate of the slope of Y with respect to X, holding the other variables Z_k constant. For example, suppose that Y is the number of motor vehicle fatalities per 10,000 vehicle miles traveled (VMT); X is the observed average speed in miles per hour; other Z_k variables (density, miles of interstates) are controlled; b is significant; and $b = .005$. Then we would say that, controlling for density and miles of interstates, each additional mile per hour is associated with .005 more fatalities per 10,000 VMT. Another way to interpret this is to say that each additional 10 miles per hour is associated with .05 more fatalities per 10,000 VMT, holding the other variables in the regression constant.

As another example, suppose that a community planner for Alpha state is examining the impact of human capital in the one hundred counties of Alpha, measured by the percent of the labor force with a high school education (X), on county economic development (Y), measured by per capita income. Holding constant other variables (such as the type of employment and industry in the county), if b is significant and $b = 832$, then the planner could say that, on the average, each 1 percent increase in high school diploma holders (e.g., from 75 percent to 76 percent) in the total county labor force is associated with an increase of \$832 in per capita income.

In program evaluation, the X variable is often a dummy variable. For example, suppose that an evaluator is comparing the impact of on-the-job training versus classroom training on the wages of female household heads who are no longer receiving Temporary Assistance for Needy Families (TANF) support in Alpha state. Then the X variable is a dummy variable, taking the value of 0 if the observation had received classroom training and 1 if the observation had received on-the-job training. The Y variable in this example is the hourly wage. Since this is a nonexperimental design, there are other Z-type control variables, such as the TANF recipient's education, number of children under age six, county of residence, and race. Suppose that b is significant with $p < .05$ and that $b = 1.78$. Then we may infer that holding constant the control (Z_k) variables in the regression, the average hourly wage of female household heads who no longer receive TANF support and received on-the-job training while on TANF ($X = 1$) is $1.78 an hour higher than the hourly wage of those who received classroom training ($X = 0$). "Holding the control (Z) variables constant" means that, for women with the same county of residence, education, race, and so on, having on-the-job training ($X = 1$) results in their earning $1.78 per hour more than having classroom training ($X = 0$) for women in the target group. When the X variable is a dummy, the change in Y for each unit change in X is equivalent to the difference in the mean of Y for those in the $X = 1$ group versus those in the $X = 0$ group; adjusted or controlling for the Z variables is included in the estimating equation. For example, $b_{yx.z} = 1.78$ is the difference in mean earnings between those in the $X = 1$ group and those in the $X = 0$ group among those at the mean on all the Z variables.

Sometimes both Y and X variables can be dummy variables. In the previous example, another outcome variable might be employment. The evaluator might examine whether on-the-job versus classroom training affects the likelihood that the TANF recipient will become employed full-time (defined as thirty-five hours or more per week) six months after the training. If the recipient is so employed, $Y = 1$; otherwise, $Y = 0$. In this case, we cannot use "regular" ordinary least squares (OLS) regression. Instead, use either logistic or probit regression.[10] If the estimate is by logistic regression, and $b_{yx.z}$ is significant and $b_{yx.z} = 1.07$, then interpret the coefficient as an estimate of the odds of being employed full-time rather than under- or unemployed given on-the-job training relative to classroom training, holding the other variables constant. The logistic regression coefficient of 1.07 is an odds ratio. It tells us that the odds of being employed full-time six months after on-the-job training (and not under- or unemployed) are about 7 percent greater than with classroom training, holding the Z variables in the regression constant. Logistic (or logit or probit) regression is also appropriate when the X variable is continuous (e.g., amount of financial support per week for day care) and the Y variable is a dummy variable (employed full-time or not).[11]

Regression coefficients associated with the control variables estimate the association of the control variables with the outcome when the program variables in the equation are held constant. They are frequently of interest to program evaluators, even if they are ancillary to the key estimates of program impact. For instance, in the previous example, suppose that the estimate of hourly wages regressed on completing high school education (one of the control variables, not the same as classroom training) is $b_{yz.x} = 4.00$. This means that completing high school is associated with higher hourly wages by $4.00 per hour. By contrast, on-the-job training appeared to raise wages by $1.78 per hour. This might suggest to program managers that completing high school could be more valuable than on-the-job training for the target group in the study. However, education is not the focal variable of the design, so it would be dangerous to regard this as a causal conclusion. Similarly, it might be important to know that the county of residence (another control or Z variable, measured by a set of dummy variables) could have a substantial association (positive or negative) with wages. For program managers, this fact may suggest that encouraging TANF recipients to move may be a better antipoverty strategy than providing training.[12]

All regression coefficients, however, have the same general interpretation. Each one is an estimate of the impact of the change in the dependent variable associated with a unit change in the relevant independent variable, holding the other variables in the equation constant. Thus, every regression coefficient has a different scale of measurement. Even though every regression coefficient in a multiple regression shares the same dependent variable, each independent variable usually has a different measurement scale. So the magnitude of regression coefficients cannot be compared.

This is important to remember. Frequently, especially in program evaluation, it is tempting to compare the impact of the program variable (X) on Y relative to the control variables (Z), or to compare the impact of one program variable ($X1$) to that of another ($X2$). Unless the variables are all measured on the same scale (e.g., dollars), evaluators cannot use the ordinary, *unstandardized* regression coefficient to make such comparisons. If X is miles per hour in counties in New York and Z is miles of interstate highway in New York state counties, and Y is the county fatality rate, the evaluator cannot compare a unit change in speed to a unit change in linear miles. Regression coefficients are even more different to compare than the proverbial apples and oranges.

To compare the impact of different variables in the same regression equation relative to one another, two strategies are possible. One strategy is to turn all the variables in the regression into standard normal Z scores and then rerun the regression. In fact, many statistical programs routinely report the result of just such a transformation as *standardized* regression coefficients, which are also called beta weights. The standardized coefficient with the highest (absolute) value "wins" in terms of relative importance among the variables in the estimating equation. A variable with a standardized regression coefficient of .38 is said to be "more important" in affecting Y (controlling for the other variables in the regression) than one in the same regression with a standardized coefficient of .20, even though both are statistically significant. And the variable with a standardized coefficient of $-.72$ in this same regression would be the most important of the three, even though it has a negative impact.

Another strategy is to turn all the variables into log form; in this case, the regression coefficients are said to be elasticities, which are estimates of the percentage change in Y for each percentage change in X (controlling for the other variables in the regression). Elasticity estimates are comparable, but they assume that such an interpretation makes sense in the context of the application. They are common in economics, but it is not clear whether they are appropriate when the relations among the untransformed variables are really expected to be linear or when the most important variables are dummy variables. Dummy variables are common in program evaluation because they often represent treatment alternatives.

Neither strategy for comparing regression coefficients is without drawbacks and criticism. It is simply awkward to use regression (or any other statistical technique) to evaluate the "horse race" among variables. However, the core of evaluation is not to conduct such a horse race but, rather, to evaluate the magnitude of impact of a program on an outcome and to use external, normative standards to judge both its own and relative substantive importance.

The intercept is sometimes relevant; it is the estimated value of Y (measured in the units of Y) when all the independent variables in the regression equal zero. If, in the real world, the independent variables cannot equal zero, the intercept is probably not meaningful. This is often the case in NE designs. However, when the independent variables in the regression are all dummy variables (as they would be in RFEs with no pretest), the intercept is the estimated average value of Y_i for the control ($X_i = 0$) case. The regression coefficient is the difference between the average Y_i for the experimental group ($X_i = 1$) and the control ($X_i = 0$) group.

Examples: Interpreting Regression Result Tables

Example 1: The Impact of Teacher Certification on Student Performance in Montgomery County Public Schools

The first example comes from the *Washington Post*, reporting the findings from an evaluation produced by the Montgomery County (Maryland) Public Schools (MCPS).[13] The study made the implicit causal claim that (fully) certified teachers were critical to improving student reading performance in MCPS middle schools. (The actual claim is more general: "Teachers make a difference in . . . how much children learn.") The data backing up this claim appear in Table 6.4.

It is clear from eyeballing the numbers in Table 6.4 that, compared with teachers in better-performing schools, fully certified teachers are less prevalent in the middle schools with the highest percentage of students who score below the eighth-grade standard. (The technical term for eyeballing data like this is the "interocular test.") The article reports no further analysis of the data. However, further analysis using regression is clearly warranted.

Based on the data in the news article, bivariate (two-variable) regression confirms the positive association between poor school performance and conditionally certified teachers. (See the results in part b of Table 6.5.) In the (bivariate) regression, Y_i is measured as the percent *below* eighth-grade reading standard (pctsub8), so that a higher value is poorer performance. Provisionally certified teachers (X_i) are measured as the percent of teachers who are only conditionally, not fully, certified (pctccert). There are thirty-six middle schools in the county, so $i = 1 \ldots n = 36$ schools in the data, but one of the schools reports no performance data, so there are only thirty-five schools in the regression analysis.

In this application, the null hypothesis is that the regression parameter is zero: $H_0: B = 0$. The alternative hypothesis is that certified teachers will improve student performance: $H_a: B > 0$. The observed simple regression coefficient is 1.15. Its corresponding t-statistic is 2.64, and the associated p-value is .01. The relatively large t-statistic (> 2.00) and the relatively small p-value ($< .05$) tell us that the probability of observing $b = 1.15$ is very small if the null hypothesis $B = 0$ were true. It is reasonable in this case to reject the null hypothesis. In this application, with a one-tailed alternative hypothesis, use a one-tailed test; consequently, the actual p-value is half of that reported: $p = .013/2 = .0065$. Thus, if the null hypothesis were true, the probability of observing $b = 1.15$ is $< .007$ (i.e., less than 7 in 1,000 repeated samples of $n = 35$ schools), which is quite small. Since the probability of observing $b = 1.15$ is small if the null were true, we reject the null in favor of the alternative. The regression coefficient tells us that for each percent increase in conditionally certified teachers, the percent of students scoring below standard goes up by 1.15 percent in the average MCPS middle school. The bivariate regression conforms to the "interocular" analysis reported by MCPS.

But the internal validity of this conclusion is suspect because certified teachers (X_i) are not randomly assigned to schools. Many argue that the most qualified teachers (X_i) go to the schools with the fewest needy students (Z_i). In the table, Z_i is the percent of students in the school receiving free and reduced-price meals (pctfarm). Using the eyeball test, the data in Table 6.4 indeed indicate that schools with the fewest well-off students (Z_i) have the highest percent who score below standard (Y_i). Figure 6.A outlines the likely situation:

Figure 6.A

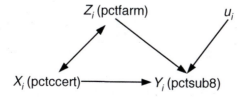

The bivariate regression omits an important confounding variable (Z_i = pctfarm); because it is omitted, it is part of the μ_i term. Consequently, μ_i is unlikely to be purely stochastic; instead, μ_i is likely to be correlated with X_i (percent of conditionally certified teachers, or "pctccert").

Table 6.4

The Data: Student Performance, Teacher Certification, and Student Free or Reduced-Price Lunch Eligibility in MCPS Middle Schools

ID	pctccert	pctfarm	pctsub8
1	1.4	2.7	7.8
2	2.2	9.8	23.0
3	5.1	12.0	17.7
4	5.3	25.4	35.7
5	5.8	29.7	25.4
6	6.0	7.3	18.4
7	6.3	20.9	19.5
8	6.3	25.3	36.1
9	7.1	5.6	14.9
10	7.5	36.4	35.2
11	8.0	8.1	10.5
12	8.2	29.7	36.2
13	9.4	39.9	NA
14	9.8	4.9	9.5
15	9.8	26.3	28.2
16	10.0	13.1	20.1
17	10.3	3.0	10.1
18	10.6	32.5	42.5
19	11.3	16.7	27.9
20	11.4	10.0	21.9
21	11.4	57.2	53.5
22	11.6	20.7	29.7
23	11.7	16.1	25.7
24	12.3	35.4	40.1
25	13.2	40.4	40.0
26	14.3	45.4	43.8
27	14.3	40.8	39.5
28	14.6	45.1	43.9
29	14.6	6.4	9.3
30	14.9	27.2	28.4
31	15.1	25.6	22.6
32	15.4	36.1	40.5
33	15.4	31.6	41.6
34	17.0	36.6	37.8
35	18.0	15.2	20.6
36	19.3	40.5	41.8

In the multiple regression, the Z_i value is actually measured, and thus it is extracted from the μ_i term. The multiple regression estimate of the impact of X_i on Y_i is far more likely to be internally valid than that in the two-variable regression; correlation between two variables is *not* causation. The bivariate regression just discussed shows clear correlation between X_i and Y_i. But the multiple regression result in part c of Table 6.5 shows that, after Z_i (pctfarm) is controlled, the impact of teacher certification (X_i) on student performance (Y_i) disappears, because it is no longer statistically significant. There, the t-statistic is $-.40$ and the associated $p = .69$, indicating that the observed coefficient of $-.08$ is quite likely to occur (seventy chances in one hundred repeated samples of $n = 35$) if the null hypothesis were true. We decide that the null hypothesis is quite likely to be true and that teacher certification apparently has no impact on student performance after student background is held constant statistically. Although

Table 6.5

Results: Student Performance, Teacher Certification, and Student Eligibility for Free or Reduced-Price Meals in MCPS Middle Schools

a. Descriptive statistics

Variable	Obs	Mean	Std. dev.	Min	Max
pctccert	36	10.69	.35	1.4	19.3
pctfarm	36	24.43	14.34	2.7	57.2
pctsub8	35	28.55	12.17	7.8	53.5

b. Simple regression: Regression of student performance on percent of teachers with conditional teaching certification

Number of obs	=	35
$F(1, 33)$	=	6.95
Prob > F	=	0.013
R^2	=	0.17
Adj R^2	=	0.15
Root MSE	=	11.23

pctsub8	Coeff.	Std. err.	t	$p > |t|$	[95 percent conf. interval]	
pctccert	1.15	.44	2.64	0.013	.26	2.04
_cons	16.18	5.06	3.20	0.003	5.88	26.48

c. Multiple regression: Regression of student performance on percent of teachers with conditional teaching certificate and percent of students eligible for free or reduced-price lunch (constant included but not reported)

Number of obs	=	35
$F(2, 32)$	=	118.51
Prob > F	=	0.000
R-squared	=	0.88
Adj R-squared	=	0.87
Root MSE	=	4.33

pctsub8	Coeff.	Std. err.	t	$p > |t|$	[95 percent conf. interval]	
pctccert	−.08	.19	−0.40	0.691	−.46	.31
pctfarm	.81	.06	13.79	0.000	.69	.93

this estimate could still be invalid (internally, statistically, or in terms of measurement), it is less likely to be invalid than the bivariate estimate.[14] In diagrammatic form (Figure 6.B), we (provisionally) conclude:

Figure 6.B

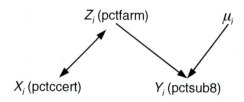

Z_i (pctfarm) μ_i

X_i (pctccert) Y_i (pctsub8)

In other words, the conclusion is that the correlation between certification and performance that was observed in the bivariate estimate reflects a spurious correlation between teacher certification and performance: Needy schools attract conditionally certified teachers, and needy schools score poorly. Consequently, we observe that conditionally certified teachers are found in poorly performing schools, but we cannot conclude that conditionally certified teachers *cause* the poor performance. Under certain circumstances, multiple regression can hold constant factors that neither our imagination nor our eyeballs can. Subsequent sections in this chapter discuss what these circumstances or assumptions are. Now, we (provisionally) conclude that the causal claim in the article regarding the importance of fully certified teachers for improved middle school student reading performance is not defensible and probably invalid.

Example 2: Does Speed Always Kill? The Impact of Speed on Highway Fatalities

Table 6.6 reports the results from an evaluation of the decision by states at various times during the 1980s and 1990s to raise the maximum rural interstate highway speed limit from 55 to 65 miles per hour (mph). Critics charged that "speed kills." They feared that higher speeds on rural interstate highways would lead to higher highway fatality rates. Supporters thought that the higher speed limit was justified for a variety of reasons. With improved highway and automobile safety, they were not so sure that speed would be as lethal as it had been. Further, when maximum speeds are fixed at 55 mph, some drivers ignore the limit, risking a ticket for speeding. Other drivers choose to drive on noninterstates, which are less safe than interstates, but allow higher speeds. Thus, one possible consequence of raising speed limits on rural interstates is to divert drivers from rural non-interstates to safer rural interstates. If the diversion expectation is to be upheld, we should observe that the 65 mph speed limit reduces fatalities on rural noninterstates and possibly on other roads as well. It is also possible that speed kills. In that case, we would observe that, compared with the previous 55 mph limit, the 65 mph speed limit raises fatalities on rural interstates and fails to divert drivers from rural noninterstates, having no impact on reducing fatalities elsewhere.

In this NE time-series cross-section (TSCS) panel evaluation, data were collected for fifty states, with fifteen years of data for each state. The units of analysis are observations for each of $i = 1 \ldots 50$ states measured over $t = 1 \ldots 15$ years, from 1981 to 1995. The number of fatalities per 1 billion vehicle miles traveled (BVMT) is the Y_{it} variable. X_{it} is the treatment variable. It equals 1 for all states and years governed by the 65 mph rural interstate maximum speed, and 0 for all states and years governed by the lower 55 mph maximum. There are numerous control variables (Z_{it}), each measured over fifteen years for each of the fifty states. Note that many of the control variables are other policy-relevant variables, which are outside the focal policy for this study.

Consider the results for the focal policy variable, the 65 mph speed limit dummy variable. First, look at whether it is significant. Decisions about significance depend on the hypotheses being tested. In this case, the null hypothesis is that the speed limit has no effect one way or another: $H_0: B = 0$. What is the alternative hypothesis? Opponents say the higher speed limit will lead to more fatalities. Supporters say the higher speed limit may divert drivers from rural noninterstates, reducing fatalities. Further, they argue that improvements in safety may mean that higher speeds on rural interstates will have no impact on fatality rates or may even reduce them, if the variance in speeds is reduced by the higher speed limit. Given the controversy, it is best to use a two-tailed alternative: $H_A: B \neq 0$. Given the many degrees of freedom in this study,[15] the probability would be "small" ($p < .05$) that the |t|-statistic will exceed |1.96| if the null hypothesis is true, where the vertical lines indicate absolute values. Thus, |1.96| is the critical value. One would reject the null hypothesis at the .05 level if the |t|-statistic exceeds the absolute value of

Table 6.6

Regression of Fatality Rate on 65 mph Speed Limit, Holding Other Variables Constant

Definitions of independent variables	
Control variables (Z_{it})	
Population density	Population per square mile of land area
Percentage of young adults	The percentage of the adult population that falls in the 18 to 24 age category
Alcohol consumption	Total consumption of alcohol in gallons per capita
Temperature	Normal daily mean temperature
Per capita income	Per capita income in 1982–1984 constant dollars
Seat belt law	A dummy variable that indicates the presence of a mandatory seat belt law: 1 represents the presence of such a state law and 0 represents the absence of one
Minimum legal drinking age	The youngest age that a person can obtain any form of alcohol
Police and safety expenditures	State government expenditures on police and safety functions per capita (in 1982–1984 constant dollars)
Focal policy variable (X_{it})	
65 mph speed limit	A dummy variable: 1 to represent a maximum speed limit of 65 mph on rural interstates and 0 to represent a 55 mph speed limit

	Pooled time-series analysis results ($N = 750$)[a]			
Variable	Rural interstate highways	Model rural noninterstate roads	Roads other than rural interstates	All roads
Population density	0.0081 (0.46)	0.0716*** (2.71)	0.0386** (2.49)	0.0255* (1.86)
Percentage of young adults	0.0316 (0.71)	0.1687** (2.46)	0.0882** (2.19)	0.0741** (2.07)
Alcohol consumption	8.1609*** (6.51)	23.2475*** (12.96)	16.2195*** (15.39)	14.5129*** (15.52)
Temperature	0.0243 (0.13)	0.2047 (0.71)	0.0437 (0.26)	0.0695 (0.46)
Per capita income	0.0001 (0.61)	−0.0004* (−1.65)	−0.0003** (−2.37)	−0.0004*** (−2.70)
Seat belt law	−1.7874*** (−3.88)	−0.9066 (−1.31)	−1.2480*** (−3.08)	−1.4119*** (−3.92)
Minimum legal drinking age	0.2864 (1.42)	0.1942 (0.64)	−0.2135 (−1.21)	−0.2379 (−1.51)
Police and safety expenditures	−0.0430* (−1.77)	−0.0405 (−1.11)	−0.0311 (−1.45)	−0.0250 (−1.32)
65 mph speed limit	0.8685* (1.90)	−3.3013*** (−4.88)	−3.5048*** (−8.81)	−2.9533*** (−8.37)
Adjusted R^2	0.78	0.72	0.81	0.83

Note: Fixed effects for states included but not reported; numbers in parentheses are *t* statistics.
*   Significant at the 0.10 level.
** Significant at the 0.05 level.
*** Significant at the 0.01 level.
[a]David J. Houston, "Implications of the 65-MPH Speed Limit for Traffic Safety," *Evaluation Review*, 23, no. 3 (1999): 310.

1.96 (absolute because the dispute requires a two-tailed test). The table has four outcome measures, but I discuss here only the results for the first two outcome measures. I leave the rest as an exercise for the student.

The first outcome measure is the rural interstate fatality rate. The t-statistic associated with the estimated impact of the 65 mph speed limit dummy variable on this outcome is 1.90, which is close to 1.96, but does not exceed it. Thus, at the .05 level, we would fail to reject the null, deciding that the speed limit had no significant impact on rural interstates. However, there is nothing magical about the .05 level. If we wish to reduce the probability of a Type II error, in exchange for a higher chance of a Type I error, we could raise the critical value of the t-statistic to, say, 1.65, which is associated with a p-value of .10 under a two-tailed test. In that case, because the computed t is 1.90, we would reject the null at the $p < .10$ level. While others might disagree, this is what the author, David Houston, decided to do.

Given that the estimated coefficient is statistically significant, it remains then to explain what it means. The estimated value of the coefficient, rounded, is .87. (Rarely is it necessary to use more than two decimal places in interpreting coefficients; neither our measures nor our methods allow more precision. Reports of estimates at four, or even seven, decimal places give an illusion of precision. The extra decimal places should be ignored.) The estimate says that, holding the other variables (including the fixed effects for each state) constant, on the average, states that raise their speed limit on rural interstates from 55 mph (where $X_{it} = 0$), to 65 mph (where $X_{it} = 1$) have .87 more fatalities per BVMT (Y_{it}) compared with states that do *not* raise speed limits. This estimate is consistent with the "speed kills" argument, but it depends on using an acceptable but slightly higher p-value than is customary.[16]

The estimate in this case also represents an important causal claim regarding the focal policy variable: Raising speed limits on rural interstate highways appears to raise the fatality rate. Compared with the causal claim in the previous example (which concluded that raising teacher certification in MCPS middle schools has no impact on student performance), the causal claim in this example is far more defensible for two reasons: It has more control variables, and, because it is a panel TSCS design, it uses fixed effects. "Fixed effects" means that the study includes a dummy variable for each state, less a reference state. Thus, it is less likely to suffer from omitted, uncontrolled confounding variables. I discuss later the confounding variables that *are* controlled. But the fixed effects represent time-invariant characteristics of states that remain unmeasured (and even unknown). This makes it possible to compare change in the outcome measure in states that change the policy to change in the outcome measure in states that do *not* change the policy. Thus, the use of fixed effects in a TSCS panel design produces an implicit difference-in-difference estimator: The coefficient of the focal policy variable is an estimate of the change (or difference) in the outcome (Y_{it}) in states that make the policy change to the change (or difference) in the outcome (Y_{it}) in states that do not make the policy change. In addition, the panel TSCS design with fixed effects supplements the implicit difference-in-difference comparison with additional statistical controls. In the absence of random assignment of speed limits, threats to causal claims about speed limits are always hazardous, but, compared with the study of schools, the design of this study yields a far more defensible causal conclusion.

Consider next the impact of the focal variable (65 mph, compared with 55 mph, speed limit for rural interstates) on the second outcome measure, fatalities on rural noninterstate roads. (See column 2 in Table 6.6.) The first question asks: Is the estimate significantly different from zero? The t-statistic of –4.88 tells us that it clearly exceeds the |1.96| critical value associated with $p < .05$. Thus, we decide that the 65 mph speed limit has a statistically significant impact on fatalities on rural interstates compared with the older 55 mph limit.

We next ask about substantive significance: What are the direction and magnitude of the impact? The value of the associated regression coefficient provides the answer. The –3.3 estimate means that, holding constant the other variables (and the fixed effects) in the regression, compared with states that do not raise speed limits on rural interstates, there are 3.3 fewer fatalities per BVMT on rural noninterstate roads in the years and states with the higher speed limits on rural interstates. That is, for the unit change in X_{it} (from 0, the 55 mph limit, to 1, the 65 mph limit), fatalities (Y_{it}) drop by 3.3 per BVMT, if the other variables in the regression are held constant. This supports the diversion hypothesis. In other words, the evidence for the first two outcomes suggests that the 65 mph limit may have raised rural interstate fatalities by less than one per BVMT, but it also reduced rural non-interstate fatalities by slightly more than three per BVMT, which is enough to offset the increase. I consider below whether to believe this inference. Before I do that, let us look at some of the other findings from the table. (Again, I concentrate only on the first two outcome measures.)

Consider first the results for the control (Z) variables in the regression for the first outcome measure, fatalities per BVMT on rural interstates. The significant control variables with $|t|$-statistics > |1.96| are alcohol consumption and the seatbelt law. The coefficient for alcohol consumption means that, holding constant the other variables in the regression, each additional gallon per person per year of alcohol consumption raises fatalities on rural interstates by an average of 8.2 persons per BVMT. (Wow! If we believe that, maybe we ought to be studying the effectiveness of programs to stop people from drinking while driving.[17]) The coefficient for the seat-belt law tells us that when states have laws that allow police to arrest drivers for not wearing seat belts as a primary offense, rural interstate fatalities drop by 1.8 per BVMT, on the average, holding the other variables in the regression constant ($p < .05$).

One other coefficient is marginally significant. Police and safety expenditures are significant at the $p < .10$ level, where the critical value is $|t| > |1.65|$. The reported t is -1.77. In this case, a one-tailed test might be justifiable; it seems reasonable to speculate that, given a null hypothesis of 0, the only alternative hypothesis that makes sense in this case is that these expenditures reduce fatalities. If we choose the one-tailed approach, then the critical value of the t-statistic at the .05 level is -1.65. Because the reported t is less than that, we can reject the null at the .05 level under a one-tailed test. Using the two-tailed test, we also reject the null, but only at the .10 level. The magnitude of the coefficient tells us that, holding constant the other variables in the regression, each additional dollar per capita of spending on police and safety reduces fatalities on rural interstates by .04 per BVMT.

What is not significant is also interesting. After other variables are controlled, raising the minimum legal drinking age appears to have no significant impact one way or another on fatalities, according to this study. Because the drinking-age policy was not the focal policy issue in this study, the evaluator should not go out and recommend changing current policies, but the results suggest that the issue warrants further evaluation.

Consider next the results for the impact of the control variables on the second outcome variable, fatalities on rural noninterstates. Three of the control variables (density, percentage of young adults, and alcohol consumption) have $|t|$-statistics that exceed the |1.96| critical value. They are significant at the $p < .05$ level under a two-tailed test. The probability of observing coefficients as large in absolute value that are actually observed in the table is very low (.05 or less), if the null hypothesis of a 0 coefficient were true. We decide to reject the null hypothesis for these variables. The coefficient for per capita income is also significant, but only at the .10 level under a two-tailed test.

Turning next to the value of the coefficients themselves, population density appears to increase the number of rural noninterstate fatalities, as does an increase in the percent of young drivers. For example, an additional percent of young drivers is associated with .17 more fatalities per BVMT. Alcohol consumption continues to be associated with an increase in the number of fatalities (by 23 per BVMT for each additional gallon per capita), while higher incomes reduce the fatality rate. Because the coefficients associated with the control variables have no causal interpretation, it is common only to mention their significance and their sign. The significance of control variables ascertains that they may have the direct effect on Y that (partly) justifies their use as a control variable in the main effort of validly estimating the direct impact of X on Y, independent of the control variables.

Summary of Examples

The first example has only one outcome indicator. In that example, the causal conclusion was that, at least in MCPS middle schools, conditionally certified teachers do not appear to adversely affect students' reading scores. This is a causal claim of *no* impact. In the second example, the causal claims pertain to significant negative or positive impacts on four outcome measures. Specifically, the conclusions are that, in the United States, holding other variables in the equation constant, raising the speed limit from 55 mph to 65 mph on rural interstates:

1. raises the number of fatalities on rural interstates by .87 fatalities per BVMT
2. reduces the number of fatalities on rural noninterstates by 3.3 fatalities per BVMT
3. reduces the number of fatalities on roads other than rural interstates by 3.5 fatalities per BVMP (from the table but not discussed)
4. reduces the number of fatalities on all roads by 2.95 fatalities per BVMT (also from the table and not discussed)

Recall that the second example has far more control variables (and a larger n) than the first example; further, it is a panel design with fixed effects, which allows estimation of the difference in outcomes between states that change the policy compared with states that do not, holding the time invariant unmeasured differences between states (the fixed effects) and the measured control variables constant. This alone makes the causal claim from the second example more credible than that from the first example.

However, there are many threats to the validity of any causal claim, especially in the absence of random assignment or a strong QE design. Hence, the big question remains: Should we believe these conclusions regarding the estimate of the focal program's effect on the outcome, summarized by the estimate of $b_{yx.z}$? More specifically,

- should we believe the parameter estimate of the effect size, $b_{yx.z}$?
- should we believe the significance test result (i.e., the p-value associated with $b_{yx.z}$)?

The remainder of this chapter discusses each of these questions. The chapter considers, first, the assumptions that must be made to defend the credibility of the estimated magnitude of program impact ($b_{yx.z}$). The chapter then lists and discusses the assumptions that must be made to defend the credibility of the significance test. In both cases, there is a brief consideration of how these assumptions can be tested, and how researchers can adjust their estimated model so that it better conforms to the requirements for valid estimates and hypothesis tests in the context of making defensible conclusions about the impact of program X on outcome Y.[18]

ASSUMPTIONS NEEDED TO BELIEVE THAT *b* IS A VALID ESTIMATE OF *B* [*E(b) = B*]

1. $E(\mu_i) = 0$

In words, this equation means that the theoretically long-run expected value of the stochastic term in the theoretical regression equation is zero. Conceptually, this means that the μ_i term in Figure 6.C that describes the theoretical regression equation contains systematic and random components whose overall impact on Y_i averages out to zero. Some factors raise values of Y_i; some lower values of Y_i; on average, the effect is zero.

Figure 6.C

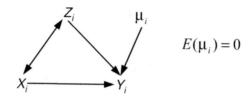

$$E(\mu_i) = 0$$

There are four sources of the random component μ_i. First, if the observations are a random sample from a specified (large) population, then random sampling error is part of the μ_i term. Second, if there is random measurement error (RME) in the Y_i variable (e.g., Scholastic Aptitude Test [SAT] or Graduate Record Examinations scores, or even sports scores, particularly when individuals, rather than classrooms or schools or teams or other aggregates, are the units of analysis), then that RME is also in the μ_i term. Third, the μ_i term also contains systematic unmeasured variables that affect Y_i but are either related or unrelated to X_i. This section focuses only on the components of μ_i that are unrelated to X_i. For example, suppose that one examines whether attending a certain type of management course (X_i) can have any impact on the participant's probability of getting a promotion (Y_i). The control variables (Z_i) may include the participant's age, race, gender, education, and so on. The μ_i term, in addition to random errors of measurement and sampling, may also include the participant's looks or social skills, assuming that people with better looks or social skills are more likely to get promoted and that "looks" and "social skills" are not measured. (A person's looks and social skills are very difficult to measure.) If looks and social skills are unrelated to the decision to attend the management course, even though they have a systematic impact on Y_i, then those variables are part of the μ_i term. There are countless variables like these that directly affect Y_i but are (probably) unrelated to X_i. The assumption is that their overall effect is zero. The fourth component of μ_i is just randomness that is inherent in human behavior. The idiosyncratic nature of human behavior is particularly apparent when individuals are the unit of analysis; the behavior of groups is more stable and predictable than that of individuals. As we pointed out earlier, the relative predictability of groups compared with individuals explains why R^2 is often very "low" when individuals are the units of analysis in a regression equation. The μ_i term contains the inexplicably quirky, seemly random component of human behavior, especially the relatively idiosyncratic behavior of individuals compared with groups.

In practice, it turns out that violations of the assumption $E(\mu_i) = 0$ are not critical for valid regression estimates. In fact, for estimates of slopes, the expected value of the μ_i term needs only to be a constant, not necessarily zero, but zero is a convenient assumption anyway. In practice, regression estimates turn out to be robust even when there are violations of this assumption.

Sometimes, researchers try to test empirically whether their data meet the assumption that $E(\mu_i) = 0$. They do this by computing the average of the *estimated* error terms e_i computed by the estimating equation to see whether that average is zero. This is *not* a test of the assumption that $E(\mu_i) = 0$. All ordinary least squares (OLS) regressions guarantee that the average of the observed (i.e., computed) error terms e_i in the estimating equation will be zero, regardless of what is going on in the real world. The zero average of the set of e_i ($i = 1 \ldots n$) in the estimating equation is inherent in the OLS formulas used to compute the estimated slopes and intercepts. The assumption $E(\mu_i) = 0$ is a statement about the unobservable μ_i that is simply not testable. Fortunately, it is usually not an important assumption either, at least in the context of program evaluation.[19]

2. No Random or Nonrandom Measurement Error in X (or Z)

Measurement error in independent variables, whether random or nonrandom, is a problem in program evaluation. Measurement error in independent variables makes regression estimates more likely to be invalid in terms of statistical validity, measurement reliability or validity, and internal validity. Chapters 2 and 3 introduced these issues while Chapter 7 explains the issue further and discusses how to reduce both random and nonrandom measurement error in more detail. What is important here is to stress again that proper measurement, especially of treatment variables, is critical for enhancing the internal validity of the estimate of program impact. In fact, for internally valid estimates of the impact of X_i on Y_i, valid and reliable measures of independent (especially X_i variables) may be arguably more important than valid and reliable measurement of Y_i variables, the usual focus.

Measurement reliability and validity are not inherently important. Rather, they are important because they are intimately related to internal validity. For example, suppose that an evaluator is interested in examining whether spending time in residential drug treatment programs (X_i) reduces recidivism to drug use (or enhances the ability to hold a legal, paying job) (Y_i). The evaluator collects relevant data (using any design). She needs to be as careful in how she measures "time in treatment" as she is in measuring the outcomes. Suppose the data for time in treatment contain random error (e.g., random sloppiness in recordkeeping by the providers) or systematic error (e.g., underestimating actual time in treatment more in short-term than in long-term facilities) in measuring X_i. In either case, estimates of program impact will be inaccurate, even if the rest of the design contains little error.[20]

3. No Nonrandom Measurement Error in Y

The paragraphs just above noted that either random measurement error (RME) or nonrandom measurement error (NRME) in independent variables results in (internally) invalid estimates of program impact. And assumption (1) notes that RME in Y_i is simply part of the stochastic term μ_i and results in lower R^2, but, while it may reduce statistical validity, it does not have major effects on the internal validity of regression estimates. However, NRME in Y_i *is* a problem because it reduces the internal validity of regression estimates of program impact.

Nonrandom error has many sources, but, in almost all cases, they result in introducing a systematic (Z_i) component to the measurement of Y_i that is likely to be related to the program variable (X_i). The consequence is an invalid estimate of program impact, unless the source of nonrandom error is identified, measured, and statistically controlled. To understand why, consider Figure 6.C. In the diagram, there is no direct relation between μ_i and X_i or between μ_i and Z_i. This is a basic requirement of the theory of regression if the regression is to produce valid estimates. What NRME in Y_i does is to make either X_i or Z_i or both correlated with μ_i, when they should not be.

For example, suppose that the race of an interviewer affects responses to a survey questionnaire in a nonrandom way, so that blacks respond differently than whites to white interviewers. Suppose further that these survey responses are the source for the outcome measure (Y_i) and that the race of the respondent is a statistical control (Z_i). If the race of the respondent (Z_i) affects the outcome measure (Y_i), then the race of the interviewer (unmeasured and part of μ_i) is confounded with the race of the respondent (Z_i). Estimates of the impact of the race of the respondent (Z_i) on the outcome (Y_i) are likely to be invalid because Z_i is now related to μ_i. More important, suppose that the race of the respondent is associated with the treatment (X_i) (e.g., a social service or anti-crime program, which may serve disproportionate numbers of racial and ethnic minorities). Then estimates of the impact of the treatment (X_i) on Y_i will also be adversely affected because X_i and μ_i are now (indirectly) related. Figure 6.D illustrates this relation.

Figure 6.D

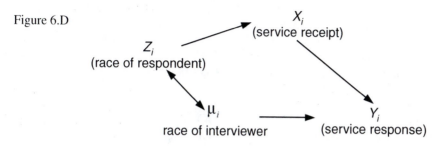

The diagram also implies the remedy, which is to anticipate the possibility that there is NRME in the measure of Y, identify the source, and control it by measuring it and then including it as a statistical control in the estimating model. Of course, such a remedy is often easier said than done, but awareness is the necessary first step. In the example, the evaluator would measure the race of the interviewer as well as the race of the respondent, including both as statistical controls.

As another example, suppose that critics allege that a measurement instrument of an outcome is racially biased. This is a charge levied against some nationally standardized achievement tests and many other tests as well. If the charge is valid and if race is also related to the treatment variable (e.g., some measure of the quality or quantity of educational services), then the estimate of the treatment on the outcome measure will also be internally invalid. Controlling for race (i.e., turning the NRME part of the μ variable into a Z variable) substantially reduces this effect. But, frequently, the source of NRME is not readily identifiable or easy to measure, so statistical controls are not a feasible solution. When evaluators have a voice in the design of instruments to measure outcomes, they should take steps to reduce NRME at the outset. Multiple indicators are often helpful in this respect also, because some indicators may be less subject to the threat of NRME than others.

In sum, when the source of NRME is known and measurable, it should be turned into a Z variable by measuring it and controlling it. Alternatively, it should be avoided by using a better measurement procedure that reduces NRME. I discuss some of these issues further in Chapter 7 (on survey question design).

4a. $E(X, \mu) = 0$: There Must Be No Correlation Between X and μ

This is an assumption of the theory of regression. In the classical regression diagram reproduced as Figure 6.E, we represent this assumption by drawing X_i and μ_i so that they are independent of each other (i.e., uncorrelated).

Figure 6.E

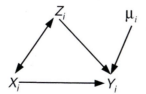

Recall from assumption (1) that μ_i contains unmeasured variables that systematically affect Y. As long as these unmeasured, uncontrolled components of μ_i are independent of the program variable X_i, they only contribute RME to Y and do not affect the internal validity of program estimates. (However, as I show here and have already noted in the chapter on RFEs, their presence reduces the statistical validity of these estimates. But, right now, the concern is internal validity.) Internal validity is threatened, however, when these unmeasured μ_i variables that affect Y_i really are related to the program variable X_i yet remain unmeasured. The presence of omitted, unmeasured variables results in omitted variable bias (OVB), which means biased, internally invalid estimates of program impact. In fact, the presence of unmeasured NRME in Y_i that we just discussed is an example of such bias, but it is not the most common example of OVB.

There are many common examples of this problem in program evaluation. I discussed them when we talked about selection bias in the chapter on internal validity. For example, if one seeks to compare the impact of public versus private schools (X_i) on educational attainment (Y_i), and fails to measure parental income, leaving it in the μ_i term, it is very likely that μ_i and X_i will be related. Wealthy parents are more likely than poor or middle-income parents to be able to afford private schools, bringing about an association between X_i and μ_i. Further, since parental wealth is partly a proxy for parent education, which directly affects the educational attainment of children, the omitted variable is part of μ_i and affects Y_i. NE (or QE) comparisons of private and public schools that fail to control for parental income as a Z_i variable are likely to be subject to OVB. The same is true when NE comparisons among public schools are made. Suppose that students in public school A perform better than those in public school B. An evaluator (or program manager) should not conclude that school A is more effective than school B, unless the parental incomes (and numerous other variables) are similar between the schools or unless statistical controls for income and other Z_i variables are included in the analysis.

In job training programs, there is always a concern that people who sign up for job training (X_i) are more motivated than otherwise comparable people who do not enroll in these programs. Motivation undoubtedly affects job outcomes (Y_i). Motivation, which is hard to measure, becomes a component of μ_i that is likely to be related to the X_i variable and, in the absence of random assignment or a good natural experiment, is often an omitted variable that can lead to biased estimates of program impact.

The problem of OVB plagues any evaluation design that is not an RFE or a high quality natural experiment PTCG: No matter how many Z_i variables that the evaluator includes as statistical controls or comparison groups, a critic can always point to one that the evaluator omitted. It is, however, the critic's responsibility to point out what the omitted variable is and why it is important.

4b. $E(X,\mu) = 0$: There Must Be No Reciprocal Causation Between X and Y

There is also a problem if the direction of causality between X_i and Y_i is uncertain. If it is unclear which comes first, the chicken or the egg, the consequence is that $E(X_i, \mu_i) \neq 0$, and estimates of program impact will be invalid. Figure 6.F explains why:

Figure 6.F

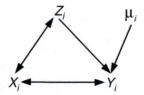

In the usual diagram for the underlying theoretical model of regression, X_i causes Y_i; the arrow has only one direction. In Figure 6.F, the direction of causality between X_i and Y_i is not certain. If Y_i causes X_i, or if the direction between them goes both ways, then μ_i and X_i are no longer independent, because μ_i causes Y_i (by definition) and Y_i causes X_i. The result is that X_i and μ_i will no longer be independent.

The problem of reciprocal causation between X_i and Y_i is common in program evaluation, where there is often a question of what causes what. For example, people with low earnings (Y_i) sign up for or are eligible for job-training programs (X_i); we observe that people who receive job training have low earnings. Which comes first? The same is true in education programs. For example, if we compare public and private schools (X_i), we realize that students are often admitted to private schools based on some aspect of their achievement (Y_i); we observe that private school students have higher achievement. But which came first? As a third example, political scientists are interested in the impact of political action committees (PAC) contributions (X_i) on the legislative voting behavior of members of Congress (Y_i), but how legislators vote may partly determine whether they get a PAC contribution. One of the thorniest examples comes from studies of police effectiveness: Where there is more crime (Y_i), there are more police (X_i); police are supposed to reduce crime. Which comes first? In all these instances, uncertainty about the causal direction between X_i and Y_i makes estimates of treatment impact subject to what is called simultaneous equation bias (SEB) and is a source of internal invalidity in estimates of program or treatment impact.

The problems of OVB and SEB are common in evaluation research. Only randomized experiments, properly designed and implemented, can rule out these two related sources of systematic error. As long as the n is large enough, random assignment to treatment and control groups representing X_i guarantees that all other factors (besides X_i) that affect Y_i are, on the average, equal between treatment and control groups or among the different treatment groups. It should be clear that the RFE turns Z_i variables into μ_i variables, so, for internal validity, they do not need to be controlled. Thus, the RFE can rule out OVB. In addition, the RFE also guarantees that the treatment comes before the outcome; it is designed so that the assignment to treatment or control group (or groups) precedes the outcome. First, units are assigned to a treatment; then, the treatments happen, then the outcome happens and is measured. Thus, the RFE can also rule out SEB.

But RFEs are not always feasible. So the first challenge is to make sure that NE designs are minimally subject to OVB, which occurs when variables that should be controlled as Z_i variables are not. In effect, OVB occurs because there are Z_i variables that lurk in the μ_i term, which, by definition, contains variables that are not measured. The next challenge is to make sure that NE designs are minimally subject to SEB, which occurs when Y_i comes before or determines X_i. In other words, if X_i causes Y_i and Y_i causes X_i, as in the diagram; or if Y_i causes X_i, but not the reverse, SEB is a problem. In both OVB and SEB, the result is a biased estimate of program impact because $E(X_i, \mu_i) \neq 0$.

Having discussed each of these sources of bias, I now suggest remedies. No one remedy works completely. Most researchers choose from this list of tools to reduce errors from OVB (and SEB, if that is necessary). They do not rely on just one weapon against these threats to internal validity, choosing instead to use several at once. The chapter first discusses numerous tools to deal with OVB. It then considers tools to reduce SEB.

Remedies for Omitted Variable Bias (OVB)

Selection bias occurs when researchers fail to control for variables in μ that are related to X and also affect Y; both conditions must be true for the omitted variable to cause selection bias.

Remedy 1. If the regression omits a suspect variable, then the validity of the estimate of *B* should be suspect, too. If an omitted variable is suspected, it should be measured and used as a control variable in the regression. Often, measurement is not possible. And it is impossible for the researcher to be aware of all omitted variables. All NE designs are subject to this threat. A critic can claim, "Oh, you omitted variable *ZJ.*" So the researcher responds by measuring it, rerunning the regression, and still finding that the original estimate is unchanged. The critic need not go away; he can now charge, "Oh, you omitted variable *Z(J + 1).*" And this can go on forever. So this remedy of measuring all *Z* variables is not very satisfactory, but it does point to the need to think about possible *Z* variables and to measure them as part of any QE or NE design.

Remedy 2. Sometimes omitted variables are *not* threats to internal validity. If the alleged omitted variable is not related to *both* X_i and Y_i, then it is not a problem. Suppose first that the alleged omitted variable is related only to Y_i. Then it is part of μ_i. It may be a possible threat to statistical validity, but it is no threat to internal validity. Second, if the alleged omitted variable is related only to X_i but has no impact on Y_i, it is best to leave it out. In this case, including it reduces statistical validity by adding an extraneous variable to the estimating model, with no addition to internal validity.

Remedy 3. When measurement of omitted variables is likely to be impossible or when important omitted variables are likely to be difficult even to identify, one way to control for these factors is to adopt QE methods. That is, preselect comparable units or time periods for NE analysis. For example, suppose that a researcher is comparing the impact of privately versus publicly administered job-training programs on relevant employment outcomes. The confounding factors that determine whether programs are publicly or privately run are too numerous to measure or even identify. A solution is to select for study publicly and privately administered training programs in the same community, with the same labor market, similar trainees, similar political overseers, similar community resources, and so on. This strategy comes at the expense of external validity but gains internal validity. As an actual example, Rivkin examines only public school students in large urban districts to reduce OVB in his study of the impact of school desegregation on black students.[21]

Remedy 4. Another strategy preserves external validity by using multiple groups and fixed effects to enhance internal validity, instead of preselection of comparable units. This design is an amplification of the TSCS multiple-group design, previously mentioned. Such a panel design collects data over time ($t = 1 \ldots T$ time periods) for each of $i = 1 \ldots n$ cross-sections. The 65 mph speed limit example is an illustration of a multiple-group design. It is also a fixed-effects design. In this design, with a large number of units of analysis, using fixed effects improves internal validity, with no sacrifice in statistical validity.

That example had multiple control variables, so it could estimate the impact of the speed limit policy change separately from the impact of other policy and environmental changes over time and controlling for differences among states. However, despite the numerous statistical controls, without fixed effects, it would still be possible that the conclusion suffers from OVB. In other words, despite the use of copious statistical controls, the estimated impact of the 65 mph speed limit on fatalities on rural and rural noninterstate highways (and on the other outcome measures) could still be internally invalid. Even with statistical controls for differences among the states, the states are still not entirely comparable. They are not comparable on many relevant *Z* variables that are hard to measure. And they are probably not comparable on many unknown but still confounding factors.

Including a fixed-effect dummy variable for each state in the analysis (less a reference state), in addition to statistical controls, reduces the threat of OVB in this kind of design. The reference group can be arbitrarily selected, or there may be a focal state that is of particular interest. The dummy variables are fixed effects. They represent the influence of what we do not know (or cannot measure) about each state. Governors matter; legislators matter; courts matter; snowstorms matter. All of these are piled into the dummy (what we do not know) variables, labeled the fixed-state effects.

Multiple-group designs like these usually have a large number of observations, equal to the sum of the number of time periods in each cross-section. Including fixed effects in TSCS designs like these usually leaves sufficient degrees of freedom for statistical validity, as long as the number of cross-sections is not too large relative to the number of time periods. It is not uncommon in fixed-effects TSCS designs to include a fixed effect for each time period (less a reference time period) as well as a fixed effect for each group (less the reference).[22]

In the example, there are 750 observations, and 10 independent variables, so adding 49 dummy variables reduces the degrees of freedom from 740 to 691, which is still more than sufficient. The estimates reported in Table 6.3 include, but do not report, these additional dummy variables for each state (less a reference state). (The estimates of rural speed limits on traffic fatalities in Table 6.3 do not include fixed effects for each time period. While fixed effects for each year could be collinear with some of the nonfocal policy variables or with the focal variable, the noncollinear fixed-time effects should be included in the model to reduce the effect of omitted time-varying factors that are common to each state, such as national policy changes.) Including fixed-effects dummy variables in TSCS designs goes far to reduce the threat of OVB in NE designs.[23] It should be standard practice in multiple-group designs, but it is not universally used.[24]

Remedy 5. Another strategy for reducing OVB in multiple-group TS (or panel) designs is to recast each variable as a difference. The outcome measure becomes $\Delta Y_i = Y_{i,t} - Y_{i,t-1}$, the program variable becomes $\Delta X_i = X_{i,t} - X_{i,t-1}$, and the control variables become $\Delta Z_i = Z_{i,t} - Z_{i,t-1}$. The estimate of the effect of ΔX_i on ΔY_i is a difference-in-difference estimator. In the usual model, *levels* of X and Z are related to each other, and as long as *levels* of Z are related to *levels* of X and may also affect *levels* of Y, it is necessary to include Z in the model to reduce the threat of OVB. But in the difference-in-difference model, it is not evident that *differences* in Z between time 1 and time 2 are systematically related to *differences* in X and Y. For example, as schools get higher socioeconomic status (SES) students between time 1 and 2, reading scores go up. This is a difference in levels. But the difference of the differences remains constant; that is, the relative differences remain constant, and hence they do not covary, reducing the OVB threat. Thus, compared with simple TSCS panel designs, difference-in-difference estimators are likely to be less subject to OVB threat. (I point out below that this approach also reduces the threat of autocorrelation and underlying trends to statistical validity.[25])

There are two (relatively minor) drawbacks to this approach. First, it means a loss of one year of observations for each cross-section. But TSCS designs usually have sufficient degrees of freedom. Second, the regression coefficient becomes somewhat awkward to interpret, because it is an estimate of the impact of a unit change in a difference variable on a difference variable. Estimating predicted change scores for specific values of the treatment differences usually avoids the problem of interpreting awkward coefficients.

Remedy 6. Often, it is not possible to use a fixed-effect, multiple-group TS design. This design requires data for multiple time periods in each of multiple groups. Often, that kind of information is not readily available. An alternative is to consider some of the better QE designs discussed in Chapter 5. Some of the single TS designs and the natural experiments are relatively strong in internal validity, although they may be weak in external validity.

Remedy 7. Another way to reduce OVB is to use lagged values of outcome variables. As Chapter 5 showed, this is a primary rationale for the pretest–posttest comparison-group (PTPTCG) design compared with the posttest-only comparison-group (PTCG) design. The presupposition is that many factors related to the nonrandom assignment to or choice of one treatment (or treatment level), and not others, and that affect Y_t, are also captured by previous values of Y, that is, Y_{t-1}. For example, educationally disadvantaged children (Z_i) may receive worse teachers than their more advantaged peers (X_i). Compared with this same group, they are also likely to have lower test scores at time $t-1$ (Y_{t-1}) and at time t (Y_{it}). We model this situation (Figure 6.G) as follows:

Figure 6.G

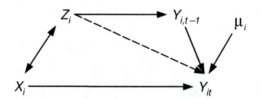

Often, we cannot identify or measure all of the confounding Z_i variables; however, many will be captured in Y_{t-1}, the lagged dependent variable (LDV). For example, Spelman uses a lagged variable with a difference-in-difference model to examine the impact of prisons (versus jobs) on crime in a TSCS analysis of Texas counties.[26] And Rivkin also uses an LDV to reduce OVB in his study of the impact of desegregation on the academic performance and earnings of black students. He also includes numerous controls and a restricted sample of roughly comparable schools in his arsenal of statistical weapons to reduce the threat of OVB.[27]

It is critical to point out the dangers of lagged endogenous variables: Under certain circumstances, they introduce more bias into the estimates of the focal policy variable than they remove.[28] First, if there is no causal theory that justifies including the endogenous variable (Y_{it}) as an exogenous variable (Y_{t-1}) on the right-hand side of the regression, then there is no reason to include it. In the example, it is very likely that previous achievement has a causal impact on current achievement: Students who failed to learn the math lessons from the first semester often never catch up in the second semester. However, it is not so clear that many aggregate level variables (e.g., current fertility rates in single- or dual-parent households) would be caused by their previous levels (either positively or negatively). Second, it is important not to confuse trend or drift in variables (e.g., revenues or expenditures) with cause: An underlying upward trend in, say, local government spending on education does not mean that spending in time t causes increases spending in time $t+1$; more likely, the cause of higher spending is higher income or tax revenues or lower prices for education inputs relative to substitute goods. In other words, if the LDV has no causal power and also shares an underlying trend with other included variables, including the LDV in the model will reduce (if not obliterate) the effect of the truly causal variables, resulting in biased estimates. (Trends are a threat to statistical validity; we discussed how to deal with them in the section on SITS and we will discuss the issue further.) Of course, sometimes LDVs really do have causal power. For example, sometimes last year's budget may have determined a choice that affects this year's budget; similarly, the very fact of doing well in, say, French or Math 101 in this semester may make it easier to do well in French or Math 102 in the next semester, respectively. It is not uncommon that outcomes are path dependent: History matters. In these cases, it may be justifiable to include the lagged dependent variable, but in the presence of serial correlation (e.g., an underlying trend), an ordinary least squares estimate of the coefficient of the focal policy variable will still remain biased (it will be too low). Thus, the solution is the same: Include the variable if it is causal, but take steps to remove the underlying trend. Using first differences (and difference-in-difference estimates) is one promising way to do this that we have already mentioned, but there are other ways as well.

Remedy 8. There is also a set of two-step procedures that researchers may use to reduce threats to OVB. These two-step procedures supplement the use of statistical controls. Reliance on statistical controls alone is hazardous in part because using statistical controls to separate the receipt of treatment (X_i) from confounding variables (Z_i) assumes that the assignment (or self-selection) process is deterministic. Yet it is far more plausible that the relation between the receipt of treatment and the confounding variables has a large stochastic component, just as the impact of treatment on the outcome has a stochastic component. Just as RME in the treatment variable X_i biases estimates of program impact, any random component in the otherwise nonrandom assignment or selection of X_i to one unit or another has the same effect.

The idea behind each of the two-step, or two-stage, procedures is to model the assignment (or selection) process in the first stage, reducing random error by measuring X_i with an *estimate* of X_i that has less error than the unadjusted observed score. We then estimate the impact of the estimated treatment score (or estimated probability of receiving one treatment versus another) in the second stage. The advantage of this approach is that it formally incorporates error into the assignment/selection or treatment (X_i) variable, reducing threats due to stochastic components (including RME) and unmeasured systematic components (including NRME) in that variable. The disadvantage is that if the assignment equation is a poor fit to the data, because it may introduce even more RME (or possibly NRME) into the treatment variable than was originally present. The result is estimates of impact that are more biased than if simple statistical controls had been used.[29]

There are three types of two-stage procedures. Two (propensity score matching and instrumental variables) either replace or supplement statistical controls to estimate treatment scores or probabilities. The third (Heckman selection) is a control for the probability of being in the study sample in the first place, regardless of the treatment that is received (or self-selected).

Remedy 8a. Propensity score matching (PSM) combines NE and QE methods. The first stage is nonexperimental. It regresses receipt of one type of treatment versus another (often a dichotomous variable so that logit or probit regression is used or multinomial logit if there are more than two unordered treatment types) on a set of confounding exogenous variables that the evaluator believes affects the type of treatment that is assigned or selected. If the model produces a reasonably good fit to the observed treatment (measured by R^2 or a maximum likelihood measure of fit), then the first-stage results produce a predicted value (and standard error) of the probability of receiving each type of treatment. This creates the categories for QE matching.

For example, there may be a set of twenty observations (out of a larger set) for which the first-stage equation predicts probability = 0.5 (or within a small standard error of that probability) of receiving public (rather than private) hospital service. Of these twenty, eight may actually have received private treatment and twelve may actually have received public. The second stage uses a QE design (effectively, a PTCG) to examine the impact of actual treatment (public versus private hospital services) on health outcomes between these twenty statistically equivalent groups. They are statistically equivalent because all twenty observations in the two groups have $p = 0.5$ as the probability of receiving public hospital services, but, in reality, twelve observations received public and eight received private hospital service. (Usually, observations that have no matching probability close to .5 are dropped from the analysis.) Similar comparisons can be made if there are other categories of matches (e.g., compare matches at other probabilities that are also close to the middle or median of the distribution). It is possible to vary how close the match is: The smaller the confidence interval of the match, the smaller the number of observations, but the "better" the match. Matches within larger confidence intervals of the predicted probability have larger ns but may be a poorer match.

Some investigators regard propensity score matching as a way to mitigate the drawbacks of using statistical controls to "mop up" errors from nonrandom assignment.[30] However, others note the limits of two-stage procedures, including propensity score matching. If the match is not close, compared with using statistical controls, propensity score matching may increase rather than reduce bias.[31] However, it is important to note that the first stage equation in propensity score matching relies entirely on nonexperimental, statistical methods to predict treatment; if the model produces a good fit to the data, so that there is a close (but not perfect!) correspondence between observed and predicted probabilities, the result will be numerous comparable comparison groups for the second stage PTCG design.[32] Propensity score matching relies heavily on the specification of the nonexperimental equation that predicts the match; rather than rely on one specification, it is useful to use several versions of the prediction equation to assess if the results depend on the specification of the first-stage, assignment equation.[33]

Remedy 8b. Instrumental variables (IVs) are close relatives of propensity scores. Propensity scores are the predicted values from an equation that models the process that is believed to determine why some choose or are selected for one treatment versus another. Propensity score matching forms QE comparison groups among those who have similar predicted values but actually receive different treatments. By contrast, using an instrumental variable, a similar first-stage equation creates the predicted values of the treatment $\hat{X}_i$. The second equation uses the *predicted* value of the treatment (called $\hat{X}_i$) and substitutes that value for the observed value (X_i) in the second-stage equation that estimates the impact of $\hat{X}_i$ on Y_i controlling for Z_i.

Instrumental variables are variables that cause assignment or selection of the treatment X_i but have no direct impact on Y_i. Instrumental variables play many roles. They can potentially reduce RME in observed values of X_i. They can also reduce endogeneity in X_i. As we will see on pages 177–178, IVs are used to reduce simultaneity between X_i and Y_i (SEB). They also help to isolate the impact of X_i from that of Z_i by reducing the stochastic component of X_i.

Like propensity score matching, the first-stage equation includes confounding Z_i variables. Unlike propensity score matching, the first-stage equation must also include at least one variable (call it W_i, the instrument) that affects the probability of selecting (or being selected for) one treatment rather than another but that differs from Z_i in that it is a variable thought to have no direct influence on Y_i. As such, W_i should not be included in a second-stage equation to estimate the impact of X_i on Y_i. But it must be included in the first-stage equation that predicts who gets one type (or level) of treatment compared with another. Figure 6.H will help to clarify.

Figure 6.H

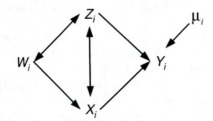

In the diagram, we are trying to estimate the impact of X_i on Y_i. W_i is a variable that helps identify X_i and to separate it from Z_i. It is like the other confounding variables, *except* that it is not part of the stochastic term for Y_i because it has no direct impact on Y_i. It is part of a stochastic term for X_i, so measuring it in the first-stage equation reduces the random component of X_i that can lead to invalid estimates of program impact.

The equations that correspond to Figure 6.H are the following:

(a)
$$X_i = a + b_1 Z1_i + b_2 Z2_i + \ldots + b_k Zk_i + cW_i + e_i'$$

(b)
$$Y_i = a + b\hat{X}_i + c_1 Z1 + c_2 Z2 + \ldots + c_k Zk + e_i$$

where
$$\hat{X} = a + b_1 Z1_i + b_2 Z2_i + \ldots + b_k Zk_i + cW_i.$$

Like propensity scores, IVs are clearly useful as a weapon in the arsenal of tools to reduce threats to internal validity. They share the disadvantages of propensity scores, too. First, if the first-stage IV equation is a poor fit to the data, it increases random error in $\hat{X}_i$ relative to X_i, thereby increasing rather than reducing threats to internal validity. (There appears to be no consensus about what distinguishes a "poor" fit from a "good" one.) Second, an identifying variable like W_i must be related to X_i but have no direct effect on Y_i.[34] Sometimes these variables are hard to find.

As an example, consider the problem of estimating the impact of participation in varsity sports (in secondary schools) on juvenile crime. Controversy surrounds this issue. Some contend that varsity sports build good character or simply reduce free time that might otherwise induce some children to get into trouble with the law. Others aver that competitive varsity sports create opportunities for "fights" that can spill over into criminal behavior. If we want to estimate the impact of participation in varsity sports (X_i) on a measure of juvenile delinquency (Y_i), we would need to control for a variety of confounding variables (Z_i), including gender, grade point average (GPA), socioeconomic status (SES), and ethnicity. But there is a large stochastic component to participation in varsity sports that emerges in the X_i measure. We need an identifying variable (or set of variables) that has no effect on Y_i but also reduces the randomness in X_i. One candidate might be whether the secondary school has a varsity sports program. The value of W_i would affect the probability that individual students participate in varsity sports. Students in high schools with no varsity sports program are less likely to participate in such a program, which means that W_i and X_i are likely to be associated. And W_i, a school-level decision, is (arguably) unlikely to directly affect whether the individual student engages in criminal activity (Y_i).[35]

As a practical matter, many studies estimate program impacts with and without instruments. That is, they estimate the conventional single-stage NE regression equation, $Y_i = a + bX_i + cZ_i + e_i$, where Z is a vector of confounding variables. They also estimate the IV version, $Y_i = a + b\hat{X}_i + cZ_i + e_i$, where $X_i = a + bZ_i + cW_i + e_i'$ and $\hat{X}_i = a + bZ_i + cW_i$.

If the estimate of b is similar in significance and magnitude using both estimates, then the defensibility of the causal claim regarding the impact of X_i on Y_i is strengthened. Once again, multiple methods are the best strategy.

Remedy 8c. Heckman selection. There are two basic types of selection threats in many designs. One type is nonrandom selection into one type of treatment or another due to OVB or SEB. Another type is selection into the observed study sample. If variables that affect the probability of being selected into the observed sample are also related to treatment score (X_i) and to the outcome (Y_i), they are confounding variables and need to be controlled. The selection equation is designed to reduce that threat.

In this case, the selection equation is a first-stage equation. It estimates the probability that each element in the potential group will be in the observed sample. The second-stage estimating equation includes that predicted probability for each observation as a control variable, in addition to including Z_i variables necessary for estimating the impact of X_i on Y_i, net of the confounding variables.

As a convenient example, consider the use of SAT and (ACT) scores (Y_i) as an outcome variable for examining the impact of teacher certification (X_i) on the academic ability of high school students. Clearly, confounding variables such as student SES, ethnicity, GPA, class size, and many other school and student characteristics would need to be controlled. But there is an additional sample selection problem in this example: Not all students take the SAT/ACT. Nonminority students with high GPA and high SES are more likely than other students to take the SAT/ACT. They are also more likely to have fully certified teachers. Consequently, in addition to the usual selection threats (OVB and SEB), there is a sample selection threat.

It is possible to reduce the threat using a two-stage procedure. In the first-stage equation, the dependent variable is based on the entire population of students in each school in the study; it is a dichotomous variable indicating whether the student took one of these exams. The independent variables in this equation would include many, if not all, of the confounding variables that were just mentioned, as well as variables that predict selection into the study sample (but that are omitted from the second-stage impact equation). For example, in this case, the number of times the school offers the exam times the average distance of students from the school may affect the probability that a student takes the exam but not the student's potential score. The second-stage estimating equation is based only on the observed subpopulation that actually did take the SAT/ACT. The probability of taking the exam, predicted by the first-stage equation, becomes a control variable in the second-stage equation to reduce a source of OVB that lurked in the sample selection process (rather than in the treatment selection process).[36]

If the sample selection process is a source of OVB, then the predicted probability of selection will be a significant variable in the second-stage estimating equation. Estimates of the impact of X_i on Y_i from an equation that includes the (significant) sample selection probability estimate (as well as Z_i variables) will be more defensible than estimates that ignore the sample selection issue.

Remedy 9. There are also some statistical tests for omitted variables. It is best to consult an applied econometrics text for procedures about how to conduct these tests. Two frequently used tests are the Ramsey regression specification error test (RESET) and the Hausman test (for TSCS panel designs only).[37] These tests, however, do have limits. The Ramsey test is very general; if it points to a specification problem, it does not tell you whether the problem is OVB or SEB or how to fix it. And the Hausman test is a test only for the presence of omitted group-level variables related to the group that defines the fixed effect. There are other sources of omitted variables; for example, there could be omitted time-related or individual-level variables to which the test is not sensitive. In general, no statistical test can eliminate the threat of OVB in NE designs. At best, the "remedies" already suggested can only reduce the threat. The best way to reduce OVB is by design: The RFE, or arguably, the natural experiment, is the gold standard in this respect.

Remedies for Simultaneous Equation Bias (SEB)

SEB occurs when there is two-way causation between X_i and Y_i or if Y_i causes X_i only (even though the researcher thinks that X_i causes Y_i).

Remedy 1. One remedy is to anticipate this issue at the design stage and take steps to make sure that measurement of X_i precedes Y_i. For instance, if Y_i is the motor-vehicle fatality rate and X_i is a law raising the minimum legal drinking age, make sure that the measurement of Y_i is at time $t + 1$ whenever X_i is measured at time t. Equivalently, measure X_i at time $t - 1$ and Y_i at time t. If the design is a TSCS panel, since the causal variable is temporally lagged, the number of observations in the study drops by the number of lags times the number of cross-sections. For instance, if the cause (X) is lagged by one year, so that the research examines the impact of $X_{i,t-1}$ on $Y_{i,t}$, there will be no observations for $X_{i,t}$ in the data. In this example, one year of data is sacrificed for each cross-section unit. But the design is structured so that the putative causal program must come before the observed effect.

In conjunction with this approach, researchers will often also lag the dependent variable (outcome measure). For example, suppose that Y_t is the dependent variable (fatalities at time t); X_{t-1} is an independent variable, which, because it is measured at time $t - 1$, precedes the dependent variable; and Y_{t-1} (the previous fatality rate) is another independent variable. Lagging the *program variable* reduces SEB. Previous sections note that lagging the *outcome* variable is intended to reduce omitted variable bias. However, previous sections have pointed out that lagged dependent variables, when there is no true causal effect, biases estimates of the focal policy variable, and the bias increases when there are underlying trends in the data. If a common trend underlies both the lagged dependent variable and the lagged policy variable, the bias is increased even more. This outcome, while it is not inevitable, is likely in many cases.

Lagging only the focal policy variable is consistent with one characteristic of causation: Causes precede effects. However, temporal precedence, known as Granger causality, is necessary but not sufficient for causation. Thus, lagging endogenous policy or program variables is a weak test for causality. Nonetheless, when the question of causal direction between X and Y is a central issue, if the result of a Granger-causality test shows that $X_{i,t-1}$ affects $Y_{i,t}$ but that $Y_{i,t-1}$ has no impact on $X_{i,t}$, that result can be quite persuasive in settling questions about causal direction. While estimates based on models with lagged policy variables may still yield invalid parameter estimates of the impact of the lagged policy variable, under many conditions this is more likely if the model also includes a lagged outcome variable.[38]

Remedy 2. Another remedy to reduce SEB is to use a two-stage least squares (2SLS) estimation.[39] As any econometrics text will explain, the idea is to estimate a first-stage equation that portrays why X_i was adopted. Many of the factors that explain why X_i was adopted will also affect variation in Y_i. However, identifying a variable that affects the selection of X_i but does not directly affect Y_i will produce an "identified" first-stage equation that predicts X (called $\hat{X}$). Now, instead of using $Y_i = a + bX_i + cZ_i + e_i$ as an equation to estimate b, a second-stage equation, which contains the predicted value of X from the first stage, can be used. The first-stage equation is:

$$X_i = a + bZ_i + cW_i + e'_i.$$

The second-stage equation is:

$$Y = a + b'\hat{X} + cZ + \varepsilon.$$

The new estimate of the impact of the predicted values of X_i on Y_i, b', will be less subject to SEB than the single-stage estimate, b.

As with its IV cousin, specifying the first-stage identification equation is often pretty tricky. For example, many empirical studies using OLS methods in the field of justice and crime have failed to find evidence that police reduce crime because of simultaneity. Simple OLS models often find, paradoxically, that hiring more police officers appears to increase crimes, but this result reflects an uncontrolled simultaneity problem. Hiring more police may well reduce crimes; however, high crime rates often lead cities to increase the number of police officers. Therefore, cities with higher crime rates (Y_i) tend to have more police officers (X_i), so that $Y_i \rightarrow X_i$, even if police reduce crime $(X_i \rightarrow Y_i)$. Using OLS to estimate the effect of the number of police on crime will thus result in a biased estimate.

In this case, a 2SLS estimate is appropriate. To estimate the first-stage equation, the key is to find a variable (or set of variables) that affects the size of the police force but not the crime rate. Steven Levitt has found that local electoral cycles have a direct impact on the size of the police force: The size of the local constabulary tends to increase in the years of mayoral or gubernatorial elections. But electoral cycles do not affect crime rates. Therefore, Levitt uses the local election year as an instrument in the 2SLS estimate.[40] In the first-stage equation, election years (and other variables) predict the size of the police force. The second-stage equation regresses the outcome measure (crime rates) on the *predicted* size of the police force (from the first stage) and on other control variables. Levitt finds that having more police does appear to lead to less crime.[41]

Final Notes and a Warning

These details should not let us forget the basic design issue at hand. In the presence of SEB or OVB, estimates of the impact of X_i on Y_i will be biased (i.e., internally invalid). Both SEB and OVB mean that $E(X_i\mu_i) \neq 0$, violating a fundamental assumption behind a theoretically valid regression model. It is important to stress that researchers can *not* test this assumption (as some are wont to do) by empirically correlating X_i with the estimated error term e_i. The formula used to estimate the coefficients in a regression also produces estimated values of e_i for each observation; that formula also guarantees that the correlation between X_i and e_i is 0 even if $E(X_i\mu_i) \neq 0$.

To elaborate the implication of this point, suppose that an evaluator generates his own data to fit the theoretical model $Y_i = 2 + 4X_i + 2.5Z_i + \mu_i$. Next, he uses the regression equation $Y_i + a + bX_i + e_i$ to estimate the impact of X_i on Y_i. He *knows* that this estimate is based on a biased estimating model (and formula) that omits Z_i, a known confounding variable. Finally, he correlates the values of X_i with the values of e_i estimated by the biased equation. Econometrics texts show the equations that prove that this correlation will be 0, even though the evaluator has used a biased estimating equation.[42] I note the point here because it is important for evaluators to know what does not work to establish internal validity as well as what does work.

5. The Underlying Model of Impact Has a Linear Functional Form

The theoretical regression equation is assumed to have the form $Y_i = A + BX + CZ_i + \mu_i$, which is a linear and additive model. Three conditions identify when this assumption will probably *not* be met: The outcome is not a continuous variable, the relation between X and Y is not a straight line, and the relation between X and Y is different for different subgroups in the sample.

Y_i Is Not Continuous

Often, the outcome variable is not continuous. In many of these cases, the outcome Y_i is a dichotomous variable. As examples, consider the following outcome measures: Trainee does or does not have a paying job; student passed or failed a test; individual did or did not vote in the last election; child does or does not attend school; respondent did or did not commit a crime in the past year. In these examples, the underlying model cannot possibly be linear, because the underlying model for a dichotomous dependent variable *must* look like one of the two cases shown in Figure 6.2.

In either of these cases, it is clear that linear regression estimates of the impact of a program on outcomes defined in this (dichotomous) way will be biased, because the underlying theoretical model of expected impact cannot be linear since the outcome is not a continuous variable. This is also true if the outcome variable is a polytomous variable, where the dependent variable is a set of (more than two) unordered categories (e.g., trainee has a paying job, has a paying job in a "sheltered" workforce, has no job).

Y_i Is Continuous, But There Is a Nonlinear Relation Between X_i and Y_i

Suppose that Y_i is continuous but the impact of X_i on Y_i is expected to depend on the value of X_i. In that case, the relation between X_i and Y_i will not be linear. For example, suppose the impact of an increment in school spending on student outcomes is expected to be greater when the funding is at very low levels than when it is at high levels. In that case, the underlying relation may look like that shown in Figure 6.3, panel (a), where the slope of Y_i on X_i is greater at lower values of X_i and becomes flatter as the values of X_i increase.

There are many other forms of nonlinear relations between X_i and Y_i. Sometimes the impact of X_i on Y_i is greater at high values of X_i than it is at lower values. For example, the impact of a cigarette tax increase on the propensity of youth to reduce or avoid smoking may be greater as the amount of the tax increases. Then, the underlying relation might look like that shown in Figure 6.3, panel (b), where the slope between Y and X becomes increasingly more negative as X increases.

Other forms of nonlinear relations between X_i and Y_i occur when the relation looks like a U or when it looks like an inverted U. In all these cases, using a linear estimating equation to estimate an underlying nonlinear impact will produce misleading, internally invalid results. The clearest example is using a linear equation to estimate what is really a U-shaped or inverted-U-shaped relation. The estimating equation will produce a coefficient of zero, when in fact the true relation is a polynomial.[43]

The Case of Statistical Interaction

Sometimes the evaluator expects the relation between X_i and Y_i to be different for certain subgroups, or the impact of X_i on Y_i may be different for different values of Z_i. For instance, the impact of training programs on job outcomes often is positive for women but appears to be zero for men. The impact of reductions in class size may have positive results on educational outcomes for educationally disadvantaged students and no impact on outcomes for their more advantaged peers. Similarly, the impact of reductions in class size on improved educational outcomes may be greater at lower grades than at higher grades. These are all examples of statistical interaction. They are cases when generalization may not be possible. In other words, if the expected value of b, representing the impact of X_i on Y_i, is expected to be different for one group than another, using one simple estimating equation, $Y_i = a + bX_i + cZ_i + e_i$, for the entire group will be biased because it estimates only one value of b for the entire sample.

Figure 6.2   **Dichotomous Outcome: Nonlinear Relations**

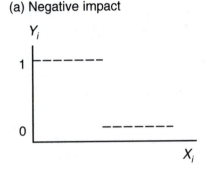

(a) Negative impact

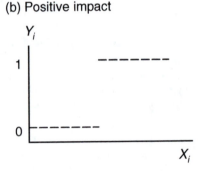

(b) Positive impact

Tests and Remedies

Aside from theoretical expectation and results from previous research, a ready empirical sign of poor functional form is when a simple linear regression produces significant independent variables with a really low R^2 or $\overline{R}^2$. This is one case when the value of R^2 must be considered in assessing the internal validity of a regression estimate. That is, while a low R^2 is not a sign of internal invalidity due to OVB, it is a sign of a possibly misspecified functional form, especially if the coefficients are significant along with the low R^2.

There are several remedies to produce a better-specified model. First, for a noncontinuous outcome measure, an appropriate maximum likelihood estimation (MLE) technique, such as those outlined in Table 6.7, should be used.

When MLE techniques are used, the sign and the significance of regression coefficients are interpreted in the same way as for simple regression. But the value of a regression estimate $b_{yx.z}$ is often not interpreted in the same way as that for linear regression. For example, the coefficient in a logit regression is the log of an odds ratio, which is hard to interpret; the coefficient in a logistic regression is an odds ratio, which is easier to interpret, but still admittedly awkward. For the general case, it is best to consult an econometrics text. Often, however, the easiest solution is to avoid direct interpretation of $b_{yx.z}$ when it is a nonlinear MLE estimate. Instead, the alternative is to estimate predicted values of Y_i for each (substantively meaningful) value of the program variable X_i, holding the values of Z_i constant at the mean (when interaction is not anticipated). This is not only a practical way to interpret regression, especially when the substantive meaning of the estimated coefficient is not clear; it is also a useful way to assess the substantive importance of a statistically significant program variable.

Figure 6.3   **The Impact of X_i on Y_i Depends on Values of X_i**

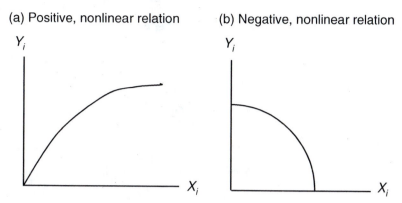

(a) Positive, nonlinear relation   (b) Negative, nonlinear relation

There are numerous examples of evaluation studies that use these MLE techniques. In the international development field, one study uses a logistic regression to estimate the impact of (continuous) measures of school quality (X_i) on early school exit in Egypt (a dichotomous Y_i). Another study uses multiple indicators of outcomes to examine the effectiveness of the Supplemental Nutrition Program for Women, Infants, and Children (WIC) in the United States. Most of the outcomes are dichotomous variables. The study uses logistic regression, along with numerous statistical controls, to estimate the effects of WIC use (itself a dummy X_i variable) on several dichotomous outcomes, including receipt of prenatal care (yes/no) and whether the baby is premature (yes/no), each of which is coded as a (1, 0) variable, just as dummy independent variables are coded. Kimball and Kropf use a negative binomial to study the impact of ballot design (X_i) in selected states in the United States on the number of unrecorded votes (Y_i), and on other countable events, along with numerous statistical controls (Z_i). The outcome variables in this study are not strictly continuous. The events can be counted, but only whole numbers can appear. Under certain circumstances, Poisson models can be used in these cases, but the negative binomial is more common.[44]

Consider next the case when both X and Y are continuous, but straight lines are not believed likely to describe the relation between X and Y.[45] In that case, simple transformations of the X or Y variables will often turn the expected curvilinear relation between X and Y into a straight line, so ordinary regression can be used to estimate b_{yx}. For example, rather than regress Y on X, controlling for Z, a researcher might regress the log of Y on X, controlling for Z. There are three possible regressions, and three interpretations of the regression coefficient correspond to each variation. Table 6.8 shows each of the three variations.

Sometimes the researcher may suspect that the relationship between Y and X looks like a U shape or an inverted U shape. The relation between private donations to nonprofit organizations and public subsidies may illustrate the inverted U. For example, Brooks believes that government subsidies to nonprofit organizations can both crowd in and crowd out private giving. At low levels of public subsidies, government support may attract private donations. However, at a certain point, an organization that receives government funds starts to look more and more like a public agency, so few citizens choose to give money to it. Therefore, in Brooks' model, Y is the private donation that the nonprofit organization received and X is government subsidies to that organization, but he also added a term of X^2 to the model. Controlling for other Z variables in the model, the coefficient of X in the regression is positive, while the coefficient of X^2 in the regression result is negative and significant, supporting his hypothesis.[46]

Table 6.7

Estimation Alternatives for Noncontinuous Outcome Measures

Estimation technique	Type of outcome measure
Logit, logistic, or probit regression	Dichotomy
Ordered logit	Ordinal (especially when there are few ordinal categories; as the number of ordinal categories increases, the outcome measure becomes more continuous)
Multinomial logit	More than two unordered categories
Tobit regression	Continuous with many zeros
Poisson or negative binomial	Event counts
Tobit regression	Percent or proportion (continuous between 0 and 100 or between 0 and 1)

Finally, if the researcher expects statistical interaction, where the impact of X on Y may depend on the value of a third variable, Z, he can still use ordinary regression to estimate program impact, but the simple form of the estimating equation, $Y_i = a + bX_i + cZ_i + e_i$, will not be properly specified. For example, suppose the expectation is that both class size (X) and measures of socioeconomic status (Z) affect student outcomes (Y), but the hypothesis is also that the impact of reduced class size on student outcomes depends on socioeconomic status. The researcher might start with the basic theoretical model, $Y = A + BX + CZ + \mu$, but this is not quite what the theory says. Rather, the expectation is that B, the impact of class size on student outcomes, will be negative for low-status students and less negative, or even 0, for higher-status students. In other words, as Z increases, the value of B will decrease (plus a random term, μ', which we assume is independent of both X and Z):[47]

$$B = B_1 + B_2Z + \mu'.$$

So, now the revised theoretical model is:

$$Y = A + BX + CZ + \mu, \text{ where}$$
$$Y = A + (B_1 + B_2Z + \mu')X + CZ + \mu = A + B_1X + B_2ZX + CZ + \mu.$$

To estimate this equation, multiply X times Z, and use their product as another independent variable in an ordinary estimating regression equation:

$$Y = a + b_1X + b_2ZX + cZ + e.$$

In this case, there is no single estimate of program impact. Rather, the estimate of program impact depends on Z:

$$b = change\ in\ Y\ for\ a\ unit\ change\ in\ X = b_1 + b_2Z.$$

Thus, no single value can describe the estimated impact of X on Y; it all depends on the value of Z. It is common to estimate b for values of Z at the mean of Z, and at one and two standard deviations above and below the mean.

Table 6.8

Three Common Nonlinear Relations in a Regression of *Y* on *X*: (Natural) Log Transformation to Make Them Linear

Transformation	Interpretation of b_{yx}
$Y \rightarrow \log Y$	Impact of unit change in *X* on relative (or proportional) change in *Y*, holding *Z* constant
	OR multiply the coefficient by 100:
	Impact of unit (absolute) change in *X* on percent change in *Y*, holding *Z* constant
$X \rightarrow \log X$	Impact of relative change in *X* on change in *Y*, holding *Z* constant:
	OR divide the coefficient by 100:
	Impact of percent change in *X* on change in *Y*, holding *Z* constant
$Y \rightarrow \log Y$ and $X \rightarrow \log X$	Impact of percent change in *X* on percent change in *Y*, holding *Z* constant (elasticity estimate)

Many similar transformations are possible in the case of statistical interaction, but this form is fairly general. It assumes that both *X* and *Z* have a direct impact on *Y*, but the impact of *X* also depends on *Z*.[48]

In conclusion, the use of a simple linear model when the underlying situation is not linear and additive will lead to internally invalid (i.e., biased) estimates of program impact. If a researcher expects a nonlinear or nonadditive (interactive) relation (based on theory and previous research), one or more of the suggested modifications to the basic model should be used. If the respecified model fits the data better (according to $\overline{R}^2$ or another measure of goodness of fit), it is probably a better model and should be used in place of, or along with, the estimate from the simple linear model.

Summary: Multiple Threats, Multiple Remedies, and Multiple Models

This section has discussed threats to the internal validity of nonexperimental estimates of program impact. In nearly each case (and especially for the threats of OVB and SEB), there are numerous methods to reduce these threats. Sometimes it is not clear which method should be used to mitigate the particular threat. For example, in a TSCS design, should the evaluator use fixed effects for each cross-section (less the reference group) but not for each year? Should she use a lagged outcome measure? Should she lag the program variable or use an instrumental variable to reduce SEB? Should she use an interactive model?

In general, the answer is at once simple and complicated: Use multiple methods. If each method or remedy yields closely similar estimates of program impact, then the defensibility of the conclusion increases accordingly. Many evaluations routinely do this. For example, Grant and Rattner appear to be uncertain whether to use ordinary regression, Poisson regression, or a negative binomial to estimate the impact of bicycle helmet laws on bicycling fatalities, so they use all three models, along with state and year fixed effects and additional statistical controls. They report consistently negative coefficient estimates. Similarly, Grabowski and Morrisey use a TSCS of states over time with multiple outcome measures, multiple specifications of combinations of fixed effects, and multiple combinations of control variables to estimate the impact of gasoline prices on motor vehicle fatalities. They consistently find that within-state variation over time of decreases in gasoline prices appears to increase motor vehicle fatalities. Rivkin also uses multiple specifications in his examination of school desegregation on outcomes for black students. The design is a cross-section (using survey data). It uses multiple outcome measures; it estimates the impact of school desegregation in models with and without a pretest score; it uses multiple combinations of control variables.[49]

In general, it is good evaluation practice to estimate as many as twenty different combinations of equation specifications, along with multiple indicators of outcomes, to provide a single estimate of overall program impact. If all the estimates tell the same story, the more convincing the story is against numerous threats. Multiple methods, in short, make causal conclusions more defensible.[50] Nonetheless, it is wise to remember that a good design (e.g., a well-designed and implemented RFE or PTCG natural experiment) reduces the requirement for the numerous statistical adjustments and variations that are demanded of most NE designs.

ASSUMPTIONS NEEDED TO BELIEVE THE SIGNIFICANCE TEST FOR *b*

Just as the use of multiple regression requires a number of assumptions for the estimate of program impact to be credible, so also is there a set of assumptions that must be met if the hypothesis test regarding the statistical significance of the regression estimate is to be credible. I list and discuss them next.

1. Independent Observations (No Autocorrelation)

The usual multiple regression *t*-test for significance (or, more specifically, the estimate of the sampling error of the parameter estimate) assumes that observations must be independent of one another. In other words, the usual test requires that the units of analysis not be able to influence one another. If individuals are the units of analysis, Joe must not be in direct communication with Jim or Sally or anyone else in the sample, and Jim cannot influence Joe or Sally, and so on for all the rest of the observations. If collectivities of individuals are the units of analysis (e.g., states in the United States), the usual test requires that what goes on in Virginia does not influence what goes on in New York or Nevada, what goes on in New York does not influence what goes on in Nevada or Virginia, and so on for other states. If units of time are the units of analysis (e.g., years, months, days), the usual *t*-test requires that what happens in one year has no influence on what happens in another year (in other words, there is no trend or path dependence). Further, what happens in year (or day, or month) t does not influence what happens in year $t + 1$ or, for that matter, year $t + j$ (where j is a positive integer). In most (not all) cases, the presence of nonindependent observations makes estimates of standard errors lower than they really are and therefore inflates *t*-statistics, making it easier to reject nulls, thereby increasing the chance of a Type I error.

The presence of nonindependence among units of analysis is particularly likely in TS data, because observations at time 1 are usually not independent of observations at time 2. This is called the problem of autocorrelation. It is also a major source of the threat to internal validity caused by maturation. That is, underlying trends in TS data are a threat to both internal and statistical validity. In general, any TS evaluation study (i.e., the SITS and any multiple-group TS or panel design, which examines time series within multiple comparison groups) should test for and expect the problem of maturation and nonindependent observations.

Tests and Remedies

The best way to deal with the problem of autocorrelation in time-series data is first to think of it as a threat to internal validity. In the case of a SITS, this is often done by including the variable of time (year, or month, or day, measured as time = $t = 1, 2, 3, 4 \ldots T$) in the regression $Y_t + a + bX_t + cT_t + e_t$. Thus, most TS designs include time or "T" (e.g., the year) as a control variable for this reason. Multiple time-series (TSCS panel) designs do the same. As an alternative in multiple time series, if time is not expected to have a linear influence, then time is included as a set of dummy variables. For example, if there are fifty states, each with ten years of data, the control for temporal effects that are invariant within states might be nine dummy year-variables (along with state fixed effects to control for differences between cross-sections), with the reference state and year reflected in the intercept.

In addition to being a threat to internal validity, nonindependence in TS data is also a threat to statistical validity. A standard test for the presence of autocorrelation as a threat to statistical validity in simple TS designs (i.e., the SITS) is the Durbin-Watson test, commonly available in standard statistical software packages. Unadjusted, it is not appropriate for multiple group time-series designs, however. The Durbin-Watson test is a test for the presence of the most likely kind of autocorrelation, called first-order autocorrelation or first-order autoregression (AR1). In first-order autoregression, values observed at time $t - j$ influence values observed in the subsequent time period, $t - j + 1$, and values observed during that period affect the next time period, $t - j + 2$, and so on.

There are other kinds of autocorrelation (e.g., a type that dies out gradually over time). In simple TS designs, regression techniques exist to estimate the form of temporal dependence and to remove it. These techniques are called autoregressive integrated moving average (ARIMA) estimates, so named because temporal data sets can have yearly dependence (autoregressive) or long-term, stored-up dependence (moving average) or both (integrated). They are discussed in many econometrics and other texts.[51]

Unadjusted, the Durbin-Watson test and ARIMA estimates are not appropriate for multiple TS or panel designs. In the case of TSCS panel designs, the best solution is to use special TSCS estimation techniques. To reduce threats to internal validity, these estimation techniques rely on standard control variables (Z), along with fixed-effects dummies for each comparison group, a dummy variable for each time period, or a single variable for trend to estimate the impact of X on Y. To reduce threats to statistical validity, they also rely on techniques that remove likely sequential (year-by-year) autocorrelation within each comparison group (or panel). These are referred to as generalized least squares (GLS) estimates, panel data estimates, TSCS estimates, linear mixed models, or hierarchical linear models and are found in many commonly used statistical software packages.[52]

Another way to reduce serial dependence in panel or TS data is to transform each variable into a difference. While levels of variables are serially dependent, first-order differences are more likely to be independent. For example, people (or countries) who are rich this year were probably rich last year, but the annual differences of differences between these persons (or countries) are probably not so regular. Thus, analysts frequently use difference-in-difference methods to reduce the threat of autocorrelation, as well as that of OVB.[53]

The Special Problem of Nonindependent Cross-Sections (Cross-Section or Spatial Autocorrelation)

Sometimes, nonindependence among units of analysis is also present in cross-section data. For example, observations on students in the same classroom (or even school) are not independent of observations of another student in the same classroom (or school). Students in the same classroom affect one another. In fact, the concept of peer influence captures the idea of nonindependent observations, and it should be expected in most studies of student outcomes that use individual-level observations, especially if they are from the same classroom (or school). The same pertains to evaluations of managerial policies that use individual workers as units of analysis, when those workers are "nested" in the same workplace across many different workplaces.[54]

The problem of nonindependence between time periods within multiple units (temporal or serial autocorrelation) is far easier to deal with than the problem of nonindependence between units of analysis at the same point in time, "nested" in different groups (cross-section or spatial autocorrelation). Temporal autocorrelation has a clear direction: Events and observations at time t affect subsequent observations or events, most likely in year $t + 1$ (or maybe dying out in subsequent years). But cross-section autocorrelation has no clear order; there is no way to know if observation n is influencing observation $n + 1$ or observation $n + 10$ or the reverse. Joe could influence Sally, or maybe it is the other way, or maybe they influence each other, or maybe Saul influences Joe and Sally, but Joe and Sally do not influence each other. Unless there is a clear order to individual paths of influence, there is no simple way to detect for and then reduce the impact of this problem in hypothesis tests.

If the evaluator can order the observations by the suspected direction of nonindependence, then the techniques appropriate for time-series autocorrelation can be used to detect and reduce this threat to statistical validity. In other words, if the direction of influence was from Joe to Suzy to Jim, then the evaluator can order the observations accordingly and use standard techniques for temporally dependent observations. But this is rarely possible.

More feasible is to regard the problem of cross-section dependence as a threat to internal validity. In that case, the evaluator can measure it and include it an independent variable. For instance, it is reasonable to expect peer influence, not only in schools but also in work groups. One way to measure peer influence is by assuming that it is represented by the influence of a group mean on individual behavior. For example, student achievement (Y_i) is influenced by education resources in the school (X_i), by the student's own SES (Z_i), and by the average SES of the students in the class ($\overline{Z}$). Thus, every student in the same class has a different SES (Z_i) score, but the same $\overline{Z}$ score.

When countries or states or other collectivities are units of analysis, it may be reasonable to expect that geographic proximity is an ordered source of cross-section dependence. For instance, welfare policies in New York may influence policy adoption and policy outcome in neighboring New Jersey. Similarly, political or other alliances make countries or states dependent on one other. There are many ways to model this type of cross-section dependence. The greatest threat is not thinking about the problem in the first place.

2. The Variance of μ Must Be Constant for All Observations

The usual method of estimating the standard error of the estimate of b_{yx} (i.e., the standard deviation of the sampling distribution of b_{yx}) requires that the variance of μ_i must be constant for all $i = 1 \ldots n$ observations, called homoscedasticity. When the variance of the stochastic term is heteroscedastic (not homoscedastic), the usual estimate of the standard error of b_{yx} is not valid. Depending on the severity of the problem, that estimate can be either too high or too low, making the t-statistic either too small or too large, respectively.

For example, the annual earnings of professionals (Y) may be positively associated with their years of working experiences (X), and, in many cases, the relation is linear. However, this might not be the case for many professional subgroups, especially those whose incomes can have extremely high variance. Consider information technology (IT) professionals. A survey of annual income of

IT professionals in 2004 may find that the variances of the income of IT professionals with five or more years of experience are much higher than those of entry-level professionals (see Figure 6.4). Some of them will be very wealthy; others will do well, but they may not have extreme wealth. At lower levels of experience, the extremes will be narrower. A regression line drawn through the data would have an upward, linear slope, but the variance of the individual observations of income increases with years of professional experience.

Some degree of heteroscedasticity should be suspected in all cross-section data. For example, when the units of analysis are collectivities or groups like schools, school districts, villages, counties, states, or countries, each unit has a different number of persons. When numbers are small, the variance of any measured statistical property of that unit will be greater than when the unit is large. Thus, the variance in average student outcomes will be larger in small than in large schools.[55] Similarly, the variance in the estimate of childhood poverty (another common outcome measure) will be larger in small counties or villages than in large ones.

Heteroscedasticity is particularly likely when individuals are the units of analysis. If the outcome measure is test scores, then the variance in test scores may be greater for some in the sample than others. For instance, the variance in responses to a standardized test may well be smaller as the age or grade of the student rises. There is probably more random error in the response of a typically wiggly third-grader to a standardized test than in the response of the typically more seasoned eighth-grader. Similarly, when outcome measures are survey responses (e.g., comparison of customer satisfaction with a private compared with publicly delivered city service), they are likely to reflect heteroscedasticity, particularly if uncertain or ambiguous beliefs might be greater for some respondents than others.[56]

Another common example of heteroscedasticity occurs when individuals are the unit of analysis in studies of consumption. Evaluators frequently study consumption. For example, they may examine the impact of taxes levied on alcoholic beverages on the consumption of alcohol or the impact of labeling on the consumption of high-calorie foods. Consumption is measured by spending on the target good (e.g., Y = spending on high-calorie foods). In a nonexperimental study, if X is labeling, then one of the control variables will be the price of the good and another will be the consumer's income. Spending on most food increases with income. However, as income goes up, the variance in the estimated error term will also go up because some rich people spend a lot on food, while other wealthy people just eat the basics (no foie gras or filet mignon). The implication is that the error term will be heteroscedastic if individual family spending on caloric foods (Y) is regressed on labeling (X), family income, price, and other Z variables. Ordinary hypothesis tests of the impact of labeling on consumption would consequently be misleading.

Even in randomized experiments, heteroscedasticity should be suspected if the number of respondents (randomly) assigned to a control group is substantially larger than the number in the treatment group. Evaluators always face a budget constraint. In an RFE, the evaluator might want to have the largest n possible. If the control group treatment is less costly than the experimental group treatment, then the evaluator might want to assign more observations (say, two-thirds of n) to the control group than to the more expensive treatment group. As long as the sample size in both groups is large (say, more than sixty in both groups), then the imbalance in sample size is no threat to internal validity. It is a threat to statistical validity because it is a source of heteroscedasticity, making the uncorrected hypothesis test invalid.

Tests and Remedies

There are numerous tests for heteroscedasticity, and all of them have various limitations.[57] One common test is to regress the absolute value of e_i on the suspect variable or variables. For example,

Figure 6.4   **Heteroscedasticity in the Relation Between Income and Experience**

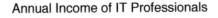

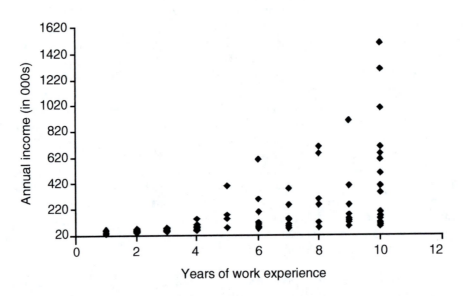

in a regression of individual student test scores on class size, grade, and parental SES, the evaluator might suspect that the variance of the error might be larger for students in lower grades and with lower SES parents. To test for this source of heteroscedasticity, the evaluator could regress the absolute value of the individual e_i scores, computed from the original regression, on grade and parental SES. If one or both of the coefficients are separately or jointly significant, the implication would be that the original hypothesis test regarding the impact of class size on test score might not be valid because of heteroscedastic error terms, resulting in invalid hypothesis tests.

Probably the most practical advice is to routinely use robust (heteroscedastic-corrected) standard errors, also known as White's heteroscedasticity-consistent variances and standard errors.[58] This procedure is useful no matter what the source of heteroscedasticity. Most statistical packages make this correction readily accessible.

When panel or TS data for multiple cross-sections are used, heteroscedasticity should also be suspect. Specifically, the variance in stochastic terms for the (time series of) observations within one cross-section is likely to be different from that for the (time series of) observations in another. Further, the variance of the stochastic terms for observations within the same cross-section is likely to be smaller than that for observations in different cross-sections. Just as evaluations that use multiple time series must routinely correct for autocorrelation *within* cross-sections (i.e., comparison groups), they must simultaneously correct for heteroscedasticity *between* cross-sections. Most regression programs specially designed for panel or TSCS data can produce estimates that correct simultaneously for both of these threats to statistical validity.

Finally, the previous example, which regresses the income of IT professionals on years of experience, suggests a very direct and simple solution to the problem of heteroscedasticity. Observed heteroscedasticity often is a sign of other problems in the model. Sometimes, it is a sign of an omitted variable. In the example, it is a sign of incorrect functional form. For instance, a regressing log of income (log Y_i) on X_i would probably go far to reduce the observed heteroscedasticity in the scatterplot. Similarly, using an ordinary linear regression model when the outcome is dichotomous, polytomous, or ordinal or when the underlying relation is not linear not only introduces the threat of biased estimates but also invites heteroscedasticity. In both cases, the best solution is first to alter the estimating model (e.g., use a logistic regression); that may fix (or reduce) the heteroscedasticity problem, too.

3. No Collinearity (or Multicollinearity)

Collinearity is the presence of such a high correlation between (or, more likely, among) independent variables that it is impossible to separate their independent impact on the outcome measure. For example, if an evaluator, using an NE design, is interested in examining the impact of workforce experience (X) among low-wage workers on wages (Y), it would clearly be necessary to control for age ($Z1$), gender ($Z2$), and race ($Z3$). But age and experience are often highly interrelated, and age, gender, and experience may also be mutually interrelated. The consequence is that the regression coefficient estimating the impact of experience (X) on wage (Y), controlling for the Z variables, is likely to be insignificant because the estimate of the standard error of the regression coefficient for experience will be high.

Multiple treatment interference is another example of collinearity. For instance, if a policy change occurs at the same time as a management change, it will be impossible to separate the impact of one from that of the other. Similarly, if experienced teachers teach small classes and inexperienced teachers teach larger classes, it may be difficult to disentangle their separate effects.

Collinearity leads to high standard errors and low t-statistics. It does not affect internal validity. Rather, it only affects statistical validity.

Evaluators sometimes worry too much about collinearity. If the regression estimates in an NE or QE design are significant, then collinearity is not likely. If all (or most) of the independent variables are significant (and especially the X_i treatment variables), collinearity is not a problem.

Tests and Remedies

When independent variables are not significant, they could be insignificant because they really do not matter in the real world or they might be insignificant because of collinearity. Then, evaluators do need to consider how to evaluate signs of collinearity. An informal, but common, sign of collinearity is when R^2 or $\overline{R}^2$ is high and no independent variable is significant or when most are not significant. A common test for collinearity is to compute the variance inflation factor (VIF) for the parameter estimates. It is a measure of the multiple correlation between the target independent variable (usually X) and the set of other independent variables ($Z1, Z2, Z3$, etc.). If one or more of the Z variables is highly related to the X variable, even after the other Z variables have been held constant, then the standard error of $b_{yx.z}$ may well be too high due to collinearity. The usual standard is that if the VIF exceeds ten, it is a sign of collinearity, but this is only an arbitrary standard, and the VIF is not the best or the only test. There are other tests for collinearity—for instance, a principal components analysis among the independent variables (a type of factor analysis). If all the independent variables appear as the same component, such that they emerge as one principal component, they are probably collinear.

An equally important point is what *not* to do as a test for collinearity. Specifically, examining a matrix of *simple* correlations between the independent variables in a regression is not a sufficient or valid test of collinearity, even though it is commonly used. Collinearity is not just a high simple correlation between two variables, but high multiple correlation among the set of right-hand-side variables in a regression.

Throwing out variables is a very poor correction for collinearity. If there is collinearity among the control (Z) variables alone or among the control and the treatment (X) variables, throwing one control variable out risks a sacrifice of internal validity for a false gain in statistical validity. The clearly superior remedy is to make an index if the control variables are collinear among themselves. For example, in examining the impact of class size (X) on student outcomes (Y), the evaluator would want to control for measures of students' race and ethnicity ($Z1$), economic disadvantage (percentage of students receiving free or reduced-price meals) ($Z2$), and ability to speak English ($Z3$), as well as other variables. Classes are often larger (X) in these economically and academically challenged environments, and these challenging (Z) environments affect academic outcomes. Since these control variables (Z) not only are related to X but also affect Y, they must be controlled to increase the internal validity of the estimate of class size on student outcomes. But these separate control variables may well be collinear in the sample. Throwing out variables to reduce collinearity is no remedy. Rather, it is easy to create an index that uses the values of all these variables, combining them to make one variable, which can then be controlled with a reduced risk of collinearity. There are many ways to create an index; simply adding or averaging the variables is one way.[59]

There are other remedies for collinearity, but none of them are entirely satisfactory. For example, if there is collinearity between the treatment and control variable, one can test the hypothesis that they are jointly significant.[60] In other words, if age and experience are collinear, the researcher can compare the fit of a model that includes *both* age (a Z variable) and experience (the X variable) to one that includes neither by using the F-statistic to test whether the two variables together have significant effects on Y. (This is also called a bloc F-test.) But this test does not help to separate the treatment from the control, so it is not an entirely satisfactory response to a collinearity problem.

Collinearity is fundamentally a problem with the sample. If a researcher anticipates that the treatment variable and one or more control variables are likely to be collinear, then there are two things she can do at the design stage. One is to make sure that the sample is large. Large samples are less subject to collinearity problems than small ones. Another is to select the sample so that one or more of the control variables is relatively invariant. For example, if she is interested in the impact of class size on academic outcomes, she can select a sample of schools that are exclusively located in economically and academically challenged neighborhoods. Class sizes will vary within these neighborhoods, so the X will vary more than the Zs, reducing their likely collinearity. Similarly, suppose that an evaluator is interested in the impact of more work experience on the wages of low-wage workers. He suspects that age and work experience are likely to be collinear, yet worries that age must be controlled. At the design stage, he can determine to select the sample within a homogeneous age group, reducing the need to control for it statistically. Even if he does need to control for age statistically, reducing its variance within the sample reduces its likely collinearity with the focal X variable, experience.

WHAT HAPPENED TO THE R^2?

There is a punch line to this chapter. No section is explicitly devoted to the R^2. Instead, while discussing how to interpret regression output, one comment was that "the R^2 (and the adjusted R^2, or $\overline{R}^2$) is the least important part of a regression table, says nothing about the validity of a regression, and should be the last thing that evaluators examine, not the first." In discussing the

Table 6.9

The Languages of Econometrics and Program Evaluation: A Crosswalk

Econometrics	Program evaluation and research design
Assumptions for internally valid parameter estimates	*Threats to internal validity*
1. No (mimimal) omitted variable bias (include potential Z variables likely to affect Y and likely to be related to X) 2. No simultaneity between X and Y 3. No RME or NRME in X 4. No NRME in Y	1. Selection/history/multiple treatment interference/contamination 2. Selection/regression artifact 3. Measurement reliability and validity of treatment variable, respectively; testing; instrumentation 4. Measurement validity of outcome measure; testing; instrumentation
Assumptions for statistically valid hypothesis tests	*Threats to statistical validity*
1. No autocorrelation; independent observations 2. No heteroscedasticity; constant variance of stochastic term 3. Little or no collinearity between X and Z	1. No maturation/underlying trend 2. (No equivalent term) 3. Multiple treatment interference; contamination

validity of regression estimates and hypothesis tests, little was said about the R^2. While the R^2 is useful for testing hypotheses about functional form and has some use for detecting collinearity, it is not fundamental because, alone, the magnitude of the R^2 says little or nothing about the validity of parameter estimates or significance tests.

- An internally, statistically valid estimate can have a low (or high) R^2
- An internally, statistically *in*valid estimate can have a high (or low) R^2

CONCLUSION

In NE designs, the central concerns are the internal validity of the parameter estimate and the statistical validity of the significance test. I summarize this chapter with a table enumerating the threats to the validity of each (see Table 6.9).[61] The table uses the language of econometrics and then translates the econometrics to the standard list of threats enumerated in texts on research design and program evaluation and discussed in Chapters 2 and 3 of this text. The language of econometrics is preferable to that of research design. It is more complete and precise, having a clear logical foundation based on the properties of the classical linear regression model. It is also more useful because it clearly applies to all regression models, no matter what the design. It makes clear that the regression model is the workhorse of all research designs, and it provides a vehicle for improving the validity of estimates of program impact. The language of program evaluation and research design is useful, too, for it provides a toolkit of alternative evaluation research designs. But a design without an estimating model is like a closet without hangers: It provides a place to put your data, but provides no frame for systematically organizing the data after they are collected. There is also evidence that the NE design, supplemented with a strong estimating model, may even produce estimates of program impact that are roughly similar to those from RFEs.[62]

This presentation in this text has moved gradually from the language of research design and program evaluation to the language of applied econometrics. Such a translation is important so that evaluators can be facile in both worlds. Nonetheless, Table 6.9 makes it clear that the language of econometrics is more complete than that of research design and program evaluation.

BASIC CONCEPTS

Definition: statistical controls
The causal model workhorse: theoretical diagram
The probable real-world diagram (in absence of RFE)
The causal model equation: theoretical
                                               estimating
Statistical controls: Why do we need them? (Hint: refer to the causal model workhorse
    diagram)
Most likely null hypothesis
Most likely alternative hypotheses
Data structures
    Cross-section
    Time series
    TSCS
Interpreting output
    R^2 and $\overline{R}^2$
Regression estimates: p-values and the two-tailed alternative
                                  p-values and one-tailed alternatives
                                  t-statistics and standard errors
                                  regression coefficients: interpretation
                                  coefficient for X_i
                                  coefficient for Z_i
Examples: correlation ≠ causation

Assumptions needed to believe that b is internally valid estimate of B [$E(b) = B$]
1. $E(\mu_i) = 0$
2. No RME/NRME in X_i (or Z_i) (see Chapters 2 and 7)
3. No NRME in Y_i (see Chapters 2 and 7)
4. $E(X_i, \mu_i) = 0$
    4a. No omitted Z_i variables (no OVB)
    4b. No two-way causation between X_i and Y_i (no SEB)
        a. Remedies for OVB
            1. Measure Z_i and use it as a statistical control
            2. Omit variables likely to have no direct impact on Y_i
            3. Preselect comparable units
            4. Use TSCS with fixed effects
            5. Use difference-in-difference estimates
            6. Use a natural experiment
            7. Use a lagged dependent variable (LDV), if it is causal
            8. Use two-stage estimation procedures
                8a. Propensity scores
                8b. Instrumental variable (IV) equation
                8c. Selection equation
            9. Use statistical tests for omitted variables
        b. Remedies for SEB
            1. Measure X_i at time $t - 1$ and Y_i at time t (i.e., lag the program variable)
            2. Use two-stage estimation procedure (2SLS) with instrumental variable (IV)

    c. CAUTION: A zero correlation between X_i and e_i (the observed residual in an estimated regression) is no test of whether $E(X_i, \mu_i) = 0$.

5. The underlying model of impact is linear (linear relation between X_i and Y_i)

    Violated if:

    a. Y_i is not continuous

    b. Y_i is continuous, but relation between X_i and Y_i is not linear

    c. Statistical interaction: impact of X_i on Y_i depends on Z_i

    Tests and remedies:

    a. Significant variables and low R^2 may be a sign of underlying nonlinear model.

    b. Y not continuous? Use MLE models

        logit/logistic/probit

        ordered logit

        multinomial logit

        tobit

        negative binomial/Poisson

    c. Nonlinear relation between X_i and Y_i? Transform variables so the relation is linear:

        $Y_i \rightarrow \log Y_i$

        $X_i \rightarrow \log X_i$

        log both Y_i and X_i

        use polynomial: add X_i^2 to estimating equation

    d. Build statistical interaction into the estimating equation:

        $Y_i = a + b_1 X_i + b_2 X_i Z_i + c Z_i + e_i$

6. Summary: Use multiple models

Assumptions needed to believe the significance test for b

1. Independent observations/no autocorrelation

    a. Examples:

        time-series data

        possible nonindependence of observations in the same group

    b. Tests and remedies

        Control for time

        Use Durbin-Watson test for simple TS data

        Use estimates corrected for heteroscedasticity between panels and

            autocorrelation within panels for TSCS data

            (or *xt* procedures in Stata)

        Model cross-section (within-group) autocorrelation

2. Variance of μ_i is constant for all observations (homoscedasticity)

    a. Examples: nonconstant error variance in cross-section data (especially individual-level observation or aggregates based on different group sizes)

    b. Tests and remedies

        Regression of absolute value of observed residual $|e_i|$ on suspect variable

        Use robust standard errors

        Correct for heteroscedasticity between panels in TSCS data

3. No (minimal) collinearity

    a. Examples: multiple treatment interference; X_i highly related with one or more Z_i variables

    b. Tests and remedies

        High R^2 and nothing significant?

Compute VIF
Principal components among independent variables
Matrix of correlations among independent variables? NO!
Toss out collinear variables? Mostly NO!
Test for joint significance
Get a large sample

What happened to the R^2?
    (We did not forget it; it is just not as useful as it is reputed to be.)

The language of econometrics and the language of program evaluation and research design
    One-to-one translation (almost)
    The language of econometrics is more complete

INTRODUCTION TO STATA

Basics

Stata is a statistical package for managing, analyzing, and graphing data. Regardless of platform, Stata can be command-driven. This brief introduction is based on personal and student experience and some content from the manual.
    The following are some of the functions most often used in Stata 8.0.

For commands (programming), type in the "Stata Command" window. The commands listed here have a period (.) in front because that is how they show up in the "Stata Results" window; you do not need to type a period when you input the commands.

---

1. Set Memory

Stata is very fast because it keeps the data in memory, so you should set a memory size large enough for its operation. The default memory size is 1 megabyte (Mb), which is good enough for homework assignments. However, if you are doing your own research project and the data set is very large, you may want to increase the memory to a larger size, say, 16 Mb:

```
.set memory 16m
```

2. Input the Data

(1) To open the data editor, click on the icon that looks like a table and is called "Data Editor." A spreadsheet opens.
(2) Input data in the cells.

Copy and paste data from the Excel spreadsheet to the Stata data editor. Copy the data from your source file; select the first cell (at the upper-lefthand corner) in the Stata data editor; then paste (ctrl-v or edit → paste). Please note that Stata does not accept some kinds of formatting in Excel; for example, if you use the 1000 separator (,), you will not be able to paste the data into Stata.

3. Examine the Data

(1)   View a description of the data set content (variables, cases, and so on.)

```
.describe
```

(2)   List the observations

```
.list
```

You should use the list command only if you have a few cases in the data set. For a large data set, you can add an "in" specification, like:

list in 1/10,

which tells Stata to list the first through tenth observations.

4. Analyze the Data

Reminder: Variable names are case sensitive.

(1) Descriptive statistics
    a.   Frequencies

```
.tab variablename
```

    b.   Mean, standard deviation, minimum, and maximum

```
.sum variablename
```

    c.   Correlation

```
.correlate var1 var2
```

(2) Generate new variables

```
.gen newvar=formula
```

For example:

```
.gen logY = ln(Y)
.gen score = (math + verbal)/2
```

Use .gen to create dummy variables. Suppose each state has a number from one to fifty in your data set, and you want to create fifty separate dummies for fixed-effects indicators. Then:

```
.gen ala = (Alabama=="01")
.gen ariz = (Arizona=="02")
.gen ark = (Arkansas=="03")
```

etc.

(3) Multivariate analysis

   a.   Linear regression

```
.regress y x1 x2 x3 x4
```

The first variable after ".regress" is treated as the dependent variable and the rest as independent variables, including the program variable(s) and the control variables.

   b.   Linear regression with heteroscedastic errors

```
.regress y x1 x2 x3 x4, robust
```

   c.   TSCS models, with correction for first-order autocorrelation over time within each group or panel, and heteroscedasticity (different variance in stochastic term in different group or panel):

```
.iis panelvarname
.tis timevarname
```

```
.xtgls y x1 x2 x3 x4, panel (hetero) corr (psar1)
```

Use .xtgee and other .xt options for 0/1, event count, and other nonlinear functional forms. They can be combined with the same commands as above to correct for autocorrelation within, and heteroscedasticity between, panels.

   d.   Logistic regression for 0/1 dependent variables (logistic generates odds ratios in Stata, while logit does not):

```
.logistic y x1 x2 x3, robust
```

You probably should use "robust" in most applications.

More Stata Use Notes

Do-file Editor

Using the command window, you can input only one command a time; Stata runs it and shows the result in the results window. The do-file editor allows you to write programs that include multiple commands and run them all at once. One significant advantage of using the do-file editor is that you can edit the commands you have input and save them for future use. To access the do-file editor, click on the "Do-file Editor" icon in the tool bar. Once you finish (part of) your program, you can (highlight the part and) click the "Do current file" icon in the tool bar of the do-file editor. Stata will run all the commands (highlighted) in your program. I recommend that you use this editor to write your commands. You can save the finished program file in .do format.

Help

Stata's help system is a very useful resource, especially if you do not have the manuals handy. To explore the syntax or other information of a specific command, you can click on "search" in the pull-down help menu and then enter the name of the command about which you are seeking assistance. In addition, you can consult a hard copy of the Stata User's Guide, which is also easy to use. You can also do an online search for more information about any Stata command.

Caution: Stata's error messages are not very informative. The pull-down help menu offers the best guidance when you make a mistake.

DO IT YOURSELF: INTERPRETING NONEXPERIMENTAL RESULTS

Note: These examples are made up. They may be loosely based on published studies, but they are designed to raise questions about design and analysis issues that can be corrected.

Gas Prices

To study whether gasoline prices are too high because there is too little competition in the retail gasoline market, a policy analyst collected the following data from a random sample of 1,000 gasoline stations in the Washington, DC, Metropolitan Statistical Area during the second week of February 2004.

Dependent variable: Posted price per gallon of regular gasoline (in $)

Independent variables: Type of station (1 = gasoline + convenience; 0 = gasoline only)
 Number of pumps available
 Hours per day station is open (1 = 24 hours; 0 = < 24 hours)
 Sum of federal + state + local gas taxes (in cents per gallon)
 Rent (rental cost per square foot, in $)
 Percent of sales sold by top four suppliers in DC; top four in Maryland; top four in Virginia
 Dummies for Maryland, DC (Virginia = omitted category)

Results

	Unstd *b*	*t*-statistic
Constant	.96	3.69
Type	.005	2.73
Number of pumps	−.02	−2.17
Hours open	−.03	−.58
Taxes	.01	7.92
Rent	.04	12.05
Percent top four	.06	3.03
Maryland	.03	1.24
DC	.02	.96

$N = 1,000$
$R^2 = .58$
F-statistic $= 200$
F-probability $= .0000$

1. Interpret the regression output, focusing on the coefficients, their significance, and the significance of the model as a whole. What do these results say about the causes of price differences between gas stations in the DC Metropolitan Statistical Area? Assuming the results in the table are valid, what light do they shed on the research question?
2. Assess the validity of the results in the table by discussing how well or poorly the most policy-relevant parts of the model meet the assumptions necessary for valid parameter estimates and hypothesis tests. How would you improve the model?

Trade

To evaluate the effectiveness of free-trade policies, an empirical study was conducted. Data were gathered on forty-four countries. The dependent variable for the regression was the average annual percentage growth rate in gross domestic product (GDP) per capita from 1990 to 1999. The independent variables were:

GDP90—the level of GDP in 1990 (in millions)
Index of restrictions—a measure of how open a country is to trade. Higher values for the index indicate the presence of more restrictions on trade, such as tariffs and quotas.
SEC—percent of the population that enrolls in secondary school
DEV—a dummy variable coded 1 if the country is classified as a developing country by the International Monetary Fund (IMF) and 0 if the country is classified as developed.

Variable	Coefficient	*t*-statistic
Constant	−.83	−.98
GDP90	−.35	−2.50
Index of trade restrictions	−1.98	−3.40
SEC	3.17	1.75
DEV	6.30	8.33

$N = 44$
$R^2 = 0.35$
F-statistic $(5,38) = 3.66$
F-probability $= .01$

1. Interpret the estimated regression equation. Specifically, what does the regression output tell you about the effects of each of the independent variables on the dependent variable? Are they significant? Be specific.
2. What, if any, are the implications of the results for the desirability of trade restrictions?
3. Do you believe the results reported in the table above? In answering, discuss how well or how poorly the model meets the assumptions necessary for valid parameter estimates and hypothesis tests.
4. How would you improve the model to produce more valid parameter estimates and hypothesis tests?

Gun Control

An empirical study of the effect of state gun-control regulations on the number of gun-related deaths reported the results shown in the following regression table. The study was based on data from each of the fifty states in the United States in 2000. The dependent variable is the number of gun-related deaths. The independent variables are:

REG   Number of gun-related regulations in the state
SIZE Population of the state in thousands
CCH   Number of crimes committed with handguns over the past twelve months
VC   Number of violent crimes over the past twelve months
HO   Handgun ownership rate (guns per 10,000) in the state over the past twelve months

Regression Results

Variable	Coefficient	t-statistic
Constant	27.22	6.10
REG	−0.02	0.33
SIZE	1.76	2.43
CCH	4.22	1.60
VC	3.12	0.99
HO	−0.02	0.25

$N = 50$
$\overline{R}^2 = 0.73$
F-statistic $(6,49) = 6.22$
F-probability $= .002$

1. Interpret the estimated regression equation. Specifically, what does the regression output tell you about the effects of each of the independent variables on the dependent variable? Are they significant? Be specific.
2. What, if any, are the implications of the results for the efficacy of gun-control regulations as a means of limiting gun-related deaths? Explain.

3. Discuss how well or how poorly the model meets the assumptions necessary for valid parameter estimates and hypothesis tests. Do you believe the results reported in the table above? Why or why not?
4. How could you improve the model? Be specific.

Charter Schools

A recent paper investigated the impact of charter schools on the quality of public schools.[63] Policy analysts have competing expectations about the likely impact. One expectation is that charter schools are merely substitutes for public schools; therefore, their presence only drains resources from public schools, reducing their quality. An alternative expectation is that charter schools complement public schools, so their presence sparks public schools to improve themselves, resulting in improved public school quality.

The investigator tested these expectations using data on 1,046 Texas school districts for each of the years from 1996 to 2002. The dependent variable is the pass rate on the tenth-grade Texas Assessment of Academic Skills (TAAS) exam; specifically, it is the percent of students who pass in traditional public schools in year t.

The main policy variable is the number of charter schools per county in which the school district is located, measured at time $t - 1$ (measured as the log of the number, written as "Ln").

The other independent variables are:

Percent of African-American students
Percent of Latino and low-income students (this is an additive index of the z-scores for each of the two variables, which are collinear)
School district enrollment (log number of students)
Average class size (number of students/number of teachers)
Percent of district revenues from state aid
Teacher experience (average number of years experience)
Teacher turnover (unit of measurement not specified)
Average daily attendance rate (percent)
Percent of full-time employees in district who are administrators

The results appear in the following table.

The Impact of Charter Schools on TAAS Pass Rates

Independent variables	Coefficient	s.e.	t-score
Ln charter schools ($t - 1$)	0.268	0.085	3.14
Class size	−0.150	0.036	−4.20
Teacher experience	0.274	0.026	10.39
Teacher turnover	−0.139	0.008	−17.75
Percent of revenue from state	−0.032	0.0025	−12.69
Bureaucracy as percent of staff	−0.11	0.039	−2.83
Attendance	3.23	0.071	45.75
African American (percent)	−0.189	0.0047	−40.76
Latino and low income	−2.05	0.032	−64.46
Log enrollment	0.49	0.068	7.04

$N = 7,245$

$\overline{R}^2 = 0.77$

$F = 1,518.47$

F-probability $= .0001$

Notes: Coefficients for annual dummy variables included but not reported.
Robust estimates of standard errors.

1. What do the specific results in this table say? (Write one sentence or phrase for each result.)
2. What light do the findings shed on the policy hypotheses that are at issue?
3. Do you believe the findings? Discuss the validity of the main finding with respect to the requirements for valid parameter estimates and hypothesis tests.
4. How would you tell the author to improve the validity of the analysis without changing the basic design? (Make a list.)

NOTES

1. Imai points to the important role of statistical controls (i.e., the NE) to "mop up" or reduce threats to internal validity that result from imperfect implementation of random assignment in RFEs. See Kosuki Imai, "Do Get-Out-the-Vote Calls Reduce Turnout? The Importance of Statistical Methods for Field Experiments," *American Political Science Review* 99, no. 2 (2005): 283–300.

2. This chapter uses uppercase letters to represent expected relations between independent X and Z variables and dependent Y; it uses lowercase letters to represent the actual empirical estimates of the relation between X and Y (and Z and Y). Previous chapters did not rely on this distinction between expected and actual coefficients, because the RFE and QE designs themselves do not rely on the econometric theory of statistical controls. In fact, in their pure form, neither the RFE nor the QE use statistical controls. Similarly, the two previous chapters represented the random component by e_i. This chapter uses μ_i to represent the theoretical stochastic term and e_i to represent the "observed" error. The chapter changes the notation to clearly distinguish the theoretically expected unknowns (given the assumptions of Equation 6.1, which this chapter explains) from the values that are actually estimated.

3. In the case of RFEs and QEs, researchers often compare units of analysis without the program or treatment to units of analysis with the program or treatment, or they compare units with treatment type 1 to similar units with treatment type 0. In these cases, the X_i variable is a dummy variable (1 or 0), and the intercept may be of interest, since it is the level of Y_i when $X_i = 0$. But even in RFEs and QEs, the regression coefficient, not the intercept, is the focus of analysis, comparable to the NE design. In most NE designs, the treatment is universal; what varies across each unit of analysis is the level or amount of the treatment. Hence, the treatment variable is not just 1 or 0; rather, it may have as many values as there are units of observation in the study.

4. Evaluators sometimes focus on correlation (r) rather than regression estimates of B. Whether computing partial correlations ($r_{xy \cdot z}$) or bivariate correlations (r_{xy}), these statistics are still correlations. Whether the correlations are partial or bivariate, they have only some of the properties of regression coefficients and are less informative. While they indicate the sign of the (linear) slope between X and Y (positive or negative), and while the partial correlation indicates the sign of the correlation between X and Y when Z is held constant, that is basically the only information in any correlation coefficient. The sign of the slope is also communicated by the sign of the regression coefficient. The magnitude of the correlation is also said to communicate the (inverse of) spread of observations around the regression line, but that information is both sample specific, and not an estimate of "noise" or error. What researchers should really want to know is the estimate of the slope, and the standard error in the estimate of the slope. The correlation coefficient does not communicate how much Y changes per unit change in X; the regression coefficient (estimate of the slope) does this, and the standard error of the coefficient gives information about the precision of the estimate. More important, because the correlation is sample specific, it does not have the generalizable properties of a parameter estimate. For example, correlation may be .20 in one sample and .85 in another,

even though the underlying impact of a unit change in X on Y is the same in the two samples. Hence, this text does not consider the use of correlations and other standardized measures of simple (bivariate) or partial association between X and Y.

5. Recall that the imaginary example of using an RFE to test pregnancy prevention programs in schools illustrated this situation. Controversy over positive or negative program impacts necessitates the use of two-tailed tests in program evaluation. Recall also from the discussion of statistical validity a nonzero (but still exact) null may often be useful. For example, an evaluator may use as a null the value of B that represents the change in Y as a result of a unit change in X that meets a cost-benefit test or that meets a politically acceptable standard of improvement.

6. It does not matter which comparison group is left out of the list of treatment dummies (but captured by the intercept). It is, however, usually convenient to compare new treatment alternatives to the current policy, so the current policy group is often the left-out or omitted dummy variable. It is referred to as the reference group.

7. In the context of a program evaluation model, the number of independent variables is the sum of the number of program or treatment dummy variables (X variables), the number of statistical controls (Z variables), plus a control for the lagged value of the output or outcome (Y_{t-1}), if there is one. So if there are three program alternatives, there will be two program dummies ($X1$, $X2$). With, say, five statistical controls ($Z1 \ldots Z5$) and a pretest or lagged outcome variable (Y_{t-1}), the total number of independent variables is eight.

8. This is the usual null. It is not necessarily the most appropriate or relevant null. Evaluators can make use of different (but exact) nulls. The usual null is 0; another null might be a higher (or lower) standard than that required by law or to meet a cost-effectiveness or cost-benefit standard. See the discussion of this issue in Chapter 2.

9. The imaginary RFE example of a dispute between controversial alternatives in abstinence education is a case in program evaluation in which, according to some, one alternative to the status quo is expected to improve outcomes while the other alternative is expected to make outcomes worse.

10. Regardless of whether the X or Z variables are dummy variables or continuous, if the outcome (Y) variable is a dummy variable, OLS regression produces internally and statistically invalid estimates. As the text shows, using OLS in this case imposes a linear functional form on a nonlinear relation and results in heteroscedastic errors. Logit (and probit) are regressions with the same logical framework of OLS regression, but they alleviate these threats to validity produced by OLS estimates. A simple transformation of direct logit estimates has the clear "odds" interpretation presented in the text. See Damodar N. Gujarati and Dawn C. Porter, *Basic Econometrics*, 5th ed. (Boston: McGraw Hill, 2009), ch. 15.

11. Ibid.

12. It is dangerous to have much confidence in a causal or impact interpretation of the coefficients associated with the confounding variables; they were included to strengthen causal conclusions about the impact of program variables. To make a causal conclusion regarding the impact of confounding variables requires a second set of control variables. Nonetheless, the coefficients do indicate association between one Z variable and Y, controlling for X (and other confounds) and may be of interest to evaluators.

13. Karen Chenoweth, "Homeroom," *Washington Post, Montgomery Extra*, September 11, 2003.

14. The example assumes that the purpose is to generalize to Montgomery County Public Schools (MCPS) middle schools. The sample is the population, less one school, and the variables are relatively stable from year to year. There is little reason to question the external validity of the result with respect to MCPS middle schools.

15. The degrees of freedom are the number of observations minus the number of coefficients to be estimated. In this study, there are 750 observations (fifty states times fifteen years for each state). There are fifty-nine unknown coefficients to be estimated. There are eight coefficients for each control variable, one coefficient for the policy variable, and an intercept (not reported, but estimated nonetheless). Also not reported are forty-nine fixed-effect estimates, representing one dummy variable for each state, less a reference state. I discuss fixed effects next. As a consequence, degrees of freedom (df) = $750 - 59 = 691$.

16. In this case, the choice of a slightly higher p-value is not unreasonable. Although the issue of marginally significant results is not raised in the article, the statistical choice in the example is between rejecting and not rejecting a substantively neutral null compared with a two-tailed alternative. One tail implies benefits (reduced fatalities), while the other implies costs (more fatalities). Risk aversion would lead an evaluator to recommend that a marginally significant positive coefficient (implying more fatalities) is substantively important. That is apparently what Houston has done.

17. This parenthetical remark is intended to highlight the importance of paying attention to the possible role of control (Z) variables in affecting outcomes (Y), holding the focal program variable (X) constant. Frequently, their significance (or lack thereof) and their magnitude may be informative about other programs and possibilities. But because Z variables are not the focal variables in the study, it is important to remember that the coefficients estimated for these variables have no causal interpretation. The results, however, may suggest that further research to examine their causal impact is warranted.

18. These are core topics in basic econometrics texts, which discuss these issues in both a larger context and much greater detail. See, for example, Peter Kennedy, *A Guide to Econometrics,* 5th ed. (Cambridge, MA: MIT Press, 2003); Gujarati and Porter, *Basic Econometrics;* W. Studenmund, *Using Econometrics: A Practical Guide,* 4th ed. (New York: Addison Wesley Longman, 2001); and Joshua D. Angrist and Jorn-Steffen Pischke, *Mostly Harmless Econometrics: An Empiricists Companion* (Princeton, NJ: Princeton University Press, 2009). These texts do not require matrix math or calculus.

19. The assumption that $E(\mu_i) = 0$ is consequential when it is important to estimate the value of the intercept. This is central in some program evaluation applications. In these applications, violating the assumption that $E(\mu_i) = 0$ is equivalent to omitting a relevant (dummy) independent variable. The issue is best considered in that context, which I will discuss.

20. If the measurement error in X_i is systematic, then it is related to Z_i and becomes an unmeasured, omitted variable; if the error is random, it (generally) attenuates the estimate of the focal regression coefficient that is intended to estimate the impact of X_i on Y_i. This has long been known, but its consequences are often ignored. See Marianne Bertrand and Sendhil Muullainathan, "Do People Mean What They Say? Implications for Subjective Survey Data," MIT Economics Working Paper 01–04 (January 2001) (http://papers.ssrn.com/paper.taf?abstract_id=260131/); R.B. Davies and B. Hutton, "The Effect of Errors in the Independent Variables in Linear Regression," *Biometrika* 62, no. 2 (1975): 383–391.

21. See S.G. Rivkin, "School Desegregation, Academic Attainment, and Earnings," *Journal of Human Resources* 35, no. 2 (2000): 333–346.

22. See, for example, Evan J. Rinquist and Tatiana Kostadinova, "Assessing the Effectiveness of International Environmental Agreements: The Case of the 1985 Helsinki Protocol," *American Journal of Political Science* 49, no. 1 (2005): 86–102. See also Christopher Carpenter, Sabina Postolek, and Casey Warman, "Public-Place Smoking Laws and Exposure to Environmental Tobacco Smoke (ETS)," *American Economic Journal: Policy* 3, no. 3 (2011): 35–61; Janel Currie, Stefano Della Vigna, Enrico Moretti, and Vikram Pathania, "The Effect of Fast Food Restaurants on Obesity and Weight Gain," *American Economic Journal: Policy* 2, no. 3 (2010): 32–63; Joseph J. Sabia, "Minimum Wages and the Economic Well-Being of Single Mothers," *Journal of Policy Analysis and Management* 27, no. 4 (2008): 848–866. See also a study similar to that discussed in Table 6.6: David J. Houston and Lilliard E. Richardson Jr., "Reducing Traffic Fatalities in the American States by Upgrading Seat Belt Use to Primary Enforcement," *Journal of Policy Analysis and Management* 25, no. 3 (2006): 645–659. These papers all use fixed effects for both cross-sections and for each time period (less a reference category in both cases).

23. There are numerous examples in policy-relevant journals such as *Social Science Quarterly, Journal of Policy Analysis and Management,* and *American Economic Review.* For examples, see Laura Langbein and Roseanna Bess, "Sports in School: Source of Amity or Antipathy?" *Social Science Quarterly* 83, no. 2 (2002): 436–454; Laura Langbein and Kim Spotswood-Bright, "Private Governments: The Efficiency and Accountability of Residential Community Associations," *Social Science Quarterly* 85, no. 3 (2004): 640–659; Kristen Butcher and Morrison Piehl, "Cross-City Evidence on the Relationship Between Immigration and Crime," *Journal of Policy Analysis and Management* 17, no. 3 (1998): 457–493. The papers by Langbein use both fixed effects and preselection of comparable groups to reduce the threat of OVB. Related approaches to using dummy variables for each group represent each group not only with a dummy variable but also with a group-specific error term. This recognizes that the location of an observation in one group rather than another is not entirely a deterministic, fixed process. This approach, referred to as hierarchical linear modeling (HLM), is useful in program evaluation for estimating the impact of whole-group reforms on individual observations within the group. HLM is useful not only with a multiple-group panel (time-series) design but also for cross-section data nested in different groups. For example, HLM can be used to analyze the impact of time-varying state-imposed cigarette tax increases on the behavior of smokers within each state. Such an analysis might require pretest information on smoking, but it does not require a full time series. See Robert Bifulco, "Addressing Self-Selection Bias in Quasi-Experimental Evaluations of Whole School Reform: A Comparison of Methods," *Evaluation Review* 26, no. 5 (2002): 545–572. See also Valentina A. Bali and R. Michael Alvarez, "The Race Gap in Achievement Scores: Longitudinal Evidence for a Racially Diverse

District," *Policy Studies Journal* 32, no. 3 (2004): 393–416. This study nests grades (scores) on multiple tests within each student who took the test, nests students within classes, and nests classes within schools, taking advantage of multiple, nonrandom hierarchies. Sarah Archibold, in "Narrowing in on Educational Resources That Do Affect Student Achievement," *Peabody Journal of Education* 81, no. 4 (2006): 23–42, uses HLM to investigate the impact of school-wide policies on students, recognizing that school policies can have different effects (that is, different estimated impact coefficients) that vary by type of school.

24. As an example of a multiple-group TSCS design that should, but does not, use fixed effects, see Gary A. Mauser and Richard A. Holmes, "An Evaluation of the 1977 Canadian Firearms Legislation," *Evaluation Review* 16, no. 6 (1992): 603–617. In addition to the studies mentioned in note 23, another example of the same design that should, and does, use fixed effects is Harrell W. Chesron, Paul Harrison, Carol R. Scotton, and Beena Varghese, "Does Funding for HIV and Sexually Transmitted Disease Prevention Matter? Evidence from Panel Data," *Evaluation Review* 29, no. 1 (2005): 3–23. This study uses eighteen annual observations for fifty states and the District of Columbia ($n = 918$), with state and year fixed effects. The authors find that funding does appear to reduce STDs. They refer to their study as a panel design. While the nomenclature is not universal, as mentioned earlier, panel designs are usually multiple-group designs with a relatively small time series (typically about 10).

25. See Bifulco, "Addressing Self-Selection Bias." Bifulco compares HLM with difference-in-difference models in that article. For an example of the use of a difference-in-difference model to estimate changes in black drop-out rates in districts that desegregated under court order to the changes in districts that faced no court order, see also Jonathan Guryan, "Desegregation and Black Drop-Out Rates," *American Economic Review* 94, no. 4 (2004): 919–943. The study also uses statistical controls. The results found that court-ordered desegregation reduced black drop-out rates significantly, by 2 to 3 percent. See also Robert Bifulco, William Duncombe, and John Yinger, "Does Whole-School Reform Boost Student Performance? The Case of New York City," *Journal of Policy Analysis and Management* 24, no. 1 (2005): 47–72, which explicitly uses difference-in-difference (with statistical controls) to reduce selection bias (i.e., OVB) in a study of three whole-school reforms in "troubled" New York City public elementary schools. The study also illustrates many other techniques mentioned in this chapter to reduce selection bias, including preselection of comparable units. For an example in the context of international development, see Esther Duflo, "Schooling and Labor Market Consequences of School Construction in Indonesia: Evidence from an Unusual Policy Experiment," *American Economic Review* 91, no. 4 (2001): 795–813. Despite the title, this is not a randomized experiment. Martha Bailey, in "'Momma's Got the Pill': How Anthony Comstock and *Griswold v. Connecticut* Shaped U.S. Childbearing," *American Economic Review* 100, no. 1 (2010): 98–129, estimates the impact of state changes in Comstock laws banning the sale of birth control bills (eliminated by the *Griswold* decision) on childbearing, showing that they are responsible for the spread of the use of contraception and declines in marital fertility. The article supplements TSCS models (with fixed effects and statistical controls) with difference (in fertility) in difference (between states with and without sales bans well after introduction of the bill) in difference (between the same states before the introduction of the pill) models (also supplemented with fixed effects and statistical controls). Another study, using a difference-in-difference (DID) model (first without and then with statistical controls), finds that a drop in traffic congestion induced by the introduction of an automated toll booth called E-Zpass (the first difference) improves infant health: The difference is larger for those who live near toll booths (the second difference). See Janet Currie and Reed Walker, "Traffic Congestion and Infant Health: Evidence from E-ZPass," *American Economic Journal: Applied Economics* 3, no. 1 (2011): 65–80. Of course, the simplest difference in difference design is just a PTPTCG design. See Eric A. Finkelstein, Kiersten Strombotne, Nadine Chan and James Krieger, in "Mandatory Menu Labeling in One Fast-Food Chain in King County, Washington," *American Journal of Preventive Medicine* 40, no. 2 (2011): 122–127, compare restaurants from one chain inside and outside King County before and after the law, finding no impact on transactions or calories per transaction.

26. See William Spelman, "Jobs or Jails? The Crime Drop in Texas," *Journal Policy Analysis and Management* 24, no. 1 (2005): 133–165.

27. Rivkin, "School Desegration."

28. Christopher Achen, "Why Lagged Dependent Variables Can Suppress the Explanatory Power of Other Independent Variables" (paper presented at the Annual Meeting of Political Methodology Section of the American Political Science Association, UCLA, July 20–22, 2000). See also Luke Keele and Nathan J. Kelly, "Dynamic Models for Dynamic Theories: The Ins and Outs of Lagged Dependent Variables," *Political Analysis* 14, no. 2 (2006): 186–205.

29. See Alan S. Gerber and Donald P. Green, "Correction to Gerber and Green (2000), Replication of Disputed Findings, and Reply to Imai (2005)," *American Political Science Review* 99, no. 2 (2005): 301–313.

30. Imai, "Do Get-Out-the-Vote Calls Reduce Turnout?"

31. Gerber and Green, "Correction."

32. See Eric Helland and Alexander Tabarrok, "The Fugitive: Evidence on Public Versus Private Law Enforcement From Bail Jumping," *Journal of Law and Economics* 47 (2004): 93–122. They use propensity score matching to estimate the impact of release of felony defendants from jail to public (or private) authorities on failure-to-appear-for-trial rates and other outcome variables. Their first-stage probability model makes ample use of fixed effects and controls for numerous potentially confounding variables. The result is a model with a good fit to the data, producing numerous close matches. Two other examples of propensity score matching are C.M. Gibson-Davis and E.M. Foster, "A Cautionary Tale: Using Propensity Scores to Estimate the Effect of Food Stamps on Food Insecurity," University of Wisconsin, Institute for Research on Poverty, Discussion Paper 1293–05; and Jason Barabas, "How Deliberation Affects Policy Opinions," *American Political Science Review* 98, no. 4 (2004): 687–702.

33. See Daniel L. Millimet and Rusty Tcherins, "On the Specification of Propensity Scores, With Applications to the Analysis of Trade Policies," *Journal of Business and Statistics* 27, no. 3 (2009): 397–415. They specify five different models to estimate impact of (comparable probabilities) of joining the World Trade Organization on environmental quality in the member states compared with (comparable) nonmember states. They also note that it is useful to "trim" the observations to the middle groups, where the predicted probabilities are not close to 1 or 0, and to see whether the results vary with the size of the trim. Another study finds that PSM, along with controls for pretest measures of the outcome, produces results that are close to results from random assignment, at least in the context of this one study. See Robert Bifulco, "Can Propensity Score Analysis Replicate Estimates Based on Random Assignment in Evaluations of School Choice? A Within-Study Comparison," Center for Policy Research, Maxwell School of Citizenship and Public Affairs, Working Paper 124 (September 2010).

34. One way to test whether W_i has no direct effect on Y_i is to ascertain that, when included in an equation for Y, the coefficient for W_i is not significant. As a practical matter, estimates from the two stages of an IV regression must be made jointly to reduce errors of statistical validity. Many statistical packages make this convenient (e.g., ivreg in STATA), but it is still necessary to explicitly specify both a first- and second-stage equation. To augment internal validity, it is also necessary to test to make sure that the instrumental variable is unrelated to the stochastic term in the second-stage equation. Joint estimation is necessary for any of the two stage equations that I mention below. Consult an applied econometrics text for specifics, such as those listed in footnote 18.

35. The are many examples of the use of IVs. One study uses IVs to investigate the impact of corruption on economic growth in the U.S. states; it estimates the impact of corruption using conventional methods with no instrument and with various IV specifications. See Noel D. Johnson, Courtney L. LaFountain, and Steven Yamarik, "Corruption Is Bad for Growth (Even in the United States)," *Public Choice* 147 (2011): 377–393. Peter Hinrichs, in "The Effects of the National School Lunch Program on Education and Health," *Journal of Policy Analysis and Management* 29, no. 3 (201): 479–505, uses a change in the federal formula for allocating funding for school lunches as an IV to identify exposure to the program: The timing and nature of the change meant that similar children born in different birth cohorts had different chances of exposure. It is unlikely that the change in the law could directly affect individual education or health outcomes, and the empirical test was consistent with that assumption. Jennifer Hunt and Marjolaine Gauthier-Loiselle, in "Does Immigration Boost Innovation?" *American Journal of Economics* 2, no. 2 (2010): 31–56, use an aggregate lagged value (1940 immigrants) to estimate the probability that contemporary immigrant college grads will receive patents (compared with natives) in a TSCS panel data set on U.S. states. Another study examines whether living near a fast food restaurant contributes to obesity by using the opening of a new interstate (in rural communities) to instrument distance from a fast food restaurant. While obese people might choose to live near a fast food restaurant, using the exogenous construction of an interstate to predict restaurant location should remove the endogenous effect of obesity on distance, because construction of an interstate is unlikely to directly affect the obesity of those who live nearby, but it does directly affect distance. The paper finds that a reduction in distance from a fast food restaurant has no effect on obesity. See Michael Anderson and David Matsa, "Are Restaurants Really Supersizing America?" *American Economic Journal: Applied Economics* 3, no. 1 (2011): 152–188.

36. See, for example, Arjun S. Bedi and Jeffrey H. Marshall, "School Attendance and Student Achievement: Evidence from Rural Honduras," *Economic Development and Cultural Change* 47, no. 3 (1999):

657–682. The dependent variable is school attendance. The main independent variable includes indicators of school quality, which is partly measured by test scores. Test scores are recorded only for those who attend, introducing a sample selection problem. The authors use a selection equation to estimate the probability of attendance and then use that estimate as a statistical control for sample selection bias. They also use instrumental variables to control for the nonrandom distribution of other school quality inputs. HeeSoun Jang, in "Contracting Out Parks and Recreation Services: Correction for Selection Bias Using a Heckman Selection Model," *International Journal of Public Administration* 29 (2006): 799–818, provides another example. The study examines whether local government contracting with private, nonprofit, or other government units affects local government expenditures; the potential selection bias problem is clear: Local governments that do no contracting in these areas will be missing from the study sample, yet contracting (or not) may affect the dependent variable and is likely to be related to the focal variable. As it turned out, the test for the absence of (Heckman) selection bias could not be rejected, and no correction is made. Had the test been rejected, the second-stage equation estimating the impact on type of contract on expenditures would require a correction for sample selection bias. Using Heckman selection is also useful to reduce bias due to nonresponse in surveys.

37. For information on the RESET and Hausman tests, respectively, see, for example, Gujarati and Porter, *Basic Econometrics*, 479–481 and 603–605.

38. On tests for Granger causality, see Gujarati and Porter, *Basic Econometrics*, 652–655. As an example of the use of lagged policy variables, see Karen L. Remmer, "Does Foreign Aid Promote the Expansion of Government?" *American Journal of Political Science* 48, no. 1 (2004): 77–92. This article uses multiple methods to reduce threats from both OVB and SEB, including (in the same model) both lagged dependent variables and lagged independent program variables. It also relies heavily on change scores rather than levels, which should reduce bias due to serial correlation (trends). It also uses a gain score as the dependent variable, with the previous level of the dependent variable as an independent variable.

The larger issue of lagged variables is related both to the question of internal validity (omitting a causally relevant lagged variable) and to the question of statistical validity due to the presence of serial or autocorrelation. For a discussion of the problems of estimating models with lagged variables, see Gujarati and Porter, *Basic Econometrics*, 412–418. The problem of invalid estimates is considerably reduced if it is reasonable to assume that the underlying model is what is called a dynamic or partial adjustment model. See also Neal Beck and Jonathan N. Katz, "Time-Series Cross-Section Issues: Dynamics, 2004" (working paper, July 24, 2004). In the context of program evaluation, this may not be an unreasonable assumption. Nonetheless, it is not advisable to use lagged variables as the only method of estimating program effects. If a researcher has the time-series data necessary for estimating models with lagged variables, a variety of estimating methods are available. If the different methods, each with different strengths and weaknesses, yield consistent results regarding the impact of the program on the outcome, then the researcher can be confident that the overall conclusion is defensible.

39. Gujarati and Porter, *Basic Econometrics*, 711–730.

40. Steven D. Levitt, "Using Electoral Cycles in Police Hiring to Estimate the Effect of Police on Crime," *American Economic Review* 87, no. 3 (1997): 270–290. Gujarati and Porter also point to the similarity between TSLS and IVs (*Basic Econometrics*, 730).

41. As another example of a study that uses 2SLS to deal with the SEB threat, see William Evans, Matthew C. Farrelly, and Edward Montgomery, "Do Workplace Smoking Bans Reduce Smoking?" *American Economic Review* 89, no. 4 (1999): 728–747. The article also discusses strategies for including more control variables to reduce the threat of OVB. In another example, Mark Lubell examines the impact of collaborative institutions on cooperation and consensus in implementing national policies regarding protecting estuaries. He notes that advocates believe that collaborative institutions build cooperation and consensus ($X_i \rightarrow Y_i$), but areas that have high levels of cooperation and consensus are more likely to build cooperative institutions ($Y_i \rightarrow X_i$). To adjust for SEB, Lubell uses a two-stage procedure. The selection model predicts the probability of choosing cooperative institutions, based on statistical controls used in both equations, and also on exogenous geographical factors that appear only in the first-stage selection model. The study concludes that collaboration appears to enhance consensus but has no impact on cooperation. See Mark Lubell, "Collaborative Environmental Institutions: All Talk and No Action?" *Journal of Policy Analysis and Management* 23, no. 3 (2004): 549–573. It is common to use IVs to reduce bias due to endogeneity: For example, high wages and employment can induce immigration, but immigration can affect wages and employment. To estimate the effect of immigration on wages, instrumenting for immigration reduces the likely endogeneity. See George J. Borjas, Jeffrey Grogger, and Gordon H. Hanson, "Immigration and the Economic Status of African-American

Men," *Economica* 77, no. 306 (2010): 255–282. Another approach is to use an exogenous policy shock that affects the focal policy variable but is unlikely to directly affect the outcome. See Jon H. Fiva, "Does Welfare Policy Affect Residential Choices: An Empirical Investigation Accounting for Policy Endogeneity," *Journal of Public Economics* 93, no. 3–4 (2009): 529–540. In addition to using an exogenous policy change to instrument the focal policy variable, reducing endogeneity, the article uses differences-in-differences to reduce omitted variable bias.

42. See, for example, Gujarati and Porter, *Basic Econometrics*, 228.

43. It is often preferable to linearize an underlying nonlinear model. For example, when a researcher seeks to estimate the impact of a percent change in X_i on the percent change in Y_i (an elasticity), and neither X_i nor Y_i are originally percents, transforming the original values of X_i and Y_i into log-scores, and using a standard linear regression of $\log Y_i$ on $\log X_i$ linearizes the original nonlinear relation. See, for example, Heather E. Campbell, "People, Devices, Prices, or Rules: The Relative Effectiveness of Policy Instruments in Water Conservation," *Review of Policy Research* 21, no. 5 (2004): 637–662. For a variety of reasons, this transformation also makes theoretical sense, particularly when the focal policy variable is price (or a proxy for price, or a component of price, such as a tax) and the outcome variable is consumption.

44. See C.B. Lloyd, S. El Tawila, W.H. Clark, and B.S. Mensch, "The Impact of Educational Quality on School Exit in Egypt," *Comparative Education Review* 47, no. 4 (2003): 444–467; M.P. Bitler and J. Currie, "Does WIC Work? The Effects of WIC on Pregnancy and Birth Outcomes," *Journal of Policy Analysis and Management* 24, no. 1 (2005): 73–91; D. Kimball and M. Kropf, "Ballot Design and Unrecorded Votes on Paper-Based Ballots," *Public Opinion Quarterly* 69, no. 4 (2005): 508–529.

45. I drop the subscript i in many of the remaining examples. It should be clear by now that X, Y, and Z describe observed values on each of these variables for each of the i units of analysis in the study.

46. Arthur C. Brooks, "Public Subsidies and Charitable Giving: Crowding Out, Crowding In, or Both?" *Journal of Policy Analysis and Management* 19, no. 3 (2000): 451–464.

47. The model for B implies that μ' is independent of Z. The other assumption is that μ' is independent of X in the full model so that $E(\mu'X) = \mu'X = 0$.

48. It is not always obvious how to interpret or test the significance of estimates of interaction terms. In general, a simple significance test for b_1 in the equation $Y = a + b_1X + b_2ZX + cZ + e$ is not correct, because the impact of X on Y depends on Z. To test if the interactive model is superior to a simple linear model $Y = a + b_1X + cZ + e$, an F-test for the difference between the R^2 for the interactive model compared with the R^2 for the linear model is usually appropriate. For a list of dos and don'ts, see Thomas Brambor, William R. Clark, and Matt Golder, "Understanding Interaction Models: Improving Empirical Analysis," *Political Analysis* 14, no. 1 (2006): 63–82.

49. See D.C. Grabowski and M.A. Morrisey, "Gasoline Prices and Motor Vehicle Fatalities," *Journal of Policy Analysis and Management* 23, no. 3 (2004): 575–593; D. Grant and S.M. Ratner, "The Effect of Bicycle Helmet Legislation on Bicycling Fatalities," *Journal of Policy Analysis and Management* 23, no. 3 (2004): 595–611; Rivkin, "School Desegregation."

50. For other examples of multiple methods, see P.B. Levine and D. Staiger, "Abortion Policy and Fertility Outcomes: The Eastern European Experience," *Journal of Law and Economics* 47 (2004): 223–244, which measures dependent variables as logs, uses multiple outcomes, is a TSCS with fixed effects for country and year, and has numerous statistical controls. See also D.N. Figlio and M.E. Lucas, "What's in a Grade: School Report Cards and the Housing Market," *American Economic Review* 94, no. 3 (2004): 591–604, which relies on numerous fixed effects (for neighborhood, school district, month, and year) for houses in Florida (a selected subsample). The authors use the subsample and multiple levels of fixed effects instead of statistical controls, which may be incomplete at best and hard to measure. The study also uses logs to measure outcomes as well as multiple measures of both outcomes and school grades. It finds that school quality indicators are capitalized into housing prices. A recent evaluation of whether No Child Left Behind (a nationwide mandate for school accountability) had no effect on student achievement, raised it, or lowered it used a TSCS panel design for the basic model, but then used varying measures of outcomes, varying measures of the treatment (e.g., as a dichotomy or as "dosage"), varying the set of controls, and testing whether the results are robust to a gradual or sudden effect. It finds consistent findings that NCLB raised student achievement among most subgroups. See Thomas S. Dee and Brian Jacob, "The Impact of No Child Left Behind on Student Achievement," *Journal of Policy Analysis and Management* 30, no. 3 (2011): 418–446. In addition to using different specifications from a basic TSCS panel design, it is often possible to reanalyze the same data with a different design. Christopher Carpenter and Carlos Dobkin, in "The Minimum Legal Drinking Age and Public Health," *Journal of Economic Perspectives* 25, no.

2 (2011): 133–156, use both a TSCS panel and a regression discontinuity design, along with numerous outcome measures and specifications to find that restricting access to drinking and driving by older teens reduces both drinking and public driving hazards.

51. For example, William H. Greene, *Econometric Analysis*, 4th ed. (Upper Saddle River, NJ: Prentice Hall, 2000), 750–751; Peter Kennedy, *A Guide to Econometrics*, 5th ed. (Cambridge, MA: MIT Press, 2003), ch. 18.

52. The speed limit example discussed earlier in this chapter (see Table 6.6) does not correct for the threat of autocorrelation; it also fails to correct for possible heteroscedasticity problems that I will discuss. Thus, while its use of controls for numerous Z variables and for fixed-effects dummies gives us confidence in the likely internal validity of the parameter estimate for the 65 mph speed limit, and the large n in the design contributes to its statistical validity, its failure to correct for autocorrelation and heteroscedasticity reduces confidence in the results of the significance tests, raising questions about statistical validity despite the large n.

53. See Bifulco, "Addressing Self-Selection Bias," and the other items in note 25 in this chapter.

54. Laura Langbein and Connie Jorstad, "Productivity in the Workplace: Cops, Culture, Communication, Cooperation, and Collusion," *Political Research Quarterly* 57, no. 1 (2004): 65–79.

55. Thomas J. Kane and Douglas O. Staiger, "The Promise and Pitfalls of Using Imprecise School Accountability Measures," *Journal of Economic Perspectives* 16, no. 4 (2002): 91–114.

56. Heteroscedasticity is particularly likely in survey responses. While heteroscedasticity is usually regarded as a statistical nuisance, it may also have substantive importance. For example, if advertising is designed to reduce uncertainty and if greater certainty can be represented by less heteroscedasticity (i.e., less variance in opinion residuals), then one can measure the impact of advertising by its impact on reducing heteroscedasticity. See M.A. Alvarez and J. Brehm, "American Ambivalence Toward Abortion Policy: Development of a Heteroscedastic Probit Model of Competing Values," *American Journal of Political Science* 39 (1995): 1055–1082.

57. Gujarati and Porter, *Basic Econometrics*, 365–411.

58. Ibid., 386–388.

59. For an example of creating a composite of collinear Z variables, see Langbein and Bess, "Sports in School."

60. For example, on using the *F*-statistic to test hypotheses about variables being jointly significant, see Gujarati and Porter, *Basic Econometrics*, 243–246.

61. The issues raised in this chapter do not exhaust the issues of NE research design. One issue that this chapter does not address is the proper level of analysis. In general, if the researcher is interested in studying individuals, then individuals should be the unit of analysis. For example, if students are the unit of analysis, then study students and not schools. Sometimes, however, data on individuals are not available and it becomes necessary to make inferences about students from data on schools. A particularly egregious example comes from a study of the effect of homework on student achievement: It uses countries as the unit of analysis to make inferences about the impact of homework on students. See David P. Baker and Gerald Letendre, *National Differences, Global Similarities: World Culture and the Future of Schooling* (Palo Alto, CA: Stanford University Press, 2005), ch. 8. The book tends to focus on correlation, with few or no statistical controls, introducing OVB. Making inferences about individuals from group-level data introduces a form of aggregation bias, which is a threat to internal validity; it may also threaten statistical validity. There is a large literature in political science concerning problems of aggregation bias and ecological inference. See, for example, Gary King, Ori Rosen, and Martin Tanner, ed., *Ecological Inference: New Methodological Strategies* (Cambridge, MA: Cambridge University Press, 2004).

Another threat to internal validity is to make inferences about program impact based on observations that are outside the range of observations in the data. For example, if no student in a sample has less than eight years of education, inferences about the impact of six versus eight years of education should not be made from the study. See Gary King and Langche Zeng, "The Dangers of Extreme Counterfactuals," *Political Analysis* 14, no. 2 (2006): 131–159.

62. David H. Greenberg, Charles Michalopoulos, and Philip K. Robins, "Do Experimental and Non-Experimental Evaluations Give Different Answers about the Effectiveness of Government-Funded Training Programs?" *Journal of Policy Analysis and Management* 25, no. 3 (2006): 523–552.

63. John Bohte, "Examining the Impact of Charter Schools on Performance in Traditional Public Schools," *Policy Studies Journal* 32, no. 4 (2004): 501–520.

7

Designing Useful Surveys for Evaluation

This chapter discusses the survey as a means of collecting useful information for evaluating public programs. The essence of evaluation is comparison, and surveys are one (but not the only) way to collect information useful for comparing programs or for comparing individual performance in a special program to individual performance in agencies or administrative units without the special program or with a different program.[1] Thus, surveys are a particularly useful source of data for cross-section experimental or quasi-experimental designs or for cross-section nonexperiments with statistical controls. For example, in evaluating education programs (or other social service programs), administrative data can be used to compare performance in similar programs (e.g., attendance rates or test scores). However, often it is useful to supplement that data with information from surveys of participants (e.g., students or their parents) or program case workers (e.g., teachers), especially when that information is not available elsewhere.[2] Surveys of the same individual over time in different programs or administrative units can be especially useful. (It is not a good use of resources to use surveys to collect information that is already available elsewhere.) The purpose of this chapter is to explain how to design a survey and use the results as one source of information to assess the effectiveness of a public program.

Many of the examples in this chapter rely on evaluation of local public education programs. The examples, however, illustrate general points that can be applied to any evaluation that relies on data about individuals. The example of education illustrates that surveys are particularly useful as a source of data for evaluating local programs in a specific place. Surveys are not reserved for national studies; while they are a useful tool for collecting data about representative national samples, they may be even more useful as a source of information for evaluating programs at the local level.[3]

Anyone can administer a survey. All you need is a word processor and a telephone; or a word processor and stamps, paper, and envelopes; or a word processor and Internet access. Special survey software is also helpful, especially with phone and Internet surveys. But poorly designed surveys can be a wasted effort. Proper design is important for three reasons:

1. To get the best possible response rate, given your survey budget
2. To get responses that are as unbiased and informative as possible
3. To turn the responses that you get into useful information

This chapter briefly discusses some of the critical steps for achieving these goals. Entire books have been written on each of these topics, so only the most important rules will be discussed here. Over the years, social scientists have learned a lot about responses to surveys, and designing surveys is increasingly becoming a science and not an art. Hence, I use the term "rules" intentionally.

THE RESPONSE RATE

Why Does a High Response Rate Matter?

Suppose you want to survey one hundred people and ninety respond. The relatively high response rate (90 percent) means that a biased response is a small potential problem. If only forty or fifty respond, then a biased response rate is potentially a larger problem. Maybe only the wealthiest of the hundred responded, and their opinions are not representative of the entire population of one hundred, or of the random sample of one hundred, that you wanted to reach. Or maybe only the activists responded, and their opinions may not represent the typical person. Any of these and other possibilities are likely sources of bias when response rates are low. The lower the response rate, the greater the potential impact on your conclusions of differences between who responds and who does not. All else being constant, a higher response rate is better than a lower one.

The actual response rate depends most critically on the kind of survey that you do. There are three basic types of surveys: the face-to-face survey, the telephone survey, and the mail questionnaire. The face-to-face (structured) interview or survey is the most expensive but usually garners the highest response rate (75 percent or better). Compared with face-to-face interviews and the telephone survey, the mail questionnaire is usually the least expensive but may wind up with a low response rate (30 to 40 percent). The telephone survey is usually in the middle on the dimensions of cost and response rate. Over the past few years, response rates to all three kinds of surveys have been declining. Internet surveys have become increasingly popular. However, their characteristics in terms of cost and response rate depend critically on the context in which they are administered and on the type of intended respondent. For example, Internet surveys of the general public usually garner very low response rates, but they may also be quite inexpensive. Internet surveys of employees may garner a reasonably high response rate, and they are not usually expensive.[4]

The general points that this chapter outlines about designing questions apply to all surveys, even those on the Internet. Some of the other points about cost and response rate tradeoffs that I make here may not apply to the Internet survey. The focus in this text is on the surveys most common in evaluation research, which are mail surveys (or Internet surveys to selected addresses, with links to a survey instrument) and telephone surveys. The focus is not on the mechanics of administering surveys; these mechanics are particularly critical in face-to-face and Internet surveys. For more information about the mechanics of surveys and on the design of survey instruments, see the texts cited at the end of this chapter.

The mail (or Internet) survey is probably the most common type of survey that program evaluators use. It is reasonably inexpensive; however, the mail survey requires money for postage and paper. By contrast, telephone surveys and face-to-face interviews take personnel time, which can be even more costly. Many communities (professional communities, localities, business communities, etc.) have access to volunteers who can administer a telephone survey. Communities also have access to volunteers who can administer a face-to-face survey. However, in the context of many communities, telephone and face-to-face surveys have a big disadvantage that national telephone and most (national) face-to-face surveys do not have: face-to-face and telephone interviews are often not really anonymous or even confidential. This may also be true of some Internet surveys. The survey respondent and the interviewer (or research sponsor) may well know each other or may have occasion to meet in the future. In that situation, respondents are unlikely to express their true opinions, reducing response rates or biasing responses. Consequently, telephone, the Internet, or face-to-face interviews may not be the best means to collect responses to a community (or office) survey unless the community population is very large or the researchers have the technical means to protect confidentiality. While the discussion in this chapter centers on ways of improving response rates to mail or Internet questionnaires, most of the examples apply to all survey instruments. The first question is one of the "real" sample size: How many people should the questionnaire be sent to, especially if the response rate is likely to be unrepresentative of the population you wish to study?

How Many Surveys Should You Send Out?

Except when the population of interest is small (e.g., under 1,000), the size of the population has no impact on the decision about how many surveys to send. Researchers who are studying large populations (e.g., the United States) and researchers who are studying smaller populations (e.g., a single state or city within the United States) usually use random samples of the same size, usually between 800 and 1,000. They use this number so that they can be confident that the sample estimate is close to the true, but unknown, characteristic of the population, called the population parameter. In most situations, samples larger than this do little to increase the level of confidence in the sample estimate or to reduce its distance from the true, but unknown, population parameter (e.g., the population percentage or mean). Larger samples do, however, add to the budget, and most researchers decide that the increase in the cost outweighs the small additional benefit in precision. In the context of local programs, however, even surveys of this size (i.e., 800 to 1,000) may be inappropriate or too expensive.

In program evaluation, even conventional samples (of 800 to 1,000 or more) are not always essential. They are critical when the task is to estimate population characteristics regarding values on a single variable (e.g., mean income) or values on a set of single variables (e.g., mean income, mean years of education, mean age, or percentage older than age sixty-five). This may be common in descriptive evaluations, including needs assessments. But in evaluating program impact, especially at the local level, the purpose is *not* to estimate population characteristics of single variables but, instead, to compare the performance of one program against another. In other words, program evaluation focuses on relations between variables. It compares values of Y_i for different values of X_i, controlling, if necessary, for values of Z_i. For example, you may want to survey teachers, asking them to estimate the percent of time that children in their classrooms spend "on task." You might then compare the survey-based time-on-task estimates (Y_i) of teachers in classrooms with a special computer-learning program to the estimates of teachers in comparable classrooms without the special program (X_i). (You could even use statistical controls to hold confounding Z_i variables constant, if the classrooms, or the teachers, are not otherwise comparable.) Or you may wish to survey parents to find out how much time their children spend at home on school-related activities (homework, art projects, music practice, writing projects) ($Y1_i$) and how much television their children watch ($Y2_i$). You might then use this survey-based information to compare the responses of parents with children in schools with a special arts program to those of parents with children in comparable schools without the program (X_i).

In these examples, you can estimate these differences with samples of fifty or sixty respondents in each of the two schools. Samples of less than thirty in each school are dangerously small: The data would need to show huge differences to claim that those differences were unlikely to have occurred by chance had they been based on data from a world in which there really was no difference between the schools. But samples in the range of fifty to sixty (or perhaps a few more) from each of the entities to be compared should be sufficient for most applications.

The main point is that program evaluators who focus on causal evaluation usually do not use surveys to estimate population parameters on single variables or sets of single variables from a sample.[5] Rather, they use surveys to collect data to compare the performance of programs or management strategies in particular locales. Thus they use surveys to examine the relation *between* variables. Because evaluators use surveys to make comparisons, the need for huge numbers of observations (usually well in excess of 800) is not necessary.[6] Recall from previous chapters that statistically valid multiple regressions, the workhorse of evaluations, rarely require that large a sample. The reason is that the purpose of the regression is to estimate program impact (i.e., a regression or relational parameter) rather than to estimate a population characteristic (i.e., a population parameter). The sampling distribution of most relational estimators (e.g., the regression coefficient) becomes normal when the sample size, minus the number of variables in the analysis, is 120 or larger.

It is, however, important to point out that, even in the context estimating the parameter relating a treatment (X_i) to a program outcome (Y_i), the relevant target sample size applies to each subgroup. If the evaluator expects interaction effects (e.g., the program is likely to operate differently in each state), the target $n = 50$ states $\times$ 120 sample in each state $= 6,000$.

What Do I Do About Nonrespondents?

Even if evaluators who use surveys do not need huge numbers of respondents, they still need to decide how many surveys they need. The question of how many to survey is related in part to the response rate. All else being constant, for a fixed budget, you often face a choice. The choice is between sending the survey once to a lot of people, getting a low (and possibly biased) response rate, and sending the survey to fewer people, while budgeting for follow-up to nonrespondents, garnering a higher final response rate and reducing the risk of bias due to atypical respondents.

There is no clear answer to this dilemma. If you survey professionals (e.g., teachers), who are likely to be interested in the topic (e.g., their schools), you can probably anticipate a relatively high response rate (60 to 70 percent or more) with just a single mailing. In that case, follow-up may not be necessary, and you can have a large number of respondents for a fixed budget. Conversely, if you anticipate a low response rate (30 to 40 percent) and a possibly biased set of responses from the first wave, a smaller initial sample with multiple (and costly) follow-up may be a better option.

If you anticipate a relatively high response rate (e.g., more than 70 percent), then you probably do not need to worry about sending out follow-up surveys, and the related issue of the sample size is quite straightforward. For example, suppose that you can afford to study a total of one hundred teachers and aides, fifty from a high school with a mentoring program and fifty from a comparable high school without the special program. If that is the entire teaching staff of each school, then you do not need to worry about selecting a random sample: Simply send a survey instrument to every teacher and aide in both schools. (These two populations do not need to be exactly equal in size. However, since the schools are supposed to be roughly comparable in all important respects except for the presence of the special mentoring program, their size should also be about the same.)

Alternatively, suppose that you wish to survey the parents of the children in these two schools and you cannot afford to survey all of them.[7] You can afford a random sample of fifty parents from each school. Assuming a high response rate, how should you select that random sample? There are several ways to do this, but one of the easiest is to list all the pupils in each school alphabetically or by the last four digits of the students' Social Security numbers or school ID numbers. If there are 1,000 pupils in each school, you will select every twentieth child from each list to get the desired sample of fifty parents—*but* pick the starting point randomly. In other words, you can start with the first pupil on the list, the second, the third, or anywhere up through the twentieth.

What makes your selection random is where you start. Pick a random number between 1 and 20 by using the last two digits (of those that are 20 or below) of the last lottery ticket you bought or the ID number on one of the bills in your wallet.[8]

So far, the assumption is that most of the people in your sample respond to your survey. But often it is reasonable to expect a low and possibly biased response rate. Then the sample size of fifty from each school (or other street-level administrative entity) may yield considerably fewer than fifty responses. Moreover, the actual respondents may be unrepresentative of the random sample that you selected. In this situation, you must select a larger random sample from each school and plan to send follow-up surveys to the nonrespondents.

For example, suppose that you are still aiming for a random sample of fifty responses (from students or, more likely, one of their parents) from each of two schools that you are comparing. You anticipate a low response rate of perhaps 40 percent after the first try and 20 percent of the remaining sample after the second try. You do not find it advisable to remind parents more than twice. The usual rule of thumb is that the response rate to a follow-up is half the response rate to the original mailing, where the halved response applies to those who did not respond in the first wave. To get fifty actual responses from each school, you should select a random sample of ninety-six from each school. This sample size was calculated in the following way:

$$0.40 \times sample\ size + 0.20 \times (1 - 0.40) \times sample\ size = 50\ actual\ responses$$
Solving for the sample size, you have 50/0.52 = 96 for the sample size.

To select 96 from the population of 1,000 pupils in each school, select every tenth student from each school list as described before (1,000/96 ≈ 10). Use a random start by picking at random a number between 1 and 10. If you actually get 50 responses from the 96 surveys that you mailed out, your overall response rate would be a respectable 52 percent (50/96 = 0.52). In that case, you could abandon the idea of a second wave.

It may be reasonable to anticipate an even lower response to the first wave (say, 30 percent) while still planning to send just one reminder. Then, to get fifty responses, you will have to select from each school a random sample whose size is calculated in the following way:

$$0.30\ (sample\ size) + .15 \times (1 - 0.30) \times (sample\ size) = .405\ (sample\ size) = 50$$
Solving for the sample size, you have 50/.405 = 123 for the actual sample size.

However, if the respondents are still likely to be very unrepresentative of the randomly selected 123, then the seemingly low response rate (50/123 = 40.5 percent) would be cause for some concern. You will need to consider the following steps for increasing the response rates. But these steps do not guarantee success, and sometimes a 40 percent response rate (or even less, like 35 percent) is just the best that you can do, unless face-to-face or telephone interviews (with follow-up to nonrespondents) are a feasible and sensible alternative.

How to Get the Best Response Rates to Mail Surveys

1. In these days of diminishing response rates to all kinds of surveys, you should probably expect to follow-up to improve response rates. For mail surveys, this means that you should send out surveys once, wait two weeks, then send out a second wave, wait another two weeks, and then possibly send out a third wave. (I discuss later whether to resend the second- and third-wave survey only to nonrespondents or to everyone.) Expect diminishing returns to each follow up. If you get 50 percent on

the first try, count on getting half of that on the second try from the nonrespondents, and half of the second-try response rate (based on the still remaining, stalwart or stubborn, nonrespondents) on the third try. Many researchers make do with just one follow-up. The assumptions about likely response rates mentioned here might be too optimistic. You will simply have to make assumptions about likely response rates based on your own and others' experience in your situation or community.[9]

2. Keep the surveys short. They should take no more than twenty minutes of a respondent's time. The longer the survey, the lower the response rate.

3. Administer surveys when it is convenient for the respondents, not when it is convenient for the researcher. For example, do not conduct surveys during holidays, when respondents are not likely to be at home or work.

4. Do not make it more costly than necessary for respondents to cooperate. Respondents are already giving you their time. Do not ask any more of them.

4a. If you use postage mail, include a self-addressed stamped envelope (SASE) that respondents can use to return their surveys to you. Some experts advise sending the survey out in an attractive and noticeable (e.g., pastel-colored) envelope, with a real stamp (even a commemorative stamp), rather than a postal imprimatur. Others advise calling the respondent's attention to the survey by sending it as a flat-mail package (e.g., using FedEx) rather than in a regular envelope.

4b. Should you pay respondents? Some researchers provide a small monetary remuneration (a dollar) to respondents, but sometimes the cost of administering such a reward makes it prohibitive. Other researchers enclose a small gift (e.g., a shiny nickel or dime) in all mail surveys, hoping that the inclusion of a gift will make likely nonrespondents feel guilty, thus turning them into respondents. There is evidence that these techniques work, but they are not a magic bullet. However, if you are surveying people in relatively homogeneous groups (e.g., teachers, professionals, or work groups) who are already interested in the topic (e.g., their jobs), you are likely to get a high response rate (assuming that you follow the other suggestions in this list) without resorting to a payment or gift. However, some sort of inexpensive gift might improve the response rate of those (e.g., parents) who are less inherently interested in the topic of your survey. Some professional survey (and market) research firms report paying incentives of as much as $150 to hard-to-get respondents, such as high-powered executives. The money is given to the respondent or to the charity of their choice.

5. Make the respondents want to cooperate, even without a reward.

5a. Tell respondents, in an introductory letter or statement, why you are doing the survey and why their response is important.

5b. Begin with questions that pertain to the survey topic. That is, do *not* begin your survey with demographic questions. If you tell teachers that you are doing this survey because you are interested in teachers' assessment of their pupils' computer skills and activities, then the first questions on the survey should *not* ask the respondent about her age, race, years of experience, and education. Such background characteristics are important: They help you interpret your findings. But save these questions for the end of the survey. Begin the demographic section (at the end of the survey) with a brief introduction, such as "Finally, the last few questions are for statistical purposes only," or "Finally, the last few questions are to help us understand your responses better." Within the demographic questions, put the most sensitive item (e.g., income or salary) at the end. Also, since you are using your surveys to compare respondents in different schools or classrooms, do not forget to ask on the survey which school (or classroom) the respondent is in. Asking demographic questions at the beginning of a survey is justifiable only when you are targeting the survey to one group of respondents or targeting different surveys to respondents in different groups. For example, in an Internet or telephone survey, if married (or employed) persons receive one set of questions (or none at all) while unmarried (or unemployed) persons receive another, then you must ask one demographic question about marital (or employment) status at the beginning of the survey.

6. Make the survey easy to answer. That is, use closed-ended (multiple-choice) response categories, rather than open-ended questions, and make sure the questions are clear. Suppose that you are surveying classroom instructors in public schools. An example of an open-ended opinion question is:

What changes should the school board make in its policies regarding the placement of computers in elementary schools?

This question is too vague and hard to answer. A closed-ended version might be:

Should the school board increase or decrease its spending on computers for elementary school classrooms?

1. increase a lot
2. increase
3. neither increase nor decrease
4. decrease
5. decrease a lot

An example of an open-ended perception question is:

What changes have you observed in how the children in your classroom use computers?

Again, this question is too vague and is therefore difficult to answer. A closed-ended version of this question on perception might include a series of specific questions with fixed response categories:

During the past school year, has computer use by the average child in your classroom increased, decreased, or stayed the same?

1. increased a lot
2. increased
3. neither increased nor decreased
4. decreased
5. decreased a lot

During the past school year, has the use of mathematical computer games by the average child in your classroom increased, decreased, or stayed the same?

1. increased a lot
2. increased
3. stayed the same
4. decreased
5. decreased a lot

Notice, first, that compared with the open-ended version of both these questions, the closed-ended version is more specific. It specifies the topic or dimension of the opinion or perception, directing the respondent to answer in respect to information the researcher wants. In these examples, the question asks about increases or decreases in spending and usage, respectively. It would also be possible to ask another closed-ended question that refers to an entirely different dimension of interest, such as opinions and perceptions about issues of equity.

In addition to using closed-ended questions, clarity is always important. For example, when appropriate, survey questions should specify the time period. There are several ways to refer to a specific time period. For example, consider the following two alternatives:

During the past year, has computer use by the average child in your classroom increased, decreased, or stayed the same?

or

During the past twelve months, has computer use by the average child in your classroom increased, decreased, or stayed the same?

The problem with using "year" as the reference time period is that it is not clear. Some respondents may refer to the calendar year (or the budget year), while others refer to the past twelve months. In general, it is preferable to use "the past twelve months" as the reference time period rather than "year." However, in the context of a question about schools, the appropriate reference is to the past academic year, which is not twelve months.

When asking questions about perceptions of recent events, a clear time period should be specified. The reference time period should not be so long that memory is distorted, nor should it be so short that the sample of events to which the respondent refers is too small. For example, it is easier to recall events during the past week than in the past twelve months. But in asking about perceptions of change, the past week may be too short. Suppose that you are asking about the amount of time that students spend using computers, and *not* about the *change* in the amount of time. In that case, the questionnaire might well ask about the past week rather than the past academic year:

During a typical day last week, about how many hours did a typical student in your classroom spend using the Internet on the computer?

The textbooks on survey research cited at the end of this chapter consider this issue in considerably more depth. For example, memory plays tricks on us: We remember the time of infrequent unpleasant events (e.g., a visit to the hospital) differently than we remember the time of infrequent happy events (e.g., weddings). Survey researchers who are collecting information about these kinds of perceptions should be aware of these problems. However, these issues are usually not typical for those who use surveys in evaluation research.

More generally, specific, closed-ended questions are harder to write, but they have several payoffs. Compared with open-ended questions, they will yield higher response rates, and they will make it much easier for you to analyze the responses to your survey. (Analyzing responses is discussed more fully later in this chapter.)

Of course, some respondents will want to comment extensively. At the end of the survey, which consists of closed-ended questions, you should include an open-ended question inviting comments on any topics raised in the survey. These comments will provide useful information about the topics in your survey that are most important to the respondents.

7. Make the survey easy to read. Do not use jargon or big words. The questionnaire should be neatly laid out, and the print should be legible and not too small. Do not try to save paper or space if the survey is online. Keep questions on the same topic together in the same section. Proofread the survey. Remember that the spell checker does not recognize properly spelled words when they are misused (e.g., "their" and "there" and sometimes "they're," are often misused, but the spell checker will not recognize the problem, and even the grammar checker misses a lot). A sloppy survey shows that the researcher does not care. If the researcher does not care, why should the respondent?

8. Make sure the responses are at least confidential, if not anonymous. Anonymity means that the researcher cannot identify the respondent. Respondents are more likely to give their honest views, answer all the questions in the survey, and return the survey when their responses are anonymous. Confidentiality means that the researcher can identify the respondent, but promises not to use that information in any personally identifying way except to separate respondents from nonrespondents so that the researcher can follow-up with nonrespondents.[10] Obviously, there is a contradiction here: Anonymity increases response rates but makes it impossible to follow-up with nonrespondents. So, depending on your budget and the type of survey, you may want to keep the survey anonymous and send follow-up surveys to everyone. In the introductory letter to the follow-up survey, thank the respondents and ask those who have not yet responded to do so as soon as possible. Ask them to use the survey that you enclose in the follow-up if they misplaced the original. (That way, they do not need to locate the original.) This method requires placing no identifying number or name on the survey instrument, guaranteeing anonymity. Once you put an identifying number on the survey and tag each number with a specific respondent, then you can separate respondents from nonrespondents, promising confidentiality—but not anonymity.

Even if a survey has no identifying information on it, it may not be truly anonymous—especially for minority respondents, who know how easily they can be identified. Once I received a survey at work asking my opinion about a university issue. Aside from my opinion, the survey asked for information about department, rank, and gender. Since, at the time of the survey, I was the only female full professor in my department, my response could easily be identified. I threw the survey in the trash. The researchers should have known better; they did not need to know the gender of the respondent for the purposes of the survey.

9. Make sure that your survey conforms to these goals by pretesting it on a small sample (e.g., ten to twenty people) drawn at random from the population you wish to study. Revise your survey based on the pretest results. For example, if the response rate to the pretest is unexpectedly low, maybe the survey is too long, confusing, or hard to answer. If there are noticeably few responses to a question, then revise the question: It is probably unclear or too hard to answer. (You will have to remove the pretest respondents from the sample that you study. That is, do not send the revised, final survey instrument that you will actually use to the pretest respondents.)

HOW TO WRITE QUESTIONS TO GET UNBIASED, ACCURATE, INFORMATIVE RESPONSES

So far, the general point is that sample survey questions should be closed-ended. Closed-ended questions raise the response rate by making it easier for respondents to respond; they also make it easier for researchers to analyze the data. But this simple rule does not deal with the problem of closed-ended questions and response categories that elicit biased, inaccurate, and uninformative responses.

Informative Questions and Responses

Use Mutually Exclusive Categories

Consider the following set of response categories to a simple question:

How many hours did you spend at your primary job last week?

1. None
2. 1–8
3. 8–16
4. 16–24
5. 24–32
6. 32 or over

Respondents whose response is "8," "16," "24," or "32" can pick one of two categories; their response will not be very informative to the researcher. For the respondent, the ambiguity of the categories makes a response difficult, increases the randomness of responses, and provides an incentive not to respond to the question or to toss the entire survey in the trash. Use mutually exclusive response categories: 1–7, 8–15, 16–23, 24–31, 32 or over. This solution is obvious, but it is a small detail that survey researchers often overlook.

Avoid Double- (or Triple-, or Quadruple-) Barreled Questions and Responses

Consider the following item, asked of a classroom teacher:

My classroom aide performed his/her tasks carefully, impartially, thoroughly, and on time.

1. Agree strongly
2. Agree
3. Neither agree nor disagree
4. Disagree
5. Strongly disagree

This is really four questions in one. The classroom aide might have been careful and impartial on the tasks she did perform, but did not do everything that was asked and was sometimes late. It would be better to break this quadruple-barreled question into four separate items, one for each adverb. The responses will be far more informative and less prone to random measurement error (RME).

Response categories can also be double-barreled. Look at the possible responses to this question:

How did you first hear about the Computers in the Classroom Program? (Select only one response.)

1. From a friend or relative
2. At a meeting of an organization to which I belong
3. At work
4. From a member of my family
5. Over TV or radio
6. From the newspaper

Respondents who first heard about the program from a friend at work or on the radio at work will not know which category to select. They will not respond, respond randomly, or check both categories (if they can), leaving the researcher uninformed, unless you have anticipated multiple responses to the same question.

If You Want to Allow Multiple Responses, Frame the Responses Accordingly

Suppose you really do not want a single response to the previous question; rather, you want to know all the sources where the respondent heard about the Computers in the Classroom program. You could allow respondents to check multiple items in the 1 to 6 response list, heading it "Check all that apply." This is not advisable, because it fails to distinguish a nonreponse from "no." Instead, the format immediately below explicitly allows for multiple responses, eases data entry and analysis (as the chapter explains next), and distinguishes nonresponses from the real response of "no."

	Yes	No
From a friend or relative	1	2
At a meeting of an organization to which I belong	1	2
At work	1	2
From a member of my family	1	2
Over TV or radio	1	2
From the newspaper	1	2

Avoid Vague Response Categories When More Precise Categories Are Readily Available

For example, consider the following three ways of responding to the same question:

How often did you assign computer projects to your students during the past month?

1. Never
2. Rarely
3. Occasionally
4. Regularly

VERSUS

1. Not at all
2. About once a week
3. Two or three times a week
4. About once a day
5. More than once a day

VERSUS

_____ times

Obviously, the second set of responses is far more informative than the first. The first set makes both the respondent and the researcher guess at the meaning of each response category: The respondent's definition of "rarely" may not be the same as yours. The second version is easy for the respondent to answer and easy for the researcher to interpret. So, whenever possible, avoid vague adjectives to describe events when numerical categories can be used instead.

What about the third alternative? It requires a specific number. The problem is that most teachers will not remember exactly how many computer assignments they gave during the last month; they will either not respond or guess. If there is a numerical response, its precision may be illusory.[11] Further, you probably do not need to know the exact number. If you need the exact number, use a more recent time frame of reference: Ask how many computer assignments the respondent gave last week, or yesterday, rather than during the last month.[12] So, overall, the second option is best. Further, asking respondents for exact numbers can introduce other problems, as the next section discusses.

Asking About Age, Income, and Other Numbers: Use Categories When Exact Numbers Are Available But Not Helpful

Using categories is often useful for collecting accurate, informative data about sensitive topics like the respondent's age or salary. Rarely does the researcher need the exact number; asking for the exact number may induce the respondent to respond randomly, to dissemble, or not to respond at all, because the exact number can reveal the respondent's identity more readily than a broad category. So it is often preferable to use categories even when exact numbers are readily available.[13]

However, in devising categories for questions about age and income, the top category is left open-ended. If that category is so large that most of the respondents fit into it, their answers will not be very informative. For example, in the case of age, you might use categories like the following: 20–29, 30–39, 40–49, 50–59, and 60 and over. However, if most respondents are over fifty-nine, then the categories provided will not suffice to describe the respondents, and it will be necessary to add more categories to the set of responses (e.g., add 60–69, 70–79, and 80 and older). It is also important to have numerous category choices when income levels among respondents vary a great deal. However, the categories should not be too small: If each category is too small, the questionnaire looks cluttered, and respondents cannot hide in the anonymity provided by a reasonably large category.[14]

Balanced Questions and Responses

It is impossible to eliminate bias from survey research—how you ask a question affects the response. But sometimes the effect of asking a question in a particular way leads to a response in a particular direction. When that happens, the bias in a question is clear and can (and should) be reduced, if not eliminated.

Avoid Social Pressures and Outside Cues

Thought to inform the respondent, researchers often use declarative statements to introduce a survey question. The consequence usually results in leading questions. Such cues do not belong in most survey research questions. A favorite example is the following question, which uses a statement of fact to introduce the survey item:

More people have seen Gone with the Wind than any other movie in history. Have you seen this movie?

1. Yes
2. No

The introductory statement leads more than it informs. Unless the respondent enjoys being contrary, there is really only one way to respond to the question.

The previous example illustrates the use of social pressure to create a leading question. The next example uses a supposedly informative, but leading, outside cue:

The (name of state) Supreme Court has ruled that spending among school districts must be equal. Do you favor or oppose this ruling?

1. Favor
2. Oppose
3. No opinion

Few people are likely to want to disagree with a state Supreme Court ruling. The question is framed to increase the proportion who favor the policy, at least compared with a less leading (and more precise) version of the same question:

Would you favor or oppose a law that requires spending among the school districts in (name of state) to be equal on a per capita basis?

1. Favor
2. Oppose
3. No opinion

Avoid Agree/Disagree Questions

Despite their popularity, agree/disagree questions should be avoided if possible. The following is a typical agree/disagree question:

On average, students in my class are more interested in their studies at the end of this school year than they were at the beginning.

1. Agree strongly
2. Agree
3. Neither agree nor disagree
4. Disagree
5. Disagree strongly

There are three problems with this set of response choices. First, the two disagree responses are not informative; disagreeing with the statement does not indicate what the respondent believes. Second, the responses confuse intensity of opinion with the position of the opinion. Does simple agreement mean that the respondent thinks that the students are *much* more interested in their studies at the end of the year than they were at the beginning (strong position) but is not very confident about this view (low intensity)? Or does it mean that the respondent thinks that the students are somewhat more interested in their studies at the end of the year compared with the beginning (moderate position) and is quite sure that this is the case (strong intensity)? And, third, the agree-disagree responses induce bias due to the tendency among many people (particularly those with less power, knowledge, or experience) to acquiesce or to be agreeable.

Using bipolar, balanced response categories avoids all these problems. Consider the following example:

Compared with the beginning of the school year, my students' interest in their studies this year has:

Increased a lot						Decreased a lot
+3	+2	+1	0	−1	−2	−3

In this example, the seven response numbers that the question provides convey the position of the response; no change (which you can label or not) is zero, a big increase is +3, a big decrease is −3, and intermediate positions are between those extremes. Alternatively, the response categories to this survey item could use five numerical options (ranging from +2 to −2) or even three (ranging from +1 to −1). Using only three choices does not allow for much variation in possible responses; it needlessly conceals information. Five responses may do the same thing: Because respondents tend to avoid extreme responses, most will not respond with +2 or −2, so the useful range of responses is really only −1, 0, and +1, again concealing useful information. By having seven response categories available, respondents (who generally like to avoid extremes) can more realistically convey their observations or beliefs. Using nine response categories is overkill, lending seeming precision to a response that, at best, is only an approximation.

This kind of bipolar, balanced question is very useful for soliciting descriptions from respondents (as in the earlier example) or for soliciting opinions:

The administrators in this school are:

Very overworked						Very underworked
+3	+2	+1	0	−1	−2	−3

My classroom aide makes my job:

A lot easier						A lot harder
+3	+2	+1	0	−1	−2	−3

Overall, the bipolar, balanced question is almost always preferable to the agree/disagree question. It clarifies the dimension of the intended response, so it produces more information. It allows for more response options (five or seven categories, rather than the three or five typical in the agree/disagree question). Finally, it is less biased. Its disadvantage is that it is harder for the researcher to write. Professional survey researchers, by their behavior, clearly find that the benefits exceed the costs, as they rarely use the agree/disagree form any more.

Placement of Items

Surveys almost always ask multiple questions about a specific topic. For example, in a survey about client satisfaction with agency services, evaluators may ask questions about how professional the caseworker was, how prompt at responding to inquiries, how helpful, how clear; how completely the problem was solved; and how quickly the problem was solved. The evaluator may also ask a summary question: *Overall, how satisfied were you with the way the caseworker handled your problem?* Each of these items can be asked as a balanced question, with a balanced response scale. But how should the items be ordered? Specifically, where should the "overall" question be placed? It matters!

In general, if the "overall" question is first in the battery of questions, you will probably get a more extreme response than if it is put at the end. In other words, if the respondent's overall experience is generally positive, the respondent will give a "very satisfactory" or "satisfactory" response to the summary question if it is first in the battery. But, if the same question is at the end of the battery, the respondent is prompted to think about specifics first. It is likely that not every contact was fully satisfactory. Each specific question prompts the respondent to think about the problems. Then, having been reminded of the problems and asked at the end to respond to the "overall" experience, the respondent will give an answer that is more negative than it would have been otherwise. The opposite happens when the respondent's overall experience with the agency was generally "unhappy."

There is no clear answer to this problem. What is important is to be aware that the order of questions in a survey affects the responses to them. For a series of related questions on a single topic, three options are available: Put the "overall" question first or last or leave it out.[15] Leaving it out is not necessarily a good solution. First, its omission reduces the number of indicators, making measurement less valid and reliable. Second, the response may be an important piece of information for the evaluation, because it is a summary view from the client. Assuming, then, that the summary question is not omitted, the best way to minimize the impact of its placement in a battery of items is to create an additive index based on all the items in the series of questions. The last part of this chapter discusses how to do this. An additional alternative is to randomly put the summary question at the beginning or the end: In half the surveys, placement is at the beginning, and in half the placement is at the end.[16]

Random Attitudes: The "No Opinion" Option

When you ask a question in a cross-section survey, most people will answer it, even if they have never thought about the question before it was asked. The consequence is a random response (random measurement error). A respondent who has never thought about the issue might give one response on one day and a different response on another day, even when the underlying "nonattitude" has not changed. Nonetheless, the analyst sees only a one-time response and mistakenly regards it as a "signal," when in fact it is "noise." In these situations, the most common practice among survey researchers is to offer a "no opinion" option. For example, suppose the following question is asked in a survey of parents:

Should the use of computers in your child's classroom be increased, decreased, or stay the same?

Increased a lot					Decreased a lot		No opinion
+3	+2	+1	0	−1	−2	−3	9

Parents who have not thought about the issue can respond with "no opinion." Parents who think computer use should stay the same can respond with a zero.

However, it is not useful to offer the "no opinion" option when respondents are likely to have an opinion. For example, in a survey asking teachers about the students in their class, the respondents are sure to have an opinion, so the "no opinion" option is not necessary. Furthermore, it invites a nonresponse when the respondent is actually hesitating between two possible responses. In other words, the respondents may say to themselves, "I can't decide between a +1 and a +2, so I'll choose 'no opinion.'" In that case, the researcher gets no information. It is better to have a response, even an unsure one, than none at all. Hence, do not offer the "no opinion" option when you can safely assume that respondents have an opinion. By contrast, to avoid random nonattitudes, you should offer the "no opinion" option when it is reasonable to expect that some respondents really have no experience with the issue or have not previously thought about it and, hence, have no opinion.[17]

Numerical Codes for Response Categories

Note that in the sample questions, each possible response word or phrase has a number beside it. Professional survey researchers put these numbers on every possible response option because using numbers rather than words makes it much easier to enter the responses into a computer database and to analyze them. Respondents should be instructed to circle the number that corresponds to their response. (Internet survey software should do this automatically.) Using numbers in surveys is no problem for respondents, the cost is low, and the benefit in time savings for the researcher is high.[18]

TURNING RESPONSES INTO USEFUL INFORMATION

One of the most important reasons to have numerical codes for every possible response option is to make it easy to enter the results from each survey into a spreadsheet like Excel or a statistical package like SPSS, STATA, or SAS.[19] Each observation is one record or one row in the spreadsheet. Check to ensure that you have entered your data properly. One way to do this is to read the numbers you have entered into the database to someone else who is reading the numbers on the corresponding completed survey form.

There are many ways to analyze your data. The previous chapters have shown how to use a basic regression model to analyze data, and, often, surveys are the (or one) source of such data. Survey data are frequently underanalyzed. Researchers use them to compute frequency distributions and bivariate, two-way contingency tables, but evaluation requires controlled comparison. For example, suppose that you wish to compare, for each question, the percent of student responses in each response category (or the mean response) between two (or more) comparison schools. Suppose further that in this quasi experiment the two schools have been selected to be comparable in most respects, except that one had a special program and the other did not. But exact comparability is rare, necessitating statistical controls for other variables, using regression to hold these variables constant. These variables include both student-level characteristics (e.g., age, IQ, demographic characteristics) and classroom characteristics (e.g., size of respondent's, average IQ of classroom peers). You would use the survey instrument to collect data on student-level output variables (Y) and the student-level Z variables. If you ask on the survey which classroom the student is in (e.g., Ms. Masters' ninth grade history of the United States), you can add to the survey database information (from the school's administrative database) about other classroom and teacher-related Z variables. (The value of these variables will be the same for all students in the same classroom. Note that the question about the respondent's classroom would be a demographic type of question, so you would probably ask it in the last section of the survey.) You know which school the respondent attends, so that gives you information about the X variable for each student. (The X variable will have the same value for all students in the same school.) The number of observations is the number of student respondents to the survey.

Both spreadsheets and statistical packages come with instructions about how to show the percentages (or means) for one type of unit (schools with the special program) and the same percentages (or means) for similar schools without the special program. Regression programs allow you to add statistical controls. Regression programs will tell you whether, holding constant the (measured) confounding differences between students and classrooms (the Z variables), the between-treatment differences (X) in outputs or outcomes (Y) are statistically significant, and the direction and magnitude of the differences.

In this example, before estimating significance, it would also be appropriate to anticipate heteroscedasticity among classrooms and schools, and to use robust, clustered (by classroom) estimates of standard errors. As Chapter 6 explained, to read the statistical information, look for the p-value or the probability level. Using conventional statistical standards, if that value is 0.05 or lower, the difference is said to be statistically significant. This means that if the samples were drawn from two schools that were really the same with respect to the outcome measures, getting a difference as large as the one that you estimate with the regression coefficient is extremely unlikely (less than five chances in one hundred, given your sample size). The implication is that it is not likely that the schools are the same; the researcher can reject that null hypothesis in favor of the alternative hypothesis that one school really is performing better (or worse) than the other. When a percentage or mean difference is statistically significant, you should also look at the magnitude of the difference. For example, holding the Z variables constant, a 1 percent difference between the comparison schools in the percent of students who report using a computer for their homework may be statistically significant, but not substantively or practically important. The statistical analysis software can report the statistical significance and the magnitude of a difference, but only the researcher can evaluate whether the magnitude of a statistically significant difference is important. In short, the information in previous chapters about design and data analysis remains unchanged when the data are survey responses.

Using Surveys to Create Indexes: Multiple Indicators and Measuring Reliability and Validity

Surveys are frequently a source of information about multiple indicators of complex output or outcome measures ($Y_1 \ldots Y_K$) or even of program variables ($X_1 \ldots X_K$) or control variables ($Z_1 \ldots Z_K$). For example, suppose that you are investigating the impact of participatory management (X) on worker productivity (Y). One might use the survey to measure both the program variable (amount of participatory management) and the outcome (productivity). Both are complex concepts that could not be reliably or validly measured with a single indicator.[20]

Consider the use of a survey to measure just the outcome or output variable, productivity. While a full measure of productivity includes assessment of value by clients, a part of productivity includes assessment of effort by the worker. Surveys of employees are a common source of information about daily workplace activities. For example, suppose that employees have two core activities that constitute their daily tasks (e.g., assisting clients on the phone and in face-to-face visits with clients at the employee's place of work). Suppose further that employees normally have two other daily activities that may appear less central to their core tasks: maintaining records about each client ("paperwork") and staying on top of the latest rules ("reading"). The employees work in field offices without direct, on-site supervision from program managers. You could use a survey to ask each employee to respond to a question like this:

Think of a typical day at work last week (or during the most recent week that you worked). About what percent of your time did you spend on these activities? (Check only one response in each column.)

	On the phone with clients	Office visits with clients	Maintaining client records	Staying informed
1. Less than 5 percent	___	___	___	___
2. 5 percent–10 percent	___	___	___	___
3. 11 percent–25 percent	___	___	___	___
4. 26 percent–50 percent	___	___	___	___
5. Over 50 percent	___	___	___	___

You could code the responses to these four questions in one of two ways (or both). One code could be a rank order, ordinal scale from 1 to 5, indicated by the numbers to the left of each response category. For example, a response of "less than 5 percent" for "on the phone with clients" would be coded 1, while a response of "over 50 percent" would be coded 5. Another code could be the percent itself, summarized by a single number placed at each category median (i.e., 2.5 percent, 7.5 percent, 18 percent, 38 percent, and 75 percent). Both choices have advantages and disadvantages. This example assumes that the ordinal codes are chosen, but the instructions for assessing reliability and validity and for creating an index do not depend on the choice. In fact, researchers should assess reliability and validity using both codes.

Regardless of the code, the goal is to measure how hard the employees work at their core tasks. No one task is sufficient to describe what employees are supposed to do. The mental model of the concept that you are trying to measure with multiple indicators looks like this:

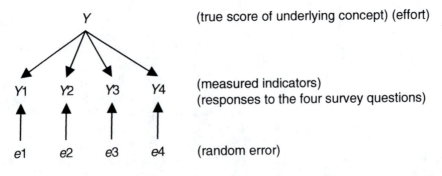

Y	(true score of underlying concept) (effort)
Y1 Y2 Y3 Y4	(measured indicators) (responses to the four survey questions)
e1 e2 e3 e4	(random error)

In other words, the underlying, unmeasured concept implies that hardworking employees exhibit certain behaviors. No one behavior alone represents the underlying concept. Compared with any single measure, taken together, these behaviors more closely represent what the researcher means when he talks about employees "working hard," rather than goofing off or shirking.[21]

Note that this is a very general model useful for examining many abstract concepts. Employee job satisfaction is such a concept; so is citizen satisfaction with city services or client satisfaction with personal services. Researchers use similar models to represent beliefs and attitudes, such as "religiosity," "liberalism-conservatism," or "willingness to take risks." The model can also be used to represent patterns of actual behavior, such as indexes of risky behavior, indexes of political participation, or the health of a respondent.

If the data conform to a model like this, then you should observe two things. First, the responses to the individual questions should be highly correlated with one another. In other words, if the responses reflect a lot of random measurement error (RME) (the $e_1 \ldots e_4$) terms, the responses will not be correlated with each other; they will simply reflect noise. This is the *reliability* component. Evaluators use a statistic called Cronbach's alpha (α) to assess reliability, the absence of RME.

Second, the responses to each (measured) question should be a linear function of the (unmeasured) underlying construct. In the previous model, this means that the coefficient on each of the four arrows between the measured response ($Y1$, $Y2$, $Y3$, and $Y4$) and the underlying concept (Y) should be positive and "large."

Note that this is not the same as the indicators' being related to one another. There are many ways in which indicators could be related to one another. They could be directly related, as in:

$$Y1 \leftrightarrow Y2 \leftrightarrow Y3 \leftrightarrow Y4$$

or, they could be related to another underlying concept (Q), and only possibly or not at all to Y:

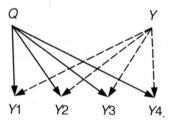

For example, if the response items $Y1 \ldots Y4$ were racially biased, they might reflect not only Y but also Q (e.g., race of respondent), because Q, along with Y, partly explains why they are related.

Clearly, I have just reintroduced the topic of nonrandom measurement error (NRME). In the example, Q is a source of NRME. But the task now is to test the hypothesis that $Y1 \ldots Y4$ are a linear function only of Y and not of each other or of Q. This is a test of *validity*. Evaluators commonly use principal components factor analysis to test this hypothesis. I first discuss Cronbach's alpha as a measure of *reliability*. I then discuss principal components factor analysis to assess the *validity* of measures. After reliability and validity have been established, I briefly discuss simple ways to construct an index.

Assessing Reliability

Cronbach's alpha is probably the most commonly used measure of reliability. Its logic is consistent with the measurement model. It is designed to assess the relative contribution of systematic covariation between pairs of indicators compared with that of a pattern of randomness. It is a coefficient that varies between 0 (random variation) and 1 (perfect covariation). Warning: An alpha of 1 should make you suspicious that you do not really have two separate indicators! The formula for the alpha is:

$$\alpha = M\rho/[1 + \rho(M - 1)],$$

where:

M = *number of items in the proposed index. (In the measurement model, M = 4.)*
ρ = *average of the [M(M – 1)/2] interitem correlations (r_{jm})*

$$= \sum_{j<m} \frac{r_{jm}}{[M(M-1)/2]} \quad (r_{jm} = each\ interitem\ correlation).$$

Since there are four items ($Y1 \ldots Y4$), there are $4 \times 3/2 = 6$ possible interitem correlations,

$$(r_{jm}) = (r_{12},\ r_{13},\ r_{14},\ r_{23},\ r_{24},\ r_{34}).$$

In the example, there are four items asking how much time each respondent spends on various tasks at work. Each task can be regarded as a partial indicator of the underlying concept "amount of effort that the respondent exerts in a typical workday." The underlying concept is unmeasured, but the separate indicators are measured. Suppose that the observed correlations[22] among the four separate indicator items, computed from the survey responses, are as follows:

	Item			
	Y1	Y2	Y3	Y4
Y1	1.0	0.6	0.5	0.4
Y2		1.0	0.4	0.4
Y3			1.0	0.6
Y4				1.0

Then

$$\rho = (.6 + .5 + .4 + .4 + .4 + .6)\ /6 = 2.9/6 = .48$$
$$\alpha = 4\ (.48)/[1 + .48\ (3)] = 1.92/2.44 = .79.$$

Usually, alphas of .70 or more are considered to mean that the scale (in this case, a four-item scale) is reliable. So, based on the computed $\alpha = .79$, you would conclude that, taken together, these four items are a reliable set of multiple indicators. They are systematically related to one another and are likely to reflect a common signal, rather than represent noise. (Note that, so far, you do not know what the signal is; you only know that the indicators are a common signal of something.) You would conclude that the four indicators together represent a reasonably reliable measure . . . of something as yet unknown.[23]

The formula for alpha also makes it clear that increaseing the number of items always adds to reliability, a point discussed in Chapter 2. In the formula for α, as M, the number of items, increases, alpha increases. More indicators mean more reliability, independent of the average interitem correlation p. In addition, as the average of the r_{jm} interitem correlations increases, reliability also increases, implying that the individual items covary systematically and not randomly. Overall, the most reliable index will have multiple indicators that are highly related to each other.

In the real world, however, some intended indicators may detract from reliability. In other words, sometimes four highly correlated indicators will be more reliable than five or six indicators. In that case, it would be reasonable to select the subset of indicators that maximizes reliability. But assessing multiple-item concepts according to reliability alone fails to consider validity, the next topic.

Assessing Validity

Factor analysis is commonly used to assess the validity of a multi-item measurement instrument. Recall that validity is the absence of NRME. A valid measure is related to the underlying concept (*Y*) that it is supposed to measure, and it is unrelated to an underlying systematic factor (*Q*) that it is not supposed to reflect. Factor analysis tests if a set of indicators is systematically related to *Y* and not related to *Q*.

Specifically, the factor analysis measurement model[24] for assessing validity separates measurement model A, with one clear underlying factor (*Y*),

Measurement model A

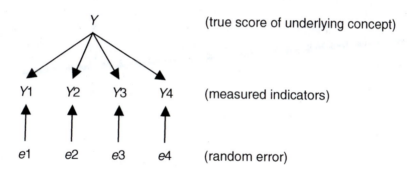

Y   (true score of underlying concept)

Y1   Y2   Y3   Y4   (measured indicators)

e1   e2   e3   e4   (random error)

from measurement model B, in which the indicators are directly related to one another, but there is no underlying unmeasured concept,

Measurement model B

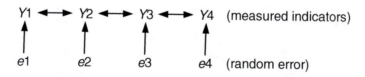

Y1 ⟷ Y2 ⟷ Y3 ⟷ Y4 (measured indicators)

e1   e2   e3   e4 (random error)

and from measurement model C, in which the indicators reflect a common underlying factor (*Q*) that is *not Y*, and in which the four indicators may (or may not) also reflect *Y*:

Measurement model C

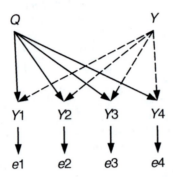

It is important to recognize that the factor analysis model assumes that model B is NOT true; under many, but not all, circumstances it can distinguish between model A and model C. Its best use is simply to test if the data are consistent with model A. If model A is inconsistent with your underlying measurement "theory," then factor analysis is probably not the best choice for assessing measurement validity. In addition, while the factor analytic model can potentially assess both reliability and validity, the focus here is only on validity, leaving the assessment of reliability to Cronbach's alpha. To uphold validity, the results from a principal components factor analysis of the selected items should look like measurement model A, producing one principal component, with each indicator showing a high "factor loading" or correlation with the underlying principal component.

For example, the results of a principal components factor analysis of the four-item set of indicators of effort might look like those in the following table, if it were consistent with measurement model A:

Results from a principal components factor analysis:

	1	2	3	4
Eigenvalue	2.87	.61	.43	.09
Factor pattern	Factor 1			
1	.91			
2	.87			
3	.75			
4	.84			

The strange terms in this table have reasonably clear explanations, and the two parts of the table are related to each other. First, consider the eigenvalue. In terms of the underlying measurement model of factor analysis, an eigenvalue represents the contribution of each potential factor to the underlying total factor space. The total factor space is always represented by the number of indicators. In the example, the total factor space is 4.00. If the factor space looked exactly like measurement model A, the eigenvalue for the first principal component would be 4.00, and the eigenvalues for the other components would be 0. If there were two underlying principal components, one eigenvalue might equal something like 1.7; the other might equal something like 1.5. The two other factors might each have an eigenvalue of less than 1 (e.g., .5 and .3), but the fact that their eigenvalues are less than 1 and relatively small suggests that these factors are not *principal* factors or components.

Since the sum of the eigenvalues must always equal the number of items in the factor analysis, and since there are four items in the example, the factor analysis will report four components or factors, but they are not all principal. In the example, the eigenvalue for the first component is 2.87;

it indicates that one component (or underlying factor, which you hope to call "effort") represents about 2.87/4.00 or 72 percent of the total factor space, which is 4.00.

Some components may be more important than others. A conventional standard for judging importance is that the eigenvalue of the component be greater than 1. However, this is a very weak condition, especially as the number of items hypothesized to reflect the same underlying concept increases. A better standard is that the eigenvalue of the important component be considerably greater than the other eigenvalues. According to this rule, there is clearly one principal component in our example.

The factor loadings reported in the factor pattern represent the correlation between each indicator and the underlying principal component. If there were two principal components, the factor pattern results would contain two columns of coefficients. In the example, there is only one principal component (labeled component or factor 1), so there is only one column of correlations in the factor pattern. In the example, these correlations range from .75 to .91; they are "high" and positive, but less than 1. Each item asked about a different aspect of effort. $Y1$ ("on the phone with clients") has the highest overall correlation with the underlying concept of "effort"; $Y3$ ("maintaining client records") has the lowest correlation, but a correlation (factor loading) of .75 is acceptable in the practice of factor analysis. Overall, the results are consistent with measurement model A.[25]

Results from a factor analysis are not always so simple. For example, it would also be possible for each eigenvalue to equal a number slightly smaller or larger than 1. (Remember, the sum of the eigenvalues is always the number of items entered into the factor analysis. In the example, the sum of the eigenvalues will be 4.00.) If each of the eigenvalues were about 1.00, it would suggest that the underlying model is *not* consistent with a single-factor model. Based on a high Cronbach's alpha, you could assume that you have reliable indicators. But if each eigenvalue were 1, or close to 1, you could not argue that the indicators validly measure the same single underlying concept. (Such a pattern might be more consistent with the second measurement model, but that model is not a factor analytic model. Factor analytic models assume that there is no direct relation between indicators. Rather, indicators in factor analytic models are correlated because of their common dependence on an underlying, unmeasured factor.)

Consider another familiar example. Suppose you hypothesize that the sum of Scholastic Aptitude Test (SAT) scores is a measure of a single underlying concept called "academic ability." This overall SAT score has three parts: a verbal score, a math score, and a writing score.[26] If you entered data on individual verbal, math, and writing scores into a factor analysis program, you would hope to get results that resembled those in the previous table. That is, there would be one principal factor, with an eigenvalue of, say, 2.3. The remaining two factors would have eigenvalues that summed to .7. Only the principal factor or component (with the relatively large eigenvalue) can be regarded as a signal. The other two factors, with small eigenvalues, are not clearly interpretable as factors at all. Technically, they are factors; substantively, they are noise.

Having decided that there is probably one underlying principal factor or component that appears to organize the data on the three separate SAT scores, you would then look at the factor pattern. You would expect, if your hypothesis were to be upheld, that each item would be highly correlated with the underlying principal or dominant factor (say, at .7 or more). Unless you had reason to believe otherwise, you would also expect that the factor loadings for the verbal, math, and writing scores on the principal component would be about the same. Results such as these would uphold your conjecture that the three scores together validly represent an underlying concept that you will label as "academic ability."

Overall then, if you hypothesize a single factor model, you should expect that a single factor dominates the factor space. The eigenvalues should indicate one dominant factor whose eigenvalue is not only greater than 1, but also dominates the factor space by being considerably larger than the eigenvalue associated with each of the other components, or factors, as it does in this example. Further, you should expect that the factor loading for each indicator variable shows a reasonably high level of correlation with the single, dominant, underlying factor, as they do in this example. Results like these would uphold your conjecture that the items in the measurement model are a valid representation of the complex concept that you are trying to measure. However, it is important to point out that, at best, factor analytic models such as these are tests of "construct" and maybe "face" validity. They are not tests of "predictive" validity.

Building an Index of Multiple Indicators

Having concluded that your four indicators are not only reasonably reliable but also appear to be a reasonably "construct-valid" reflection of a single underlying concept that you will call effort, you might then proceed to combine the indicators into an index. Because the index will comprise multiple indicators that you have shown to be reasonably reliable and valid, the index will be more reliable and valid than any one indicator alone would be.

There are many ways to construct an index. One way is to use factor analysis, which creates factor scores for each observation on each indicator and then sums the factor scores to create an overall index. The factor score is created by multiplying the original value for each observation on the indicator by the factor loading of the indicator on the principal component, and summing the weighted scores. In the example, let the factor score index be called YF_i. Then:

$$YF_i = .91(Y1_i) + .87(Y2_i) + .75 (Y3_i) + .84 (Y4_i).$$

In effect, this method weights each indicator by its correlation with the underlying variable (the factor loading). In the example, the factor score method would give values of $Y1$ the most weight and the values of $Y3$ the least amount of weight in the index. Most factor analysis programs will create factor scores on request.

While this method is theoretically preferred, common practice is often to sum the components of the index, giving each component equal weight of 1. The additive index creates a Likert scale, which has a clearer explanation than the factor score index. The basic model underlying the Likert scale is an unweighted additive index. (You can also divide the sum by the number of items in the index, but this step is not necessary. However, using the average rather than the sum of items retains the original scoring of each item in the index, making the final score easier to interpret.) The model (still our basic measurement model A) assumes that each indicator is the sum of a random component and the underlying true score:

$$Likert\ score\ index = (Y1 + Y2 + Y3 + Y4)/4 = [(Y + e1) + (Y + e2) +$$
$$(Y + e3) + (Y + e4)]/4 = (e1 + e2 + e3 + e4 + 4Y)/4 = Y + random\ error.$$

This formulation makes clear that the summative index contains random error. While the score looks like a hard number, its seeming precision contains noise. However, the assumption is that the multi-item index is more valid than any single indicator alone, because it measures more components of the underlying complex concept. Further, while the summative index score clearly retains a random component, because it is composed of multiple items, it has more information or signal than any single indicator alone. While each random component associated with each indicator is expected to be zero, that expectation could be wrong when applied to any specific indicator. One measured indicator may be a slight overestimate of its true value; the other may be a slight underestimate. However, they are more likely to equal zero together than separately.

The factor score approach is similar. It just weights each $Y1 \ldots Y4$ in the summation by its factor loading from the principal components analysis. Usually, both methods produce the same results.[27] A good practice is to use both methods. If they produce the same results, report the simple Likert-scale results. Remember, clarity counts in applied research.

FOR FURTHER READING

Earl Babbie. *Survey Research Methods*. 2d ed. Belmont, CA: Wadsworth, 1990.

Norman M. Bradburn, Seymour Sudman, and Brian Wansink. *Asking Questions: The Definitive Guide to Questionnaire Design—For Market Research, Political Polls, and Social and Health Questionnaires*. Rev. ed. San Francisco: Jossey-Bass, 2004.

Marc T. Braverman and Jana Kay Slater, ed. *Advances in Survey Research*. San Francisco: Jossey-Bass, 1996.

Jean M. Converse and Stanley Presser. *Survey Questions: Handcrafting the Standardized Questionnaire*. Beverly Hills, CA: Sage, 1986.

Don A. Dillman. *Mail and Internet Surveys: The Tailored Design Method*. 2d ed. New York: Wiley, 2000.

———. *Mail and Telephone Surveys: The Total Design Method*. New York: Wiley, 1978.

Floyd J. Fowler, Jr. *Improving Survey Questions: Design and Evaluation*. Thousand Oaks, CA: Sage, 1995.

———. *Survey Research Methods*. 2d ed. Newbury Park, CA: Sage, 1993.

Thomas W. Mangione. *Mail Surveys: Improving the Quality*. Thousand Oaks, CA: Sage, 1995.

National Science Foundation. *EHR/NSF Evaluation Handbook: User-Friendly Handbook for Project Evaluation: Science, Mathematics, Engineering and Technology Education*. National Science Foundation, Directorate for Education and Human Resource Development, www.nsf.gov/pubs/2002/nsf02057/start.htm.

Howard Schuman and Stanley Presser. *Questions and Answers in Attitude Surveys: Experiments on Question Form, Wording and Context*. New York: Academic Press, 1981.

Madhu Viswanathan. *Measurement Error and Research Design*. Thousand Oaks, CA: Sage, 2005.

BASIC CONCEPTS

Types of surveys
Response rates and types of surveys
Sample size: estimating population values for a set of variables
Sample size: estimating theoretically expected relations between variables
Sample size: when the response rate is less than 100 percent and the budget is fixed
    When to send follow-ups
    Selecting a random sample
    Actual responses vs. sample size
Increasing response rates
    Follow-ups
    Short
    Convenient timing for respondent
    Low cost for respondent
        SASE
        Payment or gift
    Induce cooperation by respondent
        Introductory letter
        Demographics at end
    Closed-ended items that are not too vague (or too specific)
    Easy to read
    Confidential or anonymous responses
    Pretest the survey

Writing questions
   Informative
      Mutually exclusive categories
      Avoid double-barreled items and responses
      Writing for multiple responses
      Specific response categories
      Avoid illusion of precision
   Reducing bias: balanced questions
      No outside cues
      Avoid agree/disagree questions
      Use bipolar, balanced response categories
      Placement of items
   Random attitudes
      Judicious use of "no opinion" option
Analysis
   Use nonexperimental (NE) methods
   Use multiple indicators
      The measurement model:
         reliability (low RME)
         validity (low NRME)
      Measurement reliability: Cronbach's alpha
      Measurement validity: one principle component
If reliable and valid: create multi-item index
   Factor scale score: weighted addition
   Likert-scale score: unweighted or equally weighted addition

DO IT YOURSELF

Along with other questions, American University used to use the survey questions listed in Figure 7.1 (following page) to assess student evaluations of teachers. Based on what you have learned about the design of useful, valid, and reliable survey questions and response categories, answer the following three questions:

1. Succinctly critique and rewrite survey items 1–6 and 8–11 in Figure 7.1.
2. The university used item 7 alone to measure the overall rating of the course and item 12 alone to measure the overall rating of the instructor. Do you think this procedure is likely to produce a valid and reliable result, or would an alternative procedure (based on the listed or revised survey items) be more valid and reliable? If you think the current procedure of using one summative item alone is the best possible use of the survey data, explain why. If you think an alternative procedure would be better, describe it and explain why you think it would produce a more reliable and valid measure of student evaluations of the course and instructor.
3. If you could add one item to the existing survey that would improve the validity of student evaluation of instructional quality, what would it be? (Focus not only on substance, but also on how you structure the question and response categories.)

Figure 7.1   American University Student Evaluation of Teaching Survey: Selected Questions

Note: Omitted are factual questions about the student and the course. The course is identified, but there is no way to identify the student. The individual responses are anonymous.

Instructions: Circle the number that best corresponds to your response.

1.   The course was well-prepared and well-organized.

| Strongly agree 1 | Agree 2 | Neither agree nor disagree 3 | Disagree 4 | Strongly disagree 5 | No opinion 6 |

2.   The course materials (textbook, assigned readings, manuals, etc.) contributed significantly to my understanding of this course.

| Strongly agree 1 | Agree 2 | Neither agree nor disagree 3 | Disagree 4 | Strongly disagree 5 | No opinion 6 |

3.   The course assignments (papers, projects, homework, discussion sections, exams, etc.) contributed significantly to my understanding of this course.

| Strongly agree 1 | Agree 2 | Neither agree nor disagree 3 | Disagree 4 | Strongly disagree 5 | No opinion 6 |

4.   The course provided an appropriate amount of interaction in the classroom.

| Strongly agree 1 | Agree 2 | Neither agree nor disagree 3 | Disagree 4 | Strongly disagree 5 | No opinion 6 |

5.   Overall, the course was demanding and required high standards of performance.

| Strongly agree 1 | Agree 2 | Neither agree nor disagree 3 | Disagree 4 | Strongly disagree 5 | No opinion 6 |

6.   Overall, I am satisfied with the amount of information I learned in this course.

| Strongly agree 1 | Agree 2 | Neither agree nor disagree 3 | Disagree 4 | Strongly disagree 5 | No opinion 6 |

7.   Overall, this course is:

| Superior 1 | Very good 2 | Good 3 | Satisfactory 4 | Fair 5 | Poor 6 |

8.   The instructor's presentations were clear.

| Strongly agree 1 | Agree 2 | Neither agree nor disagree 3 | Disagree 4 | Strongly disagree 5 | No opinion 6 |

(continued)

9. The instructor was stimulating.

Strongly agree 1	Agree 2	Neither agree nor disagree 3	Disagree 4	Strongly disagree 5	No opinion 6

10. The instructor seemed knowledgeable about the subject matter.

Strongly agree 1	Agree 2	Neither agree nor disagree 3	Disagree 4	Strongly disagree 5	No opinion 6

11. The instructor evaluated student work carefully, impartially, objectively, and in a timely manner.

Strongly agree 1	Agree 2	Neither agree nor disagree 3	Disagree 4	Strongly disagree 5	No opinion 6

12. Overall, the instructor is:

Superior 1	Very good 2	Good 3	Satisfactory 4	Fair 5	Poor 6

Source: American University, Washington, DC (2004).

NOTES

1. Other sources of information for evaluation research include routinely collected administrative, budgeting, and accounting data; direct observation; open-ended interviews; focus groups; administrative records and minutes; and newspaper items. Case studies are often regarded as yet another source of information or data for evaluation. As the discussion of quasi experiments noted briefly, I regard a case study as the use of multiple sources of data (possibly including surveys and, more often, direct observation) to collect information about comparable units of analysis with different programs. A single case is unlikely to be useful for program evaluation in most instances because there is no comparison. When there are comparative case studies, the multiple cases become a form of quasi experiment, most commonly a posttest-only comparison group with multiple measures of outcomes and perhaps with multiple measures of program variables as well.

2. For an example of the use of group-level administrative data to supplement sample survey observations, see Jennifer Stuber and Karl Kronebusch, "Stigma and Other Determinants of Participation in TANF and Medicaid," *Journal of Policy Analysis and Management* 23, no. 3 (2004): 509–530.

3. For examples of local surveys for evaluation, see Harry J. Holzer, John M. Quigley, and Steven Raphael, "Public Transit and the Spatial Distribution of Minority Employment: Evidence from a Natural Experiment," *Journal of Policy Analysis and Management* 22, no. 3 (2003): 415–441; Gregg G. Van Ryzin, "The Impact of Resident Management on Residents' Satisfaction with Public Housing," *Evaluation Review* 20, no. 4 (1996): 485–506. For examples of national surveys for evaluation, see Thomas D'Aunno, Thomas E. Vaughn, and Peter McElroy, "An Institutional Analysis of HIV Prevention Efforts by the Nation's Outpatient Drug Abuse Treatment Units," *Journal of Health and Social Behavior* 40, no. 2 (1999): 175–192; Diana C. Mutz, "Contextualizing Personal Experience: The Role of Mass Media," *Journal of Politics* 56, no. 3 (1994): 689–714; and Richard J. Murnane, John B. Willett, and Kathryn Parker Boudett, "Do Male Dropouts Benefit from Obtaining a GED, Postsecondary Education, and Training?" *Evaluation Review* 23, no. 5 (1999): 475–503; Susanne James-Burdumy, Mark Dynarski, and John Deke, in "When Elementary Schools Stay Open Late: Results From the National Evaluation of the 21st Century Community Learning Centers Program," *Educational Evaluation and Policy Analysis* 29, no. 4 (2007): 296–318, use survey data to assess results from an RFE that randomly assigned students who expressed interest in the program to a center or a control group; more people expressed interest than the number of slots available. The survey was administered to those in the treatment and control group ($n = 2,308$).

4. Professional groups may actually have higher response rates to Internet than to snail-mail surveys. Kiernan et al. used a random field experiment to examine response rates, completion rates, and bias in re-

sponses of educators who had attended a training program. They found that the Internet version performed better on all counts. See Nancy E. Kiernan, Michaela Kiernan, Mary A. Oyler, and Carolyn Grilles, "Is a Web Survey as Effective as a Mail Survey? A Field Experiment Among Computer Users," *American Journal of Evaluation* 26, no. 3 (2005): 245–252. In addition, while Internet surveys of the public may have low response rates, after appropriate weighting, recent evidence suggests that they may be representative. See Robert P. Berrens, Alok K. Bohara, Hank Jenkins-Smith, Carol Silva, and David L. Weimer, "The Advent of Internet Surveys for Political Research: A Comparison of Telephone and Internet Samples," *Political Analysis* 11, no. 1 (2003): 1–22.

5. Of course, descriptive evaluations estimate values of single variables. The focus in this text is on causal evaluations.

6. Berrens et al., "Advent of Internet Surveys," point out that Internet surveys of the public garner a large number of responses at low marginal cost. They do have a low response rate; however, they appear to have no disadvantage, relative to telephone surveys, when relations between variables are being studied.

7. "Parent" refers to the child's principal guardian at home.

8. This is slightly more complicated when a family has two or more children in the same school: Some parents will have a higher probability of being sampled than others. For more information, consult a text on survey sampling. A good place to start is Graham Kalton, *Introduction to Survey Sampling* (Thousand Oaks, CA: Sage, 1983).

9. For more detailed information on the importance of multiple follow-ups and how to make them work, see Priscilla Salant and Don A. Dillman, *How to Conduct Your Own Survey* (New York: Wiley, 1994); Don A. Dillman, "The Design and Administration of Mail Surveys," *Annual Review of Sociology* 17 (1991): 225–249; Don A. Dillman et al., "Increasing Mail Questionnaire Response: A Four-State Comparison," *American Sociological Review* 39, no. 5 (1974): 744–756; Don A. Dillman, *Mail and Internet Surveys: The Tailored Design Method,* 2d ed. (Hoboken, NJ: John Wiley, 2007).

10. The researcher must also promise not to report any personal information to the client, including individual information about who does and does not respond.

11. Recall that Chapter 2 noted that general categories sometimes have less RME than specific ones. Often, using category versions of continuous variables reduces RME. For example, asking respondents about "years of education" may elicit responses with more RME than asking about categories (e.g., highest degree). Magidson reports that reanalysis of an evaluation of the Head Start program using dummy variables rather than continuous measures of many control variables changes the estimate of program impact. This can occur because RME in independent variables reduces the internal (and statistical) validity of parameter estimates. (See Chapters 2 and 6.) See Jay Magidson, "On Models Used to Adjust for Pre-Existing Differences," in *Research Design: Donald Campbell's Legacy,* vol. 2, ed. Leonard Bickman (Thousand Oaks, CA: Sage, 2000), 181–194.

12. Note the reference period for this question. One possible choice of reference period is to "the past school year." But that timeframe may be too distant for accurate memory. There is no single rule for the appropriate temporal reference. The best choice depends on the situation.

13. This is another case in which it may be advantageous to use dummy variable, categorical responses rather than continuous measures to reduce RME.

14. Many researchers report that respondents find questions about age somewhat threatening. Oddly enough, rather than use categories to reduce the threat, the researchers get more responses if they ask the specific question, "In what year were you born?" Similarly, asking for "current annual salary from current or most recent primary job, rounded to the nearest $10,000" may garner more responses than the category form of the question. Asking the question in this manner, evoking a specific response, entails no explicit comparison and therefore may be perceived as less threatening than the categorical form of the question.

15. The summative question could be placed in the middle of the multi-item battery of questions, but that would violate the requirement that surveys have a logical, orderly flow of questions.

16. Random placement is commonly used when order may matter; this allows the researcher to statistically control for possible bias due to placement. The order of response from +3 on the left to –3 on the right could also affect responses; the solution is to randomly decide to order responses from –3 on the left to +3 on the right in half the questionnaires and to statistically control for placement when examining the responses (either as a dependent or independent variable).

17. When respondents hesitate between one response category and a neighboring one, it usually indicates randomness in the respondents' behavior or uncertainty about how to respond. These are examples of RME. RME in survey responses is not a trivial problem. Recall that RME in independent variables reduces internal

validity. RME in any type of variable reduces statistical validity. RME in outcome variables, especially if it is not constant, affects statistical validity in two ways. It adds to the noise; if the RME is greater for some respondents than others, it also adds heteroscedastic error to the random error. For example, research in political science has shown that uncertainty about one's own political perceptions and opinions is not just simple noise. Rather, it varies systematically depending on political interest and education. Further, it can be modeled as ambivalence or value conflict. See R. Michael Alvarez and Charles Franklin, "Uncertainty and Political Perceptions," *Journal of Politics* 56 (1994): 671–688; R. Michael Alvarez and Charles Franklin, "American Ambivalence Towards Abortion Policy: Development of a Heteroskedastic Probit Model of Competing Values," *American Journal of Political Science* 39 (1995): 1055–1082; R. Michael Alvarez and John Brehm, "Are Americans Ambivalent Toward Racial Policies?" *American Journal of Political Science* 42 (1998): 418–452; R. Michael Alvarez and John Brehm, *Hard Choices, Easy Answers* (Princeton, NJ: Princeton University Press, 2002).

18. Internet surveys (and computer-assisted telephone interviews, or CATI) automatically enter each response into a numerically precoded survey database. In these cases, the numerical response may not be apparent to the respondent (or the interviewer), but it nonetheless is designed into the data-recording process. Thus, it is no different from the precoding process recommended for mail surveys.

19. There are many software packages for data analysis. STATA is particularly useful for the analysis of survey responses, where problems of heteroscedasticity are likely to affect hypothesis tests. STATA provides more ready-to-use tools to test and adjust for heteroscedasticity (and disproportionate stratified random samples) than SPSS, SAS, or Excel.

20. For an example of the use of multiple indicators and indexes to measure the outcome, the theoretically important independent variables, and selected control variables, see Darren W. Davis and Brian D. Silver, "Civil Liberties vs. Security: Public Opinion in the Context of the Terrorist Attacks in America," *American Journal of Political Science* 48, no. 1 (2004): 28–46.

21. For examples of the methods suggested here, in the workplace context, see Laura Langbein, "Ownership, Empowerment, and Productivity: Some Empirical Evidence on the Causes and Consequences of Employee Discretion," *Journal of Policy Analysis and Management* 19, no. 3 (2000): 427–450; and Laura Langbein and Connie Jorstad, "Productivity in the Workplace: Cops, Culture, Communication, Cooperation, and Collusion," *Political Research Quarterly* 57, no. 1 (2004): 65–79.

22. This is a case in which it is correct to use simple bivariate Pearson correlations and not regression coefficients.

23. For an example of a reliable measure of no clear single underlying concept, see Laura Langbein, "The Validity of Student Evaluations of Teaching," *PS: Political Science and Politics* 27, no. 3 (1994): 545–553. The example in that article shows that reliable indicators may not reflect the same underlying concept, even though they are intended to do so.

24. For more on the underlying model and interpretation of factor analyses, see, in this order, Jae-On Kim and Charles W. Mueller, "Introduction to Factor Analysis: What It Is and How to Do It," Sage University Paper Series on Quantitative Applications in the Social Sciences 13 (Thousand Oaks, CA: Sage, 1978), and Jae-On Kim and Charles W. Mueller, "Factor Analysis: Statistical Methods and Practical Issues," Sage University Paper Series on Quantitative Applications in the Social Sciences 14 (Thousand Oaks, CA: Sage, 1978).

25. In simple models like that of measurement model A, the sum of the squared factor loadings equals the eigenvalue of the principal component. For the derivation of this result and the results for more general situations, see Kim and Mueller, "Introduction to Factor Analysis."

26. Ignore the fact that each component (the verbal reading, the math, and the writing scores) is itself an underlying concept composed of an index of individual measured indicators. The "math" score, for example, is the principal component of the responses to each math question; the same is true for the verbal and the writing scores.

27. Edward G. Carmines and Richard A. Zeller, "Reliability and Validity Assessment," Sage University Paper Series on Quantitative Applications in the Social Sciences 17 (Thousand Oaks, CA: Sage, 1979).

8

Summing It Up

Meta-Analysis

WHAT IS META-ANALYSIS?

Strictly speaking, meta-analysis is the one component of program evaluation that is not original research. Meta-analysis is the systematic accumulation of findings from previous evaluation studies. It is particularly useful when there have been numerous other evaluation studies and when, as is usually the case, the findings appear quite disparate. For example, there have been many studies of the impact of class size on student achievement. There have been many studies of the impact of gun control on homicides, the impact of welfare reform's transition to Temporary Assistance for Needy Families (TANF) on employment outcomes and on children, and the impact of citizen and stakeholder participation in regulatory program implementation on indicators of implementation success. There is more of a consensus of findings in some of these areas than in others, but in no case are the findings uniform. In these instances, when the findings from one study differ from those of another, policy makers and program managers want to know: What is the overall conclusion? When studies disagree, it is hard, without meta-analysis, to give a valid answer to that question.

Further, in most cases, the studies are not randomized experiments. Some studies are better designed than others; the statistical analysis is better in some studies than others; some studies are more externally valid than others. Does the choice of method affect the conclusion? Should we dispense with a study just because it is not the best possible design, even though it is nationally representative? Should we ignore a study that is well designed but is based on data from a single site? Meta-analysis can provide answers to such questions. Further, meta-analysis can help program managers understand why some programs appear to work better than others. For example, it may be able to help managers evaluate whether centralized or decentralized management of statewide programs makes programs more "effective," assuming that effective has a specific definition or set of definitions.

Meta-analysis differs from an ad hoc review of literature. In an ad hoc review of literature, what is selected for review is often a matter of convenience or bias or both. For instance, researchers review what is readily available. That includes research in journals that they subscribe to, research on the bookshelves in their office, research in the "favorites" file in their documents folder on their computer desktop, research in the local library, or research in easily accessed electronic sources. But many other studies, especially those done by state and local government agencies, by nonprofit organizations, by school districts, and so on, are not as readily available. Frequently, those studies are done for internal use, so they are not widely circulated. Moreover, researchers choose not to look at some studies because of various professional or other biases. They often overlook peer-reviewed research published in journals outside their own field. For example, economists might ignore research on public education published in political science journals, and political scientists might ignore research on the same topic published in economics journals; both ignore research in education journals, educators ignore research in political science and economics journals, and they all ignore the research in sociology journals! Dissertations are often excluded from literature searches. Studies that are not peer-reviewed are also often excluded. Studies that are, in the researcher's opinion, poorly designed are often excluded. In sum, the process for selecting previous research for ad hoc review is frequently far more sloppy and capricious than would be tolerable in the design of a specific evaluation study.[1]

Most reviews of previous research on a topic are often haphazard in reporting about methods of analysis. The finding may be quoted, but the uncertainty (or standard error) of the finding is not. The design of the study (e.g., the type of quasi experiment [QE]) may or may not be mentioned in the review. In many reviews, it is difficult to determine whether the study under review had any controlled comparison at all or what the nature of the control was. Reviewers usually indicate whether the design under review was a randomized experiment, but if the design under review was a QE or nonexperiment (NE) (or a combination), reviews of the study rarely make clear exactly how groups were matched or which variables were statistically controlled. Many other characteristics usually go unmentioned (e.g., the source of funding, the affiliation of the author), or they are haphazardly mentioned in the description of one previous study but remain unmentioned in the description of another.

Meta-analysis is different. It is far more systematic than a casual review of previous research. It is intended to meet the highest validity standards in its assessments of the studies that it reviews. Specifically, meta-analysis is the statistical (usually nonexperimental) analysis of the findings of many previous individual analyses on a particular topic, in which the sample characteristics, type of research design, findings, and so on are regarded as a complex data set, not comprehensible without multivariate statistical analysis. Usually, meta-analyses do not filter out of the data base studies whose designs are regarded as inferior or uncontrolled or studies published in non–peer-reviewed outlets. Instead, these characteristics are examined to see whether and how they affect the results.

EXAMPLE OF A META-ANALYSIS: DATA

Below, I describe what a meta-analysis might look like. This example of meta-analysis is loosely borrowed from an actual, but dated, meta-analysis of the impact of class size on achievement.[2] The database comprised studies going back twenty years, found in three places:

1. a search of documents and abstracts (e.g., ERIC, PAIS, *Dissertation Abstracts*)[3]
2. previous ad hoc reviews of studies of the class-size literature
3. bibliographies from the studies uncovered in steps 1 and 2.

This effort resulted in 300 documents; however, not all of them were usable. First, 150 were not usable because the study reviewed reported no data comparing large classes to small ones. In other words, case studies of a single class have no comparison to report. As the chapters in this text repeatedly point out, evaluation without comparison is not evaluation. Hence, studies with no comparison cannot be used in a meta-analysis of the impact of class size on achievement. Only studies that compare larger to smaller classes can be included in the meta-analysis data set. Second, seventy studies were eliminated because they looked at the impact of class size on other outcomes (e.g., school attendance, parent satisfaction), not achievement. The final result was a database of eighty studies relating class size to student achievement. Of these eighty studies, some had multiple findings. For example, a single study might include results for math achievement, reading achievement, and science achievement. Such a study would contribute three observations to the final database.

A more modern version of this same meta-analysis would be similar, with one exception: It would yield a larger original database of studies. On the first pass through this database of studies of class size and academic achievement, studies with no comparison and studies with irrelevant outcome measures would still need to be filtered out. While the numbers may vary from topic to topic and from one time to another, the basic process for selecting a database is clear. Nothing is thrown out, as long as it includes comparison and studies the program and outcomes that are relevant to the specific meta-analysis.[4]

EXAMPLE OF A META-ANALYSIS: VARIABLES

Having assembled a database of studies and of findings embedded within a study, it is then necessary to "interview" each study and to code its "responses." The interview questions include the following characteristics, and the responses (or answers) for each study are then coded in much the same way as they are in a survey. Some of these codes will be as dummy variables, some will be ordinal, and some will have continuous values.

1. Year of publication
2. Publication source (book, thesis, refereed journal, professional journal, etc.)
3. Funding source (government, interest group, business, university, no external support, etc.)
4. Amount of funding
5. Author's affiliation (academic, nonprofit, for-profit)
6. Subject taught (math, reading, science, music)
7. Duration of instruction (number of weeks)
8. Number of students in the study
9. Number of different teachers in the study
10. Student ability (probably measured ordinally as high, medium, low, or all levels)
11. Student "need" (percentage of students receiving free or reduced-price lunch, percentage of students taking English as a second language, etc.)
12. Class level (from K–12, e.g., third grade; or list of class levels in the study)
13. Type of control (random assignment, matching, prepost with or without a time series, nonexperimental statistical controls, no controls at all)
14. Method of measuring achievement (national standardized test, state standardized test, schoolwide test, ad hoc test [e.g., Ms. Johnson's arithmetic test], etc.)
15. Method of quantification of outcomes (gain scores, regression coefficient, difference of proportions, etc.). Gain scores (or differences) mean that the outcome measure is the difference between the average scores of large and small classes. Regression coefficients report the impact of adding one additional student to the classroom on the achievement score, holding other variables constant. The difference of proportions reports the differ-

ence in the proportion (or percent) of students who pass, or meet some other threshold, between small and large classes. There may be other ways that outcomes are quantified, but these are typical. Previous chapters discussed many of these measures.

16.   The size of the "small" class and the size of the "large" class
17.   The effect size, measured as:

$$\Delta = \frac{(\overline{X}_{small} - \overline{X}_{large})}{\delta_{\overline{x}}},$$

where:

$\overline{X}_{small}$ = estimated mean achievement of the smaller class;
$\overline{X}_{large}$ = estimated mean achievement of the larger class and;
$\delta_{\overline{x}}$ = sigma = estimated within-group standard deviation (or pooled standard deviation).

Having $\delta_{\overline{x}}$, that is, sigma, in the denominator means that all outcomes are measured based on, or relative to, standard deviation units, so that ACT scores, Scholastic Aptitude Test (SAT) scores, state Standards of Learning (SOL) scores, and Ms. Johnson's arithmetic test are all comparable outcomes.

18.   The confidence interval (or standard error) of the effect size
19.   Number of observations (n) in the study

Knowing Δ requires knowing basic descriptive statistics about mean achievement scores in large and small classes and about the variance around these means. When these are not reported, they can often be derived from statistics that are reported (e.g., from t-scores or z-scores or F-statistics).

Many studies report multiple results for the same outcome measure. For example, suppose that one study reports the impact of a larger class on reading, math, and science scores; further, for each measure, it reports regression coefficients for changes in each of the mean scores and for each change in the percent of students who pass, according to the state standards of learning. This information requires that six effect-size values for the same study are entered into the meta-analysis database. These six values become six observations that will share similar values on many of the independent variables (e.g., the same author, publication source). But they are *not* independent observations, and the meta-analysis needs to account for this source of nonindependent observations in the statistical analysis, perhaps with a fixed-effect indicator. In addition, the stochastic term would clearly be heteroscedastic, and robust estimates (clustered by study) of the standard error of the class size coefficient in the meta-analysis would be appropriate.

EXAMPLE OF A META-ANALYSIS: DATA ANALYSIS

The results from the meta-analysis should be displayed first as simple descriptive statistics, such as those shown in Table 8.1, which is the frequency distribution for the types of research designs in the meta-analytic database. Note that the effective n is the number of findings (the number of

Table 8.1

Distribution of Types of Control Used in the Class Sizes of the Studies Reviewed

Type of control	n of Δ s	Percent distribution
Random assignment	110	15.2
Matched/statistical controls	235	32.4
Repeated measures (before-after)	18	2.5
Uncontrolled	362	49.9
Total	725	100.0

Δs); it is not the number of separate studies. Table 8.1 shows that about half the 725 Δs reported in the (imaginary) study database have some sort of rigorous control; the other half do not. The evaluators do not throw the uncontrolled studies out of the meta-analysis. Doing so assumes that design flaws affect the findings. It is possible that design flaws have no impact on the findings; further, it is important for evaluators to know how design flaws affect the findings. If certain design flaws consistently overestimate program impact, then that knowledge informs the debate that often ensues when studies have conflicting findings.

It is important to report other univariate statistics from the imaginary meta-analysis:

- $N = 725$ Δs
- Mean $\Delta = .088$; median $\Delta = .05$
- (Infer from this that the mean achievement in small classes is greater than large classes by .088, or just under .1 standard deviation unit.)
- 40 percent of the Δs were negative; 60 percent were positive
- Standard deviation of Δs is .401
- Range of Δs is from −1.98 to 2.54

In the meta-analysis, the researcher should also regress the effect size for each of the 725 findings on the independent variables. This would provide useful information about why there are sometimes different estimates of effect sizes. For example, the regression might indicate that effect size depends on student demographics. More specifically, the regression might find that as the percentage of students receiving free or reduced-price lunch in the study goes up, the reported effect size also increases, controlling for other variables in the analysis. The regression might also find that as the number and quality of experimental and statistical controls increase, the effect size does, too, controlling for other variables. This finding would suggest that better designed studies produce stronger findings of class size effects. The results might also indicate that, controlling for other variables, as the age of the students increases, the effect size decreases. Overall, these kinds of analyses can provide useful information to program managers about why programs sometimes seem to work and why they sometimes seem ineffective.

THE ROLE OF META-ANALYSIS IN PROGRAM EVALUATION AND CAUSAL CONCLUSIONS

The example makes clear that meta-analysis is the application of nonexperimental methods to a database representing relevant characteristics of the universe of prior findings. It allows evaluators to accumulate findings from disparate studies with disparate findings. It is particularly useful to program managers who want to know what works, when, and where.

The beginning of this book stated that no one study can "prove" impact or causation. But if previous studies, all using different methodologies, come to a general conclusion, then one can act as if the causal statement had been proven. Meta-analysis provides a method for examining the findings of these different studies, which so often have different methods and different findings.

Notice that meta-analysis requires education in program evaluation, because an evaluator doing a meta-analysis needs to be able to characterize the type of research design that studies use and to understand the elements of NE research designs. Meta-analysis helps to ensure that evaluation results live on, even after the reason for the specific evaluation study has long since disappeared.

FOR FURTHER READING

Examples of Meta-Analysis

Germa Bel, Xavier Fageda, and Milred Warner. "Is Private Production of Public Services Cheaper Than Public Production? A Meta-Regression Analysis of Solid Waste and Water Services." *Journal of Policy Analysis and Management* 29, no. 3 (2010): 553–577.

Howard S. Bloom, Carolyn J. Hill, and James A. Riccio. "Linking Program Implementation and Effectiveness: Lessons from a Pooled Sample of Welfare-to-Work Experiments." *Journal of Policy Analysis and Management* 22, no. 4 (2003): 551–575.

Campbell Collaboration. *Meta-Analyses of Education RFEs.* www.campbellcollaboration.org.

David H. Greenberg, Victoria Deitch, and Gayle Hamilton. "A Synthesis of Random Assignment Benefit-Cost Studies of Welfare to Work Programs." *Journal of Benefit-Cost Analysis* 1, no. 1 (2010): Article 3.

David H. Greenberg, Charles Michalopoulos, and Philip K. Robins. "Do Experimental and Non-Experimental Evaluations Give Different Answers About the Effectiveness of Government-Funded Training Programs?" *Journal of Policy Analysis and Management* 25, no. 3 (2006): 523–552.

George Hillocks Jr. "What Works in Teaching Composition: A Meta-Analysis of Experimental Treatment Studies." *American Journal of Education* 93, no. 1 (1984): 133–170.

Janusz R. Mrozek and Laura O. Taylor. "What Determines the Value of Life? A Meta-Analysis." *Journal of Policy Analysis and Management* 21, no. 2 (2002): 253–270.

Evan J. Ringquist. "Assessing Evidence of Environmental Inequities: A Meta-Analysis." *Journal of Policy Analysis and Management* 24, no. 2 (2005): 223–247.

Douglas D. Roscoe and Sharon Jenkins. "A Meta-Analysis of Campaign Contributions' Impact on Roll-Call Voting." *Social Science Quarterly* 86, no. 1 (2005): 52–68.

Pauline Vaillancourt Rosenau and Stephen H. Linder. "Two Decades of Research Comparing For-Profit and Nonprofit Health Provider Performance in the United States." *Social Science Quarterly* 84, no. 2 (2003): 219–241.

Methods and Methodological Issues in Meta-Analysis

John G. Adair, et al. "Hawthorne Control Procedures in Educational Experiments: A Reconsideration of Their Use and Effectiveness." *Review of Educational Research* 59, no. 2 (1989): 215–228.

———. "The Placebo Control Group: An Analysis of Its Effectiveness in Educational Research." *Journal of Experimental Education* 59, no. 1 (1990): 67–86.

Harris M. Cooper. *Research Synthesis and Meta-Analysis: A Step-by-Step Approach.* Thousand Oaks, CA: Sage, 2000.

Thomas D. Cook. *Meta-Analysis for Explanation: A Casebook.* New York: Russell Sage Foundation, 1992.

John Edward Hunter and Frank L. Schmidt. *Methods of Meta-Analysis: Correcting Error and Bias in Research Findings.* 2d ed. Thousand Oaks, CA: Sage, 2004.

Mark W. Lipsey and David S. Wilson. *Practical Meta-Analysis.* Thousand Oaks, CA: Sage, 2001.

David Lopez-Lee. "Indiscriminate Data Aggregations in Meta-Analysis: A Cause for Concern Among Policy Makers and Social Scientists." *Evaluation Review* 26, no. 5 (2002): 520–544.

Frederic M. Wolf. "Meta-Analysis: Quantitative Methods for Research Synthesis." Sage University Paper Series on Quantitative Methods, No. 07–059. Thousand Oaks, CA: Sage, 1986.

NOTES

1. Many years ago, Gene Glass and Mary Lee Smith, in *Meta-Analysis of the Relationship of Class Size and Achievement* (San Francisco: Far West Laboratory for Educational Research, 1978), expressed this sentiment, and it is still true.

2. Ibid.; Gene Glass, Leonard Cahan, Mary Lee Smith, and Nikola Filby, *School Class Size: Research and Policy* (Beverly Hills, CA: Sage, 1982).

3. ERIC is the Education Research Information Clearinghouse; PAIS is the Public Affairs Information Service. They are widely available electronic databases. *Dissertation Abstracts* is published by ProQuest.

4. There is some controversy about the advisability of including randomized field experiments and other studies (quasi experiments and nonexperiments) in the same meta-analysis database. See David Lopez-Lee, "Indiscriminate Data Aggregations in Meta-Analysis," *Evaluation Review* 26, no. 5 (2002): 520–544. By contrast, David H. Greenberg, Charles Michalopoulos, and Philip K. Robins ("Do Experimental and Non-Experimental Evaluations Give Different Answers About the Effectiveness of Government-Funded Training Programs?" *Journal of Policy Analysis and Management* 25, no. 3 [2006]: 523–552) explicitly compare randomized experiments to nonexperiments to see whether, and when, they give comparable results.

Index

About the Author

Laura Langbein (Ph.D., University of North Carolina at Chapel Hill) is a professor in the Department of Public Administration and Policy at American University. Professor Langbein teaches quantitative methods, program evaluation, and policy analysis. Her research focuses on empirical applications regarding the performance of public employees, and on policy and program evaluation in various policy areas, including the environment, education, housing, criminal justice (death penalty and police), gay marriage laws, and corruption. Her recent articles have appeared in *Journal of Policy Analysis and Management, Social Science Quarterly, Journal of Public Administration Research and Theory, Evaluation Review, Public Choice, Economics of Education Review, Journal of Development Studies, International Public Management Review,* and other scholarly journals.